Anglo-Saxon Studies 23

CAPITAL AND CORPORAL PUNISHMENT
IN ANGLO-SAXON ENGLAND

Anglo-Saxon Studies

ISSN 1475–2468

General Editors
John Hines
Catherine Cubitt

'Anglo-Saxon Studies' aims to provide a forum for the best scholarship on the Anglo-Saxon peoples in the period from the end of Roman Britain to the Norman Conquest, including comparative studies involving adjacent populations and periods; both new research and major re-assessments of central topics are welcomed.

Books in the series may be based in any one of the principal disciplines of archaeology, art history, history, language and literature, and inter- or multi-disciplinary studies are encouraged.

Proposals or enquiries may be sent directly to the editors or the publisher at the addresses given below; all submissions will receive prompt and informed consideration.

Professor John Hines, School of History, Archaeology and Religion, Cardiff University, Colum Drive, Cardiff, Wales, UK CF10 3EU

Professor Catherine Cubitt, Centre for Medieval Studies, University of York, The King's Manor, York, England, UK YO1 7EP

Boydell & Brewer, PO Box 9, Woodbridge, Suffolk, England, UK IP12 3DF

Previously published volumes in the series are listed at the back of this book

CAPITAL AND CORPORAL PUNISHMENT IN ANGLO-SAXON ENGLAND

Edited by

Jay Paul Gates and Nicole Marafioti

THE BOYDELL PRESS

© Contributors 2014

All Rights Reserved. Except as permitted under current legislation no part of this work may be photocopied, stored in a retrieval system, published, performed in public, adapted, broadcast, transmitted, recorded or reproduced in any form or by any means, without the prior permission of the copyright owner

First published 2014
The Boydell Press, Woodbridge

ISBN 978-1-84383-918-7

The Boydell Press is an imprint of Boydell & Brewer Ltd
PO Box 9, Woodbridge, Suffolk IP12 3DF, UK
and of Boydell & Brewer Inc.
668 Mount Hope Ave, Rochester, NY 14620-2731, USA

website: www.boydellandbrewer.com

A CIP catalogue record for this book is available
from the British Library

The publisher has no responsibility for the continued existence or accuracy of URLs for external or third-party internet websites referred to in this book, and does not guarantee that any content on such websites is, or will remain, accurate or appropriate.

Printed on acid-free paper

Contents

List of Illustrations	vii
Acknowledgments	ix
List of Contributors	xi
Abbreviations	xiii

Introduction: Capital and Corporal Punishment in
    Anglo-Saxon England ... 1
    Nicole Marafioti and Jay Paul Gates

1. When Compensation Costs an Arm and a Leg ... 17
    Valerie Allen

2. Beginnings and Legitimation of Punishment in Early
    Anglo-Saxon Legislation From the Seventh to the Ninth Century ... 34
    Daniela Fruscione

3. Genital Mutilation in Medieval Germanic Law ... 48
    Lisi Oliver

4. 'Sick-Maintenance' and Earlier English Law ... 74
    Stefan Jurasinski

5. Incarceration as Judicial Punishment in Anglo-Saxon England ... 92
    Daniel Thomas

6. Earthly Justice and Spiritual Consequences: Judging and
    Punishing in the Old English *Consolation of Philosophy* ... 113
    Nicole Marafioti

7. Osteological Evidence of Corporal and Capital Punishment
    in Later Anglo-Saxon England ... 131
    Jo Buckberry

8. Mutilation and Spectacle in Anglo-Saxon Legislation ... 149
    Daniel O'Gorman

Contents

9. The 'Worcester' Historians and Eadric *Streona*'s Execution   165
   Jay Paul Gates

10. Capital Punishment and the Anglo-Saxon Judicial Apparatus: A Maximum View?   181
    Andrew Rabin

Index   201

List of Illustrations

Plates

Plate 3.1	Wijnaldum brooch (photograph © Fries Museum, Leeuwarden, Johan van der Veer)	59
Plate 3.2	Gold belt buckle from the ship-burial at Sutton Hoo (image © The Trustees of the British Museum)	59
Plate 3.3	Book of Durrow: MS Dublin, Trinity College Library 57, fol. 125v (image © The Board of Trinity College Dublin)	60
Plate 3.4	'Porcupine' design on a silver penny (c. 700) from the Woodham Walter hoard, Essex (image © The Trustees of the British Museum)	61
Plate 3.5	'Solomon's Knot' interlace design on reverse of a silver sceat (penny) from the Middle Harling hoard, Norfolk (ruler: Beonna, King of East Anglia) (image © Fitzwilliam Museum, Cambridge/Art Resource, NY)	62
Plate 7.1	Sharp-force trauma to the posterior of a cervical vertebra, consistent with decapitation (Skeleton 578 from Old Dairy Cottage) (photograph © Jo Buckberry)	135
Plate 7.2	Skull associated with Skeleton 1 from Walkington Wold, Barrow 1, East Yorkshire (photograph © Hull and East Riding Museum: Hull Museums)	137
Plate 7.3	Second cervical vertebra with peri-mortem 'hangman's fracture', from Iron Age Heslington, York (photograph © Jo Buckberry)	138
Plate 7.4	Healed amputation from later medieval Ipswich (photograph © English Heritage)	145
Plate 7.5	Nineteenth-century peri-mortem amputation from the Royal London Hospital (photograph © Museum of London Archaeology)	146

List of Illustrations

Figures

Figure 7.1 Anatomical regions and bones discussed in Chapter 7
(drawn by Dan Bashford)   134

Maps

Map 3.1 Compensation values for genital injury in Anglo-Saxon
and barbarian law   51

Tables

Table 1.1 Compensation values for digits in Æthelberht's and
Alfred's law codes   31

Table 3.1 Fines for inflicting genital injuries in Anglo-Saxon
and Frisian laws   54

Table 3.2 Punishments for inflicting genital injuries
in barbarian laws   70

Acknowledgments

This book emerged from a series of conference panels we organized from 2007 through 2010 at the International Medieval Congresses at Western Michigan University and the University of Leeds. The editors would like to thank the participants in those sessions – presenters and attendees alike – for their insightful contributions and unabashed enthusiasm for Anglo-Saxon punishment. We were privileged to receive financial support from the History Department of Trinity University and from John Jay College of Criminal Justice, CUNY. We are grateful to the general editors of the Anglo-Saxon Studies series, John Hines and Catherine Cubitt, for their support for this volume; to Rob Kinsey, for his invaluable assistance as we prepared the manuscript; to Rohais Haughton, for seeing the book through production; and to Caroline Palmer, for her guidance and enthusiasm at every stage of this project.

List of Contributors

Valerie Allen is a Professor of English at John Jay College of Criminal Justice in the City University of New York.

Jo Buckberry is a Lecturer in Biological Anthropology in the Biological Anthropology Research Centre, Archaeological Sciences at the University of Bradford.

Daniela Fruscione is a Research Fellow of the Institut für Rechtsgeschichte at the Johann Wolfgang Goethe Universität, Frankfurt am Main.

Jay Paul Gates is an Assistant Professor of English at John Jay College of Criminal Justice in the City University of New York.

Stefan Jurasinski is an Associate Professor of English at the College of Brockport of the State University of New York.

Nicole Marafioti is an Assistant Professor of History at Trinity University.

Daniel O'Gorman is a PhD candidate in History at Loyola University of Chicago.

Lisi Oliver is the Houston Chapter Alumni Professor of English and Director of the Interdepartmental Program in Linguistics at Louisiana State University.

Andrew Rabin is an Associate Professor of English at the University of Louisville.

Daniel Thomas is a Lecturer in English at Pembroke College of the University of Oxford.

Abbreviations

Anger's Past, ed. Rosenwein   Barbara H. Rosenwein, ed., *Anger's Past: The Social Uses of an Emotion in the Middle Ages* (Ithaca, NY, 1998)
ANS   *Anglo-Norman Studies*
ArchJ   *Archaeological Journal*
ASC A   Janet M. Bately, ed., *The Anglo-Saxon Chronicle: A Collaborative Edition*, vol. 3: *MS A* (Cambridge, 1986)
ASC B   Simon Taylor, ed., *The Anglo-Saxon Chronicle: A Collaborative Edition*, vol. 4: *MS B* (Cambridge, 1983)
ASC C   Katherine O'Brien O'Keeffe, ed., *The Anglo-Saxon Chronicle: A Collaborative Edition*, vol. 5: *MS C* (Cambridge, 2001)
ASC D   G. P. Cubbin, ed., *The Anglo-Saxon Chronicle: A Collaborative Edition*, vol. 6: *MS D* (Cambridge, 1996)
ASC E   Susan Irvine, ed., *The Anglo-Saxon Chronicle: A Collaborative Edition*, vol. 7: *MS E* (Cambridge, 2004)
ASC F   Peter S. Baker, ed., *The Anglo-Saxon Chronicle: A Collaborative Edition*, vol. 8: *MS F* (Cambridge, 2000)
ASE   *Anglo-Saxon England*
ASPR   Anglo-Saxon Poetic Records
Attenborough, *Laws*   F. L. Attenborough, ed., *The Laws of the Earliest English Kings* (Cambridge, 1922)
BAR   British Archaeological Reports
Beowulf   R. D. Fulk, Robert E. Bjork and John D. Niles, eds, *Klaeber's Beowulf and the Fight at Finnsburg*, 4th edn (Toronto, 2008)
BL   British Library
Blackwell Encyclopaedia, ed. Lapidge *et al.*   Michael Lapidge, John Blair, Simon Keynes and Donald Scragg, eds, *Blackwell Encyclopaedia of Anglo-Saxon England* (Malden, 1999)

Abbreviations

Bosworth–Toller	T. Northcote Toller, ed., *An Anglo-Saxon Dictionary Based on the Manuscript Collections of the Late Joseph Bosworth* (Oxford, 1898)
CCSL	Corpus Christianorum Series Latina
DOE	Angus Cameron, Ashley Crandell Amos, Antonette diPaolo Healey *et al.*, eds, *Dictionary of Old English: A to G* (Toronto, 2007) (online at http://www.doe.utoronto.ca/; accessed 3 January 2013)
Early Medieval Studies, ed. Baxter *et al.*	Stephen Baxter, Catherine E. Karkov, Janet L. Nelson and David Pelteret, eds, *Early Medieval Studies in Memory of Patrick Wormald* (Aldershot, 2009)
EETS	Early English Text Society
n.s.	new series
o.s.	original series
s.s.	supplementary series
EHD 1	Dorothy Whitelock, ed., *English Historical Documents*, vol. 1: *c. 500–1042*, 2nd edn (London, 1979)
EHR	*English Historical Review*
EME	*Early Medieval Europe*
Ethelred, ed. Hill	David Hill, ed., *Ethelred the Unready: Papers from the Millenary Conference*, BAR British Series 59 (Oxford, 1978)
Godden and Irvine, *OE Boethius*	Malcolm Godden and Susan Irvine, eds, *The Old English Boethius: An Edition of the Old English Versions of Boethius's 'De Consolatione Philosophiae'*, 2 vols (Oxford, 2009)
HSJ	*Haskins Society Journal*
Hurnard, *King's Pardon*	Naomi D. Hurnard, *The King's Pardon for Homicide before A.D. 1307* (Oxford, 1969)
Hyams, *Rancor and Reconciliation*	Paul R. Hyams, *Rancor and Reconciliation in Medieval England* (Ithaca, NY, 2003)
JEGP	*Journal of English and Germanic Philology*
JW	R. R. Darlington and P. McGurk, eds, *The Chronicle of John of Worcester*, trans. Jennifer Bray and P. McGurk (Oxford, 1995)
Keynes, *Diplomas*	Simon Keynes, *The Diplomas of King Æthelred 'The Unready', 978–1016* (Cambridge, 1980)
Lapidge, *Swithun*	Michael Lapidge, ed., *The Cult of St Swithun*, Winchester Studies 4.ii: The Anglo-Saxon Minsters of Winchester (Oxford, 2003)
Legal Culture	Patrick Wormald, *Legal Culture in the Early Medieval West: Law as Text, Image and Experience* (London, 1999)

Abbreviations

Liebermann, *Gesetze*	F. Liebermann, ed., *Die Gesetze der Angelsachsen*, 3 vols (Halle, 1903)
MÆ	*Medium Ævum*
MGH	Monumenta Germaniae Historica
Capit.	Capitularia regum Francorum
Capit. episc.	Capitula episcoporum
Conc.	Concilia
Epp. sel.	Epistolae selectae
Fontes iuris	Fontes iuris Germanici antiqui
LL	Leges
LL nat. Germ.	Leges nationum Germanicarum
MS	manuscript
Naked Before God, ed. Withers and Wilcox	Benjamin C. Withers and Jonathan Wilcox, eds, *Naked Before God: Uncovering the Body in Anglo-Saxon England* (Morgantown, 2003)
Oliver, *Beginnings of English Law*	Lisi Oliver, *The Beginnings of English Law* (Toronto, 2002)
Oliver, *Body Legal*	Lisi Oliver, *The Body Legal in Barbarian Law* (Toronto, 2011)
Pastoral Care, ed. Tinti	Francesca Tinti, ed., *Pastoral Care in Late Anglo-Saxon England*, Anglo-Saxon Studies 6 (Woodbridge, 2005)
PL	J.-P. Migne, ed., *Patrologiae cursus completus, series latina* (Paris, 1844–64)
Pollock and Maitland, *History of English Law*	Frederick Pollock and Frederic William Maitland, *The History of English Law before the Time of Edward I*, 2 vols, 2nd edn (Cambridge, 1898–9, repr. 1968)
Reynolds, *Deviant Burial*	Andrew Reynolds, *Anglo-Saxon Deviant Burial Customs* (Oxford, 2009)
Robertson, *Laws*	A. J. Robertson, ed., *The Laws of the Kings of England from Edmund to Henry I* (Cambridge, 1925)
S	P. H. Sawyer, *Anglo-Saxon Charters: An Annotated List and Bibliography* (London, 1968)
s.a.	*sub annum*
s.v.	*sub verbum*
Skeat, *LS* I	Walter W. Skeat, ed., *Ælfric's Lives of Saints: Being a Set of Sermons on Saints' Days Formerly Observed by the English Church*, vol. 1, EETS o.s. 76 and 82 (London, 1881–1900)
Skeat, *LS* II	Walter W. Skeat, ed., *Ælfric's Lives of Saints: Being a Set of Sermons on Saints' Days Formerly Observed by the English Church*, vol. 2, EETS o.s. 94 and 114 (London, 1881–1900)

Abbreviations

Thompson, *Dying and Death*	Victoria Thompson, *Dying and Death in Later Anglo-Saxon England*, Anglo-Saxon Studies 4 (Woodbridge, 2004)
TRHS	*Transactions of the Royal Historical Society*
Wormald, *Making of English Law*	Patrick Wormald, *The Making of English Law: King Alfred to the Twelfth Century*, vol. 1: *Legislation and its Limits* (Oxford, 1999)
Wulfstan, ed. Townend	Matthew Townend, ed., *Wulfstan, Archbishop of York: The Proceedings of the Second Alcuin Conference* (Turnhout, 2004)

Introduction

Capital and Corporal Punishment in Anglo-Saxon England

Nicole Marafioti and Jay Paul Gates

Æt þam oðrum cyrre ne si þær nan oðer bot, gif he ful wurðe, butan þæt man ceorfe him ða handa oððe þa fet oððe ægþer, be þam ðe seo dæd sig. ⁊ gif he þonne gyt mare wurc geworht hæbbe, þonne do man ut his eagan, ⁊ ceorfan of his nosu ⁊ his earan ⁊ þa uferan lippan oððon hine hættian, swa hwylc þyssa swa man þonne geræde, ða þe ðærto rædan sceolon: swa man mæg styran ⁊ eac þære sawle beorgan.

At the second offense, there is to be no other remedy, if he is guilty, but that his hands, or feet, or both are to be cut off, depending on the deed. And if he has committed further offenses, his eyes should be put out and his nose and ears and upper lip cut off, or he should be scalped, whichever of these is decided by those who must judge. Thus one can punish and also protect the soul.

II Cnut 30.4–5[1]

In the early eleventh century, Archbishop Wulfstan of York was confronted with the problem of reconciling principles of Christian mercy with the earthly obligation to punish criminals. The alignment of secular and spiritual priorities had long been an element of English law, as Christian clergy had been drafting English royal legislation since the turn of the seventh century. Yet it was only with Wulfstan's codes for Kings Æthelred and Cnut that the rhetoric of salvation was fully and explicitly integrated into Old English law. In contrast to the laws of previous Anglo-Saxon kings, which required capital punishment for a range of offenses, Wulfstan's legislation prescribed non-lethal penalties 'so that God's handiwork and his own purchase, which he dearly bought, not be destroyed for small offenses.'[2] Whereas an immediate death sentence might place the soul of the condemned beyond redemption, if he lacked the opportunity or inclination to repent before his execution, a life-sparing punishment allowed even the worst offenders enough time to make their peace with God. Whether or not they chose to be reconciled with

---

[1] All references to the Anglo-Saxon laws are from Liebermann, *Gesetze* I. All translations are our own.
[2] 'Ne forspille for lytlum Godes handgeweorc ⁊ his agenne ceap, þe he deore gebohte': V Æthelred 3.1.

the Church, under Wulfstan's program of punishment, it would not be the judge or executioner determining the condemned's fate in the afterlife, but the criminal himself.

Wulfstan did not oppose the harsh application of earthly justice, however, and the potential brutality of his life-sparing punishments silences any suggestion that he or the kings he wrote for were 'soft on crime.' The thorough mutilations prescribed in II Cnut 30 for repeat offenders would have been excruciating.[3] If the offender survived his punishment, which was by no means a certainty, he would have been incapacitated for the remainder of his life and permanently marked as a criminal.[4] Of course, exhaustive mutilation was not the only option. Less debilitating punishments, such as imprisonment, branding, or lashing, were deemed sufficient under certain circumstances, and moderate mutilation – the amputation of just a hand, for instance – was preferred in some cases. Fines might be applied alone or in conjunction with physical punishments; and non-corporal penalties, like forfeiture or exile, appeared alongside prescriptions for mutilation and execution.

Wulfstan's insistence upon non-lethal sentences in his laws leaves the impression that he was departing dramatically from existing practice, but death was certainly not the only punishment prescribed before the eleventh century, and earlier laws were not indifferent to Christian priorities. In fact, it seems that Wulfstan's legislative approach to keeping the peace and promoting salvation drew upon themes articulated more obliquely by earlier lawmakers.[5] The earliest Old English laws, issued by the kings of Kent at the turn of the seventh century, were concerned with protecting Christian clergy and ensuring that the fledgling Church could do its spiritual work in peace.[6] In the late ninth century, the punishment of the body was explicitly tied to concerns about the soul in the laws of Alfred, which required offenders to submit to penances assigned by the bishop in addition to their earthly punishment.[7] Writing the Church into the process of law enforcement may have allowed clergy greater influence and enhanced Alfred's own Christian credentials, but it also redefined punishment as necessary for the offender's own good. By the mid-tenth century, the promotion of earthly law was construed as a means of securing divine favor, with penalties designed to appease both God and men.[8] Even in legislation that did not explicitly mention the spiritual state of offenders, it is difficult to imagine that penalties were assigned in a vacuum, without reference to Christian values and interests.

---

[3] Quoted in the epigraph above.
[4] On the debilitating effects of mutilation, see Oliver, *Body Legal*, especially pp. 165–79.
[5] Patrick Wormald, 'Archbishop Wulfstan and the Holiness of Society,' *Legal Culture*, pp. 225–51.
[6] For a summary of the various approaches to the relationship between Christianity and early Anglo-Saxon written law, see Oliver, *Beginnings of English Law*, pp. 14–20.
[7] Alfred 1.2.
[8] See for example II Edmund 4, III Edgar 1.2, IV Edgar 1. These ideas were developed further by Wulfstan, who required compensation 'before God and before the world' (*for Gode and for worolde*); see for example V Æthelred 1.1, VI Æthelred 36, and II Cnut 11.1.

Introduction

Although contemporary judicial practice was evidently enough to inspire Wulfstan to reiterate the principles of Christian mercy in his laws, it is clear that earlier lawmakers did not prescribe capital and corporal punishments lightly. Even the notoriously harsh laws of Æthelstan, which applied the death penalty more frequently than any other king's legislation, reveal a process of revision and adaptation over time.[9] The prologue and opening clauses of V Æthelstan issue widespread and severe penalties after noting that the existing law was not being properly enforced; VI Æthelstan 12, by contrast, records a bishop's objections to executing twelve-year-old thieves and raises the minimum age for capital punishment to fifteen. The fact that such severe sentences were so openly rationalized indicates that punishments were not decreed arbitrarily, but rather, were carefully considered in light of contemporary concerns. Well before Wulfstan began explicitly articulating religious principles in royal law codes, Anglo-Saxon legislators demonstrated concern with assigning appropriate, commensurate justice.

This volume investigates how capital and corporal punishments developed and operated in English society between c. 600 and c. 1150, from the time of the earliest Christian Anglo-Saxon kings through the generations after the Norman Conquest. The following essays engage legal, literary, historiographical, philological, and archaeological evidence to provide a multifaceted view of how the practice and conception of punishment evolved and manifested in Anglo-Saxon society. These studies demonstrate that judicial sentencing was normally grounded in ideologies of social control, which sought to create and sustain authority at local, regional, and national levels. Despite the potential severity of criminal penalties in this period, this book contends that punishment did not ordinarily involve the unjustified subjugation of individuals or the arbitrary exercise of power. Rather than being motivated by cruelty, excess, or barbarism, judicial punishments were designed to discourage transgression, keep the peace, maintain a standard of Christian behavior, and reinforce the authority of those in power. Though violence was often a component of punishment, that violence – when applied appropriately – was considered necessary, legitimate, and even righteous.

The sources of information are varied and independently raise more questions than they answer about what Anglo-Saxon judicial violence looked like. The starting point for any consideration of punishment in pre-Conquest England is the corpus of written law, which presents the imposition of capital and corporal penalties as a legitimate response to wrongdoing. A recent handlist has identified ninety-seven laws, across twenty-four royal law codes, which involve death or dismemberment for criminal offenders.[10] This is not to imply that royal lawmakers were always involved – directly or indirectly – in criminal punishments. Moreover, it is by no means certain

---

[9] Wormald, *Making of English Law*, pp. 305–6.
[10] Reynolds, *Deviant Burial*, pp. 251–61. These ninety-seven clauses include eighty references to the criminal's death and seventeen prescriptions for mutilation.

that surviving laws were implemented as written or that they underpinned a universal understanding of how social deviance ought to be remedied. It is possible that written law reflected ideal rather than reality: the royal power which these compilations took for granted may have been little more than a literary construction. Despite kings' self-proclaimed role as givers and keepers of the law, royal officials and local magistrates must have assumed most of the responsibility for enforcing justice.[11] From the reign of Edgar, royal law codes make reference to lower courts, associated with the regional units of shires and hundreds, and it is unlikely that uniform standards of judicial procedure and practice were consistently employed across each of these institutions.[12] Nevertheless, extant records of Anglo-Saxon lawsuits indicate that the operation of justice rarely conflicted outright with the procedures outlined in royal legislation.[13] Whether the king should be credited with implementing the law or whether written legislation codified existing practice, prescriptions for physical punishment in early English law must have been considered appropriate responses to wrongdoing.

The acceptability of top-down punishment as a response to wrongdoing is confirmed by extralegal texts. A handful of Anglo-Saxon charters mention death sentences, executions, and the denial of consecrated burial, and pre-Conquest executions are also noted in Domesday Book and post-Conquest cartularies.[14] The Anglo-Saxon Chronicle provides additional examples of kings imposing physical penalties at the highest political levels.[15] Eadred had the archbishop of York imprisoned from 952 until 954, for fomenting dissent in Northumbria.[16] Æthelred II had a number of high-ranking nobles blinded and killed in 993 and 1006.[17] Cnut executed a swathe of the English nobility in 1016 and 1017, including Eadric *Streona*, who was remembered as

---

[11] Patrick Wormald, 'Charters, Law and the Settlement of Disputes in Anglo-Saxon England,' *Legal Culture*, pp. 289–311, at 304–6; compare also Thompson, *Dying and Death*, pp. 181–2.

[12] See for example III Edgar 5, II Cnut 17. Patrick Wormald, 'Giving God and King their Due: Conflict and its Regulation in the Early English State,' *Legal Culture*, pp. 333–57, at 346–7.

[13] Wormald, 'Giving God and King their Due,' pp. 346–8.

[14] These are all noted in Patrick Wormald, 'A Handlist of Anglo-Saxon Lawsuits,' *Legal Culture*, pp. 253–87, as nos 31, 43, 54, 57, 76, 100, 144, and 148. The relevant charters are S 443 (of dubious authenticity), 877, 883, 927, and 1377.

[15] The earliest mentions of kings ordering death and dismemberment reflect political conflicts rather than punishment for wrongs committed. For example, Oswiu ordered his rival Oswine to be killed; Offa had the East Anglian king Æthelberht decapitated; and Ceolwulf captured the Kentish king Præn, bound him, had his eyes put out, and had his hands chopped off. In addition, Alfred hanged two Danes who were captured after a battle. For Oswiu and Oswine: *ASC* A, B, and C, s.a. 651 (*recte* 650); *ASC* E and F, s.a. 650. Oswiu's involvement is only noted in E, while the other annals simply note that Oswine was killed (*wæs ofslægen*). For Offa and Æthelberht: *ASC* A, B, C, D, E, and F, s.a. 792 (*recte* 794). For Ceolwulf and Præn: *ASC* A, B, C, D, E, and F, s.a. 796 (*recte* 798); the mutilation is only noted in F. For Alfred: *ASC* A, s.a. 896; *ASC* B, C, and D, s.a. 897 (*recte* 896).

[16] *ASC* D, s.a. 952 and 954.

[17] *ASC* C, D, and E, s.a. 993 and 1006. See also Keynes, *Diplomas*, pp. 211–13; Elizabeth Boyle, 'A Welsh Record of an Anglo-Saxon Political Mutilation,' *ASE* 35 (2006), 245–9; Geneviève Bührer-Thierry, '"Just Anger" or "Vengeful Anger"? The Punishment of Blinding in the Early Medieval West,' *Anger's Past*, ed. Rosenwein, pp. 75–91.

having been justly punished for treason.[18] In 1036 Harold Harefoot blinded a royal rival and subjected his men to punishments prescribed for thieves and traitors in recent law codes: 'some of them were sold for money, some pitifully destroyed, some of them were bound, some of them were blinded, some mutilated, some scalped.'[19] The 1036 entry provides the only extended description of royal punishment in the Chronicle, but even brief notices of the king's justice suggest that both crime and punishment were matters of public knowledge and record.[20] The point of punishment was not simply to respond to wrongdoing but to signify that there were real consequences for transgression – thereby reinforcing the power of the crown.[21]

Old English poetry likewise offers glimpses of punishment and its machinery. Images of the gallows are particularly common. The narrator in *The Dream of the Rood* explicitly states that the cross was not a gallows for the wicked (*ne wæs ðær huru fracodes gealga*), even though the cross itself describes Christ mounting the gallows (*Gestah he on gealgan*).[22] In *Beowulf* the death of one son at the hands of another, which precluded vengeance as well as restitution, is compared to the impotence of a father watching his son hanged on the gallows (*galgan*): 'his son hangs, a comfort to the raven, and he did not have the power to help him.'[23] *The Fates of Mortals* also imagines the bodies of hanged men disintegrating on the gibbet and becoming carrion for birds of prey, confirming the infamy of the dead,[24] while *Maxims II* is clear that 'the criminal should hang, should properly repay the evil he previously did.'[25] Other punishments appear as well. Juliana, refusing marriage and the worship of pagan gods, is hung from a beam (*beam*) by her hair, beaten for six hours, and placed in prison (*to carcerne*).[26] *Fates of the Apostles* recounts two executions of martyrs with swords, three with unspecified weapons, and one by beating.[27]

---

[18] On the execution of Eadric, see the essay by Jay Paul Gates in this volume.
[19] 'Sume hi man wið feo sealde, sume hreowlice acwealde, sume hi man bende, sume hi man blende, sume hamelode, sume hættode': ASC C and D, s.a. 1036. ASC E gives the prose, but not the verse. See also Katherine O'Brien O'Keeffe, 'Body and Law in Late Anglo-Saxon England,' *ASE* 27 (1998), 209–32.
[20] There is no mention of a judicial process in the Chronicle version of this episode, but a trial is mentioned in the *Encomium Emmae Reginae* composed c. 1040: see Alistair Campbell, ed., *Encomium Emmae Reginae* (London, 1949, repr. 1998), pp. 44–7. For the judicial nature of these punishments, see Nicole Marafioti, *The King's Body: Burial and Succession in Late Anglo-Saxon England* (Toronto, 2014).
[21] On performative royal violence, see Gerd Althoff, '*Ira Regis*: Prolegomena to a History of Royal Anger,' *Anger's Past*, ed. Rosenwein, pp. 59–74; Julia Barrow, 'Demonstrative Behaviour and Political Communication in Later Anglo-Saxon England,' *ASE* 36 (2007), 127–50.
[22] *Dream of the Rood*, lines 10 and 40, in George Philip Krapp, ed., *The Vercelli Book*, ASPR 2 (New York, 1932).
[23] 'Þonne his sunu hangað, hrefne to hroðre, ond he him helpe ne mæg': *Beowulf*, lines 2435–49.
[24] *The Fates of Mortals*, lines 33–42, in Bernard J. Muir, ed., *The Exeter Anthology of Old English Poetry: An Edition of Exeter Dean and Chapter MS 3501*, vol. 1: *Texts* (Exeter, 1994), pp. 244–7; previously edited as *Fortunes of Men* in George Philip Krapp and Elliott Van Kirk Dobbie, eds, *The Exeter Book*, ASPR 3 (New York, 1936), pp. 154–6.
[25] 'Wearh hangian, fægere ongildan þæt he ær facen dyde manna cynne': *Maxims II*, lines 55–7, in Elliott Van Kirk Dobbie, ed., *The Anglo-Saxon Minor Poems*, ASPR 6 (New York, 1942).
[26] *Juliana*, lines 225–33, in Muir, *Exeter Anthology*; Krapp and Dobbie, *Exeter Book*.
[27] *Fates of the Apostles*, lines 34, 46, 59, 69, 72, and 80, in Krapp, *Vercelli Book*.

Even Judith's decapitation of Holofernes could be read as the just execution of a deserving criminal at the command of God, the supreme judge (*dema*).[28] Although these literary topoi should not be regarded as straightforward evidence for Anglo-Saxon punishment in practice, especially when they draw upon biblical material or stories of early martyrdoms, it is clear that contemporary audiences were expected to recognize and understand the impact of these imagined penalties.

Hagiographies, homilies, and other religious texts also echoed contemporary legal language and judicial practice. In addition to the numerous Anglo-Saxon adaptations of Roman-era martyrs' stories, which frequently described gruesome punishments, clerical authors and artists showed considerable familiarity with contemporary penalties. Lantfred, in his *Translatio et miracula* of St Swithun, enumerated a series of grisly punishments for theft which were likely part of a (now lost) law code of King Edgar; Ælfric of Eynsham listed similar punishments in his homily on the book of Maccabees.[29] Elsewhere, Ælfric took for granted that thieves would be put to death whether or not they repented of their sins – a position also taken by Bishop Theodred of London, who reportedly tried and hanged a group of would-be church robbers himself.[30] Bishop Ælfheah of Winchester was credited with flogging and imprisoning a thief, who confessed that he deserved the punishments decreed for him by the bishop's just judgment (*iusto iudicio episcopi*); and Archbishop Dunstan of Canterbury was reputed to have enforced harsh justice in his diocese, demanding on one occasion that the hands of convicted forgers be chopped off in accordance with the law.[31] Despite occasional clerical objections against clergy shedding blood or endorsing lethal judicial sentences, these examples suggest that high-ranking churchmen possessed a working knowledge of criminal procedure and participated, to some degree, in the execution of earthly justice.[32] Artistic renditions of biblical episodes confirm

---

[28] *Judith*, especially lines 65 and 103–11; and see also 4, 59, and 94, where God is referred to as *dema*, 'judge,' in the context of Holofernes' death: Elliott Van Kirk Dobbie, ed., *Beowulf and Judith*, ASPR 4 (New York, 1953).

[29] Lantfred's text is edited in Lapidge, *Swithun*, with this episode at pp. 312–13. For the episode's relation to Old English law, see Dorothy Whitelock, 'Wulfstan *Cantor* and Anglo-Saxon Law,' *Nordica et Anglica: Studies in Honor of Stefan Einarsson*, ed. A. H. Orrick (The Hague, 1968), pp. 83–92, at 83–7; Wormald, *Making of English Law*, pp. 125–8 and 370; O'Brien O'Keeffe, 'Body and Law,' 225–9. See also the essay by Valerie Allen in this volume. For Ælfric's homily on *Maccabees*, see Skeat, *LS* II, pp. 74–7.

[30] Ælfric's discussion of thieves appears in his homily on Ahitophel and Absolom, edited in Skeat, *LS* I, pp. 424–31. Theodred's execution of thieves was first attested in Abbo of Fleury's *Life of St Edmund*, edited by Michael Winterbottom in *Three Lives of English Saints* (Toronto, 1972), pp. 65–87, at 84. See also Nicole Marafioti, 'Punishing Bodies and Saving Souls: Capital and Corporal Punishment in Late Anglo-Saxon England,' *HSJ* 20 (2008), 39–57; Wormald, 'Handlist,' no. 157.

[31] Wulfstan of Winchester, *The Life of St Æthelwold*, ed. Michael Lapidge and Michael Winterbottom (Oxford, 1991), pp. 68–9; Eadmer of Canterbury, *Lives and Miracles of Saints Oda, Dunstan, and Oswald*, ed. Bernard J. Muir and Andrew J. Turner (Oxford, 2006), pp. 119–23. See also Wormald, 'Handlist,' nos 154 and 174.

[32] For Ælfric's own objections, see Malcolm Godden, 'The Relations of Ælfric and Wulfstan: A Re-assessment,' *Wulfstan*, ed. Townend, pp. 353–74, at 355. See also Marafioti, 'Punishing Bodies,' pp. 43–6.

Introduction

this impression, as monastic productions offer glimpses of what punishment may have looked like in Anglo-Saxon England. In the Old English Hexateuch, an illustration of Pharaoh ordering an execution provides a clear image of a post-and-lintel gallows, while Noah's wayward raven is shown scavenging a decapitated head displayed on a pike.[33] In addition, illustrations of damnation in the Harley Psalter show condemned souls with severed heads and amputated feet, with a nearby angel wielding an executioner's sword.[34] In order to convey appropriate interpretations of the biblical past and coming afterlife, these punishments must have been recognizable to the artists and their audience.

A growing corpus of archaeological evidence confirms that physical punishment was employed in Anglo-Saxon society, as the past decade has seen a surer and more extensive identification of executed bodies from the Anglo-Saxon period.[35] So-called 'deviant' burial frequently involved the inversion or violation of funerary norms, to distinguish the condemned in death from the rest of the community.[36] Executed bodies were confined to shallow, short, or shared graves; buried face-down or in positions that suggest they were thrown carelessly into the ground; and interred with their hands bound or with neck trauma that indicates death by hanging. Corpses might be buried after decomposition had set in, suggesting a period of above-ground display (on a gallows, for instance), while some individuals may have been buried before they were fully dead.[37] There is also evidence for mutilation. In some cases, execution victims show signs of having lived with an amputated limb for some time before their deaths, suggesting that they may have been repeat offenders.[38] In other instances, body parts – notably severed heads – were placed between the legs or elsewhere in the grave. Heads might also be buried separately, sometimes with greater evidence of

---

[33] MS BL Cotton Claudius B. IV, available through http://www.bl.uk/manuscripts/ [accessed 5 January 2013]; the hanging is at fol. 59r and Noah's raven at 15r. See also Milton McC. Gatch, 'Noah's Raven in Genesis A and the Illustrated Old English Hexateuch,' *Gesta* 14 (1975), 3–15. Compare the description of head stakes and the display of decapitated bodies in the Old English legend of the Seven Sleepers: Hugh Magennis, *The Anonymous Old English Legend of the Seven Sleepers* (Durham, 1994), p. 35; Catherine Cubitt, '"As the Lawbook Teaches": Reeves, Lawbooks and Urban Life in the Anonymous Old English Legend of the Seven Sleepers,' *EHR* 124 (2009), 1021–49, at 1028–9; Andrew Reynolds, 'The Definition and Ideology of Anglo-Saxon Execution Sites and Cemeteries,' *Death and Burial in Medieval Europe: Papers of the 'Medieval Europe Brugge 1997' Conference*, vol. 2, ed. Guy De Boe and Frans Verhaeghe (Zellik, 1997), pp. 33–41, at 36; Reynolds, *Deviant Burial*, p. 31.

[34] MS BL Harley 603, fols 67r and 72r, available through http://www.bl.uk/catalogues/illuminatedmanuscripts [accessed 5 January 2013]; see also Sarah Semple, 'Illustrations of Damnation in Late Anglo-Saxon Manuscripts,' *ASE* 32 (2003), 231–45.

[35] Reynolds, *Deviant Burial*, pp. 56–60.

[36] The following modes of punishment are discussed in greater depth by Reynolds, *Deviant Burial*, especially pp. 34–60; Reynolds, 'Definition and Ideology,' 34–7; Dawn M. Hadley and Jo Buckberry, 'Caring for the Dead in Late Anglo-Saxon England,' *Pastoral Care*, ed. Tinti, pp. 121–47, at 128–30.

[37] For debates surrounding live burial, see Reynolds, *Deviant Burial*, pp. 70–1.

[38] Amputations may also indicate non-judicial injuries or medical treatment: see Hadley and Buckberry, 'Caring for the Dead,' p. 130; Mary P. Richards, 'The Body as Text in Early Anglo-Saxon Law,' *Naked Before God*, ed. Withers and Wilcox, pp. 97–115, at 105–6.

decomposition which suggests that they were displayed without the rest of the body, perhaps on a stake.

In addition to the exceptional treatment of their bodies, deviant burials were often relegated to their own cemeteries, typically located in border areas which sometimes doubled as execution sites. Solitary burials, well away from inhabited areas, were also a possibility.[39] By the tenth century, as consecrated churchyard burial became standard in England for most Christians, the systematic interment of deviants in liminal and isolated areas reflects a deliberate exclusion from hallowed ground, an ideology that was first articulated in the laws of Æthelstan in the mid-tenth century.[40] Even before consecrated burial became the norm for ordinary Christians, however, the exceptional treatment of condemned bodies would have distinguished them from the rest of the population and marked them as outcasts. Under ordinary circumstances, a burial served as a focus of remembrance: the arrangement of the body and composition of the grave provided witnesses with a final, idealized image of the deceased, while above-ground markers functioned as a 'text' to be read and interpreted by contemporary survivors and future generations.[41] In cases of execution, the signifying elements of burial proclaimed a different message, marking the condemned as undeserving of a respectable Christian grave. Together, the spectacle of punishment and the mnemonic aspects of burial would have confirmed the deviant identity of the dead. For those who witnessed the execution or encountered the resulting body or grave, a memory of the punishment – and of the offense that necessitated it – would endure beyond the moment of death.

The spectacular, memorable nature of these punishments would surely have been cultivated by those decreeing and carrying out capital and corporal sentences in order to discourage future offenses, with fear of punishment functioning as an instrument of social control. Certainly, the physical pain that would accompany bodily penalties could serve as a convincing deterrent.[42] Humiliation may also have been a factor, as the prospect of a public, dishonorable death at the hands of executioners may have discouraged

---

[39] Andrew Reynolds, 'Burials, Boundaries and Charters in Anglo-Saxon England: A Reassessment,' *Burial in Early Medieval England and Wales*, ed. Sam Lucy and Andrew Reynolds, Society for Medieval Archaeology Monograph 17 (2002), pp. 171–94, at 179–83.

[40] II Æthelstan 26. For the denial of consecrated burial as punishment, see Thompson, *Dying and Death*, pp. 170–80; Reynolds, 'Definition and Ideology,' pp. 33–41; Bonnie Effros, 'Beyond Cemetery Walls: Early Medieval Funerary Topography and Christian Salvation,' *EME* 6 (1997), 1–23. For the development of consecrated cemeteries in England, see Helen Gittos, 'Creating the Sacred: Anglo-Saxon Rites for Consecrating Cemeteries,' *Burial in Early Medieval England and Wales*, ed. Lucy and Reynolds, pp. 195–208; Donald Bullough, 'Burial, Community and Belief in the Early Medieval West,' *Ideal and Reality in Frankish and Anglo-Saxon Society: Studies Presented to J. M. Wallace-Hadrill*, ed. Patrick Wormald (Oxford, 1983), pp. 177–201.

[41] See for example Howard Williams, *Death and Memory in Early Medieval Britain* (Cambridge, 2006); Martin Carver, 'Why That? Why There? Why Then? The Politics of Early Medieval Monumentality,' *Image and Power in the Archaeology of Early Medieval Britain: Essays in Honour of Rosemary Cramp*, ed. Helena Hamerow and Arthur MacGregor (Oxford, 2001), pp. 1–22.

[42] Lantfred applies this logic to Edgar's laws in the late tenth century: see Lapidge, *Swithun*, pp. 312–13; and n. 29 above.

some from lawbreaking.[43] Moreover, a criminal's execution and burial might bring his survivors shame and grief: a law of Æthelred provides conditions for removing the body of a condemned kinsman from its original grave, presumably so that the family could bury it more respectfully; while a royal charter of the 990s pardoned a reeve for allowing a thief's accomplices Christian burial, because the king did not want to sadden his reeve by ordering the bodies moved to unconsecrated ground.[44] In addition to any emotional repercussions, a criminal's punishment had material and economic consequences for his kin. A person who survived a non-lethal mutilation might have had trouble providing for his dependents with his new disability, and his injuries would also have branded him a criminal – a life-long stigma that could render him an outcast.[45] Offenders might have their property confiscated or be charged a substantial fine, whether they lived or died, and the survivors and heirs of convicted criminals might find themselves dispossessed and destitute.[46] Yet death sentences also had spiritual consequences for the condemned, as excommunication was an implicit element of capital punishment.[47] The relegation of executed bodies to liminal areas and their exclusion from hallowed ground confirmed criminals' exclusion from the Christian community, and it is conceivable that this exclusion extended to their kin.[48] Such serious and lasting consequences – for the offender himself as well as for his survivors – would have reinforced the authority and practical power of those orchestrating criminal punishments.

For the purposes of this volume, then, 'punishment' will be understood as a top-down initiative which operated within the context of judicial practice. Whether implemented by kings and their representatives, by lesser magnates, or by other individuals or institutions, 'punishment' refers to penalties imposed by those in power against those who were found responsible for transgressing the limits of what was deemed acceptable behavior and practice.[49] The objective of punishment, by this definition, was to impose order from above through the enforced regulation of established norms. Feud violence, which existed alongside judicial punishments for much of the period

[43] Execution would not fulfill the requirements for a 'good death' by Christian standards: see for example Thompson, *Dying and Death*, pp. 57–84; Frederick S. Paxton, *Christianizing Death: The Creation of a Ritual Process in Early Medieval Europe* (Ithaca, NY, 1993).
[44] The law is III Æthelred 7.1. The charter, S 883, records that the reeve was brought to court for refusing to deny the dead men consecrated graves; the king ordered that they stay buried among Christians out of mercy for his reeve, Æthelwig: 'nolens contristari Aþelwig quia mihi erat carus et preciosus.' See also Wormald, 'Handlist,' no. 54.
[45] O'Brien O'Keeffe, 'Body and Law'; Richards, 'Body as Text'; Oliver, *Body Legal*, pp. 172–6.
[46] Wormald, 'Giving God and King their Due,' pp. 339–42; Wormald, 'Charters, Law and the Settlement of Disputes,' pp. 307–8.
[47] E. M. Treharne, 'A Unique Old English Formula for Excommunication from Cambridge, Corpus Christi College 303,' *ASE* 24 (1995), 185–211, at 195–7; Thompson, *Dying and Death*, pp. 170–80.
[48] For anathema as contagious, see Elisabeth Vodola, *Excommunication in the Middle Ages* (Berkeley, CA, 1986), pp. 8 and 20–4.
[49] Penalties that were not imposed directly upon the offender's body, such as forfeiture or exile, fall within this definition of 'punishment' but are generally outside the purview of this volume.

covered in this book, is thus excluded, since feud scenarios represent 'self help' by injured parties rather than punishment by an external authority. However, commensurate retribution against an offender may be seen as punishment if it was facilitated by a third party invested with the power to intervene in private disputes. Royal legislation decreeing eye-for-an-eye justice, for instance, allowed kings to write themselves into feud and redirect horizontal 'self help' through a vertical process of law and justice.[50]

Also excluded from our definition of punishment are acts of extra-judicial violence, including warfare and attacks on individuals. The reification of the Three Orders of Society and an increasing interest in Just War theory towards the turn of the first millennium helped legitimize military activity as a Christian obligation, and prolonged Viking attacks made fighting a particularly urgent priority in England.[51] Yet armed conflict did not formally bring individual offenders to account for their misdeeds, as battlefield injury and death were by-products of war, not its objective. Likewise, assaults and killings that were not directly sanctioned by a legal authority are outside the scope of punishment as defined here. This category includes the injuries that Anglo-Saxon legislation sought to restrict, as well as violence that could be construed as justifiable – killing a thief caught in the act of stealing, for instance. Although the threat of such activity might have functioned at times as a form of social control, scenarios in which individuals privately took action against others are not within the purview of this book. As in these cases, however, punishment – when deployed as an element of judicial process – was portrayed as a legitimate application of violence. Just as it was recognized that individuals could kill in warfare and that the injured might exact revenge in feud scenarios, so punishment issued by a third party was construed by those in power as acceptable practice. Even Archbishop Wulfstan, with his professed concern for the souls of criminals, acknowledged and endorsed the role of secular punishment in keeping order on earth and bringing wrongdoers to repent. At best, earthly law would replicate divine law, and its application would reflect God's will.

The essays in this collection examine how and why attitudes and understandings of law shifted, the anxieties and aspirations of authorities regarding violence, and the moral status of punishment. Taken together, three dominant themes emerge which elaborate a narrative of judicial violence. First is the shift in Anglo-Saxon society from a culture of feud, in which wrongs were redressed by victims, perpetrators, and their kin, to a system of punishment,

---

[50] Wormald, 'Giving God and King their Due,' pp. 336–42.
[51] For the Three Orders of society in Old English literature, see Godden and Irvine, *OE Boethius* I, B.17, p. 277; Karl Jost, ed., *Die 'Institutes of Polity, Civil and Ecclesiastical': Ein Werk Erzbischof Wulfstans von York* (Bern, 1959), pp. 55–8; Timothy E. Powell, 'The "Three Orders" of Society in Anglo-Saxon England,' *ASE* 23 (1994), 103–32. For the moral obligation to fight, see Malcolm Godden, 'Apocalypse and Invasion in Late Anglo-Saxon England,' *From Anglo-Saxon to Early Middle English: Studies Presented to E. G. Stanley*, ed. Malcolm Godden, Douglas Gray, and T. F. Hoad (Oxford, 1994), pp. 130–62.

in which penalties were imposed by a third party. As noted above, for most of the period covered in this book, top-down justice instituted by kings, their agents, or local authority figures operated alongside systems of feud and compensation. However, as Valerie Allen argues in Chapter 1, one of the most significant developments in the rise of punishment was the substitution of money for blood in feud scenarios. The talionic necessity for eye-for-an-eye justice was eased by the idea that monetary payment could offer an honorable way out of a conflict and prevent violent retaliation. The substitution of money for vengeance fundamentally changed the role of the law and the status of the individual before it. The fungibility of blood and coin allowed for greater flexibility in conflict resolution and peace-keeping: it made violence an option, not a necessity.

In addition, monetary payment widened the circle of participants beyond the disputing parties, as outsiders might be called upon to mediate a fair settlement. This opened the door for aspiring authority figures – kings, clergy, or local magnates – to participate in and benefit from feud culture. Legislators were particularly eager to claim control over the process of dispute resolution, and the earliest Anglo-Saxon royal law codes include lists of compensation tariffs to be rendered to an injured party. In issuing such regulations, a king assumed the role of mediator: it was he who proclaimed the appropriate compensation for various offenses, whether or not he was personally involved in their settlement. However, it is unclear how closely written law was followed in practice, and it is likely that the earliest Anglo-Saxon tariff lists codified existing tradition. In other words, laws were informed and justified by local custom and expectations. Nonetheless, the laws were given under a king's name, allowing him to assert legal authority personally. The proportion of laws concerned with injury, especially in the earliest laws, suggests that this was a primary objective of those kings, even if concerns changed over time. The tariffs for genital injuries, examined by Lisi Oliver in Chapter 3, exemplify such custom and change. The enormous compensation required in Æthelberht's seventh-century laws finds no parallel in Alfred's ninth-century *domboc*, indicating sharply different understandings of the effects of a genital wound across two centuries. While both kings' laws recognized the need for compensation and imposed what must have been deemed an appropriate payment for the injury, this comparison demonstrates that royal responses to conflict were not monolithic. Rather, they were justified by evolving rationales and were negotiated over time.

Still, the need to justify punishment as a royal prerogative through written law reflects how fragile such claims may have been. Unlike penalties imposed by an outside authority, feud and compensation were undertaken by the disputing parties themselves and driven by notions of honor: the shame of being victimized could only be countered by an equivalent act of vengeance or a settlement substantial enough for the injured to save face.[52]

---

[52] Hyams, *Rancor and Reconciliation*, especially pp. 3–110; Patrick Wormald, '*Lex Scripta* and *Verbum Regis*: Legislation and Germanic Kingship, from Euric to Cnut,' *Legal Culture*, pp. 1–43.

In this context, the gradual introduction of third-party punishment resulted in a transition from a restitutional to a punitive legal system. In Chapter 2, Daniela Fruscione examines this shift and identifies innovations in the West Saxon royal laws which justified the application of punishment for the first time. She argues that the earliest Anglo-Saxon law codes asserted royal power only tentatively. The establishment of compensation tariffs was claimed as the king's prerogative, but there were only a handful of instances in Æthelberht's laws in which additional punishment was exacted by the king: these consisted of a fine (*wite*) to be paid in addition to the sum rendered to the victim.[53] Though they might be seen as an early form of top-down punishment, these fines were framed by feuding logic, in which the payment was rendered as compensation to the king for breaking the peace in his presence. By systematically writing the king into the process of dispute settlement, the earliest English lawmakers made private disputes royal business. Although fines may still have been understood within Anglo-Saxon feud culture as a sort of compensation to prevent the king from taking vengeance upon those who broke the peace, they set the groundwork for later rulers to establish a distinct category of crime: offenses that did not involve the king's person but which violated his law and will.[54] The fact that *wite* became a standard term for any kind of penalty – judicial fines, bodily punishment, and even hellfire – reflects a new understanding of top-down justice. Conflicts were no longer to be resolved by the disputing parties alone; they were also cause for punishment from above.

The second theme that emerges in this volume is the role of punishment in a Christian society. The law codes of tenth- and eleventh-century kings are dramatically different from those of their seventh-century predecessors, not least in their explicit concern for the souls of offenders. Physical penalties assumed an increasingly prominent place in royal legislation in the tenth century, and the laws of Æthelstan in particular broke new ground in their systematic prescription of the death penalty for thieves.[55] The legitimacy of such harsh punishments was reinforced under Æthelstan's successor, Edmund, whose laws sought to restrict unlawful violence (*unrihtlican gefeoht*) by laying out conditions for settlement of feuds within the king's peace and setting penalties for those who persisted in vendettas.[56] Even recognizing that written law may represent ideal more than reality, it seems that a royal monopoly on legitimate violence was deemed acceptable by those who composed and promulgated royal law. The fact that even the harshest Anglo-Saxon law codes were drafted by or under the auspices of clergymen, however, would have presented a quandary: how would punishment affect the spiritual state of offenders, those who carried out royal justice, and those who issued the law?

---

[53] Æthelberht 8 is explicit in its requirement of both compensation and a fine; the two-part payment is implicit in Æthelberht 11, 12, and 15: see Oliver, *Beginnings of English Law*, pp. 85 and 135.
[54] Wormald, 'Giving God and King their Due,' pp. 340–1.
[55] Wormald, *Making of English Law*, pp. 305–7.
[56] II Edmund. Compare also Hyams, *Rancor and Reconciliation*, pp. 82–4.

Introduction

In addition to constructing particular roles for those in power, the collective attempts by royal and ecclesiastical officials to define the role of punishment in Christian Anglo-Saxon society reshaped the relationship between the individual and those in authority. Judicial processes and punishments came to be associated with pastoral as well as secular objectives, creating a moral obligation for the individual before the law. Although the pastoral concerns of Anglo-Saxon legislators before c. 1000 were less explicit than Wulfstan's, most codes included provisions for their subjects' souls. In some cases there were close connections between, and mutual influence by, royal law and penitential literature. In Chapter 4 Stefan Jurasinski traces one example of this confluence. The practice of 'sick-maintenance,' in which an individual who injures another is obligated to provide or pay for his victim's care, appears both in law codes and penitentials. Yet as Jurasinski argues, the sick-maintenance clauses in Anglo-Saxon penitentials seem to have been influenced by royal legislation rather than the other way around, despite the biblical origins of the tradition. The penitential authors evidently recognized the pastoral and moral intentions behind these laws. Daniel Thomas approaches the law's treatment of souls from a different perspective in Chapter 5, investigating how judicial imprisonment drew upon penitential and monastic practices. From the ninth century, royal codes required offenders to submit to confinement and penance as part of their punishment, and even without the type of explicit explanation that would be offered by Wulfstan, it is clear that such laws sought to address spiritual and earthly offenses in tandem. Taken together, these essays demonstrate a dynamic, concurrent evolution of penitential and judicial practice, confirming that Christian ideology was not divorced from royal law.

While offenders' souls were certainly a concern, there were also questions about how severe punishments would affect those who imposed them. Canonical prohibitions against clergy shedding blood created difficulties for bishops and other churchmen who were responsible for issuing justice within their earthly jurisdictions. Perhaps clerical drafters of royal law justified their bloodier sentences by assuming that punishments would be executed by secular authorities. Nevertheless, even laymen may have balked at the spiritual consequences of implementing harsher sentences – hanging thieves as young as twelve years old, say, or amputating all of a repeat offender's extremities.[57] In Chapter 6 Nicole Marafioti considers how judicial punishments were justified in the Old English *Consolation of Philosophy*, a text produced at the turn of the tenth century, ostensibly as part of King Alfred's translation program. In comparing judges to confessors or doctors, who cure souls and bodies through superficially painful means, the *Consolation* established that issuing just punishments to deserving offenders was virtuous and even beneficial to the souls of the punishers. While such assurances would surely have eased the minds of individuals responsible for rendering justice, this argument also reinforced the idea that top-down

---

[57] II Æthelstan 1; II Cnut 30.4–5.

punishment was compatible with Christian values. If punishment was a righteous exercise that helped preserve offenders' souls, the individuals who issued and implemented the law could portray themselves as acting in accordance with God's will. From a spiritual perspective, the physical punishment of offenders offered a chance to serve a greater good.

This point leads to the third major theme of this volume: how kings and other authority figures sought to use punishment – or the threat of punishment – to enhance and centralize their power. In Chapter 7 Jo Buckberry surveys the archaeological evidence for execution and mutilation, assessing how widely the penalties prescribed in royal law codes were actually employed. The examination of deviant burials and execution cemeteries reveals patterns of osteological trauma consistent with various types of execution and corporal punishment attested in Anglo-Saxon texts. This analysis demonstrates that the harsh penalties prescribed in written legislation were in fact applied in practice, although rather less frequently than the textual evidence implies. Nevertheless, though the archaeology of the period confirms that harsh legal penalties were indeed carried out, it is unclear to what extent such action was linked to royal initiative. Were the executioners who mutilated, executed, or displayed the bodies of the condemned following the king's law or imposing a more localized brand of justice?

Discussions of this topic generally fall into two scholarly camps. The so-called 'maximalist' interpretation holds that Anglo-Saxon kings centralized and consolidated their power through the tenth and eleventh centuries, to the extent that they were largely able to implement the laws they issued in their written codes.[58] By contrast, the 'minimalist' view contends that royal legislation was more aspiration than reality, with most conflicts resolved at a lower level, either by local authorities or by the disputing parties themselves.[59] The remaining essays in this book draw upon both sides of this debate as they consider the political role of capital and corporal punishments in the construction of an Anglo-Saxon state. For kings who professed responsibility for enforcing law and order throughout their realms, physical punishments had the potential to serve not only as retribution but also as deterrents against crime and expressions of royal power. These objectives are especially evident in the punishments set for fraudulent moneyers, as Daniel O'Gorman demonstrates in Chapter 8. As prescribed in tenth-century legislation, a convicted forger would not only have his hand cut off, but would also have the severed limb displayed as a warning to others. It is significant that these were the only written laws that specifically required an amputated body part to be displayed: because kings claimed a monopoly on minting coins, forging threatened to undermine royal authority and had to be severely punished. For lawmakers concerned with protecting a unique royal prerogative, one

---

[58] See especially James Campbell, 'The Late Anglo-Saxon State: A Maximum View,' *The Anglo-Saxon State* (London, 2000), pp. 1–30.

[59] See especially Hyams, *Rancor and Reconciliation*, pp. 71–110.

which so often carried the king's image, a displayed hand unambiguously proclaimed the rights and power of the king.

Still, the exhibition of severed limbs, or of bodies, was not an unambiguous symbol of royal power. Such displays might convey a range of possible meanings; accordingly, they had to be carefully choreographed so that the intended message could be fully understood. Jay Paul Gates considers this theme in Chapter 9, assessing two interpretations of Cnut's 1017 execution of Eadric *Streona*, produced by Worcester historians in the generation after the Norman Conquest. Although both chroniclers regarded Eadric's death as an appropriate end for a traitor, their narratives offer contrasting views of royal power: one regarded the execution as a righteous exercise of royal authority and deemed the desecration of Eadric's corpse appropriate; the other portrayed the execution as an abuse of royal power, imagining a king who killed secretly and disposed of his victim's body shamefully. Even as these authors used Eadric's story to comment on post-Conquest political concerns, their diverging accounts of a seemingly straightforward event reveal how elusive the message of execution could be – even in retrospect.

While these essays tend towards maximalist narratives of bodily punishment, the volume's final piece offers a more minimalist response. In Chapter 10 Andrew Rabin reconsiders whether the archaeological evidence for judicial execution actually reflects a centralized system of royal justice. Kings were not the only beneficiaries of demonstrative penalties: lesser authorities and communities might likewise be strengthened by the process of punishing crime. The practicalities of implementing corporal sentences were rarely mentioned in royal legislation, which apparently left the logistical aspects of punishment in the hands of local authorities, and localized justice likely operated independently of royal decree in all but the most serious cases. Accordingly, variation in capital sentences in written law across the period reflects debate and negotiation among legislators and the individuals charged with enforcing the law. Despite lawmakers' efforts to frame punishment as the king's prerogative, justice was not always a royal monopoly.

This shared responsibility for keeping the peace and issuing justice reflects how substantially ideas about punishment evolved across this period. Justice was not monolithic in Anglo-Saxon society; it is impossible to identify a comprehensive philosophy of how punishment ought to operate or a single centralized apparatus for administering penalties. Rather, punishment was a product of dialogue and negotiation – between royal and local authorities, between laymen and clergy, between judges, offenders, and their communities. The essays in this volume, by identifying some of the major points of tension in these exchanges, examine how punishment came to be recognized as a legitimate form of violence and understood as an acceptable means of social control. Yet although the harshest punishments of death and mutilation are attested with regularity in the archaeological and textual record, only a small portion of the population actually endured these penalties. The provision of alternative punishments, chances for redemption, and the possibility of pardon in so many written law codes suggest that dramatic physical penalties were designed as a last resort, for offenders who could not be curbed by any other method; and the careful justifications concerning authority figures' right and obligation to enforce the law suggest that the legitimacy of top-down punishment could not always be taken for granted. In Anglo-Saxon England, capital and corporal punishments were the exception, not the rule.

1

When Compensation Costs an Arm and a Leg

Valerie Allen

It is a commonplace of nineteenth-century legal history that monetary compensation overtook feuding, and that such a development – fostered by the Church – set justice on its way towards its fulfillment in centralized regnal authority, public peace, and state-mandated punishment. Recent legal history has revised this model of linear evolution from feud to monetary compensation to punishment, and emphasized instead both the simultaneity of revenge and compensation systems, and the coexistence of opposing pro- and anti-revenge arguments. Attention has turned to the gradual change from a logic of feud (the early seventh century being the earliest date for recorded Anglo-Saxon law) to a logic of punishment as an indication of the Christianization of law, a change well underway by the eleventh century.[1] Thought of as two vectors of force, vengeance tracks a horizontal line of reciprocal violence between (roughly) equal bodies (whether kin or entire communities), while punishment thrusts vertically and unidirectionally down from top (state, ecclesiastical, or regnal power) to bottom with a mandate of authority that pre-empts, at least in theory, reprisal from family and friends of the disciplined offender.[2]

The new emphasis on corporal punishment in the later codes – a kind of Christianized violence – anticipates the twelfth-century spiritual economics of purgatory that enables pre-payment of a sinner's debt to God.[3] Theologizing of law moves social order from the compensatory to the disciplinary, as pain itself increasingly expiates wrongdoing, offering the offender the possibility of a subject position with the experiential capacity for increasingly refined *passio*.[4]

---

[1] Katherine O'Brien O'Keeffe, 'Body and Law in Late Anglo-Saxon England,' *ASE* 27 (1998), 209–32; Mary P. Richards, 'The Body as Text in Early Anglo-Saxon Law,' *Naked Before God*, ed. Withers and Wilcox, pp. 97–115.
[2] Paul R. Hyams, 'Neither Unnatural nor Wholly Negative: The Future of Medieval Vengeance,' *Vengeance in the Middle Ages*, ed. Susanna A. Throop and Paul R. Hyams (Farnham, 2010), pp. 203–20, at 217–18.
[3] Caroline Walker Bynum, 'The Power in the Blood: Sacrifice, Satisfaction and Substitution in Late Medieval Soteriology,' *The Redemption: An Interdisciplinary Symposium on Christ as Redeemer*, ed. Stephen T. Davis, Daniel Kendall, and Gerald O'Collins (Oxford, 2004), pp. 177–204, at 192. See also Jacques le Goff, *The Birth of Purgatory*, trans. Arthur Goldhammer (London, 1984).
[4] Walker Bynum, 'Power in the Blood,' p. 198.

It is open to question, however, whether the revenge/punishment distinction will hold absolutely. As Ian Miller observes, it is a fine line between handing over body parts in payment to having them taken in punishment.⁵ Later Anglo-Saxon law refashions revenge into punishment, and the example *par excellence* of this is King Edgar's law of talion, now lost but retained in II Cnut 30.4–5, where the prescribed mutilations are designed both to deter other possible offenders and to save the soul of the actual offender by provoking suffering without death.⁶ The salvific dimension of pain points us in the direction of an ancient Greek saying (*mathein pathein*), namely, that learning hurts, conversely, that punishment teaches. However, a king's motives for punishment – deterrence (that he may control his subjects), rehabilitation, prevention – need not exclude that of retribution. Separating satisfaction from motives to deter, prevent, and rehabilitate is only theoretically possible, enabling the impulse to revenge to sublimate into the aims of spiritual betterment and docile bodies.

The point leads to the question of what value pain in the earlier laws carries. Already, as Daniela Fruscione argues in this collection, punitive damages to the king exist embryonically in Æthelberht's code.⁷ And some of the scenarios for which compensation is awarded tacitly suggest punishment by mutilation administered 'horizontally,' as in loss of thumbnails. There is nothing to stop deterrence, prevention, and even rehabilitation being the net effect of pain inflicted within a culture of revenge. To the extent that revenge and punishment can coexist, feuding families and king alike pay back an action with an equal and opposite reaction.⁸

Monetary compensation sits uneasily within this narrative, either as limp substitute for revenge or ideologically inflected 'progress' towards centralized law. In demonstration of the former, the Finn episode in *Beowulf* – its textual instability notwithstanding – imaginatively demonstrates the insubstantiality of a peace negotiated between Frisians and Danes with 'rings and rich treasures of plated gold' (*sincgestreonum / fættan goldes*) when weighed in the balance against the claims of hot blood.⁹ In demonstration of the latter, Bede celebrates the mediatory role of the Church and the pacificatory appeal of monetary compensation, in speaking of how Archbishop Theodore persuaded King Ecgfrith to accept the customary 'compensation' (*pecunia*) for the killing of his brother Ælfwine rather than seek vengeance from King Æthelred of the Mercians.¹⁰

I argue, however, that monetary compensation is central to the process of justice, for it lays bare the commonality between revenge and punishment,

---

⁵ William Ian Miller, *Eye for an Eye* (New York, 2006), p. 35.
⁶ For Edgar's law, see Lantfred's *Translatio et miracula de S Swithuni*, in Lapidge, *Swithun*, pp. 310–12.
⁷ See the essay by Daniela Fruscione in this volume, pp. 35–7.
⁸ Miller, *Eye for an Eye*, p. 10, for Newton's third law of motion as a kind of revenge.
⁹ *Beowulf*, lines 1092–3.
¹⁰ Cited by Stanley Rubin, 'The *Bot*, or Composition in Anglo-Saxon Law: A Reassessment,' *Journal of Legal History* 17 (1996), 144–54, at 144.

namely, that there is a third party – an 'oddman' (*oddamaðr*) in Old Norse – mediating and controlling the exchange between opposing parties.[11] In the words of Emmanuel Levinas, 'the drama of forgiveness comprises not just two players but three.'[12] The 'self-help' justice of revenge is just as much subject to the authority of a third party as is the justice of punishment decreed by king's law, for even players in a tit-for-tat game of revenge defer to an umpire: public approval of fair play. Compensation tariffs (not to mention the additional fine (*wite*) payable for breaking the king's peace) make those rules of the revenge game explicit and, *qua* law, actively intervene between two warring factions as the third party.

Money is central, not peripheral, to the business of justice because it functions as that third party or oddman, medium of exchange, universal equivalent. Of course, Anglo-Saxon currency is not a universal equivalent in quite the sense that Marx speaks of gold, but it does have a general if limited equivalence sufficient that the tariffs should state their amounts in money as a unit of account. By being the third party, money has therapeutic value. *Pace* the Finn episode, where rings and gold cannot appease the Danes' desire to avenge their dead leader Hnæf, money does good psychic work. Coins, which can be held at arm's length, laid down, or transmuted into something else, allow anger to exit the body.

Although other English codes mention compensation payments for personal injury, two are particularly important for their comprehensiveness of coverage: those of Æthelberht of Kent (composed c. 602×3) and Alfred of Wessex (composed c. 890).[13] Before considering in more depth the monies mentioned in these codes, a related question is addressed, namely, whether or not the tariffs were adjustable. Stanley Rubin argues not, claiming that where personal injury occurred the *bot* or compensation was fixed regardless of rank, which of course determined the amount of one's wergild.[14] Rubin notes that Æthelberht's and Alfred's tariffs, in fixing the compensation amounts relative to the wergild of a *ceorl* or ordinary freeman, demonstrate a bias in favour of this humble class, which 'formed the backbone and main pillar in society.'[15] In contrast, Lisi Oliver infers from the incompleteness of circumstantial detail that the written tariffs constituted the maximum penalty and were therefore adjustable.[16] Her fictionalized case based on the code of Æthelberht explores material considerations not explicitly provided for, such as discriminating between a serious injury that does heal and

---

[11] Miller, *Eye for an Eye*, pp. 8–11.
[12] Emmanuel Levinas, *Quatre lectures talmudiques* (Paris, 1968), p. 41: 'Le drame du pardon ne comporte pas seulement deux personnages, mais trois.'
[13] See Æthelberht 34–71 [34–72]; Alfred 44–77. Æthelberht's code is cited by the numeration provided in Oliver, *Beginnings of English Law*, with the numeration from Liebermann, *Gesetze* I in square brackets. Alfred's laws follow the numeration in Liebermann, *Gesetze* I.
[14] Rubin, 'The *Bot*,' pp. 146–8, with some exceptions for clergy and for genital damage at pp. 148–51.
[15] Rubin, 'The *Bot*,' p. 148.
[16] Oliver, *Body Legal*, pp. 50–1.

a less grievous injury that does not.[17] Oliver's arguments in support of a degree of latitude in the application of the amounts seem to better support the contemporary historical conditions of scarcity of coin and the practice of substituting payment in kind.

A broader argument in favour of adjustable compensation has to do with the local nature of these laws. The tariffs are not the stuff of precedent out of which common law would be constructed after the Conquest. Though sanctioned by custom, regal authority, and the courtesy of having been written down, they do not have the metaphysical force of a legislative fiat that binds future decisions through the principle of *stare decisis*. Precedent lifts custom or local agreement to the status of the general; it makes a particular instance enshrine and apply the precept, and in doing so, provides a case or model or analogy to be followed henceforth. Customary law arises out of respect for tradition, communal decision-making, and practical wisdom – *phronesis* – rather than deriving from any abstract principle that pertains generally and applies mechanically. Justice occurs in the discursive process of establishing culpability and the performative 'composition' of a whole out of the miscellaneous parts of blood and shillings. Emphasis is on expeditious problem-solving, on achieving closure and moving on, which is why a case under Frankish law was subject to fine if not settled on the same day.[18] This essay claims that element of contingency not only for Anglo-Saxon customary law but also for the concept of value itself. For Georg Simmel, the cultural logic of the wergild 'not only makes money the measure of man, but it also makes man the measure of the value of money.'[19]

Show Me the Money

It is ironic that the very period when monetary compensation has most legal importance (roughly speaking, the period up to the reign of Alfred) is the same period when money is least standardized and least like modern money. The history of Anglo-Saxon coinage has been written many times.[20] This section describes four monetary stages: (i) pre-coinage; (ii) *thrymsas*; (iii) *sceattas*; (iv) pennies. Simplified as the account is, it should demonstrate the complex of variables that results in almost no two coins being identical – at least from the earlier period – and insofar as each coin was individually

---

[17] Oliver, *Body Legal*, p. 61.
[18] Oliver, *Body Legal*, pp. 33–4.
[19] Georg Simmel, *The Philosophy of Money*, trans. Tom Bottomore and David Frisby, 3rd edn (London, 2004), p. 385; quoted in Miller, *Eye for an Eye*, p. 41.
[20] Philip Grierson and Mark Blackburn, *Medieval European Coinage*, vol. 1: *The Early Middle Ages, 5th–10th Centuries* (Cambridge, 1986), p. 4; J. J. North, *English Hammered Coinage*, vol. 1: *Early Anglo-Saxon to Henry III, c. 600–1272*, 3rd edn (London, 1994), pp. 19–40; M. A. S. Blackburn, 'Coinage,' *Blackwell Encyclopaedia*, ed. Lapidge et al., pp. 113–16; J. R. Maddicott, 'Prosperity and Power in the Age of Bede and *Beowulf*,' *Proceedings of the British Academy* 117 (2002), 49–71, especially 51–3; Rory Naismith, *Money and Power in Anglo-Saxon England: The Southern English Kingdoms, 757–865* (Cambridge, 2012), pp. 4–9.

hammered, no two coins actually were identical.[21] The blank or flan was placed on the fixed bottom (obverse) die while the other (reverse) die was held over it. The imprint was made by means of a hammer striking flan and both dies simultaneously. Contributory variables thus include different bullion standards, weight fluctuations, place of minting, rulers, moneyers, and different permutations between the obverse and reverse images within a single issue of coin. To this, add the variability of the placement of blanks, and strength and angle of the hammer blow.

(i) Pre-coinage: From the early fifth century to around 600, there was no coin production in England, and such foreign currency as there was figured only peripherally, sometimes not even as money. A sixth-century pagan Anglo-Saxon warrior's grave at Dover reveals a bronze pan-balance and Roman coins (dating from the first to fourth centuries) used as weights.[22] In non-monetized economies, stamped coin tends to revert to ingots.

Coins were, however, in production on the Continent. The ultimate standard of imperial currency was the *aureus solidus*, introduced in the fourth century. Once insular coin production was underway, gold *solidi*, albeit highly alloyed, appear to have been struck in Kent during the 650s or 660s, although it was never the main denomination in England.[23] An object of beauty that will have been treasured and passed on at death, a seventh-century Byzantine pure gold *solidus* is set in an Anglo-Saxon gold and garnet pectoral cross, nicely illustrating how economies of monetary and gift exchange could coexist.[24]

Was retribution (i.e., payment by blood rather than money) more common during Æthelberht's era, when ready coin must have been scarce if not absent? The detail of his tariffs suggests not. The lack of currency only suggests that the computation of equivalent specie must have constituted much of the business of just settlement.

(ii) *Thrymsas*: The high value of the *solidus* and a general scarcity of gold bullion provoked heavier reliance on the smaller-value gold tremissis, worth one-third of the *solidus*. Merovingian France minted their own from the sixth century, while England made them the main insular currency: *thrymsas*, better known as shillings (OE *scillingas*).[25] Although various coins and coin-like objects have been discovered from the late sixth century, it was not until the 630s and 640s that sustained coin production took place in Kent, so the purse of Merovingian tremisses, discovered in Mound 1 of the seventh-century Sutton Hoo burial treasure and probably deposited in the 620s or 630s, pre-dates this robust period of insular minting.[26] The Sutton Hoo find certainly

---

[21] Philip Grierson differentiates between the regularization of the late period and the lack of it in Offa's time: 'Some Aspects of the Coinage of Offa,' *Numismatic Circular* 71 (1963), 223–5; reprinted as no. 26 in his *Dark Age Numismatics* (London, 1979), pp. 1–9, at 5–6.
[22] Jonathan Williams, ed., *Money: A History* (London, 1997), p. 67, fig. 94e.
[23] Grierson and Blackburn, *Medieval European Coinage*, p. 163.
[24] Williams, *Money*, p. 66, fig. 94a. For the dangers of an over-stated polarization between the two economies, see Naismith, *Money and Power*, pp. 260–1.
[25] Williams, *Money*, pp. 64–5; Grierson and Blackburn, *Medieval European Coinage*, p. 157.
[26] Grierson and Blackburn, *Medieval European Coinage*, pp. 124–5.

attests to stamped gold coin as the wealth of royalty and as a store of value that could be stockpiled and buried, but its very luxury calls into question the extent to which it participated in the daily business of ordinary justice among ordinary folk.

The Crondall hoard in Hampshire, dating from c. 645, yields a mix of Frankish and Anglo-Saxon gold tremisses, and appears to represent a complete wergild of 100 shillings, which sum Æthelberht 24 [21] sets as an ordinary man-price in Kent.[27] Only 93 of the coins, however, are tremisses. Philip Grierson imagines how the sum might have been assembled:

> The owner originally disposed of ninety-four Frankish and Anglo-Saxon coins [twenty-four Frankish and sixty-nine Anglo-Saxon], one of these being a counterfeit. To these, in order to make up a hundred, he added six more pieces of the appropriate weight, three roughly struck so as to imitate coins and three simply left blank. When the sum came to be paid, it was discovered that one of the coins was a counterfeit. It had consequently to be replaced by a small Byzantine coin detached from a necklace, perhaps belonging to the owner's wife. Only in some such way can one account for the presence in the group of one exceptional coin, an import from much further afield and struck to a different weight system.[28]

Face value is scarcely possible with blanks included in the shilling hoard, and weight unable to serve as a fundamental measure, being only approximate from one 'coin' to the next. The point is 'not the making up of a certain *weight* of gold, but a certain *number* of coins or their equivalents.'[29] Coin's chief virtue here is sheer partibility rather than any absolute shilling value, quanta to be counted rather than stuff to be measured.

The Crondall hoard suggests the possibility that such shillings, rare finds among coins, were reserved for compensation (or other ceremonial tributes), but their scarcity can equally imply that not all compensation was rendered as currency, especially for light injuries, such as bruises or seizing a man by his hair.[30]

(iii) *Sceattas*: With continuing debasement, English gold money 'evolved' into silver, with some pieces so transitional one is hard put to know whether to call them shillings or pennies.[31] From the 670s and by the 690s, the gold shilling had effected its transition to the silver penny (OE *pening*), now commonly known as the *sceat* (pl. *sceattas*), an erroneous designation 'based on a misinterpretation of an Anglo-Saxon word for weight.'[32] The *sceattas* mentioned in Æthelberht's code are not anachronistic, for they denote not the coins minted decades later but a weight of gold equivalent to one-twentieth of a shilling. The first reference to actual coin *sceattas* or pennies is not until the

---

[27] For the Crondall hoard, see Williams, *Money*, p. 67, plate 94g.
[28] Philip Grierson, 'The Purpose of the Sutton Hoo Coins,' *Antiquity* 44 (1970), 14–18, at 15; repr. as no. 9 in his *Dark Age Numismatics*.
[29] Grierson's comment refers to the Sutton Hoo tremisses, although the point applies equally to the Crondall hoard; see also Philip Grierson, *The Origins of Money* (London, 1977), pp. 30–1 and 33.
[30] On compensation for small injuries, see Æthelbert 33 [33] and 61.3–61.4 [59–60].
[31] Grierson and Blackburn, *Medieval European Coinage*, p. 164.
[32] North, *English Hammered Coinage*, p. 20.

late seventh-century law code of Ine of Wessex. As to the rate of silver *sceattas* to the old gold shillings: in Wessex five; in Mercia four; in Kent twelve – a reminder of how value was subject to local custom.[33]

From c. 710 to c. 740, during what is known as the secondary phase of the *sceattas*, the coinage spread from the southeast of England, where it was already in use, into the midlands, suggesting significant commercial use of money. Of all the coin finds from the entire pre-Conquest period, *sceattas* number most. Yet perhaps even more important is the lack of uniformity, for the uneven distribution of *sceattas* finds suggests 'a wealthy and monetised economy in the east and a wealthy but unmonetized one in the west.'[34] The increase in coin use suggests double-edged possibilities for the payment of compensation, facilitating currency payment in some regions and simultaneously in others reinforcing what Marc Bloch calls the 'frequent disparity between the standard and the instrument of payment.'[35] The imbalanced distribution resulted from the location of the entrance points of Continental silver bullion into the island, namely, the trading ports stretching down the east coast from York to Hamwic (Southampton), where silver was exchanged for exports in the form of high-quality cloth, slaves, and possibly hides.[36]

(iv) Pennies: *Sceattas* were pennies, but early ones, chunky and small. Their spread in the first half of the eighth century coincided with their debasement in the 730s and 740s.[37] Whether debasement alone was the cause, a new kind of penny emerged, broader and flatter in fabric, and with it came the age of the penny, which lasted to the later Middle Ages. In contrast to the mostly anonymous *sceattas*, these new pennies were stamped with the king's name as a standard.[38] The expansionist and ambitious Offa, king of Mercia (r. 757–96), is most famously associated with the currency reform, which had been implemented by c. 792, and his coins bear his image and/or name on the obverse and sometimes the moneyer who issued it on the reverse.[39] Offa's innovations were preceded, however, by the transitional coin of Beonna (king of the East Angles), dating from the mid-eighth century, and by Continental monetary reforms initiated by Charlemagne's father. Northumbria also reformed its currency early (c. 740), as attested by the royally stamped coins of King Eadberht, although the design of the stumpy *sceattas* was retained.[40]

---

[33] Grierson and Blackburn, *Medieval European Coinage*, p. 157; Naismith, *Money and Power*, pp. 264–5.
[34] Maddicott, 'Prosperity and Power,' pp. 60.
[35] Marc Bloch, 'Natural Economy or Money Economy: A False Dilemma,' *Land and Work in Mediaeval Europe: Selected Papers by Marc Bloch*, trans. J. E. Anderson (London, 1967), pp. 230–43, at 238.
[36] Maddicott, 'Prosperity and Power,' pp. 52–4.
[37] Naismith, *Money and Power*, p. 6.
[38] There are some notable earlier instances, such as the gold shilling from the reign of Æthelbert's son, Eadbald of Kent (r. 616–40), held at the British Museum; see http://www.britishmuseum.org/explore/highlights/highlight_objects/cm/g/gold_tremissis_shilling_of_e.aspx [accessed 5 January 2014].
[39] North, *English Hammered Coinage*, pp. 26–7.
[40] North, *English Hammered Coinage*, pp. 28–9; Naismith, *Money and Power*, pp. 6–7.

Regnal control over coinage and its bullion content will eventually minimize the presence of foreign coin, yet Offa's beautifully designed pennies borrow freely from foreign models even to the point of imitating an Islamic gold dinar (Arabic for Latin *denarius*), with 'Offa Rex' stamped on it (upside down relative to the Arabic script, it has to be said).[41] While coinage now indexed regal power, it was the moneyer who was visible at the local level, and the supply of silver originated more from wealthy individuals and merchants than from state coffers. Nonetheless, the impact of coinage now stamped in the king's name is significant when compensation is made in currency, for the very act of payment attests to a royal presence mediating the transaction.

From the later eighth century onwards we see serious efforts to increase regnal control of coinage, raise the bullion content to stable standards, and standardize design. It is with the tenth century, however, that the most sophisticated and centralized management of money emerges. With Edgar in the late tenth century comes a monetary system that was the most advanced in Europe. By the naming of both mint and moneyer, a more reliable bullion standard is ensured, for if the silver content were found deficient the culprit was clearly identifiable.[42] One of the reasons for the increased productivity of the mints was the high demand placed on monetary reserves by the payment of gelds to the Vikings.

Governmental control was manifested also by recall and reissue. Every few years (three to six), coins had to be updated, and only current coin was acceptable for certain transactions. An estimated fifty successive new issues occurred between c. 973 and 1125.[43] With the broad penny, a pattern prevails of restoration of theoretical standards of silver, departure from that standard, and then another restoration or raising of the silver standard.[44] By the tenth century, the decline of weight standard appears to have been manipulated 'to encourage people to bring coin and bullion into the mint throughout the life of the issue. This would have been achieved by offering a better exchange rate, i.e. more coins to the pound of silver.'[45] Although there was thus constant tension between the value of a coin in tale (or face value) and in specie (or bullion value), the frequency of recall and reissue creates the illusion of consistently maintained purity, even when fluctuations in bullion content are actually the reality. 'Consumers' were required to change their old coin for new with the moneyer, inevitably for a fee (*seigniorage* being the post-Conquest term for it), much as one now buys foreign currency when crossing an international border.

---

[41] http://www.britishmuseum.org/explore/highlights/highlight_objects/cm/g/gold_imitation_dinar_of_offa.aspx [accessed 5 January 2014]. Marc Bloch notes the association between gold coins and Arabic letters and between silver coins and Latin script: 'The Problem of Gold in the Middle Ages,' *Land and Work in Mediaeval Europe*, pp. 186–229, at 199–200.

[42] Williams, *Money*, p. 73, fig. 101.

[43] Blackburn, 'Coinage,' pp. 113–15.

[44] Grierson and Blackburn, *Medieval European Coinage*, pp. 270–1; North, *English Hammered Coinage*, p. 40.

[45] Blackburn, 'Coinage,' p. 115.

In sum, the Anglo-Saxon period ends with a precociously sophisticated and centralized fiscal policy in place, having begun with total dependence on foreign coin for such currency as was available. The chronological distance between law-givers Æthelberht and Alfred also measures a shift in attitudes towards money, perhaps best captured in the following contrast. The etymology of Old English *feoh* shows how money derives conceptually from cattle (compare Latin *pecus* [cattle] and *pecunia* [money]). Yet a law of Æthelstan measures the value of a sheep at 5 pennies, a pig at 10, and a cow at 20.[46] The original measurement of money in cattle as the base unit of value (OE *feoh*) reverses itself into the measurement of cattle in money as the base unit of value. Some general comments are called for in order to understand how Anglo-Saxon money in particular is defined on the scale from primitive to modern, how it figures in the tariffs, and how other specie, whether blood or commodity, function as money. We need a more theoretical understanding of money in the compensation tariffs than as a pile of standard-issue coins to be dug up when the unforeseen occurs.

Symbolic Economy

The following discussion is based on seven main characteristics of money in general identified by Richard Seaford, which, once situated in our Anglo-Saxon context, demonstrate the permeability among coin, commodity, and blood.[47] Modern money has its worth determined by state 'fiat' rather than by any worth in its physical composition (paper, coin), which, except in extraordinary circumstances such as hyperinflation, is less than that determined by the face value. In contrast to fiat money, which is a sign only of pure exchange value and universally exchangeable, Anglo-Saxon money lacks universal exchange value and possesses intrinsic value, both use-value and aesthetic value, as in the *solidus*-jewel, mentioned above. Coins are bullion as well as a sign of value. Seaford uses the place-holder 'X' as that which operates as money in the most general of cases; for our discussion, imagine a more specific scenario, as when some quantum – whether coin, produce, livestock, armor, body parts, slave(s), or even one's own freedom – is handed over to an aggrieved party to satisfy the debt. Rather than asking, 'which specie count as revenge and which as compensation?' we ask, 'In what ways do all the above renderings behave like money?'

First, in order to function as money, compensation must satisfy social obligation, a concept to be distinguished from the direct satisfaction of need by payment rich in use-value (as when laborers are paid in food and board). Compensation is made primarily to restore peace, only secondarily to satisfy material need, and in doing so keeps the transaction distinct from a sale or

---

[46] VI Æthelstan 6.2.
[47] Richard Seaford, *Money and the Early Greek Mind: Homer, Philosophy, Tragedy* (Cambridge, 2004), pp. 16–20.

barter. It has often been noted that medieval Latin *paga*, and Old French *paie*, from which derives modern English 'pay,' all descend from Latin *pacare*, to make peace.[48] Hence when we pay for something we make peace with the one from whom we received (or took) the item. It makes sense then to state these compensations in coin rather than, say, livestock, for in so doing the imperative to satisfy social obligation, in this case restitution, is foregrounded.

Second, the compensation must answer to the question, *quot*? There must be agreement that compensation has been made in the right quantum: not too much, not too little. Quantification of both debt and compensation enables closure for a community, at least 'for a while.'[49] The statement of *bot* or compensation in terms of partible coin answers the *quot*-question in the way no cow can, as when Alfred 71 stipulates that for the loss of a hand a payment of 66 shillings, 6 pennies, and one-third of a penny is required. Coins themselves are divisible as the demand for small denomination was usually satisfied by chiseling pennies into halves or quarters along the axes of the crosses hammered on the reverse, but since no thirds of pennies have ever been found, the fraction here seems not to denote metal money so much as connote quantitative exactness of whatever specie be rendered.[50]

Third, the compensation rendered can be quantified as a unit of account that serves as a common measure between other kinds deemed incommensurable by the contending parties. For example: in representing compensation as currency, Alfred 71 mediates between the injured party who, say, wants the aggressor's hand in compensation, and the aggressor, who understandably prefers to offer a slave. The law codes neatly fulfill this requirement that money function as a unit of account, for payments were only on occasion rendered in coin. By providing shillings and pennies as a measure of value, the tariffs represent the transaction in theoretical terms. The virtual distinction between the terms in which something is valued and the terms in which value is rendered becomes in the Anglo-Saxon tariffs a distinction made real. In small communities where stamped coin might be scarce, these amounts would have to be commuted into payments made in kind.[51] An example of this comes from c. 700 in Ine of Wessex 54.1, which states that although wergild is measured in shillings, the means of payment can include a slave and weapons. Miller astutely notes that 'In his [Ine's] way of thinking such weaponry was an extension of the human body anyway.'[52] No linear evolution from bodies, living or dead, to the abstractions of money prevails here, but rather a deep-seated metonymic interrelation between flesh and metal, where money gets reverse-exchanged into bodies. The statement of *bot* as a

---

[48] Grierson, *Origins of Money*, pp. 21–2. Subsequently, Miller, *Eye for an Eye*, p. 15; Hyams, *Rancor and Reconciliation*, p. 205.
[49] Miller, *Eye for an Eye*, p. 16.
[50] Grierson and Blackburn, *Medieval European Coinage*, p. 270; Naismith, *Money and Power*, p. 267. For a cut 'farthing' see http://www.britishmuseum.org/explore/highlights/highlight_objects/cm/c/cut_farthing_of_edward_the_con.aspx [accessed 5 January 2014].
[51] Oliver, *Body Legal*, pp. 47–9.
[52] Miller, *Eye for an Eye*, p. 26.

monetary unit of account implicitly recognizes the reciprocal interchange between blood and coin.

Fourth, the more of the following four functions that compensation performs, the more it behaves like money: payment, exchange, store of wealth, and measure of value. Seaford speaks of 'special purpose money' in which the currency is heavily restricted to a case in point where only one specie will do. The classic example is the law of talion – an eye for an eye and a tooth for a tooth – that 'makes eyes into forms of money, or money-like substance.'[53] In the case of Alfred 25, in which the slave who rapes a slave is castrated (no monetary redemption being allowed as it is for free men), the phrase 'bete mid his eowede' literally means, 'he shall pay with his testicles.'[54] The law requires the slave's testicles as the only specie acceptable for payment, so while they are indeed a measure of value as well as a form of payment, they can hardly be a store of value, nor do they have exchange value beyond the given instance, for this grisly 'money' proves useless in any other transaction. To that extent, they are special purpose money, as are all body parts demanded in recompense for injury. To redescribe revenge as compensation, Alfred's law is formulated with a certain grim wit: the slave will 'pay' (*bete*) with his testicles. As 'special purpose money,' the slave's *eowede* have exclusive acceptability, meaning that only with his body parts can he reckon the debt.

Fifth, the compensation rendered even though it might command exclusive acceptability in the given instance cannot function as money proper unless it also commands general acceptability. Modern fiat money commands both, being both universally accepted as payment and the only acceptable specie of payment in most transactions. This double characteristic sets it apart from all other commodity. No Anglo-Saxon currency can be described as money in this sense, for insofar as payment in kind (or in blood) can be rendered in lieu of money, coin does not enjoy exclusive acceptability; and even if coins enjoy general acceptability, they can never not be a commodity – bullion.

Thus far Seaford's characteristics of money are sufficiently capacious to include payments made in alternative specie, but his final two characteristics pertain specifically and exclusively to stamped currency (feature six), and sufficient fiscal centralization to control the terms on which organized money is issued and used (feature seven).

Stamped coinage marks a conceptual transformation in the development of money, away from money-as-commodity towards money-as-sign. The value of a piece of gold or silver is whatever its nature or *physis* is taken to be. Stamp that same piece, however, and its value is reassigned to the rule of *nomos*. That piece of stamped metal becomes the bearer of promises, both of 'future acceptability' and 'promiscuous exchangeability.'[55] This process, by which a fixed conventional value stamped on pieces of metal trumps its intrinsic

---

[53] Miller, *Eye for an Eye*, p. 31.
[54] Compare Alfred 32, which sets the excision of the tongue as minimum 'payment' for slander, with the possibility of monetary redemption.
[55] Seaford, *Money and the Early Greek Mind*, p. 6.

value (ascertained by weight or assay), is what Seaford calls 'fiduciarity.'[56] Fiduciarity refers to the future acceptability of stamped coin, which in turn leads to another crucial function of money, namely, its potential to be a store of value. Such fiduciarity requires a significant degree of economic centralization, which can be posited by the mid-tenth century, when II Æthelstan 14 proclaims 'that there shall be one coinage throughout the king's realm.'[57]

As monetary payment becomes a real possibility through a coinage generally acceptable, available, and trustworthy by virtue of controlled bullion-content, its status as compensation for personal injury weakens in favour of a legal code oriented more towards discipline and punishment than payment. Payment legally and culturally matters most when its possibility of being rendered in good coin is most problematic in fiduciary terms. The consequence of this is not simply that payment in kind often replaces coin when the latter is in short supply, but also that coins themselves belong to the honor culture just as men do, where worth is locally measured and reputation easily lost. That elision between the ethical stature of coins and bodies is the focus of the next section.

Man-Money

No longer being minted, the gold shilling during the age of the penny was simply a unit of account, no actual shilling coin being issued until the sixteenth century.[58] So compensation in this era if paid in current coin would be rendered in silver pennies, the value of which was considerable. With much more spending power 'than was needed for one loaf of bread or one litre of wine,' a penny is not an efficient instrument for small transactions, despite the occasional minting of half-pennies, so the need for small change was met by breaking the pennies or by the base-metal Northumbrian *styccas* still minted in the style of the old *sceattas*.[59] Inherently 'noble,' the bearer of reputation and value, the penny existed less to facilitate petty consumerism and quicken trade with slippery coin than to set a standard and mark the worth of a community.

Coins were vulnerable in many ways despite their durability. Like bodies, they grew old and died through fair wear and tear – indeed, the good died young, for the higher the bullion content, the softer the metal and the more prone it was to abrasion. Coins could also be debased by either reduction of weight (a maneuver easy enough to detect with a balance scale) or of the silver content while retaining weight through the addition of alloy. Only assay can detect this method. Even if the coin left the mint new and 'true,' it could be clipped by anyone – a process that involved shaving minute amounts of metal off its edges. With milling of edges not experimented with until the sixteenth

---

[56] Seaford, *Money and the Early Greek Mind*, p. 7.
[57] 'Þæt an mynet sy ofer ealle ðæs cynges anwealde.'
[58] John Chown, *A History of Money from AD 800*, 2nd edn (London, 1996), p. 23.
[59] Naismith, *Money and Power*, pp. 288–9.

century, and not required until the seventeenth, clipping of hammered coin was frequent because it was hard to detect. The hammer did not always hit the die with perfect accuracy, and an off-center image offers opportunity for discreet clipping on the blank edge and further grounds for suspecting a coin not to be all it claims.

A stamped coin acquires language. Trust in a coin is a matter of careful balancing between the bare metal in specie and the stamped promise in tale. An individual or community is faced with the task of balancing what a coin 'does' (weigh too lightly or mix its precious metal with base) against what it 'says' (present its stamped face value). Just as in adjudging guilt, practical reason is needed to conduct this measuring and interpret the result aright. How does a small community, no moneyer in sight, believe what a coin 'says'? Who would not suspect it of 'light' behavior and feel inclined to put it to the test? In ways strikingly similar to people, coins in Anglo-Saxon England were subject to the same social expectations and regulations. Subjecting an object to the judgment of the scales is akin, notes Miller, to subjecting a person to the ordeal.[60] Where a community trusted the 'metal' of a coin, they could take it at face value, but where a coin had traveled abroad (through trade or tribute payments), it was a stranger, regarded with mistrust. Hence an eleventh-century silver penny of Cnut (r. 1016–35), found in Scandinavia, probably having arrived there through the geld raised in 1018 to pay off the Vikings, is defaced by having been 'pecked,' that is, stabbed with a knife-point to assay its purity.[61] Thousands of such English coins have turned up in Scandinavian hoards, many pecked, bearing their scars as permanent witness to their ordeal of assay.[62] Although pecking was largely a Scandinavian practice conducted in the absence of standard coinage, it was also used in the Danelaw; thus insular pecking occurs on Anglo-Saxon coin, maimed 'victims' of which are found in the Cuerdale hoard.[63] Coin's analogy with humans is demonstrated in the laws of Cnut, which lay out discrete procedures for assaying the word of the trustworthy man (*getreowe*), the untrustworthy (*ungetreowe*), the thoroughly untrustworthy (*swyðe ungetreowe*), the friendless (*freondleasan*) and the foreigner (*feorran cumenan*). Reputation in these laws has an objective solidity, which, once lost, is hard to reconstitute. Like an unfamiliar coin in Sweden, the foreigner who turns up like a bad penny, lacking friends of good standing to swear on his behalf, must be assayed by ordeal.[64]

Of all body parts, hands and face are where value concentrates, and in two varieties of ordeal, both used in Anglo-Saxon England, it is by the hand that the accused are judged: by fire, in which they must grip burning iron, and by boiling water, into which they must immerse the arm. In both cases if after

---

[60] Miller, *Eye for an Eye*, pp. 2–3.
[61] Williams, *Money*, p. 71, fig. 97g.
[62] North, *English Hammered Coinage*, p. 38.
[63] Grierson and Blackburn, *Medieval European Coinage*, p. 318.
[64] II Cnut 35; see also Robert Bartlett, *Trial by Fire and Water: The Medieval Judicial Ordeal* (Oxford, 1986), pp. 30–2.

three days the wounds suppurated, the accused were declared guilty.⁶⁵ Like assayed coins, hands in particular bear the burden of proof in ordeal. They are central to the entire legal process, for the hand is the swearing member that lays itself on a holy object as it reaches out to God as witness. I turn in the last section to the particular connection between coins and hands, and to the consideration of hands – as distinct from coins – as the measure of value.

Hands Off

The hand figures large in the tariffs of the Anglo-Saxon legal codes. Highly reticulated as a body part worthy of redemption and ransom, it is a 'compendium of the individual digits.'⁶⁶ Hands are also consistently equated with feet, eyes, and ears, the common denominator perhaps being that all can be severed from the body without necessary loss of life. In their partibility, hands do the job of coins.

Regarding manual or digital injury, Æthelberht's and Alfred's codes differ in some details. Where Alfred 71 stipulates a payment for the loss of a whole hand, Æthelberht's code does not state an amount, although we can surmise 50 shillings, which is both the sum of the loss of the individual digits and the *bot* for loss of a foot, a commensurable body part (Æthelberht 69 [69]).⁶⁷ What is interesting about Alfred's code is how it fetishizes the fingers by rendering the sum of digital parts greater than the manual whole: 83 shillings versus 66 shillings, 6 pennies and one-third of a penny.⁶⁸ Cheaper to chop off the whole hand.

The fetishization of fingers in Alfred's code seems to be associated with their aestheticization, a point suggested by the increased value of the ring finger relative to its lesser worth in Æthelberht's code (see Table 1.1). The bearing of a ring is no extraneous matter of ornament, for rings are often inscribed with runic spells, have amuletic agency, and extend the body's power beyond that afforded by physique alone.⁶⁹ Each digit has its own personality, value, and function. In both codes, the thumb is much the most valued, for it enables prehension.⁷⁰ Also common is the middling value of the forefinger, which enables precision or dexterity-requiring manipulations such as shooting. The pinkie allows the hand to cup liquid, wield weapons, and stretch to maximum span, while the middle finger … well, the *impudicus* allows one to use Anglo-Saxon words with the mouth shut.⁷¹

---

⁶⁵ David Rollason, 'Ordeal,' *Blackwell Encyclopaedia*, ed. Lapidge *et al.*, pp. 345–6; Bartlett, *Trial by Fire and Water*, pp. 1–3 and 13–33. For a miracle story that brings the process to life, see Lantfred's *Translatio et miracula de S Swithuni*, in Lapidge, *Swithun*, pp. 308–11.
⁶⁶ Oliver, *Body Legal*, p. 141.
⁶⁷ For valuation of digits, see Miller, *Eye for an Eye*, pp. 122–9.
⁶⁸ Alfred 56–60. Compare Alfred 69, which requires 40 shillings for maiming half of a hand. Compare also the essay by Lisi Oliver in this volume.
⁶⁹ For example the Kingsmoor ring: http://www.britishmuseum.org/research/collection_online/collection_object_details.aspx?objectId=88694&partId=1 [accessed 5 January 2014].
⁷⁰ For digital functions and names, see Oliver, *Body Legal*, pp. 143–53.
⁷¹ Miller, *Eye for an Eye*, pp. 124–6, on *impudicus*. On the naming of fingers and functions, see Oliver, *Body Legal*, pp. 143–58.

When Compensation Costs an Arm and a Leg

Table 1.1 Compensation values for digits in Æthelberht's and Alfred's law codes

Digit	Æthelberht 53–8 [54–54.5]		Alfred 56–60	
	Value (shillings)	Rank	Value (shillings)	Rank
thumb	20	1	30	1
index ('shooting') finger	9	3	15	3
middle finger	4	5	12	4
ring ('gold') finger	6	4	17	2
pinkie ('little') finger	11	2	9	5

The hand is also the limb that is predominantly struck off in punishment under barbarian law.[72] Theft is the obvious deed for which loss of the hand is required as punishment – and punishment rather than payment seems the right term here. For stealing in church, the hand that committed the deed is required (Alfred 6). By severing the hand that committed the deed the law probably ensures that the offender loses the dominant hand, even though no code throughout the barbarian corpus differentiates between the dominant and subordinate hand.[73] One law connects hands with coins in a singular manner: II Æthelstan 14, the law that proclaims that there should be one coinage throughout the kingdom, spells out in its first subsection the penalties for counterfeit:

> ꝼ gif se mynetere ful wurðe, slea mon of þa hond, ðe he ðæt ful mid worhte, ꝼ sette up on ða mynetsmiððan; ꝼ gif hit þonne tyhtle sy, ꝼ he hine ladian wille, ðonne ga he to þam hatum isene, ꝼ ladige þa hond, mid ðe mon tyhð, ðæt he þæt facen mid worhte.
>
> And if a moneyer is found guilty [of issuing base or light coins], the hand shall be cut off with which he committed the crime, and fastened up on the mint. But if he is accused and he wishes to clear himself then shall he go to the hot iron [ordeal] and redeem the hand with which he is accused of having committed the crime.[74]

As the personal production of the moneyer (even if he is not the one actually to strike the hammer blow), a stamped coin sheds something of the symbolic in the direction of the artisanal. And if in accordance with the tariffs a moneyer should hand over his minted coin as compensation for some other injury inflicted, then money undergoes the strangest reversal from a unit of account to payment in kind, the unalienated substance of one's labor, the produce of one's hand.

Much is known about these moneyers as a group because of the identification requirements on coins. The fact that the same moneyer's names could

---

[72] Oliver, *Body Legal*, p. 141.
[73] Oliver, *Body Legal*, p. 141.
[74] Translation from Attenborough, *Laws*, pp. 134–5. Compare also II Cnut 8.1; and Daniel O'Gorman's essay in this volume.

appear on the coins of successive rival dynasties suggests that they were men who were prominent in the local community rather than political appointees, and they have been identified in later Old English documents as witnesses to charters, lawmen, and thegns.[75] Guilty of counterfeit, a moneyer loses more than his hand and reputation, for his ability to up*hold* the law by swearing with his hand is compromised, and he can no longer grip a weapon.[76] A man without a hand cannot protect himself or defend another, not only because he literally cannot bear arms but also because, thinking more symbolically, his *mundbyrd* – that zone of personal guarantee, safety, and protection bounded by the ambit of a hand – is violated.[77]

A handless or fingerless man is unmanned in many ways, but perhaps most fundamentally, it leaves him unable to count or measure, whether by spanning thumb to pinkie or by gauging the breadth of four fingers.[78] True, it is unlikely that ordinary folk were familiar with what Bede refers to as 'that useful and easy skill of flexing the fingers,' whereby, starting with the left hand, transferring to the right at 100, and then co-opting chest, neck, belly, thigh, hip, and groin into the effort of reckoning the dates of Easter, two hands can tot up to a million.[79] But counting with the body is an ancient and widespread technique, not exclusive to Christian monks. This concrete mathematics quantifies a collection of objects by bijection, that is, by mapping it onto a known model collection of, for example, rosary beads, tally sticks, or fingers.[80] In a society used to counting by pace lengths and arm spans, where one measures the world against the body, hands are the basic portion of value, trusty as scales, and you never leave them at home by mistake. *Sans* compass and ruler, *sans* universal standard, *sans* agreed common measure, hands reach out to put reiterable pattern on commodity, thereby setting value on the world. Reading Alfred 71 (and any other of the tariffs) we take hands to be worth a certain number of pennies, and take the penny, in 'the age of the penny,' as the common measure of value; but the value-function is reversible, permitting one to regard a pile of pennies and think, 'those coins are worth my hand.'

We have learned to consider value like Cartesian space, as an even plane upon which we plot the worth of a coin. In this paradigm value is an abstract 'thing' anterior to any concrete valuable thing just as space itself is prior to objects in it. If however we think of value more in line with classical natural place, where no empty container stands awaiting its contents, then we come closer to the world of these tariffs, where value is instantiated as and inheres

---

[75] M. A. S. Blackburn, 'Moneyers,' *Blackwell Encyclopaedia*, ed. Lapidge *et al.*, pp. 324–5.
[76] On the significance of the right hand, see Valerie Allen, 'On the Nature of Things in the Bayeux Tapestry and its World,' *The Bayeux Tapestry: New Interpretations*, ed. Martin K. Foys, Karen Eileen Overbey, and Dan Terkla (Woodbridge, 2009), pp. 51–70.
[77] Miller, *Eye for an Eye*, p. 137.
[78] Oliver, *Body Legal*, p. 145.
[79] Bede, *The Reckoning of Time*, trans. Faith Wallis (Liverpool, 1999), pp. 9–11.
[80] Georges Ifrah, *The Universal History of Numbers: From Prehistory to the Invention of the Computer*, trans. David Bellos *et al.* (New York, 2000), pp. 10–22.

in valuable things. As money becomes increasingly standardized over the course of the Anglo-Saxon period, value itself gains in autonomy from and authority over the objects that embody it. As law becomes increasingly theologized, the value of pain extends beyond the fringes of mortal life itself, unbuttoning the closure that payment brings. As royal power becomes increasingly centralized, the king, in defending the aggrieved party, increasingly becomes the aggrieved party. As power actively to undo a wrong with payment decreases, what can an offender do now but deliver himself up to undergo the punishment that comes down upon him from on high?

2

Beginnings and Legitimation of Punishment in Early Anglo-Saxon Legislation From the Seventh to the Ninth Century

Daniela Fruscione

One should not take punishment in the Early Middle Ages for granted. As the various German publications on *Die Geburt der Strafe* [the beginning of penalty] show,[1] most scholars who have researched this field place the beginning of criminal law in the late Middle Ages.[2] However, the question remains of how these results correlate with Karl Siegfrid Bader's well-known quotation: 'punishment as a reaction has always been present, because without it no law would be possible.'[3]

Here I intend to use Anglo-Saxon law to show that both positions are problematic. Although Anglo-Saxon legislation has so far played only a minor role within this large body of research on the beginning of punishment,[4] as a matter of fact, written Anglo-Saxon legislation, starting from its beginnings in the seventh century, offers a good field for analysis of the beginning of punishment. First of all, being written in the vernacular and not in Latin, it is the only early medieval legislation that offers insight into an early vocabulary of punishment. In addition, the under-studied Anglo-Saxon laws allow us

---

[1] Many of them sponsored by the *Deutsche Forschungsgemeinschaft* (DFG), the main German research institution, which has created a *Sonderforschungsbereich* [a special field of research] in the development of criminal law. See for instance: Dietmar Willoweit, ed., *Die Entstehung des öffentlichen Strafrechts* (Cologne, 1999); Jürgen Weitzel, ed., *Hoheitliches Strafen in der Spätantike und im frühen Mittelalter* (Cologne, 2002); Klaus Lüderssen, ed., *Die Durchsetzung des öffentlichen Strafanspruch* (Cologne, 2002).

[2] Viktor Achter, *Geburt der Strafe* (Frankfurt, 1951); Hans Hattenhauer, 'Über Buße und Strafe im Mittelalter,' *Zeitschrift der Savigny-Stiftung für Rechtsgeschichte, Germanistische Abteilung* 100 (1983), 53–74; and see also Heinz Holzhauer, 'Geburt der Strafe,' *Acta Universitatis Szegediensis de Attila József Nominatae*, Acta Juridica et Politica 42 (Szeged, 1992), pp. 3–17; Heinz Holzhauer, 'Zum Strafgedanken im frühen Mittelalter,' *Beiträge zur Rechtsgeschichte*, ed. Heinz Holzhauer, Stefan Chr. Saar, and Andreas Roth (Berlin, 2000), pp. 112–26.

[3] 'Strafe als Reaktion war immer da, weil ohne sie eine Rechtsordnung nicht möglich ist': Karl Siegfrid Bader, 'Zum Unrechtsausgleich und zur Strafe im Frühmittelalter,' *Zeitschrift der Savigny-Stiftung für Rechtsgeschichte, Germanistische Abteilung* 112 (1995), 1–63.

[4] One exception is Roger D. Groot, 'Proto-Juries and Public Criminal Law in England,' *Die Entstehung des öffentlichen Strafrechts*, ed. Dietmar Willoweit (Cologne, 1999), pp. 23–39. Moreover, the issue of the relationship between strict liability and the idea of guilt has been introduced by Paul Mikat, 'Erfolgshaftung und Schuldgedanke im Strafrecht der Angelsachsen,' *Festschrift für Hellmuth von Weber zum 70. Geburtstag*, ed. Hans Welzel (Bonn, 1963), pp. 9–31.

to observe the progression between two methods of dealing with offences: restitutive, which is typical of family-centred societies; and punitive, which is typical of civilizations where a central power is emerging.[5] Lastly, in relation to the interaction of Germanic law with a converted Christian order, it shows that the influence of Christianity marked a turning point in developing notions of crime and punishment.

Before Punishment: Æthelberht of Kent

When we look at the Kentish king Æthelberht's first Anglo-Saxon law code from the very beginning of the seventh century, we can see no traces of corporal punishment, only of monetary penalties.[6] Most of his laws consisted of personal injury tariffs (33–71.1 [33–71]) and a list of offences (1–31 [1–31]) that were to be compensated to the victim by a particular sum of money, which was calculated based on the social status of offender and victim. The detailed descriptions of offences and the large number of acts demanding compensation indicate that Æthelberht's laws were basically designed to assure both the wholeness or physical integrity[7] of the person, and the safety of property (as articulated in the clauses on theft, and breaking and entering into a man's dwelling or enclosure).[8]

Æthelberht's first Kentish law does not focus on punishing the offender but on compensating the victim. An overwhelming number of the personal injury laws end with *gebete* or *forgelde*, meaning 'let him make restitution.'[9] In the family-based society described in most of Æthelberht's sentences, responsibility falls to the kin of the offender. Two Kentish decrees deal explicitly with the role of the family in conflict resolution. In Æthelberht 24.2 [23], the family helps with the application of the compensation rules: if

---

[5] Jürgen Weitzel, 'Strafe und Strafverfahren in der Merowingerzeit,' *Zeitschrift der Savigny-Stiftung für Rechtsgeschichte, Germanistische Abtheilung* 111 (1994), 66–147.

[6] Here I follow the edition and translation of Oliver, *Beginnings of English Law*, with reference to Liebermann, *Gesetze* I, in square brackets. On the Kentish legislation see also Patrizia Lendinara, 'The Kentish Laws,' *The Anglo-Saxons from the Migration Period to the Eighth Century: An Ethnographic Perspective*, ed. John Hines (Woodbridge, 1997), pp. 211–43. See also Valerie Allen's essay in this volume.

[7] Oliver, *Body Legal*; Oliver, *Beginnings of English Law*, pp. 99–105; Heinrich Brunner, *Deutsche Rechtsgeschichte*, vol. 1 (Berlin, 1961), pp. 671–8. A focus on the body can be found in the essays edited by Withers and Wilcox, *Naked Before God*; see especially Mary Richards, 'The Body as Text in Early Anglo-Saxon Law,' pp. 97–115. See also Katherine O'Brien O'Keeffe, 'Body and Law in Late Anglo-Saxon England,' *ASE* 27 (1998), 209–32, although this deals with later material.

[8] Oliver, *Beginnings of English Law*, pp. 93–6.

[9] The focus on damage and victim is also expressed by the semantics and the syntax of the sentences, which rarely mention denominations for crimes, but emphasize the offended part of the body. As Oliver has shown in her unpublished PhD dissertation, 'The Language of the Early English Laws' (Harvard University, 1995), pp. 178–80, the subject of the protasis is generally the wounded part of the body, whereas the perpetrator is the unexpressed subject of the apodosis. The injury has scope over the entire person. For both passive and stative sentences, the offender disappears together with his fault; the result is a sense of deresponsabilization of the subject.

a murderer flees the country, his family is responsible for paying half the wergild. In Æthelberht 65.1 [65.1], the family appears as mediator in the case of personal injury with disability. Moreover, in the second Kentish law of Hloþhere and Eadric 3 [5], written around 680, the family emerges as oath supporters; should the offender escape, his family group has to compensate the victim or, in the case of his death, his kin.[10] The Kentish legislation thus describes a symmetrical situation: not only is restitution paid to the kin in the case of the victim's death, but the kin is also responsible for payment in the case of the offender's disappearance.

In the relationship between two groups of free men, compensation was the preferred method of coping with offences, and physical punishment had no place. Compensation can be considered one of the aspects of a system in which families themselves exacted punishment for offences. Feud is another aspect of the same system but, unlike in the Continental and Nordic legislation, there is no mention of it in the Kentish laws.[11]

Very few of Æthelberht's sentences (8 [2], 12 [6], 15 [9]) cite a third party who would impose a penalty or punishment on the offender. However, there are occasional references to fines, monetary penalties rendered to a third party as punishment rather than compensation. Two types of fines are indicated in Æthelberht's laws – *wite* and *drihtinbeag* – with quite different connotations. *Wite* was the fine paid to the king in cases of theft (15 [9]). *Wite* has a common etymology with Latin *videre* and Gothic *witan* 'observe'; its meaning advanced from 'observe,' 'perceive,' or 'notice,' to 'punish.'[12] The word came to imply the existence of a controlling power with the authority to punish, and in the Christian period *wite* was the common term for suffering in hell in all Germanic languages (except Gothic *balweins*). However, only in the West Germanic languages did it become a general legal term for punishment, and Karl von Amira is of the opinion that this word is the oldest denotation for 'death penalty,'[13] although in the earliest Kentish laws *wite* had not yet assumed this meaning, but denoted only a punitive fine.

---

[10] Hloþhere and Eadric 3 [5] could refer as easily to a neighbour; see Daniela Fruscione, 'Zur Familie im VII. Jahrhundert im Spannungsfeld zwischen verfassungsgeschichtlicher Konstruktion und kentischen Quellen,' *Verwandtschaft, Name und soziale Ordnung (300–1000)*, ed. Steffen Patzold and Karl Ubl (Berlin, forthcoming).

[11] On feud as a 'live process' that differs from institutions established by law givers, see Hyams, *Rancor and Reconciliation*, p. xvi. However, even if the laws view the social order from the top down, both later Anglo-Saxon laws and Lombard legislation mention feud with the purpose to limit it. William Ian Miller does not believe that there was a sharp distinction between retributive justice and revenge: *Eye for an Eye* (Cambridge, 2006), pp. 4–5.

[12] *Wite* is part of a large family of Germanic words all going back formally to *weid-*: they concern chiding and punishing, but also pointing out and establishing. The semantics are discussed in Helmut Rix *et al.*, eds, *Lexikon der indogermanischen Verben* (Wiesbaden, 1998), s.v. 'weid-,' n. 24. See also Julius Pokorny, *Indogermanisches Etymologisches Wörterbuch* (Bern, 1959–69), pp. 83–92. This development parallels Latin *animadvertere* which changed in meaning from 'notice' to 'punish': Klaus von See, 'Strafe im Altnordischen,' *Zeitschrift für deutsches Alterthum und deutsche Literatur* 108 (1979), 283–98.

[13] Karl von Amira, *Grundriss des germanischen Rechts* (Strassburg, 1913), p. 240.

Beginnings and Legitimation

The second type of fine, *drihtinbeag*, has a different background. This compound is a *hapax legomenon*, and represents a fine which was due to the king when a free man was killed (12 [6]). Originally this archaic term denoted a payment to a lord for the killing of one of his men, with *drihtin* indicating 'lord' and the second component, *beag*, referring to the practice of using rings as payment.[14] It is an early form of monetary penalty which emerged during a period in which the size of a lord's retinue was of great importance.[15] While *wite* is directly associated with a controlling authority, *drihtinbeag* represents a link between restitutive and punitive methods of offence regulation. The compound *drihtinbeag* indicates that an absolute demarcation between compensation and punishment cannot be substantiated. Third-party penalties could not develop in a kin-based compensation system, where the redress of all forms of injury was resolved exclusively between the parties themselves. They could, however, develop within a group of free men in the transitional society of the migration period, where the interests of a military lordship (*drihtin*) were relevant to a larger community.

The absence of capital and corporal punishments in Æthelberht's laws reflect practical concerns of the migration period.[16] At the core of his legislation are binding rules for a group of free men, whose honour would be humiliated by violation of their bodies and physical integrity.[17] Moreover, in an environment of expansion and warfare, numbers of physically able warriors were crucial; physical punishment and the death penalty, which would reduce a community's able-bodied population, would have been detrimental to new settlers fighting British and other Germanic groups.[18] Preserving a robust number of active warriors and farmers in the foreign environment was particularly relevant during the Germanic migration and settlement in Britain.

---

[14] T. Capelle, 'Ring und Ringschmuck,' *Reallexikon der germanischen Altertumskunde*, vol. 25 (Berlin, 2003), pp. 16–9.

[15] Daniela Fruscione, '*Drihtinbeag* and the Question of the Beginnings of Punishment,' *Textus Roffensis in Context: Law, Language and Libraries in Early Medieval England*, ed. Bruce O'Brien and Barbara Bombi (Turnhout, forthcoming).

[16] The idea that punishment was unfamiliar in the Germanic tradition is well explained by Jürgen Weitzel, 'Der Strafgedanke im frühen Mittelalter,' *Der Strafgedanke in seiner historischen Entwicklung*, ed. Eric Hilgendorf and Jürgen Weitzel (Berlin, 2007), pp. 21–34. Thus, the oldest legislation of the Germanic peoples in England does not support the various theories propounded by the old German research, namely the idea of a Germanic death penalty, as suggested by Karl von Amira, *Die germanische Todesstrafe: Untersuchungen zur Rechts- und Religionsgeschichte* (Munich, 1922); and by Heinrich Brunner's theory of *Friedlosigkeit*, in his 'Abspaltungen der Friedlosigkeit,' *Zeitschrift der Savigny-Stiftung für Rechtsgeschichte, Germanistische Abtheilung* 11 (1890), 62–100 (called a 'magnificently systematic picture' by Julius Goebel, *Felony and Misdemeanor: A Study in the History of Criminal Law* (New York, 1937), p. 27).

[17] Oliver, *Body Legal*, pp. 165–79; Günter Jarouschek, 'Buße, Strafe und Ehre im frühen Mittelalter,' *Karl von Amira zum Gedächtnis*, ed. Peter Landau, Hermann Nehlsen and Mathias Schmoeckel (Frankfurt, 1999), pp. 231–42.

[18] Holzhauer, 'Geburt der Strafe,' pp. 3–17; Jürg Helbling, 'Sozialethnologie,' *Ethnologie: Einführung und Überblick*, ed. Bettina Behr and Hans Fisher (Berlin, 2006), pp. 125–56.

Daniela Fruscione

Christianization and Punishment: Wihtred

Composed approximately ninety years after Æthelberht's laws, the legislation of Wihtred of Kent took a very different approach to remedying offences: compensatory restitution was no longer the main feature of Kentish law; rather, fines appear more frequently and corporal and capital punishments have been introduced.[19] In the course of the seventh century, Kentish law began to place a greater emphasis on procedure. Whereas Æthelberht's laws rarely touched on procedure, his successors' legislation introduced a more complex judicial apparatus in the form of judges, witnesses and judicial proceedings.[20] The laws of Hloþhere and Eadric, composed in the latter half of the century, reflect this move towards procedure by situating the regulation of offence in the king's hall (*to cyngæs sele*) or before the altar (*in wiofode*).[21] Such procedure provides the prerequisite for penalties, since it moves the location of offence regulation out of the inter-segmentary space of horizontal transactions between family groups.[22] Punishment was no longer decided solely in negotiations between families, but was enforced against the families by a higher authority such as king or clergy.[23] The laws of Wihtred took this transformation further by merging ecclesiastical and secular powers and functions.[24] Between the reigns of Æthelberht and Wihtred, the role of the king developed from that of military chieftain to Christian leader.[25] Of twenty-three clauses, only seven do not focus on Church matters.[26] While the determiner of legal subjectivity in Æthelberht's laws was social and family rank, in Wihtred's laws, religious identity has become the most important factor.[27] This resulted in the introduction of a group of clauses which addressed transgression of the Christian commandments.[28] The permeation of the Christian moral in the legislation of Wihtred is reflected

---

[19] W. Schild, 'Todesstrafe,' *Reallexikon der germanischen Altertumskunde*, vol. 31(Berlin, 2006), pp. 16–20.
[20] Oliver, *Beginnings of English Law*, pp. 117–50.
[21] Hloþhere and Eadric 11.1 [16.1], 11.2 [16.2]; see also Wormald, *Making of English Law*, pp. 101–3; Uwe Wesel, *Frühformen des Rechts in vorstaatlichen Gesellschaften* (Frankfurt, 1985).
[22] Niklas Luhmann, *Rechtssoziologie* (Opladen, 1980), p. 160.
[23] Wesel, *Frühformen des Rechts*, p. 211; Henry Campbell Black, *Black's Law Dictionary*, 4th edn (St. Paul, MN, 1968), p. 445: 'Crimes are those wrongs which the government notices as injurious to the public and punishes in what may be called a "criminal proceeding".'
[24] Wormald, *Making of English Law*, pp. 101–3.
[25] Oliver, *Beginnings of English Law*, pp. 152–180.
[26] The first five laws of Æthelberht addressed Church property. This only reflects the fact that the application of the technology of writing to law was introduced by the Church. As a matter of fact Christianity was absolutely not central to Æthelberht from an ideological point of view, as his chapters on the position of women, marriage and family show; see Patrick Wormald, '*Inter cetera bona ... genti suae*: Law-Making and Peace-Keeping in the Earliest English Kingdoms,' *Settimane di Studio del Centro Italiano di Studi Sull'Alto Medioevo* 42 (1995), 963–93.
[27] Lisi Oliver, 'Royal and Ecclesiastical Law in Seventh-Century Kent,' *Early Medieval Studies*, ed. Baxter *et al.*, pp. 97–112.
[28] Jürgen Weitzel, 'Diskussion um ein frühmittelalterlich-fränkisches Strafrecht,' *Festschrift für Gerd Kleinheyer zum 70. Geburtstag*, ed. Franz Dorn and Jan Schröder (Heidelberg, 2001), pp. 540–67.

also in the vocabulary. The word *riht*, for instance, used both as a noun and as an adjective, covers in Wihtred everything connected with the divine order and its maintenance, whereas the evil opposed to it was referred to as *unriht* (unlawful).[29]

It is in Wihtred's legislation that we find the earliest examples of Anglo-Saxon norms which issue punishment without compensatory restitution to an injured party. We read, for example, that a slave or servant who works on the Sabbath, makes offerings to idols, or eats meat during a fast has to pay a fine of 6 shillings.[30] If he is unable to scrape together the necessary amount of money, he pays with a flogging. Nevertheless, at the end of the seventh century it was still problematic to violate the physical integrity of a free man; the object of physical punishment in Wihtred is almost always the slave.[31] There was only one exception: if a thief was caught red-handed, the choice of punishment fell to the king, who could have the thief put to death, have him sold into exile as a slave, or allow him to buy his life with his wergild.[32] In Wihtred 21 [26], the expedient factor which introduces the possibility of punishment for a free man is the fact that he has been caught red-handed.[33] This principle, which may have its roots in the spontaneous killing of the thief as a form of vengeance, is common to many medieval (not only early medieval) legislations, and also to early Roman law.[34] The increasing juridification of this custom in Kent is connected to the aim of the secular power to curtail acts of private vengeance.[35] Being caught stealing makes both self-defence and judicial defence impossible for the wrongdoer.[36]

The influence of Christianity thus marked a turning point in developing notions of crime and punishment. In particular, Christianization accompanied the disintegration of the principle of group responsibility, which had been typical of early Anglo-Saxon society, and it also marked the birth of the notion of individual responsibility.[37] Family solidarity was the chief obstacle to ecclesiastical regulation of society, but it also prevented any central

---

[29] Daniela Fruscione, '*Riht* in Earlier Anglo-Saxon Legislation: A Semasiological Approach,' *Historical Research* 86 (2013), 498–504.
[30] Wihtred 8 [9]; 10 [13]; 11 [14].
[31] As regards the different treatment of punishment for free men and slaves, this has also been studied in the Continental *leges* and the opinion of various German scholars is that this is the turning point for the introduction of punishment and the beginning of criminal law; see Gustav Radbruck, *Elegantiae iuris criminalis: Sieben Studien zur Geschichte des Strafrechts, der Ursprung des Strafrechts aus dem Stande der Unfreien* (Basel, 1938); Jarouschek, 'Buße, Strafe und Ehre,' pp. 231–42.
[32] Wihtred 21 [26]. On theft see J. R. Schwyter, *Old English Legal Language: The Lexical Field of Theft* (Odense, 1996).
[33] Wolfgang Schild, 'Handhafte Tat,' *Handwörterbuch zur deutschen Rechtsgeschichte*, II.12, cols 741–8.
[34] D. Werkmüller, 'Handhafte Tat,' *Reallexikon der germanischen Altertumskunde*, vol. 13 (Berlin, 1999), pp. 614–6.
[35] Joachim Gernhuber, *Die Landfriedensbewegung in Deutschland* (Bonn, 1952), pp. 153–6.
[36] Gerhard Dilcher, 'Die Zwangsgewalt und der Rechtsbegriff vorstaatlicher Ordnungen im Mittelalter,' *Rechtsbegriffe im Mittelalter*, ed. Albrecht Cordes and Bernd Kannowski (Frankfurt, 2002), pp. 111–53, at 131–2.
[37] Jürgen Weitzel writes 'Ohne Schuld keine Strafe' [No punishment without fault]: 'Diskussion um ein frühmittelalterlich-fränkisches Strafrecht,' p. 552.

authority from holding a monopoly on penalties for breaking the peace.[38] The Church hierarchy's intention to undermine ties of kinship among the laity (as articulated in the questions of Augustine to Pope Gregory[39]) corresponded with the interests of the secular power.[40]

The influence of the Church in developing the idea of individual responsibility was gradual. The first step was the annulment of kin as the legally responsible unit.[41] This differentiation of individual from kin-group was, for example, an essential prerequisite for defining marriage as the exclusive union of two separate beings. Reflecting the growing influence of the Christian Church, Wihtred's legislation repeatedly condemns illicit unions, indicated as *unrihthæmed*, a compound word where *unriht* emerges with the meaning of 'unlawful' beside the past participle *hæmed* which means 'union/relation.'[42] We know from the historical sources that illicit unions are unconsecrated, bigamous, and, above all, unions within forbidden degrees of kinship.[43] That the degrees of consanguinity permitted in marriage constituted a vital question for both the legislator and the Church indicates that these authorities were attempting to redefine the primary relational bond in Kentish society.

Strategies of Legitimation: Alfred the Great's Road to Punishment

Nearly three hundred years after the first Germanic legislation was composed in Britain, the legislation of the West Saxon king Alfred shows further legitimation of punishment.[44] We can begin to trace this development by making a comparison: where the fine for violating the king's protection under Æthelberht was 50 Kentish shillings, the fine under Alfred was five pounds of silver pennies – a much greater value.[45] As Patrick Wormald has pointed out: 'Alfred doubled the price of royal "protection".'[46] Doing this, Alfred ascribed a greater value to the king's person and authority.[47]

---

[38] Hans Würdinger, 'Einwirkungen des Christentums auf das angelsächsische Recht,' *Zeitschrift der Savigny-Stiftung für Rechtsgeschichte, Germanistische Abteilung* 55 (1935), 105–30.

[39] Bede, *Ecclesiastical History of the English People*, ed. Bertram Colgrave and R. A. B. Mynors (Oxford, 1969), book I, ch. 27.

[40] Paul Meyvaert, 'Bede's Text of the *Libellus responsionum* of Gregory the Great to Augustine of Canterbury,' *England before the Conquest: Studies in Primary Sources Presented to Dorothy Whitelock*, ed. Peter Clemoes and Kathleen Hughes (Cambridge, 1971), pp. 15–33.

[41] Stephanie Hollis, *Anglo-Saxon Women and the Church: Sharing a Common Fate* (Woodbridge, 1992), p. 38.

[42] Wihtred 3–5 [3–6].

[43] In the Hertford council cited in Bede, *Ecclesiastical History* IV.5, we read: 'Ut nulli liceat nisi legitimum habere coniugium; nullus incestum faciat.' See also M. Tangl, ed., *Die Briefe des heiligen Bonifatius und Lullus*, MGH Epp. sel. 1 (Berlin, 1916), no. 57.

[44] Here I follow the edition of Liebermann, *Gesetze* I.

[45] Alfred 3; Wormald, *Making of English Law*, p. 279.

[46] Wormald, *Making of English Law*, p. 279.

[47] Sarah Foot, 'The Making of *Angelcynn*: English Identity before the Norman Conquest,' *TRHS*, 6th series 6 (1996), 25–49.

Even though Alfred's position was stronger than Æthelberht's had been, in his legislation we witness a real strategy to legitimize punishment. This starts with his long prologue, which contains the Ten Commandments and other precepts from Mosaic Law.[48] Death penalties abound, imposed for murder, copulation with cattle, and sacrifices to false gods.[49] A man could even be killed for failing to enclose a dangerous ox.[50] In Mosaic severity, Alfred finds a justification for a more widespread use of punishment by bodily injury[51] and death.[52]

In the Mosaic prologue to his laws, Alfred makes no mention of punishment for offences against kingship. However, in the final part of his prologue, he turns to the New Testament and canon law stating that ecclesiastical councils had declared the payment of a fine a viable alternative to the death penalty. Synods had deemed the payment of *bot* [compensation] acceptable for almost every offence except betrayal of a lord, for which no mercy could be expected, because 'almighty God assigned no compensation for those who despised him, nor did Christ, God's son, assign any compensation to the one who betrayed him to death, and he commanded each to love his lord as Himself.'[53] The Old English text of this exception reads: 'buton æt hlafordsearwe hie nane mildheortnesse ne dorston gecweðan,' [only for lord-betrayal do they dare decree no mercy]. The term *hlafordsearo* is used to indicate treachery against a lord.[54] Here, Alfred anticipates his own legislation,[55] as treachery is the subject of the fourth chapter of his law:

> Gif hwa ymb cyninges feorh sierwe, ðurh hine oððe ðurh wreccena feormunge oððe his manna, sie he his feores scyldig ond ealles þes ðe he age.[56]
>
> If anyone plots against the life of the king, either on his own account or by harbouring outlaws or men belonging to the king himself, he shall forfeit his life and all he possesses.

Anyone plotting against the life of the king, either by himself or with the help of his men or fugitives, is to lose his life and possessions unless he can exculpate himself by swearing an oath equivalent to the king's wergild. The

---

[48] On King Alfred and the Mosaic tradition, see Wormald, *Making of English Law*, pp. 416–29; see also Stefan Jurasinski, 'Slavery, Learning and the Law of Marriage in Alfred's Mosaic Prologue,' *Secular Learning in Anglo-Saxon England*, ed. László Sándor Chardonnens and Bryan Carella, Amsterdamer Beiträge zur älteren Germanistik 69 (Amsterdam, 2012), pp. 45–64; Stefan Jurasinski, 'Violence, Penance, and Secular Law in Alfred's Mosaic Prologue,' *HSJ* 22 (2010), 25–42.
[49] Alfred Prol. 13, Prol. 31, Prol. 32.
[50] Alfred Prol. 21.
[51] Alfred Prol. 19.
[52] Wormald, *Making of English Law*, pp. 416–29.
[53] Alfred Prol. 49.7
[54] Liebermann, *Gesetze* II, p. 116.
[55] On the relationship between Alfred's prologue (which represents a fifth of the *domboc* and is the longest preface of any OE law code) and the body of his laws, see Michael Treschow, 'The Prologue to Alfred's Law Code: Instruction in the Spirit of Mercy,' *Florilegium* 13 (1994), 79–110.
[56] Alfred 4.

same liability is established *ge ceorle ge eorle*, that is, for every social order of freeman, for anyone plotting against the life of his lord, with parallel exculpation to the value of his lord's wergild.[57] Alfred established support for his law in the continuity between divine principles and his own legislation: Mosaic law provided legitimation for the use of the death penalty, while Christian law legitimized his focus on treachery against a lord. Alfred raised the idea of lordship specifically so that he could legitimate his own.[58]

Alfred was the first king in England to introduce a treason law; nothing in earlier Anglo-Saxon codes corresponded to the Lombard, Alaman, and Bavarian treason laws, which show to various degrees the influence of the Roman *laesae maiestatis*.[59] Continental Germanic law includes details of procedure and penalty, such as the confiscation of the traitor's property and the practice of denying his heirs their inheritance, which were adopted from the Roman legislative tradition.[60] Alfred's legislation shows that in England, Roman influence was conveyed later, via the Church. In the particular case of the Roman treason law, the Church supported the fight against those who were guilty of treason in an almost ideological way. A canon published in 838 states that the *rei maiestatis* must be punished more severely than other offenders, because those who offend the honour of the lord also offend the other members of the community.[61] Moreover, after 850 the Church punished the *rei maiestatis* with excommunication.[62] These canons offer an extremely important recognition that kingship had public significance and thus legitimize the penal activity of the king. The influence of the Church on Alfred's legislation is clear, and is laid out by the king to legitimize his law-giving ability and his introduction of corporal punishment and death penalty.

Furthermore, even though fines were more frequent, horizontal restitution was still very widespread in Alfred's code. His compensation system shows that the progression from compensation to penalty was not linear. Besides, some of Alfred's compensation norms show interesting anomalies which

---

[57] Alfred 4.2.

[58] Foot, 'Making of *Angelcynn*,' pp. 25–49.

[59] The offence of *laesae maiestatis* was created in the third century BC as an amalgam of many different ideas: *laesae maiestatis* could be a military act hostile to the state or an act of maladministration; it could also refer to various kinds of insults to the emperor, his family, or any representative of public power. The laws relating to treason in Classical Rome were confirmed by Justinian and through his *corpus juris civilis* were available to the various Germanic states; see Floyd Seyward Lear, 'Treason in Roman and Germanic Law,' *Collected Papers* (Austin, 1965), pp. 3–72. However, as Jürgen Weitzel has shown in an extensive article, the Germanic Continental states kept only one aspect of the *maiestas* offence, that is the *infidelitas*: 'Das Majestätsverbrechen zwischen römischen Spätantike und fränkischem Mittelalter,' *Hoheitliches Strafen*, ed. Weitzel, pp. 47–83. See also the essay by Daniel Thomas in this volume, pp. 96 and 102–5.

[60] The legislation that displays the greatest debt is probably the Visigothic *Breviarium*, but the concept of the protection of the king's life at the very beginning of the Lombard laws was also influenced by the Roman *crimen laesae maiestatis*: see Gerhard Dilcher, 'Überlegungen zum langobardischen Strafrecht,' *Festschrift für Klaus Lüderssen, zum 70. Geburstag am 2. Mai 2002*, ed. C. Prittwitz *et al.* (Baden-Baden, 2002), pp. 165–77.

[61] Albert Werminghoff, ed., *Concilia aevi Karolini*, MGH Conc. 2.2 (Hanover, 1908), p. 841.

[62] Weitzel, 'Das Majestätsverbrechen', p. 68.

accompany the emergence of penalty.[63] If we turn to Alfred 36 on 'negligence with a spear' (*be speres gemeleasnesse*), for instance, we read:

> Eac is funden: gif mon hafað spere ofer eaxle, ond hine mon on asnaseð, gielde þone wer butan wite.

> It is further enacted: if a man has a spear on his shoulder and anyone is transfixed thereon, he shall pay the wergeld without a fine

The law continues:

> Gif beforan eagum asnase, gielde þone wer, gif hine mon tio gewealdes on ðære dæde, getriowe hine be þam wite ond mid ðy þæt wite afelle, gif se ord sie ufor þreo fingre þonne hindeweard sceaft. Gif hie sien bu gelic, ord ond hindeweard sceaft, þæt sie butan pleo.[64]

> If the spear transfixes in front of his eyes he has to pay the wergeld; if someone accuses him of deliberate intention in the act, he shall clear himself with an oath according to the fine and in this way the fine falls down, if the point is higher than the end of the shaft by the width of three fingers. If they are both on a level, the point and the end of the shaft, the man with the spear shall not be regarded as responsible for causing danger.

This law, which deals with a very specific situation, was considered by Wormald to be a judgment on a particular case.[65] But Lisi Oliver is not convinced that this is case law.[66] She rather thinks that the issue here is one of intentionality. Wounding someone while carrying a spear is deemed either an intentional or unintentional wrong, depending on the position of the weapon. Two words point to the idea of intentionality: *gewealdes* 'intentional,' and *pleo* 'without dangerous intention.'[67]

Pollock and Maitland were of the opinion that Anglo-Saxon society did not distinguish between intentional and unintentional wrongs, as all that was required for responsibility was for the perpetrator to have inflicted harm or injury on another.[68] However, I see here a discriminative attitude towards intentional and accidental harm.[69] In order to determine liability,[70] this norm,

---

[63] St. Ch. Saar, 'Strafe, Strafrecht,' *Reallexikon der germanischen Altertumskunde*, vol. 30 (Berlin, 2005), pp. 58–67.
[64] Alfred 36.2.
[65] Wormald, *Making of English Law*, p. 282.
[66] Pers. comm.
[67] That this norm is a legislative enactment becomes clear if we compare it with a chapter of the thirteenth-century Frisian laws with a similar phrasing: 'Si homo quislibet telum manu tenet, et ipsum casu quolibet inciderit super alium, extra voluntatem eius qui illud manu tenet, in simplo iuxta qualitatem vulneris componatur.' [If a man holds an arrow in his hand, and it injures another by accident, against the will of the one holding it in his hand, he pays a singular fine according to the nature of the wound.]: *Lex Frisionum* 3.69, ed. Karl August Eckhardt and Albrecht Eckhardt, MGH Fontes iuris 12 (Hanover, 1982), pp. 96–7. Compare Lisi Oliver's essay in this volume, pp. 63–7.
[68] Pollock and Maitland, *History of English Law* I, pp. 53–4.
[69] Elmar Wadle, 'Die Entstehung der öffentlichen Strafe,' *Perspektiven der Strafrechtsentwicklung: Ringvorlesung im Sommersemester 1994 an der Universität des Saarlandes*, ed. Heike Jung, Heinz Müller-Dietz, and Ulfrid Neumann (Baden-Baden, 1996), pp. 9–30.
[70] Joel Feinberg, *Doing and Deserving* (Princeton, NJ, 1970); Ekkehard Kaufmann, *Die Erfolgshaftung: Untersuchung über die strafrechtliche Zurechnung im Rechtsdenken des frühen Mittelalters* (Frankfurt, 1958).

though relatively isolated, is concerned with distinguishing between the different circumstances in which a wrong occurred. It therefore represents an attempt to differentiate harm and crime.

A further reason to believe that Alfred's spear clause does not necessarily represent a reaction to a specific case can be found in Alfred's introduction to his code. As for other issues of particular relevance, Alfred here anticipates in a programmatic way the topic of guilt and liability. A distinction between an intentional and an unintentional wrong can be seen in Alfred's prologue:

> Se mon se ðe his gewealdes monnan ofslea, swelte se deaðe. Se ðe hine þonne nedes ofsloge oððe unwillum oððe ungewealdes, swelce hine God swa sende on his honda, ond he hine ne ymbsyrede, sie he feores wyrðe ond folcryhtre bote, gif he friðstowe gesece.[71]

> If a man kills his hired man intentionally, let him pay with death. He who kills him out of necessity or unwillingly or accidentally, as God puts in his hands, and he does not premeditate it, let him keep his life and pay lawful compensation, if he seeks sanctuary.

The development of an idea of individual responsibility was relevant to the issue of guilt and an important step towards the implementation of criminal law as a law of crimes rather than harm.[72] Therefore while crime is punished by the king with death, harm ought to be compensated through restitution.

In addition, Alfred's legislation reflects the king's efforts to obtain a monopoly on the legitimate use of force. Alfred's England was not a country in which the king could claim an exclusive use of force,[73] but the first steps in that direction are certainly recorded in his laws.[74] For instance, Alfred 37 states:

> Gif mon wille of boldgetale in oðer boldgetæl hlaford secan, do ðæt mid ðæs ealdormonnes gewitnesse, þe he ær in his scirefolgode. Gif he hit butan his gewitnesse do, geselle se þe hine to men feormie CXX scillinga to wite: dæle he hwæðre ðæt, healf cyninge in ða scire ðe he ær folgode, healf in þa ðe he oncymð. Gif he hwæt yfla gedon hæbbe ðær he ær wæs, bete ðæt se ðe hine ðonne to men onfo, ond cyninge CXX scillinga to wite.

> If a man wishes to go from a district to seek service in another he shall do it with the cognisance of the ealdorman, to whose jurisdiction he has previously been subject. If he does so without his cognisance, he who takes him into his employment shall pay a fine of 120 shillings; but he shall divide the payment half to the king in the district where the man has been residing, and half in that to which he has come. If he has committed any manner of offence in the place where he has been, he who now takes him into his employment shall pay compensation for it, and a fine of 120 shillings to the king.

---

[71] Alfred Prol. 13.
[72] Paul Hyams, 'Does it Matter When the English Began to Distinguish between Crime and Tort?' *Violence in Medieval Society*, ed. Richard W. Kaeuper (Woodbridge, 2000), pp. 107–28. On crime and tort in a later period, see Charles Donahue Jnr, 'The Emergence of the Crime–Tort Distinction in England,' *Conflict in Medieval Europe*, ed. Warren Brown and Piotr Górecki (Aldershot, 2003), pp. 219–28.
[73] Hyams speaks of 'romantic literary exaggeration of royal authority': 'Crime and Tort,' p. 122.
[74] On this, see also Patrick Wormald, 'A Handlist of Anglo-Saxon Lawsuits,' *Legal Culture*, pp. 253–87.

Beginnings and Legitimation

This clause, which aims to control the territory and the movements of residents in order to prevent the protection of offenders and criminals, addresses the need to keep the monopoly on the legitimate use of force.[75] Offenders who sought private protection not only placed an unwanted limitation on the king's jurisdiction, but could also help create a dangerous reservoir of military power against the king in case of treachery.[76]

It was not only physical violence which represented a threat to a lordship. As Alfred's law expressly stated, verbal violence and slander were also considered offences which did not deserve a light punishment:

> Gif man folcleasunge gewyrce, ond hio on hine geresp weorðe, mid nanum leohtran ðinge gebete þonne him mon aceorfe þa tungon of, þæt hie mon na undeorran weorðe moste lesan, ðonne hie mon be þam were geeahtige.[77]
>
> If anyone utters a public slander, and it is proved against him, he shall make amends on no lighter terms than the excision of his tongue, which shall not be ransomed at a cheaper price than estimated according to the wergild.

This norm, where the punishment fits the crime, corresponds to cutting off hands for theft and money counterfeiting; it is clear that public slander was considered a serious disturbance of the peace.[78] As Wormald has noted, the loss of one's tongue for *folcleasung* is a punishment that also appears in the Theodosian Code,[79] and the topicality of this issue in the ninth century is evident in its appearance in a forged decretal[80] and in the writings of Hincmar.[81] Like the introduction of capital punishment for traitors, this principle of a controlled *poena talionis* must be considered as a further gateway to the physical punishment of free men. Alfred refers to the *poena talionis* in his prologue, providing a precious genealogy for his laws and a strong legitimation for the introduction of punishment.

Summary and Conclusions

Far from portraying criminal law as an ensemble of norms and structures perfectly entwined, the early Anglo-Saxon legislation shows an aggregation of

---

[75] Reinhard Wenskus, *Stammesbildung und Verfassung* (Cologne, 1977), pp. 371–2.
[76] The fact that this law aimed to protect the power of the king is made evident by a Continental parallel: at the beginning of the same century, Charlemagne issued a very similar rule in the *Capitulatio de partibus Saxoniae*, ch. 24; see Daniela Fruscione, *Das Asyl bei den germanischen Stämmen im frühen Mittelalter* (Cologne, 2003), p. 185.
[77] Alfred 32.
[78] Wormald, *Making of English Law*, p. 283. On *poena talionis* in the Continental *Decretio Childeberti*, see Hermann Nehlsen, 'Entstehung des öffentlichen Strafrechts bei den germanischen Stämmen,' *Gerichtslauben-Vorträge: Freiburger Festkolloquium zum 75. Geburstag von Hans Thieme*, ed. Karl Kroeschell (Sigmaringen, 1983), pp. 3–16, at 8: 'Das Prinzip der kontrollierten Gleichvergeltung erweist sich, wie schon an dieser Stelle erkennbar, als Einfallstor für die peinlichen Strafen gegenüber Freien.' Compare also the essay by Daniel O'Gorman in this volume.
[79] Wormald, *Making of English Law*, p. 282, citing the Theodosian Code X x 2.
[80] Pseudo-Angrilamm 44: Paul Hinschius, *Decretales Pseudoisidorianae et capitula Angilramni* (Leipzig, 1863), p. 765.
[81] Hincmar of Reims, *Opusculum LV capitulorum*, PL 126, cols 377–8.

norms which take two significant directions. First, an increasing importance was placed on individual penalties; second, a greater prominence was given to the king's right to punish and to receive increasingly valuable payments for offences not directly made to his person.

From a semantic point of view, the earliest punitive fines of the Kentish legislation are based on the existence of a controlling power (*wite*) and on the difference of status within a group of warriors (*drihtinbeag*). These fines, which appear intermittently in legislation otherwise dominated by compensation, show how limited Æthelberht's power was. In most cases, the resolution of conflicts did not involve the king; compensation itself would be collectable from and payable to a kin-group. It was only after regulation was relegated to areas of higher authority – a church or royal residence – that vertical fines and physical punishments could be implemented in disputes between two groups of equivalent status. There are several possible explanations for the remarkable absence of physical punishment in the earliest Kentish legislation. One obstacle to the introduction of punishment was the idea that violation of the body was detrimental to the honour of free men; another is that corporal punishments inflicted on healthy adults might endanger the survival of a community in times of migration and war. Moreover, individual penalties were not compatible with the idea of communal responsibility in family-based conflict resolution.

In the first legislation with a clear Christian background, issued under Wihtred, these objections to punishment are bypassed by a two-pronged strategy. In punishing religious offences, Wihtred introduced a double-tracked penalty system: a fine for free men and the death penalty for slaves. There is only one exception to the policy of subjecting only slaves to physical reprimand: thieves caught red-handed may also be condemned. By focusing on the bodies of slaves and of thieves killed in revenge, Wihtred's laws legitimized corporal punishment.

A different strategy was adopted by Alfred the Great in the ninth century. Seeking legitimation through continuity with divine principles, Alfred is the first king in England to be influenced by the Roman concept of *laesae maiestatis* (*hlafordsearo*), brought to England through the Church. The prohibition of treachery is part of a group of laws pertaining to kingship which together aimed to protect the king and his power. Public slander, for instance, was considered a serious disturbance of the peace that Alfred sought to regulate through both restitutive and punitive means, while the provision that prevents the detrimental protection of offenders represents the king's attempt to establish a monopoly on the legitimate use of force.

The emergence of a centralized political authority and the construction of a group of wrongs that are primarily offences against the public, to be prosecuted and punished by public authority, is only one aspect of the beginnings of punishment. Pollock and Maitland have stated that the notion of crime could not arise until another condition was satisfied: the refinement and slow adoption of a discriminatory attitude differentiating intentional and accidental harm. A trace of this can be found in Alfred, and also semantically traced back in the vocabulary: *gewealdes/ungewealdes* [intentional/unintentional], and *pleo* [without dangerous intention]. The idea that humans possess a soul, have control over their actions, and can incur guilt, originated as an ecclesiastical rather than as a legal concept. This Christian attitude towards personal responsibility is contrary to the principle that Anglo-Saxons understood only harm, rather than the concepts of crime and guilt.

Although the king was the nominal producer of law, the early Anglo-Saxon legislation shows that the Church stood behind some of these aspects and developments. The legislation of the Christian king Wihtred is the first to give a moral direction, and also the first to punish those who were living in sin. Moving society closer to a Christian ideal thus allowed the king to make assumptions and decrees concerning right (*riht*) and wrong (*unriht*). Two centuries after Wihtred, Alfred's legislation is a further representation of the influence of the Church on law. In the introduction to his code Alfred provides the genealogy for his laws and shows himself to be clearly aware of the potential of the Christian model for his own purposes. Alfred's preface was dominated by biblical commandments that established the concept of lordship on a Christian foundation and justified capital punishment for those who violated it. Therefore, from an ideological point of view, it was the protection of the Christian common good which first gave Anglo-Saxon legislators the legitimacy needed to punish.

3

Genital Mutilation in Medieval Germanic Law*

Lisi Oliver

This paper provides a somewhat oblique approach to this volume's titular focus on the difference between corporal and capital punishment in Anglo-Saxon England. The analysis focuses on how laws regulating injury to male genitalia assess the damage either as an immediate wound to the victim, or as an injury preventing him from producing offspring. In a broader sense, tying in to the theme of this collection, these fines can be seen as regarding the injury either as 'corporal' (the victim is maimed) or 'capital' (potential offspring cannot be engendered and thus are denied life). Both competing views appear in Anglo-Saxon laws; their sources and disseminations provide a case study into what medieval law can tell us about the transmission, both oral and written, of early medieval laws across the North Sea, linking the Ingvaeonic territories of Anglo-Saxon England and Frisia through several centuries.

Anglo-Saxon and Continental Barbarian Regulations

The Anglo-Saxon laws under consideration are those of Æthelberht of Kent, written in Old English around 600, and those of Alfred the Great, similarly written in the vernacular, and compiled towards the end of the ninth century, following the Viking wars.[1]

The laws of Æthelberht represent the first laws written in the Anglo-Saxon territories. Unlike their cousins on the Continent, the Germanic peoples across the Channel chose to record their laws in the vernacular rather than in Latin. Æthelberht's rulings on damage to male genitalia read as follows:

64 [64]. Gif man gekyndelice lim awyrdeþ, þrym leudgeldum hine man forgelde.

---

* First, I would like to thank Rolf Bremmer for his thorough and invariably helpful reading of various drafts. I presented a short version of this paper at the 47th International Congress on Medieval Studies at Kalamazoo in 2011 and would like to thank the participants in that session for their comments, as well as Paul Brand for pointing me to the genetic study and to Charlie Donahue for the suggestion of pre-Christian retention. I am also indebted to Marianne Elsakkers and Katherine Willis for comments and suggestions on previous drafts. Questionable interpretations or conclusions are attributable to me alone.

[1] For Æthelberht, see Oliver, *Beginnings of English Law*, pp. 74–5; for Alfred, Liebermann, *Gesetze* I, pp. 84–5.

Genital Mutilation

64.1 [64.1]. **G**if he þurhstinð, VI scill gebete.
64.2 [64.2]. **G**if man inbestinð, VI scill gebete.²

64. If a person damages the genital organ, let him pay him with three person-prices.
    64.1.   If he stabs through [it], let him pay [with] 6 shillings.
    64.2.   If a person stabs into [it], let him pay [with] 6 shillings.

Although the *gekyndelice lim* would seem, by use of the term *lim*, to mean specifically the penis, it seems unlikely that the regulations for piercing through and piercing into – and particularly the latter – refer to the penis, as these wounds would require weaponry more delicate than common in Anglo-Saxon England. The two sub-rulings thus, with their considerably lesser reparations, probably imply damage to the scrotum which would not prohibit future procreation; these contrast the main clause, which – by nature of its enormous fine – implies an injury that incapacitates the genitals. The calculation of recompense for this greater injury seems to be based upon three children the victim can no longer create.³

The only other clauses regarding genital damage in Anglo-Saxon legislation are found in the laws of Alfred the Great:

65. Gif mon sie on þa herðan to ðam swiðe wund, þæt he ne mæge bearn [gestrienan], gebete him ðæt mid LXXX scill.
67. Gif sio lendenbræde bið forslegen, þær sceal LX scill. to bote.
    67.1.   Gif hio bið onbestungen, geselle XV scill. to bote.
    67.2.   Gif hio bið ðurhðyrel, ðon*ne* sceal ðær XXX scill. to bote.⁴

65 If a man is wounded so greatly on the testicles, that he cannot [engender] a child, let him be compensated with 80 shillings.
67. If the loins are (?scrotum is) struck off, 60 shillings shall be paid as compensation.
    67.1.   If it (?the scrotum) is pierced into, let him pay 15 shillings as compensation.
    67.2.   If it is pierced through, then 30 shillings shall be paid as compensation.

In his prologue to his laws Alfred states that he kept those which he liked and, with consent of his counselors, emended or replaced those which he did not.⁵ For sub-clauses 67.1 and 67.2, emendation was the choice. While Æthelberht equates the fines for piercing into and through the scrotum,

---

² Text and translation from Oliver, *Beginnings of English Law*, pp. 74–5. The manuscript of Æthelberht's laws is written continuously with no breakdown into clauses. The clause numbers given above come from Oliver's edition, in which the clause numeration is based on linguistic analysis; the number in [square brackets] represents the clause number from Liebermann's edition in *Gesetze*, cited in earlier scholarship.
³ See discussion in Oliver, *Beginnings of English Law*, p. 99.
⁴ Text from Parker manuscript (E), Liebermann, *Gesetze* I, pp. 84–5, translation my own. Clause 66, which separates these two rulings, concerns striking off the arm below the elbow.
⁵ See Liebermann, *Gesetze* I, pp. 46–7. For translation see Attenborough, *Laws*, p. 63.

Alfred doubles the required compensation for the latter.⁶ (Of the barbarian laws, these are the only two texts to address injury resulting from piercing the genital organs.)⁷

In the regulation of damage great enough to destroy the ability for procreation, Æthelberht and Alfred demonstrate a substantive difference: here Alfred has replaced rather than emended his model. For damage to the penis, Æthelberht requires a payment of three wergilds, presumably to compensate the victim for children he could no longer engender. By the definition provided earlier, this is viewed as a 'capital' offense. Alfred, in contrast, stipulates a fine of 80 shillings (40% wergild) for damage to testicles so that a man cannot procreate, and 60 shillings (30% wergild) for damage to the loins or scrotum. Despite the fact that Alfred, unlike Æthelberht, specifically invokes the inability of the victim to engender children, his laws calculate the recompense according to the physical injury to the victim himself. Unlike Æthelberht's 'capital' reading, Alfred's must be seen as a 'corporal' interpretation: the victim is compensated for present injury without financial consideration of longterm consequences.

Other barbarian laws⁸ concur with the 'corporal' interpretation of such major injury, as demonstrated by Map 3.1 below:⁹

As indicated above, all Continental barbarian territories rule that damage to genitals should be judged only as an injury to the individual: that is, the fine is assessed as a percentage of the victim's wergild. The injury is thus evaluated as corporal damage.

For the earliest of the barbarian laws, those of Salian Francia, the text in one version reads:

29.17. Si quis ingenuous ingenuum castrauerit aut uiriliam transcapulauerit, unde mancus sit ... solidus cc culpabilis iudicetur.¹⁰

29.17. If someone castrates a freeman or cuts through his ?manhood, so that it is maimed ... let him be judged culpable for 200 *solidi*.

This recension requires a fine equal to the wergild for incapacitating the genitals: in some sense, when a man is unmanned he ceases to exist (or at

---

⁶ The standard wergild for a freeman in Kent was 100 shillings, in Wessex 200 shillings. Thus we must double the amount of Æthelberht's fines to match the percentage of wergild demanded in Alfred's.

⁷ This concord substantiates Alfred's claim that he had access to the text of his predecessor Æthelberht. The only other ruling to show unambiguous influence from Æthelberht is the ruling on skull injuries, is that which similarly differentiates the Anglo-Saxon rulings from other barbarian regulations: see Lisi Oliver, 'Æthelberht's and Alfred's Two Skulls,' *Heroic Age* 14 (2010), online at https://www.mun.ca/mst/heroicage/ [accessed 5 January 2014]. *Lex Salica* also includes a fine for piercing through a man's ?scrotum, but lacks the ruling, peculiar to the Anglo-Saxon laws, for damage incurred by piercing into it: see Karl August Eckhardt, ed., *Lex Salica*, MGH LL nat. Germ. 4.2 (Hanover, 1969), p. 88.

⁸ Scholars differ in their definitions of which early medieval laws should be defined as 'barbarian.' Some include either or both early medieval Celtic laws and later Scandinavian laws. Here and elsewhere, I limit the term to those territories using a linguistic Western Germanic dialect.

⁹ From Oliver, *Body Legal*, p. 232.

¹⁰ Eckhardt, *Lex Salica*, p. 88. Unless otherwise noted, all translations are my own.

Genital Mutilation

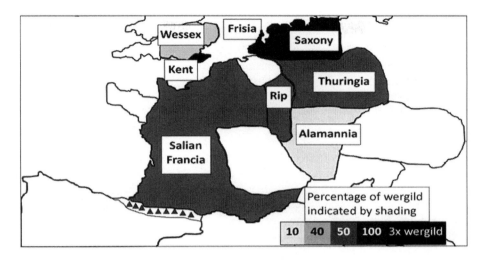

MAP 3.1 Compensation values for genital injury in Anglo-Saxon and barbarian law

least to function as a man). However, wading through the morass that is the manuscript tradition of *Lex Salica*, one finds also clauses that require only 100 *solidi* (i.e., 50% wergild) for the damage described above, or even split clauses in which castration is fined by 100 *solidi* but amputation of the penis by 200 (a full wergild).[11] Under any manuscript reading, however, this ruling must be seen as a 'corporal' fine: the restitution is for damage to the victim up to the full amount of his wergild, but does not add a surcharge for the inability to create new offspring.

The most common judgment throughout the barbarian territories was to require compensation equal to 50% wergild for the loss of one testicle. *Lex Saxonum* (c. 785) adds that if both testicles are struck off, the fine should equal the man's wergild; we can assume that this stipulation held tacitly in other Continental regions. *Lex Frisionum* (785×803) further demands a full wergild for striking off the penis.[12] In all these regulations, the maximum penalty is limited to the wergild of the victim – he is recompensed for his personal injury, but not for the loss of any – now inconceivable – future children.

While the laws of Æthelberht require three times the wergild for incapacitating damage to the genitals – compensating for three children who might otherwise have been conceived – all other barbarian laws fine the same offense with a fraction (up to 100%) of the victim's wergild, understanding the wound as an injury to present capabilities rather than future potential.

---

[11] For the former, see Eckhardt, *Lex Salica*, p. 88; for the latter, Katherine Fisher Drew, *The Laws of the Salian Franks* (Philadelphia, PA, 1991), p. 94.

[12] For *Lex Saxonum*, see Karl August Eckhardt, ed. and trans., *Die Gesetze des Karolingerreiches, 714–911* (Weimar, 1934), Germanenrechte III.2.3, pp. 18–19; for *Lex Frisionum*, see pp. 98–101 of the same volume.

Alfred's approach matches the tactic taken by the Continental laws, and any of them could have provided the theoretical model (although the actual amount of fine varies across regions).

For comparative reasons we might look towards Frisia as the specific exemplum for Alfred's 'corporal' interpretation of major injury to the genitals, although this hypothesis is hardly unproblematic. *Lex Frisionum* has a somewhat vexed cultural and textual history. We have no medieval witness – the collection remains only in a text printed by Johann Herold in 1557, from a manuscript now lost. Editors have dated the Latin collection of Frisian legal rulings to 795×803, compiled under Carolingian influence; they point to the Aachen assembly of 802 as the most likely date.[13] This compilation thus represents a chronological midpoint between the Kentish laws of Æthelberht, composed around 600, and the West-Saxon laws of Alfred, composed between 890 and 901. But Rolf Bremmer cautions against using *Lex Frisionum* as an actual code of contemporary legal practice in Frisia:

> The *Lex*, despite its modern title, never was given the status of Lex, but is rather like 'materials towards a Lex'; only one copy survived, and is now lost – it can't have been very popular, it was never imposed by Charlemagne, nor was Frisia very literate in Alfred's time – at least, we have no [such] evidence.[14]

Nonetheless, comparative evidence provides a strong argument that even if (as seems likely) Alfred did not have access to a copy of *Lex Frisionum*, he was legislating in the light of similar legal tradition, at least in regard to personal injury tariffs. In a recent essay I presented connections between the personal injury laws in *Lex Frisionum* and those of Alfred.[15] Salient equivalences – crucially, unmatched in other barbarian laws – include the primacy of the ringfinger in legal valuation of the digits of the hand; the valuation of teeth according to functional worth rather than visible prominence; the use in Alfred's laws of the Anglo-Frisian term *tusk* (the reflex of which provides the Modern Frisian word for tooth) as the only instance of reference to human – as opposed to bestial – teeth in Old English prose; and regulation of synovial fluid escaping a damaged joint. These non-trivial similarities are bolstered by other parallels which, although not themselves determinative, nonetheless provide additional substantiation of the association of the early laws of Frisia and Anglo-Saxon England, including the laws of Æthelberht. Further correspondences include a considerably greater number of regulations for damage to the face and to the torso compared to

---

[13] The most recent edition of *Lex Frisionum* is in Eckhardt, *Gesetze des Karolingerreiches*, pp. 62–127. For dating, see Karl von Richthofen, ed., *Lex Frisionum*, MGH LL 3 (Hanover, 1863), pp. 640–55; see also Harald Siems, *Studien zur Lex Frisionum* (Ebelsbach, 1980) for discussion of dating, origins and influences. A brief introduction in English can be found in Rolf H. Bremmer Jnr, '"The Children He Never Had: The Husband She Never Served": Castration and Genital Mutilation in Medieval Frisian Law,' *Castration and Culture in the Middle Ages*, ed. Larissa Tracy (Woodbridge, 2013), pp. 108–30.

[14] Rolf Bremmer, pers. comm.

[15] Lisi Oliver, 'Who Wrote Alfred's Laws?' *Textus Roffensis in Context: Law, Language and Libraries in Early Medieval England*, ed. Bruce O'Brien and Barbara Bombi (Turnhout, forthcoming).

Genital Mutilation

other barbarian laws.[16] The less specific comparanda distinguish the laws of the Anglo-Saxon (not specifically West-Saxon) and Frisian territories from those of the rest of Germania. These personal-injury rulings demonstrate a relationship between the territories of Anglo-Saxon England (at least from the time of Æthelberht to that of Alfred) and the cross-Channel region of Frisia in judicial regulation.[17]

It thus seems pertinent to examine *Lex Frisionum*'s rulings on damage to male genitalia, which read as follows:

57. Si veterum quis alium absciderit, weregildum suum componat.
58. Si unum testiculum excusserit, dimidium weregildum, si ambo, totum componat.
59. Si testiculus exierit per vulnus, et iterum reimittitur in locum suum, VI solidus supra compositionem vulneris componatur.[18]

57. If someone strikes the penis from another, he should pay with his wergild.
58. If he strikes off one testicle, let him pay a half wergild, if both, a full.
59. If a testicle emerges from the wound and can be replaced in position, let him pay 6 *solidi* above the compensation for the wound.

Like most of the barbarian laws, Frisia reckons the destruction of a man's ability to procreate as equivalent in gravity to his killing: both offenses require a full wergild. Interestingly, Alfred – whose legislation is the last that historians include among the 'barbarian' laws – reduces this fine substantially to 40% of the victim's wergild. This difference does not, however, negate the fact that Alfred's laws, like the *Lex Frisionum*, employ the 'corporal' approach as

---

[16] See Oliver, *Body Legal*, chs 3–5; Oliver, 'Who Wrote Alfred's Laws?.'

[17] Interestingly (and disappointingly), a subsequent study of the *hapax legomena* in the non-personal injury laws of Ine and Alfred against the Riustringer and Brokmer codices turned up nearly empty – in fact, fewer concordances exist than one would have predicted by chance in two such closely related languages. Even more tellingly, considering the similarity of the content, the Alfredian and Riustringer clauses regulating the liability of a man carrying a spear over his shoulder on which someone impales himself have an astoundingly total disjunt in terminology:

Alfred 36: 'Eac is funden: gyf mon hæfð spere ofer eaxle, {7} hine man onsnæseþ, gylde þone wer buton wite …' [Likewise it is determined: if a man has a spear over his shoulder, and someone is impaled on it, let him pay the wergild without the fine]. Text from Parker Manuscript (E), Liebermann, *Gesetze* I, pp. 68–71.

Riüstring IV.12: '… ieftha ther werth en ergere dede urbek eden mith bekwardiga wepne and bi unwille …' [or if a serious injury is done behind the back with a weapon carried backwards, but without intention]. Text from Wybren Jan Buma and Wilhelm Ebel, eds, *Das Rüstringer Recht* (Göttingen, 1963), p. 50.

Legal relationship between these territories thus seems mostly limited to the personal injury tariffs. Patrick Wormald has suggested for the injury schedules that they 'were in some sense the defining factor in any one *lex*, expert knowledge of which thus identified the legal specialist … A tariff recognizable as one's own was perhaps itself an ethnic marker': Patrick Wormald, 'The *Leges Barbarorum*: Law and Ethnicity in the Medieval West,' *Regna and Gentes*, ed. Hans-Werner Goetz et al. (Leiden, 2003), pp. 21–53, at 41. The discussion above might be adduced as substantiation for Wormald's hypothesis that the personal injury tariffs – above and distinct from any other rulings – were, indeed, central to a present and lasting sense of identity among the Ingvaeonic peoples.

[18] Eckhardt, *Gesetze des Karolingerreiches*, pp. 98–101.

Table 3.1 Fines for inflicting genital injuries in Anglo-Saxon and Frisian laws

Law	Date	Language	Fine (as a percentage of the victim's wergild)	Corporal/Capital
Æthelberht	c. 600	Old English	Incapacitating damage: 300% Scrotum pierced into: 6% Scrotum pierced through: 6%	Capital
Lex Frisionum	790×803	Latin	1 testicle off: 50% 2 testicles off: 100% Penis off: 100% Testicle knocked out, replaced: 3%	Corporal
Alfred	890×901	Old English	Testicles incapacitated: 40% Loin/scrotum off: 30% Pierced into: 7.5% Pierced through: 15%	Corporal

opposed to the 'capital' reading of Æthelberht. Table 3.1 lays out the relevant data for the early medieval Ingvaeonic laws, which provide the focus of the initial comparison of this study.

Although Æthelberht's version is unique among early barbarian legislation, it may have had longer-lasting impact. The following discussion proposes that a strong early connection between Anglo-Saxon England and Frisia in respect to the formulation of personal injury laws can be traced even after the disruption of that association by the subordination of Frisia to the Carolingian empire in the early ninth century. The similarities between Alfred and *Lex Frisionum* discussed above represent echoes of this association in Anglo-Saxon legislation until the late ninth century. On the Frisian side, remnants of rulings seen first in the laws of Æthelberht reach, remarkably, as far as the first recorded laws in the vernacular in the late thirteenth century, and most strongly in the 'capital' interpretation of suitable recompense for destroying a man's ability to procreate.

Evidence for Early Anglo-Frisian Connections

This section presents evidence for the foundational connections between the Frisian and English territories during the early Middle Ages. Although Rolf Bremmer has argued against a major Frisian presence in the *adventus Saxonum*,[19] recent investigations combined with previous studies provide

---

[19] Rolf H. Bremmer Jnr, 'The Nature of the Evidence for a Frisian Participation in the *Adventus Saxonum*,' *Britain 400–600: Language and History*, ed. Alfred Bammesburger and Alfred Wollmann (Heidelberg, 1990), pp. 353–72.

a conglomerate indication of continuous association between the insular Anglo-Saxon and Frisian peoples from the fifth to ninth centuries.

Linguistic

In the design of the West-Germanic family tree, linguists establish an Anglo-Frisian node, differentiating these two languages from the remainder of the Continental Germanic languages. One defining feature is the raising and fronting of West-Germanic /a/ to Anglo-Frisian /æ/ (as in Old High German *tag* compared to Old English *dæg* and Old Frisian *dei* (with later, further raising)). Roger Lass claims this Anglo-Frisian brightening 'probably dates from around the early fifth century.'[20] Further phonological comparanda are the rounding of a → o before nasals and the loss of nasals before voiceless fricatives with compensatory lengthening of the preceding vowel (for both, compare Old High German *zan* to Anglo-Frisian *tōþ*).[21]

Well-known morphological parallels include one single form used throughout the present plural indicative, and the collapse of the dative and accusative forms for first- and second-person personal pronouns.[22] Æthelberht 60 [L56] provides another early morphological similarity. This clause assigns a fine for causing the *lærestan wlitewamme* [least disfigurement of the appearance]; the first term appears elsewhere in Old English as *læs(es)t*. Old Frisian alone among the Germanic vernaculars shares this alternation between the options *lerest* and *lest* for Modern English *least*, the superlative (and suppletive) form of 'little.'[23]

Historical and Genetic[24]

Bede I.15 famously describes the migrant troops crossing the Channel in the fifth century as consisting of Angles, Saxons, and Jutes, but recent archaeological research has demonstrated that other Germanic peoples, including Frisians and Scandinavians, were also included.[25]

The Byzantine historian Procopius in the middle of the sixth century described the island of *Brittia* as being populated by '*Angili, Frissones,* and *Brittones,* the last being named from the island itself.' Procopius's claim was made from a considerable distance, and finds little regard in recent

---

[20] Roger Lass, *Old English: A Historical Linguistic Companion* (Cambridge, 1994), p. 42. See also R. Derolez, 'Cross-Channel Language Ties,' *ASE* 3 (1974), 1–14.

[21] See Rolf H. Bremmer Jnr, 'Old English–Old Frisian: The Relationship Reviewed,' *Philologica Frisica 618* (1981), 79–91.

[22] Bremmer, 'Old English–Old Frisian,' p. 81.

[23] For linguistic analysis of these forms, see Lisi Oliver, 'The Language of the Early English Laws' (unpublished PhD dissertation: Harvard University, 1995), pp. 160–4.

[24] A useful historical overview can be found in H. A. Heidinga, 'The Wijnaldum Excavation: Searching for a Central Place in Dark Age Frisia,' *The Excavations at Wijnaldum: Reports on Frisia in Roman and Medieval Times,* vol. 1, ed. J. C. Besteman *et al.* (Rotterdam, 1999), pp. 1–16, at 5–10.

[25] See Bede, *Ecclesiastical History of the English People,* ed. Bertram Colgrave and R. A. B. Mynors (Oxford, 1969), pp. 50–1 and p. 50 n. 1. See also the following essays in John Hines, ed., *The Anglo-Saxons from the Migration Period to the Eighth Century: An Ethnographic Perspective* (Woodbridge, 1997): Ian Wood, 'Before and After the Migration' and 'Discussion,' pp. 41–54 and 55–64; Walter Pohl, 'Ethnic Names and Identities in the British Isles' and 'Discussion,' pp. 7–31 and 32–40.

scholarship.²⁶ However, arguments for the presence of Frisians in the migration have been bolstered by recent evidence from genetics. A 2002 study by Michael E. Weale and Deborah A. Weiss examined Y-chromosomes from males of Central England, Norway, Wales, and Friesland and found that 'the Central English and Frisian samples were statistically indistinguishable.' They conclude that 'the best explanation for our findings is that the Anglo-Saxon cultural transition in Central England coincided with a mass migration from the continent.'²⁷ Since only Frisian data was used from the southern Germanic regions, this study does not speak to the makeup of the peoples migrating from other areas of the North Sea littoral; it does, however, provide evidence for a strong Frisian population in early Anglo-Saxon England.²⁸

In the early Merovingian period, Frisia became an important trading center. Coins minted in Dorestad crossed the English Channel,²⁹ and Bede recounts the story of the nobleman Imma who was sold as a slave in London to a Frisian merchant. Colgrave and Mynors comment on this tale:

> Slave dealing seems to have been one of the earliest forms of continental trading in Anglo-Saxon times and the slave boys seen by Gregory in Rome were probably taken there by Frisians. A number of early coins inscribed with the name of London have been found on ancient dwelling sites in Holland.³⁰

A further, though extremely slight, thread binding the two regions across the Channel is the fact that, of Germanic ship burials excavated to date, only two place the ship over the burial chamber: Sutton Hoo Mound 2, and the Hedeby boat burial in Frisia. But, as van de Noort points out, 'the Hedeby boat ... is dated to the middle of the ninth century, about 250 years after the Mound 2 ship was interred at Sutton Hoo.'³¹ If we are to include, however tentatively, these finds among the archaeological evidence for an Anglo-Frisian connection, we must assume that they represent some early common (and now lost) shared ritual meaning that persisted longer on the Continent than in Britain.³²

---

[26] See Nicholas Higham, *An English Empire: Bede and the Early Anglo-Saxon Kings* (Manchester, 1995), p. 131 for citation, discussion, and references to scholarly literature.

[27] Michael E. Weale *et al.*, 'Y Chromosome Evidence for Anglo-Saxon Mass Migration,' *Molecular Biology and Evolution* 19 (2002), 1008–21, at 1008 and 1018. I am indebted to Paul Brand for this reference.

[28] In the early medieval period Frisia may not have been distinguished from other territories under Frankish domination. This discussion, however, does not depend on the sense of Frisia as an autonomous region, but rather as the locus of the Ingvaeonic legal tradition. On early history of Frisia, see Ian Wood, *The Merovingian Kingdoms, 450–751* (London, 1994), pp. 293–306.

[29] For discussion of Dorestad as trading centre, see Ruth Mazo Karras, 'Seventh-Century Jewellery from Frisia: A Re-Examination,' *Anglo-Saxon Studies in Art and Archaeology* 4 (1985), 154–177, at 173–4.

[30] Bede, *Ecclesiastical History*, pp. 404–5 and n. 2.

[31] Robert van de Noort, *North Sea Archaeologies* (Oxford, 2011), p. 212.

[32] Van de Noort adduces the hypothesis of Egon Wamers 'that this practice [of burial below the ship] was possibly specific to the burial of Scandinavian kings who had been christened but had then reverted, wholly or partly, to the pagan ideas of Valhalla': *North Sea Archaeologies*, p. 212. But the attribution of these under-ship burials to a generalized Scandinavian tradition does not account for the fact that the only two occurrences appear in Ingvaeonic territories.

Genital Mutilation

If the original movement between the English and the Frisians was westward across the Channel, the locus of influence was reversed in the succeeding centuries, as Anglo-Saxon missionaries concerned themselves with the conversion of the pagan Frisians. Bede V.9 describes the early efforts of an otherwise unknown Wihtberht, who, towards the end of the seventh century, left his hermitage in Ireland and 'spent two whole years preaching the word of life to that nation [Frisia] and to its king Radbod, but he reaped no fruit for all this labor among the barbarians who heard him.'[33] (Radbod apostatized when he discovered that, as a Christian, he would spend eternity in heaven separated from his pagan ancestors.) Wihtberht's work was continued by Wilfrid in the late 670s, although a permanent settlement was not established until the mission led by Willibrord in 690. He went on to Rome to seek the pope's approval for his plan for converting the pagans. While he was there, the Anglo-Saxons in Frisia sent Swithberht back to Britain to be consecrated bishop by Wilfrid.[34] In 696, Pippin II, the Frankish Mayor of the Palace, had Willibrord consecrated archbishop of the Frisians as part of his effort to bring Frisia back under Frankish control; the episcopal see was located in Utrecht, where Willibrord remained bishop for thirty-six years.[35] The last of these were plagued by skirmishes between Frisia and Francia, and in 716 a brief, supportive visit was paid by the West-Saxon monk Wynfrith, later given the name Boniface. He returned to spend the years from 719 through 722 helping Willibrord rebuild the Christian mission in Frisia. Boniface remarked on a less-than-salubrious connection that set the two peoples apart from their contemporaries: the tendency towards excessive drinking and intoxication, 'for neither the Franks, nor the Gauls, nor the Lombards, nor the Romans, nor the Greeks have it.'[36] It was in Frisia that Boniface and fifty-three companions met their deaths at the hands of unconverted pagans.[37] Once Frisia was conquered by Francia in the early ninth century, the historical record becomes vague, or even non-existent – at least in regard to any connections across the English channel. The archaeological record provides an apt metaphor, as it was around this time that Frisians began to build dykes, creating 'a transition from an

---

[33] Bede, *Ecclesiastical History*, pp. 478–81.
[34] Bede, *Ecclesiastical History*, pp. 484–5. See discussion in Joanna Story, *Carolingian Connections: Anglo-Saxon England and Carolingian Francia, c. 750–870* (Aldershot, 2003), pp. 42–4 and 50.
[35] Bede, *Ecclesiastical History*, pp. 486–7. For commentary on Bede's discussion of the Frisian mission see J. M. Wallace-Hadrill, *Bede's Ecclesiastical History of the English People: A Historical Commentary* (Oxford, 1988), pp. 180–5.
[36] Amy Hagen, cited in Y. Sablerolles, 'The Glass Vessel Finds,' *Excavations at Wijnaldum*, ed. Besteman *et al.*, pp. 229–52, at 241.
[37] See Roger Collins, *Early Medieval Europe: 300–1000*, 2nd edn (Hampshire, 1999), pp. 255–8; Story, *Carolingian Connections*, p. 96, and also 131 for the short visit in Utrecht of Aluberht. W. Groenman-van Waateringe suggests (very tentatively) that the leather remains that may be from a heel-tongued shoe could be remnants of this fashion brought from Durrow by the Anglo-Saxon missionaries: 'The Leather Finds,' *Excavations at Wijnaldum*, ed. Besteman *et al.*, pp. 299–304.

environment under marine influence to a landscape without direct marine influence';[38] the natural channel of communication was literally walled off by the new technology.

Artistic and Artifactual

The early association between these two territories is further substantiated by artistic and artifactual similarities. Ruth Mazo Karras describes Kentish elements in many of the Frisian jewelry finds dating to the seventh century, leading her to postulate:

> The craftsman or men who worked in Frisia in the seventh century had such a familiarity with Kentish work that at least one must have trained in England. If the Frisian workshop remained active over the course of several decades, as seems likely judging from the quantity and range of the jewellery, it must have had access over the whole period to Kentish pieces as models, or craftsmen must have travelled frequently back and forth.[39]

The most spectacular of these Frisian adornments is the Wijnaldum brooch (Plate 3.1). Mazo Karras claims that, 'The cloisonné studs and the lower half of the cloisonné design look very Kentish. The upper half, with Style II animal ornament, has no Kentish parallels.'[40] However, J. Schoneveld and J. Zijlstra consider that the Frisian brooch has sufficient properties characteristic of the school of Sutton Hoo to postulate that 'it may well be possible that an apprentice of the Sutton Hoo workshop was working for a king in Frisia.'[41] Schoneveld and Zijlstra also point to comparable design elements in the somewhat later Book of Durrow (Plate 3.3), proposing an artistic trail from Sutton Hoo (c. 625) through Wijnaldum (< 650) to Durrow (c. 680).

On the artisanal side, specifically clay vessels, the excavations on the Wijnaldum-Tjitsma terp in Frisia have produced 'predominately hand-made, stonegrid tempered "Anglo-Saxon" pottery' beginning in c. 425, although the percentage diminishes around 600.[42]

---

[38] Van de Noort, *North Sea Archaeologies*, p. 118.
[39] Mazo Karras, 'Seventh-Century Jewellery,' p. 174.
[40] Mazo Karras, 'Seventh-Century Jewellery,' p. 168.
[41] J. Schoneveld and J. Zijlstra, 'The Wijnaldum Brooch,' *Excavations at Wijnaldum*, ed. Besteman *et al.*, pp. 191–201, particularly at 198–199. It is important to keep in mind that these artistic renditions loom far larger in importance than in size: Schoneveld and Zijlstra point out that 'in this part of the country, the early Middle Ages do not excel in producing monumental works of art in the field of architecture, sculpture or painting. Characteristic of the art of the early Middle Ages is the making of small objects, particularly using precious metals' (p. 191).
[42] D. A. Gerrets and J. de Koning, 'Settlement Development on the Wijnaldum-Tjitsma Terp,' *Excavations at Wijnaldum*, ed. Besteman *et al.*, pp. 73–123, at 96–7. Curiously, we find a dichotomy between pottery and glass finds. Y. Saberolles reports that 'It is remarkable that the 5th–7th century vessels from Wijnaldum are all "Frankish" imports. There are no fragments of glass vessels which are considered typical products of Kentish glass workshops ... As far as glass vessels are concerned, the excavations at Wijnaldum have not been able to substantiate the idea that Frisia played and intermediary role between Scandinavia and Anglo-Saxon England': 'The Glass Vessel Finds,' *Excavations at Wijnaldum*, ed. Besteman *et al.*, pp. 229–52, at 242.

Genital Mutilation

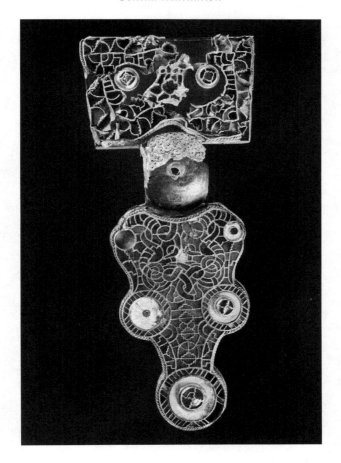

PLATE 3.1 Wijnaldum brooch (photograph © Fries Museum, Leeuwarden, Johan van der Veer)

PLATE 3.2 Gold belt buckle from the ship-burial at Sutton Hoo (image © The Trustees of the British Museum)

PLATE 3.3 Book of Durrow: MS Dublin, Trinity College Library 57, fol. 125v (image © The Board of Trinity College Dublin)

Numismatic

Final evidence for the cross-Channel connection to be presented here is from the field of numismatics. The porcupine coinage design (Plate 3.4), had its origins in Frisia, which was then a center of trade in Western Europe.[43] Although this pattern was common throughout early medieval Europe, it was especially prominent in Anglo-Saxon England in the sixth to eighth centuries. More tellingly, the simple quatrefoil 'Solomon's Knot' design (Plate 3.5) was shared only by Anglo-Saxon England and Frisia.[44]

The foregoing discussions adduce evidence for a close connection between the early medieval territories of Anglo-Saxon England and Frisia, including data from linguistics, history, archaeology, genetics, numismatics, and legal regulations. Although none of these data provide incontrovertible proof in isolation, the conglomeration offers a fairly convincing picture for a strong early association.

PLATE 3.4 'Porcupine' design on a silver penny (c. 700) from the Woodham Walter hoard, Essex (image © The Trustees of the British Museum)

---

[43] See Wood, *Merovingian Kingdoms*, pp. 296–303.
[44] Anna Gannon, *The Iconography of Early Anglo-Saxon Coinage: Sixth to Eighth Centuries* (Oxford, 2003), pp. 177–9 and 164–5. See also A. Pol, 'Medieval Coins from Wijnaldum,' *Excavations at Wijnaldum*, ed. Besteman *et al.*, pp. 217–28, at 220–1.

Lisi Oliver

PLATE 3.5 'Solomon's Knot' interlace design on reverse of a silver sceat (penny) from the Middle Harling hoard, Norfolk (ruler: Beonna, King of East Anglia c. 749–60) (image © Fitzwilliam Museum, Cambridge/Art Resource, NY)

The Relationship Ends

Once Frisia was subsumed by the Franks early in the ninth century, this relationship came to a close. Indeed, the clauses in the personal injury laws of Wessex that resemble those in *Lex Frisionum* probably already represent an echo of the early connection rather than an ongoing association. Anglo-Saxon legislation following Alfred increasingly and deliberately draws upon literary models, and the insular laws quickly abandon their early, more orally influenced, phraseology.[45]

Rolf Bremmer suggests that it may have been precisely the subordination to Francia that accounts for enduring linguistic parallels between England and Frisia:

> When the Frisians were annexed by the Franks, in the course of the eighth century, one of their ways of resistance would have been to withstand linguistic innovations that spread from the more central Frankish cultural centres. England remained outside this sphere of influence, because of its insular position. Secluded from the inland by vast marshes and oriented towards the sea, Frisian likewise escaped the fate of falling victim to Franconian; compared to the neighbouring Germanic languages, it has preserved many original Ingvaeonic features.[46]

[45] Oliver, *Beginnings of English Law*, pp. 33–6 argues for an oral basis for most of the laws of Æthelberht. For the increasingly literary style of composition, see Lisi Oliver, 'Documentary Culture and Legal Tradition,' *Cambridge History of Early Medieval English Literature*, ed. Clare Lees (Cambridge, 2012), pp. 499–529.
[46] See Bremmer, 'Frisian Participation.'

Genital Mutilation

To paraphrase and slightly adapt Bremmer's assertion, language features shared by Old English and Old Frisian might be attributed to common retention of earlier phrases which were lost in the Frankish dialects that predominated in most of early medieval western Europe.⁴⁷ That is, arising from a common geographical center and legal tradition, words, phrases, and even rulings follow their own individual paths to appear in the isolated regions in which were composed the ninth-century laws of Alfred and the thirteenth-century laws of Frisia. The ancient Near East provides a model for a central locus of legal culture of which elements can be traced in the linguistically disparate laws of Mesopotamia, Anatolia, and the Old Testament.⁴⁸ Nor would long-lasting linguistic retention be unusual: a classic example is the *Rig Veda*, which has retained for millennia our oldest versions of Sanskrit. Composers of law (and poetry) are notorious for preserving archaic terminology, both in oral and written transmission. These two methods seem to overlap in the earliest codex of vernacular Frisian law – the *Riustringer Riucht* – which is, somewhat oxymoronically, known as the *Asega buch*, 'Book of the Lawspeaker.'⁴⁹ I argue below that although no known codex of law is composed in the Frisian vernacular until the thirteenth century, both phrasal and substantive remnants from a far earlier period remained frozen in oral transmission for over six centuries.

Phrasal Echoes Across the Gap

Shared wording between the laws of Æthelberht and the late laws of Frisia provide evidence for persistence of legal phraseology.⁵⁰ Æthelberht's personal injury tariffs begin with a fine for *feaxfang* [seizing hair]. This regulation is

---

⁴⁷ Care must be taken here about interpreting the term 'linguistic,' by which Bremmer surely intends phraseology rather than phonology. With all their considerable efforts, the Académie Française has been unable to stop the natural process of language change in France, and early medieval Frisia had no such strong central linguistic watchdog.

⁴⁸ See Jonathon Burnside, *God, Justice and Society: Aspects of Law and Legality in the Bible* (Oxford, 2010), pp. 2–8.

⁴⁹ According to legend, Charlemagne asked twelve *asegas* to choose the laws for Frisia, which are not necessarily equivalent to the collection in the *Lex Frisionum*. See discussion in Rolf H. Bremmer Jnr, 'Dealing Dooms: Alliteration in the Old Frisian Laws,' *Alliteration in Culture*, ed. Jonathan Roper (Basingstoke, 2011), p. 77. For the role of the lawspeaker elsewhere, see Oliver, *Beginnings of English Law*, p. 35 and citations therein. For the *Riustringer Riucht*, see Buma and Ebels, *Rüstringer Recht*; for dating, pp. 11–21. In 1805, T. E. Wiarda published this codex under the title of *Asega-Buch: Ein alt-friesisches Gesetzbuch der Rüstringer* (Berlin, 1805).

⁵⁰ There are, of course, numerous terminological overlaps. Cognates to the Old English terms *goldfinger, scytefinger, protbolla, widuban* (among others) all appear in Old Frisian laws; a listing comparing Æthelberht and Riustringer terminology can be found in Wiarda, *Asega-Buch*, p. viii. But these represent standard nomenclature which can be found elsewhere in Old English, in Old Frisian, and in other Germanic vernaculars. These terms are thus irrelevant to this particular comparative examination. Horst H. Munske discusses a list of legal terms shared between Old English and Old Frisian laws, including those from the personal injury sections discussed above. Moving beyond these tariffs, in several other cases he adduces specific semantics restricted to legal contexts: 'Angelsächsisch–altfriesisch Beziehungen in der Rechtsterminolgie für Missetaten,' *Flecht op 'e koai: Stúdzjes oanbean oan Prof. Dr. W. J. Buma ta syn sechstichste jierdei*, ed. Teake Hoekema et al., Fryske Akademie 382 (Groningen, 1970), pp. 40–52.

not unique to early Kent. Although *Lex Frisionum* and Alfred both lack this stipulation, similar clauses are found in the *Lex Saxonum* and the *Lex Burgundionum*, the latter of which increases the fine if the opponent's hair is seized with two hands rather than one.[51] The purport of these clauses is obvious: a fight often begins by one contestant pulling the other close to him in order to be able to land a blow.[52] Even if no actual injury results, the regulation punishes intent. When Frisian laws begin to be couched in the vernacular, they also start with fines for *faxfeng/faxfang(is)*.[53] The linguistic correspondence between the Old English and Old Frisian compounds is obvious. As far as I know, this collocation is not found in any other vernacular Germanic texts. This absence constitutes, however, an argument from silence for the laws of Saxony and Burgundy: since they were composed in Latin, we have no access to the native terminology. The crucial issue is not the uniqueness of the phrase, but the persistence of its vernacular use over seven centuries of non-written legal practice.

Another parallel can be found in the collocation *bánes bite* [bite of/into a bone] in Æthelberht 35.[54] The same phrase occurs in the Riustringer injury schedule as *benes bīti*.[55] The shared metaphor of 'biting' into a bone is, excusing the pun, striking. One possible explanation for the preservation of both *feaxfang* and *bánes bite* is the alliterative nature of the formulations. With similar internal alliteration, the vernacular compound *wlitewamm* is attested (*mutatis mutandis*) in the early Saxon and Thuringian laws, in Æthelberht 60, and in the *Additiones* III.16 to the *Lex Frisionum*. Similar to the compound *feaxfang*, the component elements alliterate: *wlite* [countenance], and *wamm* [shame], with a combinatory sense of a visible bruise/damage to the face.[56] This collocation has a slightly wider early range than the two listed above, persisting into the Riustringer and later codices.[57]

Other parallels abound between alliterative phraseology elsewhere in Old English and Old Frisian legal texts. As Bremmer points out:

> A particular form of a lexical unit is the (more or less) fixed alliterative formula, of which Old English shares some 25 exclusive items with Old Frisian (Bremmer 1982), such as OE *mærke and mære*/OFris *mār and mark* 'boundary and division'

---

[51] See Oliver, *Body Legal*, pp. 108–111.
[52] Higham, *English Empire*, p. 236, suggests that this fine represents the insult to noblemen of pulling the long hair which only they were allowed to wear; I do not concur with this hypothesis, as the personal injury tariffs generally protect ranks down to that of the *ceorl*, and the clause itself is not restrictive.
[53] For editions of later Frisian laws, see Han Nijdam, *Lichaam: Eer en Recht in Middeleeuws Friesland* (Hilversum, 2008), with editions provided on accompanying CD-ROM. Specific examples can be found in *Boeteregister van Leewarderadeel* §§8 and 13; *Boeteregister van Dongeradeel* §§1 and 2; and *Riustringer Riucht* §6.1a: see Nijdam, *Lichaam*, pp. 539 and 547; Buma and Ebels, *Rüstringer Recht*, p. 68.
[54] Oliver, *Beginnings of English Law*, pp. 70–1.
[55] Buma and Ebels, *Rüstringer Recht*, §§6.7c and 6.12f, pp. 70 and 76.
[56] A very interesting discussion of this compound and its context can be found in Stefan Jurasinski, 'Germanism, Slapping and the Cultural Contexts of Æthelberht's Code: A Reconsideration of Chapters 56–58,' *HSJ* 18 (2006), 51–71.
[57] See Munske, 'Angelsächsisch–altfriesisch Beziehungen,' p. 46.

to establish boundaries between landed properties; OE *beornan and brecan*/OFris *breka ieftha barna* 'to break and/or burn' with reference to a penal expedition.⁵⁸

Shared does not, however, mean inherited (nor does Bremmer imply this). Justified skepticism has been voiced by Dorothy Bethurum (for Old English) and by Bremmer himself (for Frisian) in claiming alliteration as evidence for antiquity in Germanic legal phraseology.⁵⁹ Since the early studies of Eduard Sievers, alliteration has been recognized as a feature of Common Germanic poetic style,⁶⁰ and many readers have been tempted to regard alliterative phrases in the laws as remnants of older, oral transmission. But both Bethurum and Bremmer argue convincingly that many instances of the poetic device of alliteration were introduced later into legal terminology, influenced by Latin and Germanic written models.

Indeed, alliteration as a mnemonic technique is rarely found in the laws of Æthelberht, which substantiates the claim that phrases linked by sound patterns can generally be attributed to later stylistic innovation.⁶¹ But this hypothesis forces us to look particularly carefully at the three phrases which do appear: *feaxfang*, *bánes bite*, and *wlitewamm*. Their alliteration stands out stylistically within the remainder of Æthelberht's text, and it is to precisely this prominence that I would attribute their persistence into the much later recording of Frisian vernacular laws.

A Side-Trip to Saxony

The thirteenth century saw the emergence on the Continent of laws written in Germanic vernaculars (a practice instituted in the British Isles some seven centuries earlier!).⁶² Before turning to the rulings on genital mutilation in the vernacular Frisian laws, I would like to consider the regulations from the *Sachsenspiegel* (Saxon Mirror), composed by Eike von Repkow in the early or mid-thirteenth century in Saxony, a territory bordering on Frisia. The *Sachsenspiegel* differs in a legal sense significantly from the laws discussed above in that it was a private, not public, legal compilation, although this collection became a model for law throughout the later medieval German territories, extending into eastern Europe.⁶³ Eike first

---

⁵⁸ Rolf H. Bremmer Jnr, *An Introduction to Old Frisian: History, Grammar, Reader, Glossary* (Amsterdam, 2009), pp. 126–7; see also Bremmer, 'Dealing Dooms,' pp. 87–8; Bremmer, 'Old English–Old Frisian,' pp. 83–5.
⁵⁹ Dorothy Bethurum, 'Stylistic Features of the Old English Laws,' *Modern Language Review* 27 (1932), 263–79; Bremmer, 'Dealing Dooms.'
⁶⁰ Eduard Sievers, *Altgermanische Metrik* (Halle, 1893).
⁶¹ For this development in later Anglo-Saxon laws, see Oliver, 'Documentary Culture.'
⁶² Irish laws were also from their earliest recording written in the vernacular, as were the later laws of Welsh kingdoms.
⁶³ See Rolf Lieberwirth, *Eike von Repchow und der Sachsenspiegel* (Berlin, 1982), pp. 41–50. Emendations introduced in individual territories are laid out in C. G. Homeyer, 'Die Extravagenten des Sachsenspiegels,' *Abhandlungen der Königlichen Akademie der Wissenschaften* (1861), 221–66.

wrote a Latin version (now lost to us), and subsequently, at the request of Count Hoyer von Falkenstein, translated it into the vernacular Saxon. He drew not only on Germanic practice but also from the Bible and biblical commentaries.[64] Even if the text itself postdates the Frisian compilations (the exact order may not be recoverable, but they are near contemporaries), the Frisian jurists may have had access to the geographically close sources from which Eike drew.

The rulings in the *Sachsenspiegel* are considerably more complex than their predecessors. The pertinent clauses are as follows:

> 2.16.2. Swer den anderen lemet oder wundet, wert her des beredet, man sleit eme die hant af ... 5. Den munt, nasen und ogen, tungen und ore, und des mannes gemechte, hende und vute, dirre iewelk, wert de man dar an gelemet unde scal man it eme beteren, men mut it eme gelden mit eneme halven weregelde ... 9. Wundet man enen man an en led, dat <it> em vergulden is vor gerichte, howet man it em suver af ...[65]

> 2.16.2. Whoever maims or wounds another, if that be proven here, let his hand be cut off ... 5. The mouth, nose and eyes, tongue and ears, and the man's genitals, hands and feet: for each of them, if a man is wounded there and one can make restitution for it, one must compensate with one half wergild ... 9. If one wounds a man on a limb, so it is proven of him before the court, one must strike it off him himself.

The three rulings contained in this paragraph seem inherently contradictory, and scholars have varied in their interpretations. I find most convincing the proposal by Victor Friese in his outstanding and (in terms of legal theory) still remarkably pertinent 1898 study, *Das Strafrecht des Sachsenspiegels*.[66] His hypothesis is that the perpetrator's hand is struck off for a serious wound not covered by the later clauses. He then suggests that §5 applies to a wound inflicted without intention: the man responsible can compensate his offense with a fine of half the victim's wergild (echoing the general ruling of the earlier barbarian laws). §9 then addresses the case of intentional amputation of a primary sensory organ, or a hand or foot, or a man's genitals. An assailant who deliberately strikes off one of these crucial organs has the corresponding organ amputated himself. The *Schwabenspiegel*, written in southern Germany in the latter part of the thirteenth century, echoes the *Sachsenspiegel* in these draconian regulations.[67]

---

[64] For an introduction to the *Sachsenspiegel* and its dating, see Frank Both, *Der Sachsenspiegel aus dem Leben gegriffen: ein Rechtsbuch spiegelt seine Zeit*, Archäologische Mitteilungen aus Nordwestdeutschland, Beihefte 14 (Oldenburg, 1996); also Lieberwirth, *Eike von Repchow*. For biblical influences see Guido Kisch, *Sachsenspiegel and Bible: Researches in the Source History of the Sachsenspiegel and the Influence of the Bible on Mediaeval German Law* (Notre Dame, IN, 1941).

[65] Karl August Eckhardt, ed., *Sachsenspiegel Landrecht*, 2nd edn, MGH Fontes iuris n.s. 1.1 (Göttingen, 1955), pp. 146–8. Translation mine.

[66] Victor Friese, *Das Strafrecht des Sachsenspiegels* (Breslau, 1898), especially pp. 145–60 and 221–37. See also Lieberwirth, *Eike von Repchow*, pp. 39–40.

[67] The clauses in the *Schwabenspiegel* read: 'Swem der munt wirt ab gesniten oder ougen uz gestochen oder oren ab gesniten oder (di) zunge wirt uz gesniten oder unter den peinen wirt versniten oder im sus der deheinez wirt verterbet swer diu dinch dem andern tut dem

Genital Mutilation

These high-medieval vernacular German laws consider damage to genitals as a corporal injury upon the victim, similar to the wounding of any other major body part. Unlike earlier laws, they distinguish between accidental and deliberate infliction of the wound. The first demands monetary punishment, the second physical. Although the pattern resembles the biblical principle of talion in demanding an eye for an eye, most scholars reject this model as a principle source, assuming rather that the purpose behind the punishment was to mirror the crime itself.[68] These penalties may be seen in some sense as representing a lesser version of treating intentional homicide with the reflective punishment of death. I am not personally convinced that the two explanations are mutually incompatible. In any event, we must now add to the previously discussed alternation between compensation for present injury or for future loss a third option: mutilation equaling mutilation. In regard to the 'corporal' and 'capital' distinction discussed above, the financial and mutilative rulings clearly assign the German *Spiegels* to the corporal category.

A Return to the Ingvaeonic Territories: Late Medieval Frisia

Laws began to be written in the Frisian vernacular at about the same time that Eike was translating his Latin compilation into Saxon. In the Frisian laws, however, we find a surprising return to the 'capital' interpretation of incapacitating genital damage, not seen since the laws of Æthelberht some seven centuries earlier. Yet the claim for continuity across such a wide chronological gap is not as dramatic as it may appear. First, these attestations are contained in the first Frisian laws to appear in the vernacular; the Anglo-Saxons were the only (early Germanic) barbarian peoples to couch their laws in their own, non-Latin language. Second, the foregoing discussion has demonstrated a close connection between Frisia and England in the early legislative period. Finally, while both of the vernacular Frisian clauses adduced below match Æthelberht in the 'capital' nature of this assessment, one of them also matches in the particular of number.

---

sol man daz selbe hinwider tun': *Landrecht* 176A (MSS Ks, Kb), in Karl August Eckhardt, ed., *Schwabenspiegel Kurzform*, MGH Fontes iuris n.s. 4.1/2 (Hanover, 1974), p. 256. See also Rudolf Grosse, *Schwabenspiegel Kurzform* (Weimar, 1964), pp. 155–6. This is emended in later versions of the Sachsenspiegel: see, for example, Maria Dobozy, trans., *The Saxon Mirror: A Sachsenspiegel of the Fourteenth Century* (Philadelphia, PA, 1999), p. 98, where the translation reads: 'A man is to be compensated when he suffers permanent injury to any one [of the following]: the mouth, nose, eyes, tongue, ears, his sexual organs, hands or feet. One must pay him a compensation that is half of his established wergeld … As many times as a person injures a disabled person in a different part of the body, that many times shall he compensate that person with half his wergeld individually for each injury … If someone is injured by another in a body part that has already been redressed by the court, even if it is severed completely, he may sue for no higher compensation than his composition tariff.'

[68] For castration as punishment in Old Frisian laws, see Bremmer, 'Castration and Genital Mutilation.'

The earliest of these Frisian clauses occurs in the *Emsingoër Boetregister*, the Old East Frisian law for which the first manuscript dates around 1400 although the text itself originated much earlier:

91. Huersa hir en mon thruch sine mechte vundad werth, thet hi nauuet tia ni mughe: nioghen mark to bote fora tha nioghen bern hi tia machte.
92. Het hi ac bern etein, sa nime ma hit of ta berena and retze hit tha vneberene.[69]

91. Whenever a man is wounded here [in the Emsingo territory] through his genital organs, so that he cannot engender children: 9 marks compensation for the nine children that he could have engendered.
92. If he has engendered children, then one should take that from the born and give it to the unborn.

This clause provides an answer to the heretofore unasked question of how many children a man could expect to engender in high-medieval Frisia. The answer is nine: if a man is damaged in his genitals, his compensation is calculated as 9 marks minus 1 mark for every child he has already fathered. Thus, a victim who has fathered three children receives 6 marks; one who has fathered seven children receives 2 marks. (The enumeration is not clear as to whether it encompasses all children engendered or only children who survived the often difficult process of medieval childbirth.)

The second and more directly parallel ruling comes from the *Boeteregister van Leeuwarderadeel*, Old West Frisian law, for which the first manuscript dates to the thirteenth century:

Hweer so thi man scethen werth thruch sine machten thruch dat fel, thio bote en pund, hit ne se thet hi ferra wolle spreka. So mey hi habba sine sinekerf. Thio aersta thio stiapsine and thio waldsine and thio fruchtsine. Hir moth hi fan tigia thria onnameda morth, tha ach ma allerick toe betana also dyora alse an manslachta, iefta xij-sum onswerra.[70]

If a man is shot through his genitals, through the skin, then compensation is one pound, unless he wants to press charges further. Then he can claim compensation for three cut-through tendons/sinews. The first is the 'uphigh/steep sinew,' and the 'wield/strength sinew' and the 'fruit sinew.' This way he can make a claim for three unborn children, which one must compensate equally as for a murder, or the accused must swear himself free as one of twelve oath-helpers.

---

[69] Nijdam, *Lichaam*, p. 275. I would like to thank Christine Kooi for translation of this and the succeeding passage, and Rolf Bremmer for some corrections. This paragraph ends with assertion that 'if he has retained the left testicle and lost the right one, yet he can beget children. Does he not have the left one (any longer), though he (still) has the right one, then he is unable to beget because of that.' The superiority of the left testicle over the right is also attested in Irish law; however, this Old Frisian clause contradicts the ruling elsewhere that the right testicle is to be compensated with six pounds and the left with five-and-a-half. For discussion (and the citation above) see Bremmer, 'Castration and Genital Mutilation.'

[70] Nijdam, *Lichaam*, p. 26; the manuscript attestations date between 1475 and 1530 (p. 485). Bremmer, 'Castration and Genital Mutilation,' discusses the equivalent clause in the *Weterlauwerssches Recht*, 28.239, and also addresses the interpretation of the three sinews.

Genital Mutilation

This clause provides an even closer parallel to Æthelberht: the recompense, as specifically stated, is for unborn children; the restitution is in wergilds; and the stipulation of three wergilds matches exactly. The loss of the unengendered child is specifically designated as equivalent to murder (a capital offense), and the father is recompensed for each child with a full wergild.

Rolf Bremmer persuasively proposes the following hypothesis to explain the three sinews described in the Leeuwarderadeel law:

> According to Constantinus the African (1017–1087), author of the *Pantegni* – the first comprehensive medieval anatomical treatise that brought fame to the Salernitan school – the penis is a *cauda nervorum* [tail of nerves], which is 'concave so that with the arrival of appetite it is filled with air and becomes erect. Lateral muscles on both sides prevent it from bending, so that the sperm is ejaculated directly into the vulva.' According to this description, the penis is hollow and consists of a duct through which the sperm flows and two muscles, one on either side of the penis. The *Anatomia vivorum* [Anatomy of the Living], for example, written in Paris in the first half of the thirteenth century expands on Constantinus's description and explains that the penis 'has two ducts, one for the sperm from the testicles and the other for the urine from the bladder which join at the neck of the penis. It also has two pairs of muscles (*lacerti*), one which governs the length and extension of the erection and the other which keeps it straight.' The Frisian classification of the three 'sinews' must have been inspired by knowledge derived from such medical treatises, the *stiapsine* referring to the muscle that takes care of the erection, while the *wieldsine* reflects the one that keeps the penis straight. The *fruchtsine*, then, must be identified with the duct that guides the sperm from the testicles to the neck of the penis. If this interpretation is right, the absence of the urine duct from the Frisian regulation must be accounted for. There are two possible explanations for this. First of all, a tripartite division tallies with the three children he will never have; secondly, the inability to create offspring is a much more serious handicap than having difficulty discharging urine and the focus of this particular regulation is on a man's fertility.[71]

Both model texts mentioned by Bremmer considerably post-date the laws of Æthelberht but pre-date the laws of Frisia. But the omission in the Old West Frisian clause of the urinary duct, however it might be explained, points to a focus on the sinew count of three. I postulate that the discussion of these three sinews is a later addition to the original source ruling, inserted according to recent anatomical studies to account for the three wergilds that genital incapacitation traditionally required as compensation.

Conclusion

A summation of the laws discussed above as regards restitution for injury to genitals is provided in Table 3.2 in chronological order:

Three different groupings appear in this chart:

- The early medieval fines based on a corporal interpretation found in *Lex Frisionum* and Alfred.

---

[71] Bremmer, 'Castration and Genital Mutilation,' pp. 123–4; and see Bremmer's article for citations therein, which have been omitted in this quotation.

Table 3.2 Punishments for inflicting genital injuries in barbarian laws

Law	Date	Language	Punishment	Corporal/Capital
Æthelberht	c. 600	Old English	Fined 300% wergild	Capital
Lex Frisionum	790×803	Latin	1 testicle off: fined 50% wergild 2 testicles off: fined 100% wergild Penis off: fined 100% wergild	Corporal
Alfred	890×901	Old English	Testicles incapacitated: fined 40% wergild Loin/scrotum off: fined 30% wergild Loin/scrotum pierced: fined 7.5% wergild Loin/scrotum pierced through: fined 15% wergild	Corporal
Sachsenspiegel	Early 13th century	Old Saxon	Fined 50% wergild, or castrated	Corporal
Schwabenspiegel	Later 13th century	Old Schwabian	Fined 50% wergild, or castrated	Corporal
Emsingoër Boeteregister	13th century	Old Frisian (East)	Fined 1 mark per 'lost' child (9 children maximum)	Capital
Boeteregister van Leeuwarderadeel	13th century	Old Frisian (West)	Fined 300% wergild	Capital

Alfred's model was not the insular laws of his ancestor Æthelberht, but apparently the contemporary Continental Frankish tradition. The specific source could have been Frisia, but no evidence definitively refutes or substantiates this hypothesis. However, other parallels between the personal injury tariffs in Alfred and *Lex Frisionum* give some weight to the postulation of Frisian influence here also.

- The later medieval corporal punishment, mirroring the injury itself.

    The approach of demanding a limb for a limb is common throughout the later medieval vernacular laws that draw their source from the *Sachsenspiegel*. This regulation on injury to major organs was employed east of Frisia in later medieval German and eastern European territories.[72]

- The very early and late medieval fines based on the interpretation of castration as an offense rendering future offspring literally inconceivable.

This discussion ends with a revisitation of Æthelberht's ruling on damage to the 'procreative organ' as a 'capital' offense. The only other territory

---

[72] See, for example, Homeyer, 'Extravaganten des Sachsenspiegels,' p. 260.

and time in which a 'non-corporal' ruling appears is late medieval Frisia, as the Frisians start recording their laws in the vernacular in the thirteenth century. It would seem that these regulations are, in fact, related: both stemming from an early Anglo-Frisian (or Ingvaeonic) connection which appears in both regions in the first laws recorded in their respective vernaculars. It may stretch the boundaries of credulity that a ruling whereby a man damaged in the genitals receives three times his wergild to compensate him for unborn children might persist in oral transmission over seven centuries and across the English Channel. But given the strong early connections between Anglo-Saxon England and Frisia evidenced by linguistic, numismatic, historical, archaeological, and genetic data; scattered retained common phraseology in Old English and Old Frisian laws; the lack of any similar stipulation for damage to genitals elsewhere in time or location throughout the barbarian and later Germanic territories; and the specificity of the resemblance between the clauses themselves, I find the solution of archaic retention more plausible than the unlikely hypothesis of individual and unconnected origins. In the words of Sherlock Holmes: 'when you have eliminated the impossible, whatever remains, *however improbable*, must be the truth.'[73]

Beyond the Word of the Law: Further Implications

The difference between the Anglo-Saxon/Frisian and Continental rulings raises two fascinating possibilities, which, however, I propose very tentatively. Portions of the laws of Æthelberht likely represent the closest equivalent to a pre-Christian (and pre-literate) legal system that we have received from the Germanic regions.[74] We might thus assign the 'capital' ruling of genital mutilation to this period, in which case recompense for the inability to create future offspring that we see in the Anglo-Saxon and Frisian laws is one of the last remnants of a pagan tradition. Children carry on the family line, the importance of which function is demonstrated by the genealogies that appear frequently both in literary works such as *Beowulf, Battle of Maldon*, and the Old High German *Hildebrandslied*, and historical records such as Bede's *Ecclesiastical History* and the Anglo-Saxon Chronicles. In a metaphysical sense, the immortality of the pagan was determined by two factors: the reputation achieved while living, and the procreation of offspring to carry on the lineage. It is possible, then, that what we find in the vernacular Frisian laws is the last vestige, not only of the Ingvaeonic connection, but also of an alternative, pagan tradition in relation to genital damage which prevents procreation.[75]

Although we cannot rule out the possibility that both 'capital' and 'corporal' approaches existed simultaneously in pre-Christian laws, we should

---

[73] Sir Arthur Conan Doyle, 'The Sign of the Four,' *The Annotated Sherlock Holmes*, ed. William S. Baring-Gould (New York, 1967), p. 638.
[74] See Oliver, *Beginnings of English Law*, pp. 34–51.
[75] I owe this suggestion to Charlie Donahue, pers. comm.

not ignore the fact that only the 'corporal' interpretation appears in the post-Christian Salian laws and all the barbarian laws that follow; the 'capital' interpretation disappears except for the rulings in the very early laws of Æthelberht and the late-medieval laws of Frisia. Upon reading this paper, Katherine Willis suggested that a possible explanation of the shift in the Continental laws could be based in the teachings of the early Christian church:

> In ancient Jewish culture, having children meant not just the continuation of a specific family line but the continuation of the entire people and therefore of God's covenant. The primary purpose of marriage was procreation. In the first centuries of the church, however, early Christians came to understand marriage and children differently: the primary purpose of marriage was now to reflect the relationship between God and the church. Having children was still important, but it was no longer the primary purpose of marriage nor a means of ensuring an immortality for the individual and the family line. Eternal life comes through Christ.[76]

Regarding this new Christian approach, Catharine Ross claims that, 'Between St Paul and the twentieth century, the best in Christian teaching on marriage is represented by St John Chrysostom.'[77] St John, ordained Bishop of Antioch in 398, presents the patristic consensus on the new Christian attitude towards marriage and children in his 'Sermon on Marriage':

> At the beginning, the procreation of children was desirable, so that each person might leave a memorial of his life. Since there was not yet any hope of resurrection, but death held sway, and those who died thought that they would perish after this life, God gave the comfort of children, so as to leave living images of the departed and to preserve our species ... But now that resurrection is at our gates, and we do not speak of death, but advance toward another life better than the present, the desire for posterity is superfluous. If you desire children you can get much better children now, a nobler childbirth and better help in your old age, if you give birth by spiritual labor.[78]

In the medieval Christian understanding, the union of husband and wife mirrors the marriage of Christ to the church, and the children they create by bringing them to the church become more important than those they beget physically. The eternity of the church trumps the eternity of earthly lineage. Paul Evdokimov elaborates that 'The marriage-procreation concept of old was *functional*, subordinated to the cycles of generations and tending toward the coming of the Messiah. The nuptial marriage-priesthood is *ontological*, the new creation that saturates human time with eternity.'[79]

---

[76] Katherine Willis, pers. comm.
[77] Catharine P. Roth, 'Introduction,' in St John Chrysostom, *On Marriage and Family Life*, trans. Catharine P. Roth and David Anderson (Crestwood, NY, 1986; repr. 1997), pp. 7–24, at 11.
[78] St John Chrysostom, *On Marriage and Family Life*, pp. 85–6.
[79] Paul Evdokimov, *The Sacrament of Love: The Nuptial Mystery in the Light of the Orthodox Tradition*, trans. Anthony P. Gythiel and Victoria Steadman (Crestwood, NY, 1985), p. 47.

Genital Mutilation

This early medieval approach still dominates Christian thinking on marriage and procreation, as demonstrated by the Encyclical Letter of Pius XI, *On Christian Marriage* (1930):

> [Love] must have as its primary purpose that man and wife help each other in forming and perfecting themselves in the interior life, so that through their partnership in life they may advance ever more and more in virtue; ... this mutual inward moulding of husband and wife ... can in a very real sense be said to be the chief reason and purpose of matrimony.[80]

No mention here is made of procreation; marriage centers on the relationship of husband and wife and their mutual growth towards eternal life.

How does this relate to the shift in legal penalties for rendering a man unable to create offspring? Willis provides a possible answer: '[I]t makes sense for pagan law to prefer capital penalties: if one's immortal legacy is at stake, then the ability to produce offspring is far more important from a pagan perspective than a Christian one. It is, one might say, a matter of *eternal* life and death.'[81] That is, when offspring are crucial to immortality, law might adjudge genital damage in terms of the children who can no longer be created. But when Christianity introduces the concept that the crucial function of marriage is to create a bond between husband and wife parallel to that of Christ and the church, and 'children' can be seen as religious rather than physical offspring, the law might shift its ruling on damage to male genitalia to reflect corporeal injury to the individual rather than permanent loss to the lineage. The godson that a Christian man brings to the church need not be created of his own flesh.

As a linguist and non-Christian, I swim here in waters deeper than I can tread. I certainly find these hypotheses interesting, but they must be substantiated by scholars familiar with the textual transmission of Christian writings in early Germanic Europe. I proffer these suggestions in the hope that other, future researchers will be able to use these data when investigating the influence of Christian philosophy on early medieval law.

---

[80] William J. Gibbon, S.J., ed., *Seven Great Encyclicals* (New York, 1963), p. 84.
[81] Katherine Willis, pers. comm.

4

'Sick-Maintenance' and Earlier English Law

Stefan Jurasinski

This chapter is concerned with a form of reconciliation attested in Irish and other Indo-European traditions and arguably present in some Anglo-Saxon legislative evidence as well. Its most familiar occurrence, however, is in a text far removed from early medieval Europe:

> When individuals quarrel and one strikes the other with a stone or fist so that the injured party, though not dead, is confined to bed, but recovers and walks around outside with the help of a staff, then the assailant shall be free of liability, except to pay for the loss of time, and to arrange for full recovery.[1]

That it has become customary to refer to Exodus 21:18–19 as an instance of 'sick-maintenance' shows how decisively our understanding of this institution has been shaped by studies less interested in the biblical ordinance than its supposed analogues within various branches of Indo-European.[2] The term 'sick-maintenance' is a close translation of the Irish *folog n-othrusa*, and although they conceivably postdate the events of Exodus by millennia, Irish ordinances have long been held to preserve a more archaic form of the institution than is found even in the laws of Moses. According to D. A. Binchy, whose article of 1934 remains the authoritative discussion of the subject,

> the Old Irish law preserves for us ... the relics of a more primitive system [than is found in Exodus]. In the earliest texts we find that the injurer, instead of paying the "leech-fee", must undertake the duty of nursing his victim back to health and providing him with medical attendance.[3]

---

[1] Exodus 21:18–19, quoted from Michael D. Coogan, ed., *The New Oxford Annotated Bible*, 3rd edn (Oxford, 2001).

[2] For example, Doris Edel refers to 'the institution of sick-maintenance, which is also found in the early Germanic laws and in the Old Testament (Exod. 21:18–19), albeit in modernized form': 'The Status and Development of the Vernacular in Early Medieval Ireland,' *The Dawn of the Written Vernacular in Western Europe*, ed. Michèle Goyens and Werner Verbeke (Leuven, 2003), pp. 351–78, at 355 n. 17. For an overview of the Göttingen school of legal history, in which the methods of comparative philology were first wedded to historiography, see Daniela Fruscione, 'Liebermann's Intellectual Milieu,' *English Law Before Magna Carta*, ed. Stefan Jurasinski, Andrew Rabin and Lisi Oliver (Leiden, 2010), pp. 15–26. The foundation of nineteenth-century historical jurisprudence in Indo-Europeanist studies such as those of Sir Henry Maine is asserted in Lawrence Krader, 'Introduction,' *Anthropology and Early Law*, ed. Krader (New York, 1966), p. 7.

[3] See D. A. Binchy, 'Sick-Maintenance in Irish Law,' *Ériu* 12 (1934), 78–134, at 78.

Sick-Maintenance

An ordinance composed in Hittite (1500 BCE) suggests that the customs described above have roots deep in the Indo-European past:

> If anyone injures a [free] person and temporarily incapacitates him, he shall provide medical care for him. In his place he shall provide a person to work on his estate until he recovers. When he recovers [his assailant] shall pay him six shekels of silver and shall pay the physician's fee as well.[4]

Similar provisions in sources as far-flung as the code of Manu led Calvert Watkins in 1976 to label sick-maintenance 'an inherited feature of Indo-European customary law.'[5] Though this conclusion has since found wide acceptance, the views of Binchy and Watkins are not always repeated without reservations in present-day scholarship.[6] Given the absence of a genuinely cognate term to describe the institution in the various Indo-European witnesses, one recent commentator has noted the 'rather weak linguistic basis for the reconstruction of a Proto-Indo-European rule of sick-maintenance.'[7]

The assumption that traces of Indo-European sick-maintenance are evident in Anglo-Saxon materials is, I argue, still less certain.[8] The written output of Anglo-Saxon England, which neither Binchy nor Watkins considered in any detail, does not in fact offer much support for this conclusion. Of the four attestations of sick-maintenance within the corpus of Old English prose, three occur in texts relying in some fashion on the language of Exodus 21:18–19. Of these, two are translations of the biblical text, the earliest occurring in the preface to the laws of King Alfred and the second in the much later Old English Heptateuch. Each translates the Vulgate version of Exodus rather differently.[9] Alfred's preface reads:

> Gif hwa slea hys ðone nehstan mid stane oððe mid fyste, ᛣ he þeah utgongan mæge bi stæfe, begite him læce ᛣ wyrce his weorc þa hwile þe he self ne mæge.[10]
>
> If someone should strike his neighbor with a stone or with a fist, and the latter may nonetheless walk about with a staff, let [the attacker] obtain a physician for him and perform his work while he is unable.

---

[4] Harry Angier Hoffner Jnr, ed. and trans., *The Laws of the Hittites: A Critical Edition* (Leiden, 1997), p. 23.
[5] Calvert Watkins, 'Sick-Maintenance in Indo-European,' *Ériu* 27 (1976), 21–5.
[6] For affirmative considerations of these arguments see Stefan Zimmer, 'Glimpses of Indo-European Law,' *The Law's Beginnings*, ed. Ferdinand Joseph Maria Feldbrugge (Leiden, 2003), pp. 115–136, at 127–8; J. P. Mallory and D. Q. Adams, eds, *Encyclopedia of Indo-European Culture* (Chicago, 1997), s.v. 'medicine.'
[7] Zimmer, 'Glimpses of Indo-European Law,' p. 128. See also the word of caution in Ferdinand Joseph Maria Feldbrugge, *Law in Medieval Russia* (Leiden, 2009), p. 9.
[8] Binchy, 'Sick-Maintenance,' p. 78, n. 3; Watkins, 'Sick-Maintenance,' p. 23.
[9] The Vulgate version is as follows: 'Si rixati fuerint viri et percusserit alter proximum suum lapide vel pugno et ille mortuus non fuerit sed iacuerit in lectulo: si surrexerit et ambulaverit foris super baculum suum innocens erit qui percusserit ita tamen ut operas eius et inpensas in medicos restituat.'
[10] Alfred Prol. 16. The version given here is the transcription of MS E, the 'Parker Manuscript' (MS Cambridge, Corpus Christi College 173), in Lierbermann, *Gesetze*. Unless otherwise noted, all translations are my own.

And the Old English Heptateuch:

> Gif men cidað and hira oðer hys nextan mid stane wyrpð oþþe mid fyste slicþ, and he dead ne bið ac lið on bedde seoc, gif he arist and ut gæþ mid his stafe, he bið unscildig þe hine sloh; gylde swa þeah his weorc and þæt hine man hæle.[11]

> If men quarrel, and one of them throws a stone at the other or beats him with his fist, and he is not dead but lies sick in his bed; if he rises and goes out with his staff, he who injured him is without blame; let him pay nonetheless for his work and so that he may be healed.

Another Old English treatment of sick-maintenance is found in the penitential edited by Benjamin Thorpe as the *Confessionale Pseudo-Egberti* and known since the pioneering studies of Allen Frantzen as the *Scriftboc*.[12] Of all the Old English treatments of sick-maintenance, it is by far the most detailed, and the strangest:

> Swa hwylc man se ðe in gecynde oðerne gedo wánhalne oððe hine womwlite on gewyrce, forgylde him þone womwlite, and his weorc wyrce oð þæt seo wund hal sy, and þæt læcefeoh ðam læce gylde, and fæste twa æfestena oððe þreo; gyf he nyte hu he hit gylde, fæste XII monað.[13]

> Whoever renders a man injured in his genitals or inflicts *womwlite* upon him, let him compensate his victim for the *womwlite*, and let him perform his victim's work until the wound has healed, and let him make payment to the physician, and let him fast for two or three of the ordained fasting periods; if he does not know how he might make compensation for the injury, let him fast for twelve months.

Though the *Scriftboc* also relies in some measure on Exodus, here the biblical provisions have been filtered through another layer of influences. This portion of the *Scriftboc* relies on one of the many virtually identical clauses circulating in Latin penitentials that adapted the language of Exodus 21:18–19 to the realities of post-conversion Europe. Some, but not all, of the *Scriftboc*'s peculiarities are traceable to this tradition, as will be shown later.[14]

The rest of the evidence is limited to single words occurring in texts at opposite ends of the Old English period: one in the seventh-century laws of King Æthelberht, and another surfacing in the Old French *Leis Willelme* – a text composed perhaps a century after the death of William the Conqueror that

---

[11] Richard Marsden, ed., *The Old English Heptateuch and Ælfric's Libellus de Veteri Testamento et Novo*, vol. 1: *Introduction and Text*, EETS o.s. 330 (Oxford, 2008), p. 117.

[12] Benjamin Thorpe, ed., *Ancient Laws and Institutes of England*, vol. 2 (London, 1840), pp. 148–9, ch. 22. On the *Scriftboc*, see Allen J. Frantzen, *The Literature of Penance in Anglo-Saxon England* (New Brunswick, 1982), pp. 133–4.

[13] Robert Spindler, *Das altenglische Bussbuch* (Leipzig, 1934), p. 186, ch. XIX.20.d.

[14] The most recent discussion of this clause may be found in Lisi Oliver, 'Sick-Maintenance in Anglo-Saxon Law,' *JEGP* 107 (2008), 303–26, at 326: 'The extant Germanic clauses lack the third requirement of Hittite and Old Irish sick-maintenance clauses that the perpetrator either provide a man to work in the wounded man's stead or compensate the work … The one Old English instance that we seem to have, from the *Confessional of Egbert*, turns out to have been borrowed from the Irish penitential tradition, which itself had been influenced by Irish secular law.'

probably contains few authentic descriptions of pre-Conquest law.[15] While the occurrence of the word *cearwund* in the laws of Æthelberht offers some indication that sick-maintenance was an element of English law, there is at best a trace of the institution in this compound; one perhaps unrecognized by those who devised the ordinance in which it occurs, as this clause imposes on the assailant no obligation beyond payment of 30 shillings to a man so wounded.[16] In spite of its lateness, the *Leis Willelme* is the only English source referred to in the studies of Binchy and Watkins, both of whom mention its use of the term *læcefeoh* (if only in the garbled form *leceof*), but nothing else.[17] The relevance of this text to the history of sick-maintenance has recently been called into question by Lisi Oliver. For Binchy, the *conditio sine qua non* of sick-maintenance legislation in Ireland and throughout the Indo-European world was the presence of an incapacitating injury: 'it is obvious that before any question of increased liability for the defendant can arise, the condition of his victim must be sufficiently serious to demand medical attention and nursing over a period of time.'[18] Yet as Oliver notes, the injuries referred to in the *Leis Willelme* must have been of little lasting significance. Her conclusion is borne out by the brief text itself, which requires that the plaintiff swear he is not exaggerating the seriousness of his wounds, a condition presupposing a victim who was not, as in Exodus, hovering between life and death:

> [10] Si hom feit plaie en auter e il deive faire les amendes, primereinement lui rende sien lecheof. [10a] Et li plaez jurra sur seinz, que pur meins nel pot feire ne pur haur si cher nel fist.[19]

---

[15] On the date of the *Leis Willelme* and the various theories concerning its composition, see Ralph V. Turner, 'Roman Law in England before the Time of Bracton,' *Journal of British Studies* 15 (1975), 1–25; repr. in Ralph V. Turner, *Judges, Administrators, and the Common Law in Angevin England* (Rio Grande, OH, 1994), pp. 45–69, at 49–50.

[16] Oliver discusses at length the hapax legomenon *cearwund* attested in Æthelberht 63, and builds on the suggestions of earlier scholars that this compound must mean 'wound causing a person to be bedridden,' which indicates (given the apparently cognate Old Norse term *kǫr*, 'sickbed') awareness in seventh-century Kent of 'an inherited regulation of sick-maintenance': 'Sick-Maintenance,' pp. 308 and 311.

[17] See Watkins, 'Sick-Maintenance,' p. 23: '[W]e must recognize the primitive institution of sick-maintenance as a feature of Indo-European customary law, remarkably preserved intact in Irish and Hittite, and in other cognate Indo-European legal systems commuted, with Binchy, to the later "leech-fee" alone (OEng. *læce-feoh*, Skt. *samutthāna-vyayam* Manu 8.287).' Watkins does not mention the source of the Old English compound, which occurs in legislation only in the likely irrelevant *Leis Willelme*, as Binchy notes: 'Sick-Maintenance,' p. 78.

[18] Binchy, 'Sick-Maintenance,' pp. 91–2. A convalescence in excess of nine days qualified a victim for sick-maintenance in Irish law, which shows just how severe injuries of this sort needed to be: see Fergus Kelly, *A Guide to Early Irish Law* (Dublin, 1988; repr. 1991), p. 130. That the *Leis Willelme* have little in common with Irish law is also evident in the latter's requirement that a victim's entitlement to sick-maintenance be first determined upon a physician's examination, a feature discussed in Robin Chapman Stacy, *Dark Speech: The Performance of Law in Early Ireland* (Philadelphia, PA, 2007), p. 34.

[19] Liebermann, *Gesetze*, pp. 498–501. The translation given here owes something to that of Robertson, *Laws*, p. 259. The passage has been most recently discussed in Oliver, 'Sick-Maintenance,' p. 315 n. 40: '[A]lthough the term *lecheof* echoes (probably unrelatedly) Egbert's ruling on sick-maintenance, this stipulation from this *Leis Willelme* would seem to apply to all injuries inflicted by another, whether debilitating to the point of incapacitation or not. The clause that follows even implies that at least in some instances the damage might even have been healed so quickly that the perpetrator could not himself bear witness to the cure.'

> If a man injures another and is obliged to make amends, first let him render [to the victim] the leech-fee. And the injured party must swear on the holy relics, that it could not be done for less nor has he made [the amount] so expensive because of hatred.

Ultimately, there is no way out of the difficulty that what little survives of sick-maintenance in Anglo-Saxon England seems the product of influences external to the British Isles. With the application of the 'leech-fee' to injuries much less significant than those meriting sick-maintenance in Irish law, what remains of the institution seems far removed from the provisions either of Mosaic or Irish law. And even if *cearwund* and *lecheof* suggest an awareness of sick-maintenance in Anglo-Saxon law, the possibility that such a practice arrived via Exodus cannot be disproved, and indeed seems probable given its influence upon early ecclesiastical law.[20]

Such a conclusion is surely disappointing should our aim be to find in English law traces of Indo-European antiquity. If, however, we accept the limitation that sick-maintenance as it existed in England was thoroughly contaminated by ecclesiastical canons originating in the laws of Moses as described in Exodus, I think the Old English evidence described above may still have much to offer the historian of pre-Conquest law. The independence of Anglo-Saxon thought concerning sick-maintenance is evident in the fact that no two Old English discussions of this institution agree as to its form, even though each translates a text, whether Exodus 21:18–19 or the penitential clauses derived from it, whose authority should have made divergent translations unlikely. If those who translated these passages were indeed recording distinctly English views in their departures from source material, the evidence afforded by the *Scriftboc* – evidence which has so far received the least attention in studies devoted to the history of sick-maintenance – would seem to be the most revealing. That its translator renders independently even norms of ecclesiastical law that were likely seen as binding upon his contemporaries suggests that its clause on sick-maintenance may well record something of the customs of his time. The result, as I hope to demonstrate in what remains of this chapter, is a clause showing how biblical, ecclesiastical, and secular norms combined to establish a punitive institution unique to pre-Conquest England that has yet to be acknowledged. That the description of sick-maintenance in the *Scriftboc* shows some agreement with the other Old English texts discussed above makes the existence of an independent English variant of sick-maintenance highly likely.

---

[20] The earliest references to sick-maintenance extant in ecclesiastical law occur in the penitential of Cummean, a likely source of the *Scriftboc*'s provision that will be discussed in more detail below. Though the Cummean to whom this penitential was attributed by tradition has been lost to history, it may be assumed that this text antedates considerably the cycle of Theodorean penitentials, given the latter's partial reliance upon Cummean for some of its provisions. The penitential of Cummean is thus in all likelihood a work of the seventh century. On the debt of Theodore's penitential to Cummean, see Roy Flechner, 'The Making of the Canons of Theodore,' *Peritia* 17–18 (2003–4), 121–143, at 129–130.

Exodus and the Latin Penitentials on Sick-Maintenance

Making sense of what the *Scriftboc* and other Old English texts have to say about sick-maintenance requires that we consider again the biblical clause that served as the template for all later ecclesiastical legislation. All treatments of sick-maintenance in the Latin penitentials derive in some manner from the Vulgate version of Exodus 21:18–19:

> Si rixati fuerint viri et percusserit alter proximum suum lapide vel pugno et ille mortuus non fuerit sed iacuerit in lectulo: si surrexerit et ambulaverit foris super baculum suum innocens erit qui percusserit ita tamen ut operas eius et inpensas in medicos restituat

The Douay-Rheims version translates this passage as follows:

> If men quarrel, and the one strike his neighbor with a stone or with his fist, and he die not, but keepeth his bed; if he rise again, and walk abroad upon his staff, he that struck him shall be quit [*innocens erit qui percusserit*], yet so that he make restitution for his work [*restituat ... operas eius*], and for his expenses upon the physicians [*inpensas in medicos*].

This phrasing is echoed particularly closely in the penitential of Cummean, whose clause on sick-maintenance likely served as a basis for what occurs in the *Scriftboc*:

> Qui per rixam ictu debilem uel deformem hominem reddit, inpensa in medicos curat et maculae pretium et opus eius donec sanetur restituat et dimidium anni peniteat. Si uero non habeat unde restituat haec, .i. annum peniteat.[21]

> He who by a blow in a quarrel renders a man incapacitated or maimed shall meet [the injured man's] medical expenses and shall make good the damages for the deformity and shall do his work until he is healed and do penance for half a year. If he has not the wherewithal to make restitution for these things, he shall do penance for one year.

We should note the overall aims of this clause. Some of the changes Exodus has undergone in Cummean's penitential are plainly meant to accommodate the understanding of violence characteristic of Christian teaching in post-conversion Europe. In Exodus, the assailant had been considered *innocens* if his assault did not result in the death of his victim. The arrival of Christianity brought with it an understanding that violence of this sort was prompted by sinful lusts, and thus such a formulation is unacceptable to the author of Cummean's penitential, who adds to the clause quoted above, perhaps to ensure that there is no ambiguity, a penance even for those acts of violence from which no injury results: 'Qui ictum proximo suo dederit et non nocuit, .i. uel .ii. uel .iii. xlmis in pane et aqua peniteat' [He who gives a blow to his neighbor without doing him harm, shall do penance on bread and water one or two or three forty-day periods].[22] Imposition of a year of penance on an assailant unable to undertake the obligations of 'sick-maintenance' similarly

---

[21] Ludwig Bieler, ed. and trans., *Irish Penitentials* (Dublin, 1963), pp. 120–1.
[22] Bieler, *Irish Penitentials*, pp. 120–1.

targets as of primary importance the spiritual condition that caused the penitent to do harm, while concern for the material condition of his victim retreats into the background.

These additions result in an understanding of sick-maintenance different from what may have obtained in ancient Israel, the Hittite empire, or even early Ireland. In the Penitential of Cummean, sick-maintenance serves less as a legal remedy than as a means of restoring the soul of the penitent by compelling him to help a man he has wronged and thus curing with its opposite the spiritual ailment that brought about his evil act.[23] Along with the obvious debt to the Vulgate version of Exodus manifest in its use of the verb *restituere* and the phrase *inpensa in medicos*, the presence of such ideas suffices to disprove Thomas Oakley's suggestion that sick-maintenance appears in Latin penitentials solely as a result of influence from Irish secular law.[24] We will see later that Cummean's understanding of sick-maintenance as an avenue towards moral improvement, so far unremarked in scholarship on these texts, will determine as well the peculiar treatment of sick-maintenance found in the *Scriftboc*.

Pastoral ends also lead Cummean to broaden the range of injuries to which the remedy of sick-maintenance may be applicable. Now an injury that renders a victim *deformem* [maimed] rather than bedridden may entitle him to sick-maintenance. A somewhat different set of motives is suggested by the penitential's reference to the *maculae pretium*, probably an allusion to the system of payments assigned in Frankish and British secular law to various injuries.[25] Adding a requirement to pay the *maculae pretium* may perhaps be

---

[23] On this tendency, see John T. McNeill, 'Medicine for Sin as Prescribed in the Penitentials,' *Church History* 1 (1932), 14–26, especially 16–18. Here McNeill considers the belief, characteristic of most penitentials, that sins are to be cured with their opposites. Being derived ultimately from early medical thought, McNeill traces this *topos* into the writings of Cassian and thence to the Celtic church, where such thinking finds its first expression in the British Isles.

[24] The point that these phrases show indebtedness to Exodus is made in Oliver, 'Sick-Maintenance,' p. 319. On supposed Irish influence, see Thomas P. Oakley, 'The Cooperation of Medieval Penance and Secular Law,' *Speculum* 7 (1932), 515–24, at 522: 'Of particular interest are provisions concerning reparations for wounds. Of Irish origin, and subsequently incorporated into penitentials elsewhere, these demanded that he who wounds another must pay for his medical treatment, do the work of the injured until his recovery, and perform penance, as well as pay the regular secular compensation ... The custom is apparently derived from the requirement of "sick-maintenance" [in Irish secular law].' Oakley's description of the practice as maintained in the penitentials is misleading. While his language would suggest that 'do[ing] the work of the injured' is characteristic of all of them, in fact this obligation is required of a penitent only in the *Scriftboc*, which Oakley cites (as 'Conf. ps. Egb.') alongside those of Bede and Uinniau as if it were a member of the Latin tradition (which Oakley may indeed have taken it to be). The penitential of Uinniau, in any case, does not prescribe anything beyond compensation fixed by an arbiter in cases of wounding, and is thus irrelevant to the present discussion: see Bieler, *Irish Penitentials*, pp. 76–7, chs 8–9.

[25] The penitential of Theodore (*PT* I.iv.1) similarly makes concessions to secular custom concerning compensation, lessening the penances of those who pay the 'pecuniam æstimationis,' taken by McNeill and Gamer to refer to 'the "wergeld" or value in law of the slain man': John T. McNeill and Helena M. Gamer, trans., *Medieval Handbooks of Penance* (New York, 1938), p. 187 n. 53. See also the *Iudicia Theodori*, ch. 88, wherein the treatment of the offender unable to pay is close to that of Cummean's provision on sick-maintenance: 'Qui

considered an improvement upon Exodus rather than an outright departure from it. The injuries for which one might have expected compensation in Frankish laws of this period – severed digits, ears, noses, and the like – might easily have delayed one's return to labor even if the victim was not bedridden, and so this ordinance may be seen as preserving the logic of Exodus while making its provisions more merciful. An alternative reading of this clause might see in it some early trace of the tendency of secular legislation to offer remedies for the shame attached to visible injuries.[26] At all events, inclusion of the *maculae pretium* is rather different from the changes so far discussed, for here it is secular legal tradition rather than pastoral concern that shapes the raw materials of Exodus into a provision distinct from its source.

More resistant to categorization are the other remedies assigned by this clause. The problems involve the meaning of *restituat*. We have seen that the translators of the Douay-Rheims version were content to translate *restituat* in a pecuniary sense – 'make restitution' – in spite of the fact that the verb may have the meaning 'restore,' 'replace.' In Cummean, as in the Vulgate, the objects of *restituat* are *inpensa in medicos* and *opus eius*. While *inpensa in medicos* would lend itself to a monetary understanding of the obligation implied by this verb, *opus eius* does not seem to do so with equal ease. Bieler's translation gets around this problem by assigning two meanings to the verb ('shall meet [the injured man's] medical expenses … and shall do his work'). The translation offered by MacNeill and Gamer does the same, but their version of an identical passage occurring in the penitential ascribed to Bede gives 'make compensation for his work while he is recovering,' which suggests that their views on how to render this verb may have wavered.[27]

Some of the ambiguity that twentieth-century scholars have perceived in Cummean's ordinance may be owing to their having followed Oakley in assuming this text to rely upon the Irish tradition of sick-maintenance. As Binchy has shown, while an offender was obliged in 'the earliest [Irish] texts … [to] undertake the duty of nursing his victim back to health and providing

---

homicidium vel furtum comisserit et non composuit illis quibus nocuit quando confessus fuerit aepiscopo vel presbitero peccata sua debet illis aut propria reddere vel componere. Si vero non habuerit substantiam unde conponere potest vel nescierit quibus nocuit penitentia plus augeatur' [He who commits murder or theft and fails to make composition with those whom he has injured, when he has confessed his sins to a bishop or a presbyter, ought either to render them his property or to make composition; if indeed he has not the substance with which to make composition or does not know whom he has injured, his penance is to be the more increased]; Latin text from Paul Willem Finsterwalder, ed., *Die Canones Theodori Cantuariensis und ihre Überlieferungsformen* (Weimar, 1929), p. 246; translation from McNeill and Gamer, *Medieval Handbooks of Penance*, p. 216.

[26] This aspect of earlier English legislation is considered in Mary P. Richards, 'The Body as Text in Early Anglo-Saxon Law,' *Naked Before God*, ed. Withers and Wilcox, pp. 97–115; the article is a response to Katherine O'Brien O'Keeffe, 'Body and Law in Late Anglo-Saxon England,' *ASE* 27 (1998), 209–32.

[27] MacNeill and Gamer, *Medieval Handbooks of Penance*, pp. 107 (Cummean) and 225 (Bede). Given the provision in Cummean (*Si uero non habeat unde restituat …*), which suggests that sick-maintenance involves giving of one's possessions rather than one's time or efforts, I see no reason to think that the intended meaning of this provision differs at all from Exodus. Bieler renders this clause as 'If he has not the wherewithal,' as do McNeill and Gamer.

him with medical attendance,' later 'the more primitive obligation to provide sick-maintenance was commuted for a fixed payment, thereby approximating to the practice of the other systems.'[28] The shift from personal care to payment in Irish law seems to have happened well in advance of the year 700, though it is doubtful that the former practice died out completely.[29] Bieler's translation seems to have in mind the earlier practice, and the same may be the case for McNeill and Gamer. But I think we may be sure that nothing other than a pecuniary obligation is implied by the penitentials of Cummean or Bede, whose understanding of sick-maintenance seems in any case rooted in the language of Exodus, and which were set to writing well after the obligation to provide sick-maintenance in person had been commuted to a payment in Irish law.

The situation is perhaps clarified by the language of *Pseudo-Cummean* (c. VI.23), which diverges from the language of Cummean's penitential: 'Si laicus per scandalum sanguinem effuderit, reddat illi tantum, quantum nocuit, et si non habeat unde reddat, solvat opera proximi sui, quamdiu ille infirmus est et postea XL dies peniteat in pane et aqua.'[30] The verb *solvere* typically refers to payment in normative texts of this period.[31] I think we may understand the word to have this meaning here as well: if the culprit cannot afford to compensate his victim in accordance with the value assigned the wound in secular law, let him at least pay him for his lost work as long as he is incapacitated, then proceed to forty days' penance on bread and water. Of course, the culprit's lack of means may suggest that he would in this case have been expected to render penance with labor. In secular law, offenders unable to compensate their victims might become their slaves, and some temporary period of bondage may be implied by this clause if *solvat* is to be understood as meaning something other than 'pay,' which is unlikely but nonetheless conceivable.[32] Should *solvat* here mean 'give' rather than 'pay,' it should in any event be noted that this portion of *Pseudo-Cummean* describes a situation rather different from what we find in Cummean and elsewhere. In Cummean, the person unable to pay is assigned a longer penance but is thereby relieved of any obligation to his victim. Thus the supposedly traditional obligation of 'sick-maintenance' is somewhat overshadowed by the necessity of penance.

Sick-Maintenance in the Scriftboc

We may now revisit the portion of the *Scriftboc* referred to at the outset of this chapter. Here the provisions of Exodus acquire still more traces of local

---

[28] Binchy, 'Sick-Maintenance,' p. 79.
[29] Oliver, *Beginnings of English Law*, p. 105; Stacy, *Dark Speech*, p. 35.
[30] F. W. H. Wasserschleben, ed., *Die Bussordnungen der abendländischen Kirche* (Halle, 1851), p. 480.
[31] See, for example, the *Pactus lex Alamannorum*, wherein this usage is ubiquitous (as in ch. 21, 'Si quartus digitus truncatus fuerit, solvat solidos 5'): Karl Lehmann, ed., *Leges Alamannorum*, MGH LL nat. Germ. 5.1 (Hanover, 1966), p. 22 and *passim*.
[32] See Heinrich Brunner, *Deutsche Rechtsgeschichte*, vol. 2 (Leipzig, 1892), p. 477.

custom as they enter a third textual tradition. About this clause Spindler had little to say beyond remarks on possible sources in the penitentials referred to above; he says nothing about the sweeping changes made by the translator.[33] These deserve extended consideration. Elsewhere I have shown that, in his clause on *morð*, the translator of the *Scriftboc* was concerned to adapt his materials to the terms and customs of English folk-law.[34] The ordinance on sick-maintenance as well, drawn from the same subsection of this text (*De homicidiis vel livoribus que in homine perfecta sunt*), likely adapts its materials in a purposeful way. However, determining how the *Scriftboc*'s changes assist a priest in the care of souls is not nearly as straightforward a matter as is the case with Cummean.

Before forming some conclusions about the Old English translator's purposes, it will be necessary to describe these changes in some detail. The strangest is the rendering of *debilem ... reddit* as *in gecynde oðerne gedo wánhalne*, a phrase rendered by Thorpe as 'alium in genitalibus debilem fecerit.'[35] It is hard to say why causing someone to be 'disabled in his genitals' would have established the necessity of sick-maintenance. Given belief among ecclesiastics in the sinfulness even of marital sexuality, no priest would have regarded the injured party as much harmed by a brief respite from the begetting of children. At all events, the reference seems oddly specific: why offer sick-maintenance only to those who have sustained injuries to the genitals?

The evidence of secular law is not as illuminating as might be hoped. The somewhat more voluble descriptions of genital wounding in the laws of Æthelberht and Alfred point to injuries that would have been of permanent consequence for the victim but would not in all instances have met Binchy's criterion for sick-maintenance.[36] In the first of these, compensation remedies not the suffering entailed by the injury itself but the harm done to the victim's kin-group, whose numbers the injured party is left unable to augment: the fine of multiple wergilds thus takes the place of persons never born.[37] Some trace of this idea may have attached itself to sick-maintenance within the Irish tradition, for assailants were sometimes required to compensate their bedridden victims for the fact of their being unable to conceive children while incapacitated.[38] These provisions of Irish law, however, do not refer to injury to the genitals; they respond instead to the fact that the victim was

---

[33] Spindler, *Das altenglische Bussbuch*, p. 58.
[34] See 'The Old English Penitentials and the Law of Slavery,' *English Law before Magna Carta*, ed. Jurasinski *et al.*, pp. 103–4.
[35] Thorpe, *Ancient Laws and Institutes*, p. 149.
[36] Wounds to genitals are considered in ch. 64 of Æthelberht's laws, the most severe of which is assigned three wergilds as compensation; to have merely pierced the genitals entails the much less significant payment of 6 shillings. Alfred's provision (ch. 65) prescribes a substantially lighter penalty than had Æthelberht for the destruction of one's reproductive capacity: 80 shillings is the same amount to be paid for loss of an arm (ch. 66). See also Lisi Oliver's essay in this volume.
[37] As is made explicit in Alfred 65.
[38] Kelly, *Guide to Early Irish Law*, p. 131.

expected to recover away from his wife within the culprit's home.³⁹ At all events, since the *Scriftboc* refers in this instance to a wound whose effects will come to an end (*oð þæt seo wund hal sy*), it seems unlikely that injuries as severe as those described in the laws of Æthelberht or Alfred are what the author has in mind. Perhaps a better question, to be turned to later in this chapter, is why the genitals appear to have been targeted for injury so routinely as to occasion tariffs in royal legislation.

No less puzzling is the transformation of *deformem ... fecerit* as *womwlite on gewyrce*. There is no easy explanation for the translator's substitution of an injury specifically to the face. Like *morð*, *womwlite* is a legal *terminus technicus* of the first order, attested in Frisian as well as English sources and thus likely a shared inheritance of some antiquity.⁴⁰ Occurring only in legislation (in the transposed form *wlitewamm*), it designates bruises or other minor wounds to visible parts of the body. The nature of such injuries is perhaps evident from a handful of interrelated clauses occurring in the laws of Æthelberht which I have discussed elsewhere.⁴¹ Here, the least *wlitewamm* is a minor mark or bruise, the greatest a deep bruise or evidence of having been slapped.⁴² As is evident in the examples given above, injuries implied by the term *wlitewamm* are physiologically minor, being remunerable with no more than 3 to 6 shillings in the laws of Æthelberht – the same amount required for a pierced ear or lost tooth. Given the trivial compensation occasioned by *wlitewamm*, it would seem that restitution was advised in Æthelberht's laws – and thus, perhaps, in the *Scriftboc* – as much for slights to one's honor as wounds to one's body. That the referent is something more abstract than bodily injury is implied by the element *wamm/wom*, which may according to Bosworth and Toller's *Dictionary* have the meanings 'moral stain, impurity, uncleanness, defilement'

---

[39] Kelly, *Guide to Early Irish Law*, p. 131. While the Irish norm, if present, would give an unexpected meaning to the *Scriftboc*'s requirement that the assailant 'do the work' of the wounded party, it is unclear how such a remedy, if performed by his attacker, would have offered much relief to the convalescing victim.

[40] See Horst Haider Munske, *Der germanische Rechtswortschatz im Bereich der Missetaten* (Berlin, 1973), pp. 51, 128–9, and 246.

[41] The discussion of *wamm* here is somewhat indebted to remarks made in my 'Germanism, Slapping, and the Cultural Contexts of Æthelberht's Code: A Reconsideration of Chapters 56–58,' *HSJ* 18 (2006), 51–71.

[42] That slapping could result in a visible and therefore shameful wound is evident in the probably contemporaneous *Excerpta de libris Romanorum et Francorum*, datable perhaps to the sixth or seventh century and edited as the 'Canones Wallici' in what remains the standard edition. The relevant clauses, drawn from versions 'A' and 'P' of this text, are as follows: 'Si quis alterius in faciem alapam percusserit ut sanguis aut libido appareat, se ancellam nouerit rediturum' [If anyone strikes another with a slap in the face so that blood or a bruise appears, he shall be prepared to pay a female slave]; 'Si alterum in faciem alapa ferierit sic ut sanguis aut liuido appareat, argenti libram unam reddat' [If anyone strikes another with a slap in the face so that blood or a bruise appears, he shall pay one silver pound]. Both texts are given in Bieler, *Irish Penitentials*, pp. 138–9 and 154–5, respectively. On the date of this text, see Léon Fleuriot, 'Un Fragment en Latin de très anciennes lois bretonnes armoricanes du VIᵉ siècle,' *Annales de Bretagne* 78 (1971), 601–60; David Dumville, 'On the Dating of the Early Breton Lawcodes,' *Études celtiques* 21 (1984), 207–21.

as well as 'blot, disgrace, damage, hurt' when appearing independently.[43] In its verbal form, the word refers almost exclusively to the sexual defilement of women, as it does elsewhere in the *Scriftboc*.[44] A curious passage in the Exeter Book poem known as *Maxims I* suggests the association of *wamm*, whatever it may have been, with one's appearance: 'word gespringeð, oft hy mon wommum bilihð / hæleð hy hospe mænað, oft hyre hleor abreoþeð' [word spreads, often she is encompassed with shameful [accusations] / men speak of her insultingly, often her appearance becomes marred].[45] Some light on this passage, which may show early English thought to depend on notions of causality rather foreign to our own, is shed by Liebermann's assertion that *wlite* might have been understood at this time to designate something more abstract than the face, perhaps having instead the meaning 'appearance.'[46] However strange, this text suggests that the injury referred to in the *Scriftboc* need not be understood as the consequence of a necessarily physical assault on the victim (which does not, of course, require us to assume that the victim in the *Scriftboc* has received his injury by the same means as the 'roving woman' in *Maxims I*). However this injury has been realized, it is plain that by the time sick-maintenance arrives in the *Scriftboc* the situation is far removed from that in Exodus, whose victim must be near death in order to qualify for payment of his physician's fee.

The idiosyncrasies of the *Scriftboc* are perhaps clarified by direct comparison with Cummean's penitential. With the use of the term *womwlite*, the *Scriftboc* moves further in the direction intimated by Cummean and its congeners of applying the remedies of biblical sick-maintenance to injuries that do not render victims bedridden or otherwise incapacitated. That the *Scriftboc*'s translator knew what he was doing is suggested by the penance he imposes on the assailant. While in his source the penitent was obliged to

---

[43] The clauses in Æthelberht's code are numbered 60–61.4 in Oliver, *Beginnings of English Law*, p. 72; they are chs 56–60 in Liebermann's edition.

[44] See Spindler, *Das altenglische Bussbuch*, p. 177, ch. V.6.a, where according to Spindler *wemman* renders *maculans* in the penitential of Bede: 'Læwede man him wife agende gyf he oðres ceorles wif wemme oððe fæmnan, fæste an winter' [If a married layman should seduce another man's spouse or an unmarried woman, let him fast for a year]; see also Bosworth–Toller, s.v. 'wamm.'

[45] See George Philip Krapp and Elliott Van Kirk Dobbie, eds, *The Exeter Book*, ASPR 3 (New York, 1936), p. 159. See also Clare A. Lees and Gillian R. Overing, 'The Clerics and the Critics: Misogyny and the Social Symbolic in Anglo-Saxon England,' *Gender in Debate from the Early Middle Ages to the Renaissance*, ed. Thelma S. Fenster and Clare A. Lees (New York, 2002), pp. 19–41, at 22–3.

[46] Liebermann, *Gesetze* III, p. 12: '"Angesicht" im besonderen heisst Ags. *andwlite*, nicht (wie allerdings in anderen German. Dialekten) *wlite*.' Thus the standard gloss of cognate forms of this term in Continental legislation – *deformitas faciei* – should be used with caution when making sense of the English evidence: 'facies weiter "äussere Gestalt" bedeuten kann' [*facies* can more broadly be defined as 'outward appearance']. The reference is to Karl August Eckhardt and Albrecht Eckhardt, eds, *Lex Frisionum*, MGH Fontes iuris 12 (Hanover, 1982), p. 84, §16: 'Si ex percussione deformitas faciei illata fuerit, quae de XII pedum longitudine possit agnosci, quod *wlitiwam* dicunt, ter IIII solid[is] componat[ur]' [If, because of a beating, a *deformitas faciei* will have been occasioned that can be recognized from a distance of 12 feet – which they call *wlitiwam* – let [the offender] pay thrice 4 *solidi*].

undertake a half-year of penance upon completing the obligations of sick-maintenance, the *Scriftboc* imposes on him the two or three quadragesimas required in Cummean of an assailant whose attack results in no injury at all. Imposition of such a penance suggests that the *wanhalne* done to the victim's genitals is of no more lasting physiological consequence than the *womwlite*.

No less suggestive of deliberate aims on the part of the *Scriftboc*'s author is the rendering of *opus eius ... restituat*. We have seen that, at the time extant manuscripts of the *Scriftboc* were being prepared, the translator of the Old English Heptateuch regarded this portion of Exodus as a reference to a specifically monetary obligation, as is evident from his rendering: 'gylde swa þeah his weorc ⁊ þæt hine man hæle' [let him pay nonetheless for his work and so that he may be healed]. The *Scriftboc* instead obliges the penitent 'his weorc wyrc[ean] oð þæt seo wund hal sy' [to do [the victim's] work until the wound is healed] – even though neither wound is likely to have been incapacitating, as the translator is sure to have understood given his substitution of a penance applied in his source only to attacks resulting in no injuries. This change is of particular interest given its occurrence in the partial translation of Exodus taking up most of the preface to Alfred's *domboc* or 'book of judgments,' wherein the attacker faces a similar requirement: 'wyrce his weorc þa hwyle he sylf ne mæge' [let him do his [the victim's] work while he is unable].[47] In both cases, this remedy is not prescribed for a culprit unable to afford compensation, as it arguably was in *Pseudo-Cummean*. I am not sure that this coincidence is best explained by assuming that *restituat* – a term understood by the author of the Old English Heptateuch to refer to payment – was misunderstood both by Alfred and by the author of the *Scriftboc*;[48] and while one may speculate that their substitution shows evidence of Irish tradition, such a possibility is complicated by the fact that Irish law, as was mentioned earlier, came to adopt monetary substitutes for personal care of the wounded well in advance of the composition of Alfred's laws. Moreover, Irish law always required that the culprit 'provide a substitute to perform the normal work of the victim,' as had been the case in Hittite law; he was not obliged to undergo the humiliation of doing the work himself.[49]

---

[47] Liebermann offers no comment on this aberrant translation in Alfred's *domboc* beyond a description of it in *Gesetze* II, s.v. 'Arbeit': 'Wer jemanden bis zur Arbeitsunfähigkeit verletzt, muss für ihn arbeiten während derselben: aus Exodus AfEl 16 [auch in Bussbüchern, z. B. Merseburg c. 40].' Liebermann seems mistaken in his assertion that the requirement to perform the work of an injured man is found in penitentials; the one that he mentions (now known conventionally as Merseburg aM) is little different from those so far discussed, requiring of the culprit that he 'reddit inpensam in medicum et maculae pretium et opus eius, donec sanetur, restituat et dimidium annum peniteat'. See Raymond Kottje, L. Körntgen, and U. Spengler-Reffgen, eds, *Paenitentialia minora Franciae et Italiae saeculi VIII–IX* (Turnhout, 1994), p. 145. I am not sure what Liebermann is referring to in the passage quoted above, since there are various Merseburg penitentials, and in none of them does ch. 40 give an ordinance on personal injury.

[48] Spindler offers no comment on the changes made by the author of the *Scriftboc* to his source, assuming instead the influence of at least four penitential canons, not one of which comes close to the provisions of the *Scriftboc*.

[49] Kelly, *Guide to Early Irish Law*, p. 131.

Thus there is nothing particularly Irish about what Alfred and the *Scriftboc* do with *restituat*.

The other points of similarity between Alfred's preface and the *Scriftboc*, none of which has been noted in published scholarship, all seem to derive from the tradition of penitentials rather than Irish secular law. For instance, Alfred has omitted any suggestion that the assailant is *innocens* if he fails to kill his victim, an adaptation made as well by Cummean and related penitentials. That Alfred omits such language in the immediately following clause shows this to be a deliberate change.[50] And while Exodus had been clear that the assailant was obliged to provide sick-maintenance until his victim was able to walk with a staff – i.e., was no longer bedridden – Alfred appears to assert that the obligation begins while the victim is able to walk, as is also the case in the penitential of Cummean and those derived from it.

This failure to render *restituat* as 'pay, compensate for,' and the insistence instead that the assailant act as a substitute for the victim, may perhaps also be explained as a development of tendencies manifest in Latin penitentials that reach their fulfillment in these vernacular texts. We have seen that Cummean's penitential was concerned to establish penalties affecting the soul as much as the purse. By removing money from consideration altogether, the *Scriftboc* and Alfred's laws may have sought to add emphasis to this aspect of the pastoral remedy, perhaps because pecuniary remedies advantaged the affluent.

We are still left, however, with the problem that the injuries referred to in the *Scriftboc*, and perhaps in Alfred, are not necessarily incapacitating, and thus would not have obliged the assailant to perform sick-maintenance in any of the legal environments in which this tradition is attested. Given its appearance in the *Leis Willelme*, this tendency to assign the payment of medical expenses even in cases of milder injuries may be seen as characteristic of sick-maintenance as observed in English law. Unlike the *Leis Willelme*, however, both Alfred's preface and the *Scriftboc* insist on a remedy that was probably more demeaning for the assailant than those imposed in other legal traditions even for injuries of greater severity. For an explanation, it may be necessary to dispense with the notion of sick-maintenance altogether, which had by this point already been transformed by the likeliest textual influences on Alfred and the *Scriftboc* into a device serving the inner needs of the penitent more than the physical needs of the victim.

The recommendations of Alfred and the *Scriftboc* may perhaps best be explained by the peculiar attitudes that seem to have surrounded acts of violence in Anglo-Saxon England and the wider Germanic world. Scholars have noted the tendency of injuries in Anglo-Saxon England (and, no doubt, much of pre-modern Europe) to act as signifiers of one's social status or lack thereof. Beatings were reserved for slaves, women, and children: persons who were in a sense feminized by their regularly acting as the objects rather

---

[50] This clause is discussed in great detail in Stefan Jurasinski, 'Violence, Penance and Secular Law in Alfred's Mosaic Prologue,' *HSJ* 22 (2010), 25–42.

than originators of violence, as Carol Clover has demonstrated most vividly.[51] Even in cases of graver and more lasting wounds, shame seems to have outweighed the suffering and hardship of living with an enfeebled body as a motive for the pursuit of compensation.

This is most strikingly the case in chapter 77 of Alfred's laws, wherein one who endures paralysis as a result of an injury is described as *gescynded*, which Oliver has correctly rendered as 'shamed' (over Attenborough's 'wounded').[52] In such an environment, it is hardly surprising that a class of injuries arose whose sole purpose was to inflict shame (often without appreciable bodily injury at all), as is the case with penalties for forcibly tonsuring a man or cutting off his beard 'on bismor.'[53] Anglo-Saxon law furnishes no parallel to a form of abuse familiar from accounts of saga-age Iceland – the lopping off of a rival's buttocks, usually in the heat of battle – but similar acts of ritual humiliation attested in Alfred's laws suggest that both England and Scandinavia shared an understanding of injury as a way of diminishing the social status of rivals as well as inflicting pain and fear upon them.[54] As is suggested alike by the forcible shaving of beards in England and by the prohibited insults of the Norwegian 'Gulaþing' law, one of which was to call a man a 'mare,' the means of inflicting injury to one's status were dependent upon prevailing notions of masculinity and femininity.[55] Though they are not typically described as having this function, the tendency to see injury as a means of feminizing victims may reach its apogee within the Germanic world in the wounds to the genitals that surface in the laws of Æthelberht and Alfred. Such, at any rate, would seem to be implied by the usage of *macht* to designate the genitals in Old Frisian ordinances concerned with wounding.[56] Such assaults, of which the forcible shaving of beards was probably a lesser variant, make good on the threats hinted at in the prohibited forms of defamation.

---

[51] Carol Clover, 'Regardless of Sex: Men, Women and Power in Early Northern Europe,' *Speculum* 68 (1993), 363–87.
[52] Oliver, 'Sick-Maintenance,' p. 325.
[53] See Alfred 35.3–5. These provisions have recently found a remarkable parallel in the behavior of a renegade Amish sect: Erik Eckholm and Daniel Lovering, 'Hair-Cutting Attacks Stir Fear among Ohio Amish,' *New York Times*, 17 October 2011.
[54] Hrólf's attack on King Aðils of Sweden, which culminates in his slicing off the latter's buttocks, has for some time been regarded as an instance of 'symbolic sexual domination of one man by another': Carl Phelpstead, 'The Sexual Ideology of *Hrólfs Saga Kraka*,' *Scandinavian Studies* 75 (2003), 1–24, at 11–12.
[55] R. Keyser *et al.*, eds, *Norges gamle love indtil 1387*, vol. 1 (Christiania, 1846), p. 70.
[56] 'Hversar en man vndad werth ynna sina machte, thet hi nawt tia ne muge, niogen merc to bote for tha niogen bern, ther hi tia machte.' [If a man should be wounded in genitals [literally, 'in his power'], so that he may procreate not at all, [the assailant shall pay] nine marks as a remedy for the nine children whom he might have conceived.] Wybren Jan Buma and Wilhelm Ebel, eds, *Das Emsiger Recht*, Altfriesische Rechtsquellen 3 (Göttingen, 1967), p. 187, ch. 200. Thus my view of the social significance attached in Anglo-Saxon England to the male generative organ differs somewhat from that argued for in Jay Gates, 'The *Fulmannod* Society: Social Valuing of the (Male) Legal Subject,' *Castration and Culture in the Middle Ages*, ed. Larissa Tracy (Woodbridge, 2013), pp. 131–48. I am grateful to the author for providing me a copy of this essay in advance of its publication.

Sick-Maintenance

Given the associations of the term elsewhere in Old English prose, some sort of 'feminization' of the victim is probably implied by the *Scriftboc*'s reference to *womwlite*. The *wanhalne* done to the genitals likewise seems inseparable from notions of gender familiar in the written remains of North Sea peoples. The goal of these injuries was to humiliate the victim, and thus the equally humiliating remedy arrived at by Alfred and the *Scriftboc* cures more effectively the spiritual defect of the penitent, by forcing upon him the shame of acting for a time as his victim's laborer and thus occupying the same category as the women, children, and slaves of his victim's household.

Some light on why this would be the preferred remedy is shed by the *Leges Henrici Primi*, a post-Conquest summary of Anglo-Saxon law as understood by a Norman immigrant. Its author imagines pre-Conquest law imposing punishments on both 'qui verberat et qui verberatur, ut nec malefaciens inpunitate superbiat nec contumeliatus fedis emendationibus insolescat' [he who beats and he who is beaten, so that the malefactor will not be made proud in his impunity nor he who is shamed become accustomed to the disgraceful receipt of compensation].[57] The agreement of this clause with the vernacular laws discussed earlier shows it to be more than its author's invention. While he may have gotten wrong some of the particulars of Anglo-Saxon legislation, the unknown Anglo-Norman author of the *Leges* knew the centrality of shame to the understanding of violence that prevailed in early England. We may therefore take seriously his assertion that one who beat or injured another might have been understood by his confessor as stained by the sin of pride (*superbia*). If such a view prevailed during the composition of the *Scriftboc* – and there is no reason to suppose it did not – it is unsurprising that this text should present the culprit rather than victim as in need of the 'medicine' of penance and should seek a cure for his *superbia* in humiliation, the direct opposite of the passion that led him to injure his neighbor.

Such aims may explain why this punishment came to be attached in both secular and ecclesiastical law to injuries that are not incapacitating and, in the case of *womwlite*, physiologically trivial. In an environment in which to be injured at all was so humiliating that even a paralytic was regarded as 'shamed' by his condition, the physiological severity of an injury could not alone determine the remedy prescribed. That compensation amounts in the secular laws of this period do not correspond to the gravity of an injury but instead reflect a sense of its social effects has long been known.[58] We should therefore not be surprised that the *Scriftboc* would complete the tendency of its source to assign 'sick-maintenance' for injuries less grave than those in Exodus, here apparently going so far as to apply it to wounds whose 'severity' was tied to their capacity to inflict shame.

---

[57] L. J. Downer, ed. and trans., *Leges Henrici Primi* (Oxford, 1972), pp. 260–1, ch. 84.1. The *Leges* are not actually the legislation of Henry I, but rather a twelfth-century compilation of statements from Anglo-Saxon legislation. That the author was familiar with the treatment of visible wounds in pre-Conquest legislation is evident from p. 293, ch. 93.1.

[58] For a discussion of this principle, see Oliver, *Beginnings of English Law*, p. 100.

Stefan Jurasinski

English Sick-Maintenance?

The foregoing has shown that the physician's fee in the *Scriftboc* was very likely superfluous, a meaningless appendage left over from the origins of this clause in Latin penitentials and, ultimately, the laws of Exodus. If the translator of the *Scriftboc* was willing to alter so many other aspects of his anchor text, we may ask why he did not change this one as well. The *Leis Willelme*, which impose, as in the *Scriftboc*, the *læcefeoh* on an offender whose attack has not left his victim bedridden, suggest that this penalty survives in the *Scriftboc* not because of the influence of its source but because payment of the leech-fee had become the norm in secular law for relatively minor injuries. Moreover, the *Leis Willelme* follows this clause with one showing a clear understanding of the ideology of violence peculiar to pre-Conquest texts:

> De sa[r]bote, ceo est de la dulur: Si la plaie lui vient el vis en descuvert, al pouz tuteveies VIII den.; u en la teste u en auter liu, u ele seit cuverte, al puoz tuteveies IIII den.[59]

> With regard to *sarbot*, that is [compensation] for a wound: If he is wounded on the face, on a part which is visible, for every inch 8 pence shall be paid in every case; if on the head or any other place where it is hidden, for every inch 4 pence shall be paid in every case.

The language of the provision shows the faultiness of the gloss. Whatever it was, *sarbot* was concerned with more than mere *dulur*, or at least involved an understanding of suffering broad enough to encompass the humiliation of bearing on one's face the visible effects of having been beaten. And this is made clear from the provision that follows, which describes the manner in which compensation is to be paid: 'Puis a l'acordement si lui metera avant honurs' [Then at their reconciliation the attacker shall, in the first place, show honor to the wounded man]. The legal environment described in this text, one which made wounds remunerable in accordance with their visibility and which required of the attacker above all that he humble himself before his victim, differs little from that of the *Scriftboc*.

Though they are less than ideal witnesses, both the *Scriftboc* and the *Leis Willelme* would seem to offer, along with the Alfredian passage discussed earlier, some sense of the form assumed by sick-maintenance in pre-Conquest English law. In all three of these texts, sick-maintenance is applicable to injuries that are not incapacitating, and might even be trivial, and all three require of the culprit that he undertake a more humiliating remedy than mere payment, perhaps because acceptance of the latter was held to be a sign of cowardice and thus offered to the assailant a chance to further humiliate his victim.[60] It would be simplistic to describe the *Scriftboc* as engaging here in

---

[59] Liebermann, *Gesetze* I, pp. 500–1, ch. 10.1; trans. Robertson, *Laws*, p. 259. For Liebermann, the source of this ordinance was 'probably Anglo-Saxon' [*wohl Angelsächsisch*].

[60] Contempt for the acceptance of compensation is ubiquitous in much saga literature; see, for example, Jón Jóhanneson, ed., *Austfirðinga sögur*, Íslenzk fornrit 11 (Reykjavík, 1950), p. 17: 'Þorsteinn hvíti kvazk eigi vilja bera Þorgil, son sinn, í sjóði' [Þorsteinn the White said that he would not bear Þorgil, his son, in [his] purse].

the sort of 'cooperation' of penance and secular law Oakley perceived in some penitentials of this period. Rather, the *Scriftboc* has absorbed secular norms only to reframe them so that they furnish priests with a remedy for violence suited to the associations it seems to have had within the Anglo-Saxon world. That the other witnesses to the tradition of early English sick-maintenance, both of which belong ostensibly to the tradition of 'secular' ordinances, seem to agree with the penitentials' manner of dealing with wounds in their concern to affect the spiritual condition of the culprit, suggests that ecclesiastical laws did more than merely support laws promulgated by the secular 'state.'[61] In this case, the understanding of sick-maintenance developed within the penitential of Cummean seems to have served as the template of supposedly secular laws on wounding.

The foregoing has also afforded some clues as to the place of the *Scriftboc* in the chronology of the Old English penitentials. That the *Scriftboc* insists upon service in the victim's household over payment suggests that its author might not have looked favorably on the practice known as 'commutation,' which permitted affluent penitents to hire others to perform the obligations they incurred.[62] In the corpus of Old English penitentials, this practice is isolated to the *Penitential* and *Handbook*; while commutations are acknowledged in the so-called 'Old English Introduction' that precedes the *Scriftboc* in MS O (MS Cambridge, Corpus Christi College 190), the 'Introduction' seems to have been added to the *Scriftboc* at a late phase of its transmission and is thus of little relevance to the contents of the penitential.[63] Though composed with pastoral aims in mind, the *Scriftboc* affords in this instance a view of early English practice more detailed than that which may be found in any legislation.

---

[61] Paul Hyams has considered skeptically claims for 'the sharp division of royal government (that is, "the state") and society,' suggesting instead that 'assertive royal aspirations [were] compelled to co-exist with something much less than an actual monopoly on the means of violence': *Rancor and Reconciliation*, p. 73. Neither penitentials nor Oakley's thesis figure in Hyams's study.

[62] Similar claims (though without reference to the clause that is of primary concern in this chapter) are made in Frantzen, *Literature of Penance*, p. 138.

[63] Commutations in the Old English penitentials are considered in Carole Hough, 'Penitential Literature and Secular Law in Anglo-Saxon England,' *Anglo-Saxon Studies in Archaeology and History* 11 (2000), pp. 133–41, at 139. On the relation of the 'Introduction' to these texts, see Frantzen, *Literature of Penance*, p. 135; Spindler, *Das altenglische Bussbuch*, pp. 165–9.

5

Incarceration as Judicial Punishment in Anglo-Saxon England*

Daniel Thomas

The Old English translation of the *Soliloquies* of St Augustine contains the following passage on the different experiences of those who set out to seek wisdom:

> swa hit bið æac be þam wisdome: ælc þara þe hys wilnað and þe hys geornful byt, he hym mæg cuman to and on hys hyrede wunian and be lybbam, þeah hi hym sume nær sian, sume fyer. swa swa ælces cynges hama beoð sume on bure, sume on healle, sume on odene, sume on carcerne, and lybbað þeah æalle be anes hlafordes are.[1]

> so it is too concerning wisdom: each of those who desires it and is eager for it, he may come to it and dwell and live in its company, yet some of them shall be near to it and some further off. Just so in the estate of every king there are some in the chamber, some in the hall, some in the threshing house, some in prison, and nevertheless they all live according to a single lord's grace.

One of a series of analogies in the Old English text drawn from the courtly world of Anglo-Saxon England,[2] the reference to a royal prison in this passage is recalled subsequently in the text when the translator likens the helpless situation of the damned to that of a man confined in a king's prison:

> Ac hym byð þonne swa swa þam mannum þe her beoð on sumes kincges carcerne gebrohte, and magon geseon ælc dæge heora freond and geahsian be heom þæt þæt hy willað, and ne magon heom þeah na nane gode ne beon.[3]

> But it will be for him then as for those men who are here brought into a king's prison, and they may see their friends each day and ask what they will of them, and yet they [the friends] may not be any use to them.

Neither passage relates directly to anything in the ostensible Latin source of the *Soliloquies*, and the casual references to the existence of royal prisons might at first glance be taken as evidence for the contemporary practice of

---

* I am grateful to Professors Anne Duggan and Malcolm Godden for reading and commenting upon drafts of this paper. Remaining errors are, of course, my own.

[1] Thomas A. Carnicelli, ed., *King Alfred's Version of St Augustine's Soliloquies* (Cambridge, MA, 1969), p. 77, lines 15–19. Hereafter cited as *Soliloquies*. Translations are my own throughout.

[2] Malcolm Godden, 'The Player King: Identification and Self-Representation in King Alfred's Writings,' *Alfred the Great: Papers from the Eleventh-Centenary Conferences*, ed. Timothy Reuter (Aldershot, 2003), pp. 137–50, at 148–50.

[3] *Soliloquies*, p. 96, lines 8–11.

incarceration and the availability of prison facilities in Anglo-Saxon England in the late ninth or early tenth centuries.[4]

However, these passages actually raise more questions than they answer. While some familiarity with the idea of imprisonment is implicit in these accounts, there is no indication of how common such a practice might have been. At the same time, there is nothing in either passage to indicate the nature of the incarceration envisaged. The text might attest the role of incarceration within Anglo-Saxon legal procedure – either as a custodial or as a punitive measure – but it might equally well attest the use of imprisonment as a summary punishment for those out of royal favour. In the same way, there is nothing in the text to show whether imprisonment might habitually have been of indefinite duration, perhaps dependent upon the favour of the king, or whether prisoners might have served particular and limited prison sentences, perhaps in relation to the manner of their offence.

The purpose of this study, therefore, is to reconsider the evidence for the use of incarceration in Anglo-Saxon England, with particular focus on the legal process. My aim is to provide answers, where possible, to questions such as those raised above, and to discuss some of the broader issues surrounding the understanding and interpretation of incarceration as a judicial punishment in this period. What follows falls into two parts: the first half of the essay examines evidence for the practice of incarceration and considers how familiar it would have been in the centuries before the Conquest; the second half focuses on the prescription of incarceration as a judicial punishment in extant Anglo-Saxon legislation, particularly in the *domboc* associated with King Alfred. It also considers the relationship between such normative prescriptions and the evidence considered in the first part, and asks what role incarceration might have played in the conception of the law in the late ninth and tenth centuries.

Before proceeding, however, it is necessary to say a word regarding the definition of incarceration with which I am working. The distinctions between incarceration and other forms of restraint (such as stocks or binding), or the imposition of non-physical restrictions on personal freedom (such as exile), are very fine. My interest in what follows is in incarceration in a strict sense, involving the use of a structure that might be identified as a prison.[5] I have,

---

[4] On the sources of the *Soliloquies*, see Malcolm Godden, 'The Sources of the Old English Soliloquies (Cameron B.9.4.2),' *Fontes Anglo-Saxonici: A Register of Written Sources Used by Anglo-Saxon Authors*, online at http://fontes.english.ox.ac.uk/ [accessed 6 January 2014]. For a reconsideration of the date of the translation and of the traditional attribution to King Alfred, see M. R. Godden, 'Did King Alfred Write Anything?' *MÆ* 76 (2007), 1–23; Malcolm Godden, 'The Alfredian Project and its Aftermath: Rethinking the Literary History of the Ninth and Tenth Centuries,' *Proceedings of the British Academy* 162 (2009), 93–122.

[5] Excluding the descriptive compounds found in vernacular verse renditions of Latin hagiographical narratives, the Old English lexicon contained two words that specifically denote the prison: *carcern* and *cweartern*. The latter term is restricted primarily to late West Saxon prose texts and was apparently a later formation than *carcern*. Both terms appear to represent compound borrowings, combining the Old English element *–ærn* ('building') with Latin *carcer* and (more doubtfully) *quarterium*. Cf. *DOE*, s.v. 'carcern' and 'cwearten'.

therefore, largely limited my analysis to instances in which the use of such a facility is either explicitly mentioned, or might reasonably be inferred.

Incarceration in Anglo-Saxon England

The evidence for the practice of incarceration in Anglo-Saxon England is at best ambiguous. As a custodial measure for the detention of those accused of a crime, or as a summary measure by which kings and lords might remove personal or political threats, it seems implausible that confinement of some form was not practised throughout this period. Clear evidence for the role of the prison in custodial or summary detention is, however, surprisingly elusive. For custodial purposes, incarceration is attested in Anglo-Latin hagiographical texts such as Lantfred of Winchester's *Translatio et miracula S. Swithuni*.[6] Written shortly after the translation of Swithun's relics into the Old Minster at Winchester in 971, Lantfred's enthusiastic account of the miracles performed through the saint's intercession includes the liberation of a man accused of theft from the prison in which he awaited execution, and another similarly miraculous release said to have occurred in France.[7] However, the value of such accounts as evidence for historical practice is questionable. From as early as the sixth century, the liberation of prisoners and captives was, like the healing of the sick, an established element of the hagiographical miracle stories with which Lantfred was clearly very familiar.[8] Despite Lantfred's claim that the liberation of prisoners through Swithun's intercession constitutes a remarkable proof of his sanctity, these accounts are in fact highly typical of medieval hagiography from across Europe.[9]

The same might be said of hagiographical accounts of the summary incarceration of Anglo-Saxon saints themselves. Stephen of Ripon's early eighth-century *Vita Wilfridi*, for example, describes at length the bishop's imprisonment by Ecgfrith of Northumbria in the late seventh century and the miracles associated with his incarceration.[10] However, despite Stephen's

---

On the derivation of *cweartern*, see Helmut Gneuss, '*Anglicae linguae interpretatio*: Language Contact, Lexical Borrowing and Glossing in Anglo-Saxon England,' *Proceedings of the British Academy* 82 (1993), 107–48, at 140 and n. 130.

[6] Edited in Lapidge, *Swithun*, pp. 217–333.
[7] On the date of the text, see Lapidge, *Swithun*, pp. 218–24 and 235–7, chs 27 and 39.
[8] Edward M. Peters, 'Prison Before the Prison: the Ancient and Medieval Worlds,' *The Oxford History of the Prison: The Practice of Punishment in Western Society*, ed. Norval Morris and David J. Rothman (Oxford, 1995), pp. 3–47, at 24–5; Guy Geltner, *The Medieval Prison: A Social History* (Princeton, NJ, 2008), pp. 86–8. On Lantfred's knowledge of hagiographical texts, see Lapidge, *Swithun*, p. 234.
[9] Lapidge, *Swithun*, pp. 235–7, ch. 39. The European tradition of saintly liberation would have been particularly familiar to Lantfred, himself apparently of Frankish origins, and it is possible that the text was in fact written for a Continental rather than an English audience. See further Rachel Koopmans, *Wonderful to Relate: Miracle Stories and Miracle Collecting in High Medieval England* (Philadelphia, PA, 2011), pp. 47–59.
[10] Bertram Colgrave, ed. and trans., *The Life of Bishop Wilfrid by Eddius Stephanus* (Cambridge, 1927), chs 34–9.

unusually detailed account of the life of Wilfrid, the historicity of the narrative of his imprisonment is open to question. The chronology of Wilfrid's imprisonment in Stephen's text does not accord with the evidence of other sources and it is likely that the account of the incarceration – which may, in fact, be a later addition to the *Vita* – again reflects conventional hagiographical tropes for the depiction of endurance and suffering more than it does the realities of Anglo-Saxon England in the late seventh and early eighth centuries.[11]

Beyond hagiographical texts such as these, Anglo-Saxon accounts of the detention of criminals awaiting trial or punishment, or of political threats, are ambiguous regarding the nature of the detention involved and provide no clear evidence for the use of dedicated prison facilities. Typical in this regard is the reference in the E-text of the Anglo-Saxon Chronicle to the detention of the widow of the powerful Northern ealdorman Sigeferð in 1015.[12] Following Sigeferð's death at the hands of Eadric *Streona* – an outrage in which the king may well have been implicated – Æthelred ordered that this unfortunate woman be seized and taken to Malmesbury (*het nimon Sigeferðes lafe ⁊ gebringon binnon Mealdelmesbyrig*).[13] This is almost certainly a reference to the summary detention of a potential political threat – and indeed the threat that Sigeferð's widow posed to Æthelred is indicated by the fact that she was quickly taken from Malmesbury by the king's rebellious son Edmund 'Ironside,' who subsequently married her in an apparently successful attempt to gain both the support of the aristocracy of the Five Boroughs and the lands and goods previously belonging to Sigeferð.[14] There is, however, no mention of incarceration in the Chronicle entry, and there is nothing to indicate the type of detention involved.

It is perhaps because the practice of custodial or summary incarceration was so ubiquitous that it fails to merit explicit mention in the surviving documentation. However, it is also possible that custodial and summary detention were habitually practised without recourse to dedicated prison buildings, or that alternative strategies were employed to avoid the need for such facilities.[15] For temporary custodial purposes, it is possible that the prevalence of systems of surety and oath-swearing in Anglo-Saxon legal

---

[11] D. P. Kirby, 'Bede, Eddius Stephanus and the "Life of Wilfrid",' *EHR* 98 (1983), 101–14, at 110; Patrick Sims-Williams, 'St Wilfrid and Two Charters Dated AD 676 and 680,' *Journal of Ecclesiastical History* 39 (1988), 163–83, at 176–7. On the role of summary incarceration in medieval hagiography, see Megan Cassidy-Welch, *Imprisonment in the Medieval Religious Imagination, c. 1150–1400* (Basingstoke, 2011), pp. 37–41. On the historical value of medieval hagiography more generally, see Susan J. Ridyard, *The Royal Saints of Anglo-Saxon England: A study of West Saxon and East Anglian Cults* (Cambridge, 1988), pp. 8–16.

[12] ASC E, s.a. 1015.

[13] ASC E, s.a. 1015.

[14] P. A. Stafford, 'The Reign of Æthelred II: A Study in the Limitations on Royal Policy and Action,' *Ethelred*, ed. Hill, pp. 15–46, at 35–6.

[15] Margaret Deanesly, *The Pre-Conquest Church in England* (London, 1961), p. 330. Andrew Reynolds states somewhat equivocally that a dedicated prison structure 'might be expected at a royal estate centre and was surely a necessity, although fettering within any secure building could have served such a purpose adequately': *Deviant Burial*, p. 12.

practice reduced the need for the physical detention of those suspected of crimes.[16] Similarly, the availability of more cost-effective methods for the control of political opponents – exile, mutilation, enforced tonsuring, or confinement within a monastery – may account for the lack of explicit references to summary incarceration during this period.

As a non-summary judicial punishment, however, incarceration is explicitly prescribed for a range of offences in a small number of extant Anglo-Saxon legal codes.[17] The use of incarceration for the punishment of the laity was opposed by the Church until as late as 1298.[18] However, where Anglo-Saxon law-codes mention imprisonment it is clearly as a specifically punitive measure.[19] The earliest such reference is in the late ninth-century *domboc* issued in the name of King Alfred (r. 871–99).[20] The first statute of the *domboc* establishes the need for every man to fulfil his oath and pledge faithfully (*þæt æghwelc mon his að ⁊ his wed wærlice healde*).[21] The punishment for failing to do so is set out in clause 1.2:

> Gif he þonne þæs weddige þe him riht sie to gelæstanne ⁊ þæt aleoge, selle mid eaðmedum his wæpn ⁊ his æhta his freondum to gehealdanne ⁊ beo feowertig nihta on carcerne on cyninges tune, ðrowige ðær swa biscep him scrife, ⁊ his mægas hine feden, gif he self mete næbbe.

> If he pledges that which it is right for him to perform, and does not fulfil that, he shall give his weapons and possessions humbly into the keeping of his friends and shall spend forty nights in prison in the king's town, and he shall suffer there what the bishop prescribes for him. And his kinsmen shall feed him, if he himself has no food.

In the early decades of the tenth century this punishment for oath-breaking was endorsed in the legislation of Alfred's son Edward the Elder (r. 899–924). In the prologue to Edward's first code the authority of the *domboc* is endorsed in a general way in the statement that the king expects his reeves to pronounce in accordance with the existing legislation (*⁊ hit on ðære dombec stande*).[22] More specifically, the first of the Alfredian statutes is directly endorsed in a later code of Edward's, associated with Exeter, which states that anyone who

---

[16] John Hudson, *The Oxford History of the Laws of England*, vol. 2: *871–1216* (Oxford, 2012), p. 195.
[17] All references to Anglo-Saxon legal codes are from Liebermann, *Gesetze*. Much-needed re-editing of the corpus of surviving codes issued up until 1215 is to be undertaken for the Early English Laws project. For details of the project, see http://www.earlyenglishlaws.ac.uk [accessed 6 January 2014].
[18] Guy Geltner, '*Detrusio*: Penal Cloistering in the Middle Ages,' *Revue Bénédictine* 118 (2008), 89–108, at 89.
[19] The statement in Frederick Pollock and Frederic William Maitland's monumental history of early medieval English law that '[i]mprisonment occurs in the Anglo-Saxon laws only as a means of temporary security' is at odds with the evidence presented here; see Pollock and Matiland, *History of English Law* I, p. 49.
[20] See Wormald, *Making of English Law*, pp. 265–85; David Pratt, *The Political Thought of King Alfred the Great* (Cambridge, 2007), pp. 214–41. On the question of Alfred's direct involvement in the construction of this code, see Alfred P. Smyth, *King Alfred the Great* (Oxford, 1995), p. 238; Godden, 'Did King Alfred Write Anything?' p. 6.
[21] Alfred 1.
[22] I Edward Prologue.

breaks his oath and pledge (*his að ⁊ his wæd brece*) is required to 'atone for it as the *domboc* teaches' (*bete swa domboc tæce*).[23]

Subsequently, two codes issued during the reign of Alfred's grandson Æthelstan (r. 924–39) make provision for the incarceration of offenders.[24] The code known as II Æthelstan, or the Grately code, prescribes a term of forty nights' imprisonment as a punishment for theft involving goods worth more than 8 pence:

> Gif mon ðeof on carcerne gebringe, ðæt he beo XL nihta on carcerne, ⁊ hine mon ðonne lyse ut mid CXX scll'; ⁊ ga sio mægþ him on borh, ðæt he æfre geswice.[25]
>
> If a thief is brought to prison, [we declare] that he shall be forty nights in prison, and then let someone bail him out with 120 shillings; and his kin shall stand surety for him, that he will renounce such acts forever.

The prescriptions for theft in II Æthelstan are complex. In the first place, the code states that thieves caught red-handed must be put to death (II Æthelstan 1). Presumably, therefore, the prescription of imprisonment legislates for those convicted of theft but not apprehended in the act. Moreover, the same code prescribes a longer term of 120 nights' imprisonment under the same conditions of release for those accused of causing death through sorcery, of arson, or of taking personal vengeance against a thief, if they are convicted through a threefold ordeal (II Æthelstan 6–6.3); those frequently accused of a crime and convicted through the simple ordeal suffer the same punishment if they are unable to find anyone willing to stand surety for them (II Æthelstan 7).

Finally, the later, London-based, composite code known as VI Æthelstan explicitly refers back to the Grately legislation on the imprisonment of thieves. On the one hand, the code begins by extending the death penalty to cover all those over the age of twelve convicted of stealing goods worth more than 12 pence, regardless of whether or not they are caught in the act (VI Æthelstan 1.1). On the other hand, a postscript to the same code modifies this draconian statute by declaring that those under the age of fifteen caught stealing should be spared capital punishment if they do not resist arrest, and should instead be imprisoned in the manner laid down in the Grately legislation (*do hine man on carcern, swa hit æt Greatanlea gecweden wæs*).[26] The statute goes on to clarify the procedures by which such a youth might provide sureties for his conduct, if there is no available prison in which he might be confined (*gif he in carcern ne cume, ⁊ man nan næbbe*).[27]

In each of these codes incarceration is clearly envisaged as a punitive measure and an alternative to other forms of punishment such as financial penalties, exile, or execution. The recognition in VI Æthelstan that prison

---

[23] II Edward 5.
[24] On the legislation of Æthelstan's reign, see Wormald, *Making of English Law*, pp. 290–308; Sarah Foot, *Æthelstan: The First King of England* (New Haven, CT, 2011), pp. 136–48.
[25] II Æthelstan 1.3.
[26] VI Æthelstan 12.1.
[27] VI Æthelstan 12.2.

facilities may not be available when needed does suggest that such facilities were uncommon, but it also indicates that it is incarceration within such dedicated facilities – rather than more general forms of confinement – that is envisaged here. The reference in the *domboc* to the existence of a prison *on cyninges tune* may also be significant. On the one hand, this reference seems to support the casual allusions to the habitual presence of a prison on a royal estate that we have seen in the Old English *Soliloquies*.[28] On the other hand, the phrase *cyninges tune* may refer here more specifically to the particular type of administrative site reflected in the survival of 'Kingston'-type place-names. Such an identification has recently been suggested in a discussion of the function of 'Kingston' sites by Jill Bourne, who speculates not only that a 'Kingston' was 'an easily identifiable site where some aspect of royal activity took place or royal power was enforced,' but also that such sites might have been the habitual location for Anglo-Saxon prison facilities.[29] However, the extent to which the punitive measures attested in these law codes were applied in practice remains unclear: the existence of prison facilities is not supported by either archaeological or – with the exception of the references in the *Soliloquies* – documentary evidence; nor is the normative prescription of judicial incarceration in these codes reflected in surviving narrative sources.

From an archaeological point of view, the lack of evidence for prison facilities in this period is not surprising. The difficulties associated with the interpretation of excavated Anglo-Saxon structures is indicated by the case of the unexplained circular structure located close to what is believed to have been the main gateway of an Anglo-Saxon palace excavated at Cheddar in Somerset. Associated with a period of construction before c. 930, this feature has been tentatively interpreted as 'a gaol, some kind of temporary cage structure.'[30] This interpretation is largely based on conjecture, however, and the feature in question may equally well have been 'some rick-like structure for hay-drying.'[31]

Documentary evidence is scarcely more helpful. Despite Pugh's assertion that 'the Normans found a number of prisons in the England they invaded,' the earliest clear evidence for the existence of such facilities post-dates the Norman invasion.[32] It is in the years after the Conquest, for example, that the Anglo-Saxon Chronicle begins to record the unambiguous use of prison facilities, and it is perhaps telling that it is the Anglo-Norman term *prisun* rather

---

[28] It is this combination of evidence that presumably lies behind Frank Stenton's statement that 'the *cyninges tun* usually contained a prison': *Anglo-Saxon England*, 3rd edn (Oxford, 1971), p. 482.

[29] Jill Bourne, 'Kingston—The Place-Name and its Context,' *Sense of Place in Anglo-Saxon England*, ed. Richard Jones and Sarah Semple (Donington, 2012), pp. 260–300, at 270–2 and 280. I am grateful to Professor John Blair for bringing this reference to my attention.

[30] Philip Rahtz et al., *The Saxon and Medieval Palaces at Cheddar: Excavations 1960–62*, BAR British Series 65 (Oxford, 1979), pp. 120–1, and cf. 49–51. For an argument in favour of a slightly later date for Rahtz's period 1, see John Blair, 'Palaces or Minsters? Northampton and Cheddar Reconsidered,' *ASE* 25 (1996), 97–121, at 109–20.

[31] Rahtz et al., *Saxon and Medieval Palaces at Cheddar*, p. 121.

[32] Ralph B. Pugh, *Imprisonment in Medieval England* (Cambridge, 1968), p. 3.

than the late West Saxon *cweatern* that is most frequently employed in these late annals.[33] A century after the Conquest, the Assize of Clarendon made provision for the construction of prisons only in those counties which did not already have such facilities, but this is hardly evidence for the existence of prisons in the period before the Norman invasion.[34] Of more relevance to the pre-Conquest period, perhaps, is the early twelfth-century *Winton Domesday*. Commissioned by Henry I to enquire into the lands previously held in Winchester by Edward the Confessor, this survey contains a reference to 'the *balcheus* of the king, where thieves used to be placed in custody' (*le balcheus regis, ubi latrones ponebantur in prisone*), a feature that has been interpreted as 'a fenced gaol compound or prison cage.'[35] The form *balcheus* seems to support an Anglo-Saxon origin for this feature. The first element of the compound is apparently the rare Old English noun *balc*, which is elsewhere twice attested referring to a means of punishment or constraint apparently equivalent to fettering.[36] However, in the light of the date and imprecision of this reference, the identification of this feature as a pre-Conquest prison facility cannot be asserted with any great confidence.[37]

In spite of the prescriptions of the legal codes discussed above, therefore, the evidence for the existence of prison facilities during the Anglo-Saxon period is hardly overwhelming. Neither is there clear evidence among extant narrative sources for the actual imposition of imprisonment as judicial punishment. One possible example from the mid-tenth century is the apparent detention of Archbishop Wulfstan I of York by King Eadred recorded in the entry for 952 in the D-text of the Anglo-Saxon Chronicle:

> Her on þyssum geare het Eadred cyning gebringan Wulstan arcebiscop in Iudanbyrig on þam fæstenne, for þæm he wæs oft to þam cyninge forwreged.[38]
>
> In this year King Eadred ordered Archbishop Wulfstan to be brought into the stronghold in Iudanbyrig, because he was frequently accused to the king.

The wording of this entry is ambiguous. The noun *fæsten* most usually refers to a protective enclosure, and it is possible to read the phrase *on þam fæstenne* in this passage as a reference to the stronghold at the otherwise

---

[33] *ASC* D, s.a. 1076; *ASC* E, s.a. 1086, 1112, 1137, and 1140.

[34] David C. Douglas and George W. Greenaway, eds, *English Historical Documents*, vol. 2: *1042–1189*, 2nd edn (London, 1981), pp. 440–3, at 441–2. Cf. Christopher Harding et al., *Imprisonment in England and Wales: A Concise History* (London, 1985), pp. 4–5.

[35] Frank Barlow et al., *Winchester in the Early Middle Ages: An Edition and Discussion of the Winton Domesday*, Winchester Studies 1 (Oxford, 1976), pp. 37 and 75, and see also 37 n. 19.3, 236, and 305–6 on the interpretation of this feature. See also, Ralph B. Pugh, 'The King's Prisons Before 1250,' *TRHS* 5th series 5 (1955), 1–22, at 1. I am grateful to Nicole Marafioti for bringing this example to my attention.

[36] Cf. *DOE*, s.v. 'balc,' 2; Michael Korhammer, 'Old English *Bolca* and *Mægþa Land*. Two Problems, One Solved,' *Words, Texts and Manuscripts: Studies in Anglo-Saxon Culture Presented to Helmut Gneuss*, ed. Michael Korhammer (Cambridge, 1992), pp. 305–24, at 307–9.

[37] The surviving toponyms Balkerne Hill and Balkern Gate in Colchester might similarly suggest an association with prison facilities, but again the earliest extant references to these place-names date from the middle of the twelfth century: see P. H. Reaney, *The Place-Names of Essex*, English Place-Name Society 12 (Cambridge, 1935), pp. 369–70.

[38] *ASC* D, s.a. 952.

unidentified Iudanbyrig to which the archbishop was summoned. However, as the *Dictionary of Old English* attests, there is also limited evidence for the use of *fæsten* as a term for a place of confinement, and more specifically for a structure otherwise identified explicitly as a prison.[39] This is, at any rate, how the wording of the Chronicle account was interpreted in the twelfth century by John of Worcester and William of Malmesbury, both of whom draw upon the version of these events recorded in the D-text, and recount that Wulfstan was imprisoned by the king.[40]

That Eadred would wish to delimit Wulfstan's capacity for political action at this time is not implausible given the archbishop's largely subversive influence on Northumbrian politics in the 940s and early 950s.[41] It is of particular interest, therefore, that while the annal for 952 is somewhat vague about the precise justification for the (possible) imprisonment of the archbishop, an earlier entry records that Wulfstan had, together with the Northumbrian *witan*, sworn an oath of allegiance to Eadred, and that they had subsequently reneged on their pledge (*hit eall alugon, ge wed ⁊ eac aþas*).[42] The wording here recalls that of the statutes on oath-breaking contained in the *domboc* and II Edward.[43] It is possible to infer, therefore, that the offence of which the archbishop was repeatedly accused before the king might have been oath-breaking. If so, it is also possible that the entry for 952 describes the enactment of a legal principle encoded more than half a century previously in the legislation of Alfred's reign.

This is, however, an isolated and perhaps tentative example.[44] The exhaustive catalogue of Anglo-Saxon law-suits compiled by Patrick Wormald

---

[39] See *DOE*, s.v. 'fæsten,' 3.b. and 3.b.i.

[40] JW, pp. 402–3; R. A. B. Mynors, R. M. Thompson and M. Winterbottom, eds, *William of Malmesbury: Gesta regum Anglorum, The History of the English Kings*, vol. 1 (Oxford, 1998), pp. 236–7. The incident is also recounted by William in his *Gesta pontificum Anglorum*, though here the king in question is said to be Eadred's predecessor Edmund; see M. Winterbottom and R. M. Thompson, eds, *William of Malmesbury: Gesta pontificum Anglorum, The History of the English Bishops*, vol. 1 (Oxford, 2007), pp. 376–7.

[41] A. Campbell, 'Two Notes on the Norse Kingdoms in Northumbria,' *EHR* 57 (1942), 85–97, at 91–5; Alfred P. Smyth, *Scandinavian York and Dublin: The History and Archaeology of Two Related Viking Kingdoms*, vol. 2 (Dublin, 1975–9), pp. 90–4, 155–7, and 161–2.

[42] ASC D, s.a. 947. Cf. JW, pp. 400–1. The *Historia Regum* associated with Symeon of Durham records this treachery twice: firstly, drawing on an otherwise unknown chronicle for the years 888–957 that recorded the perfidy of the Northumbrian people without specifically indicating Wulfstan's complicity; secondly, following John's account and specifying Wulfstan's role in the betrayal. See Thomas Arnold, ed., *Symeonis Monachi opera omnia*, vol. 2 (London, 1882–5), pp. 94 and 126–7; cf. David Rollason, ed. and trans., *Symeon of Durham, Libellus de exordio atque procursu istius, hoc est Dunhelmensis, Ecclesie: Tract on the Origins and Progress of this the Church of Durham* (Oxford, 2000), pp. xlviii–1.

[43] For the suggestion that the legalistic pairing of *að* and *wedd* in fact originated in the Alfredian legislation, see E. G. Stanley, 'On the Laws of King Alfred: The End of the Preface and the Beginning of the Laws,' *Alfred the Wise: Studies in Honour of Janet Bately on the Occasion of Her Sixty-Fifth Birthday*, ed. Jane Roberts, Janet L. Nelson, and Malcolm Godden (Cambridge, 1997), pp. 211–21.

[44] The chronology relating to Wulfstan's possible imprisonment is at best confused. Cyril Hart has argued that the Chronicle is inaccurate in its dating of the events of the early 950s and that Wulfstan's arrest in fact took place in 951: *The Early Charters of Northern England and the North Midlands* (Leicester, 1975), pp. 376–7. When Wulfstan might have been released is likewise

contains no certain instance of the incarceration of offenders.[45] Indeed, although Wormald does record a case of oath-breaking from the end of Alfred's reign, the punishment recorded for this offence was not imprisonment but forfeiture.[46] The significance of these facts is difficult to ascertain given the general discrepancy between the normative prescriptions of Anglo-Saxon law-codes and surviving records of actual judgments,[47] and to argue from negative evidence is, of course, always a dangerous approach. However, the striking scarcity of evidence for incarceration during the Anglo-Saxon period does at least suggest that this was not a commonplace judicial measure. With this in mind, therefore, it is worth examining in more detail those law-codes that do provide for the imprisonment of offenders.

Incarceration and the Nature of Anglo-Saxon Law

Characteristic of Anglo-Saxon legal writing is a desire to promote the idea of continuity and tradition, through which – according to Dorothy Bethurum – the statutes claim their force of authority.[48] This is evident in the construction of the *domboc* itself, in which the laws attributed to King Alfred are prefaced by a translation of the Mosaic Commandments and followed by a late seventh-century code attributed to Alfred's distant West Saxon predecessor Ine. It is also evident in the preamble to the Alfredian laws, recorded in the king's

---

unclear. The Chronicle does not explicitly mention his release but records that Wulfstan was restored to his episcopal duties in 954: *ASC* D, s.a. 954. John of Worcester explicitly links this restoration to the release of the Archbishop, and Smyth has seen a connection between the release of Wulfstan and the final expulsion of Eric Bloodaxe from Northumbria in this year: see *JW*, pp. 402–3; Smyth, *Scandinavian York and Dublin*, p. 173. However, that the archbishop was at liberty earlier than this is indicated by his witnessing a charter issued by Eadred in 953: see Hart, *Early Charters*, p. 377; Simon Keynes, 'Wulfstan I,' *Blackwell Encyclopaedia*, ed. Lapidge *et al.*, pp. 492–3. It seems likely, therefore, that any imprisonment was – in common with the stipulations in the laws of Alfred and Æthelstan – of relatively short duration.

[45] Patrick Wormald, 'A Handlist of Anglo-Saxon Lawsuits,' *Legal Culture*, pp. 253–87. Wormald does describe one case of the '[f]logging and imprisonment of a thief' (p. 274, no. 158), but this refers to an episode in ch. 46 of Wulfstan of Winchester's *Vita Æthelwoldi* in which the reference is in any case to the use of stocks rather than to incarceration.; see Wulfstan of Winchester, *The Life of St Æthelwold*, ed. Michael Lapidge and Michael Winterbottom (Oxford, 1991), pp. 68–9.

[46] Wormald, 'Handlist,' no. 27. The case is recorded in a charter of Edward granting the forfeited land (or part of it) to one Æthelwulf; see Pratt, *Political Thought*, pp. 239–40, who notes that additional penalties may have applied that were not relevant to the context of the charter.

[47] See Patrick Wormald, '*Lex Scripta* and *Verbum Regis*: Legislation and Germanic Kingship, from Euric to Cnut,' *Legal Culture*, pp. 1–43, at 21 and n. 97; Wormald, *Making of English Law*, p. 264. For Wormald's claim, on this and other evidence, that the written codes were not in fact intended to be used as guides for the practical application of the law, which depended instead upon oral pronouncement, see, for example, 'The Uses of Literacy in Anglo-Saxon England and its Neighbours,' *TRHS* 5th ser. 27 (1977), 95–114, at 111–13. In response, see Simon Keynes, 'Royal Government and the Written Word in Late Anglo-Saxon England,' *The Uses of Literacy in Early Medieval Europe*, ed. Rosamond McKitterick (Cambridge, 1990), pp. 226–57, at 235–45.

[48] Dorothy Bethurum, 'Stylistic Features of the Old English Laws,' *Modern Language Review* 27 (1932), 263–79, at 268.

voice, which describes how the king both endorsed many existing laws, and avoided recording too many of his own original laws out of concern for the judgment of posterity (Alfred Prologue 49.9). The assumed humility of this statement may, it is true, reflect an established legal *topos*.[49] However, whilst very few – if any – of the Alfredian laws can in fact be shown to have been taken over without modification or adaptation from pre-existing legislation, Wormald states that some 75% of these laws may, in a general way, be said to have been '"borrowed" from earlier English legislation.'[50]

If, however, the *domboc* as a whole displays a notable 'anxiety not to seem innovative,' this does not mean that innovation is totally absent from the Alfredian laws.[51] The opening law on oath-breaking, which is not paralleled in earlier Anglo-Saxon legislation, is a case in point. According to Wormald's stylistic analysis, the Alfredian code taken as a whole is strikingly traditional in its use of simple syntax and statements of consequence and value.[52] Deviations from this traditional legislative style, therefore, deserve closer examination. The first clause of the law on oath-breaking is just such a deviation, in that it constitutes a statement of principle, a feature identified by Wormald as characteristic of a more developed legislative style:

> Æt ærestan we lærað, þæt mæst ðearf is, þæt æghwelc mon his að ꞇ his wed wærlice healde.[53]
>
> We stipulate first, that which is most necessary, that each man should carefully fulfil his oath and his pledge.

In the clauses that follow, the inclusion of procedural detail relating to the prescription of incarceration similarly suggests a more ambitious legislative intention. We learn, for example, that prisoners without the means of providing food for themselves and without family to provide for them are to be the responsibility of the king's reeve (Alfred 1.3), that prisoners recaptured after an attempted escape from prison are to serve their full sentence (Alfred 1.6), and that those who succeed in making their escape are to be exiled and excommunicated (Alfred 1.7).

Wormald concludes from his stylistic analysis, and from the lack of direct precedent for the law on oath-breaking, that this law belongs among a group of about two dozen of the Alfredian statutes that 'were legislative in the sense that they seem to establish new legal principles.'[54] Indeed, as an innovation in Anglo-Saxon law-making the statute on oath-breaking may have had far reaching consequences. The endorsement of the Alfredian statute in II Edward refers specifically to an oath and pledge given by the whole population (*ðe eal ðeod geseald hæfð*),[55] by which is apparently meant an oath of loyalty

---

[49] Wormald, *Making of English Law*, pp. 277–8.
[50] Wormald, *Making of English Law*, pp. 281–2.
[51] Wormald, *Making of English Law*, p. 281. Cf. Pratt, *Political Thought*, pp. 238–41.
[52] Wormald, *Making of English Law*, pp. 271–2.
[53] Alfred 1. For the suggestion that the linguistic pairing of *að* and *wedd* also reflects the innovative nature of this statute, see above, n. 43.
[54] Wormald, *Making of English Law*, p. 282.
[55] II Edward 5.

to the king similar to that recorded later in the tenth century in the laws of Edmund (III Edmund 1). While such an oath is not necessarily implied in the wording of the Alfredian law, it is possible that the practice of extracting oaths of allegiance may have begun in England towards the end of Alfred's reign, possibly under the influence of Carolingian practice.[56] Such a practice would explain the prominence of the stipulation against oath-breaking in the *domboc* and the significance there attached to it. It may also explain the apparent influence of this law evident not only in II Edward but also in the legislation of Æthelstan's reign.

According to Wormald, the Alfredian law marks a turning point in the history of early medieval English law in that it for the first time equates criminal activity – particularly theft or connivance in theft – with a breach of fidelity.[57] Significantly, this same equation has also been noted by Sarah Foot in the legislation of Æthelstan, both in his own apparent use of oaths of loyalty and specifically in his laws concerning theft:

> To Æthelstan, as to his grandfather, Alfred, crime (and for Æthelstan, especially thieving) led to the disturbance of the peace and hence to disloyalty against the king himself and to his office. Breach of the peace became in his eyes tantamount to treachery, the breaking of a man's oath to the king, his lord.[58]

In this context, therefore, it is worth emphasizing the similarities between the Alfredian law on oath-breaking and the Grately legislation on theft. The Grately legislation does not begin with a statement of principle in quite the same way as the Alfredian statute, but it certainly starts with a forceful statement of intent:

> Ærest þæt mon ne sparige nænne þeof þe æt hæbbendre honda gefongen sy, ofer XII winter ˥ ofer eahta peningas.[59]

---

[56] Wormald, 'Handlist,' p. 284. See also Wormald, 'Oaths,' *Blackwell Encyclopaedia*, ed. Lapidge et al., pp. 338–9; Hudson, *Laws of England*, pp. 163–4.

[57] Wormald, *Making of English Law*, p. 148. Wormald's argument is merely hinted at here and elsewhere in his published writings, and was to be addressed in more detail in the projected second volume of his *Making of English Law*, unpublished at the time of his death. The direction that his argument was taking is indicated by draft material for what was to be chapter nine in this second volume, now part of the collected papers held by King's College London Archives (ref. K/PP148 Box 11): the wording of the Alfredian statute is 'appropriate for solemn and binding agreements' and seems to imply 'something more formal and specific than the duty to be a man of one's word' (22); the innovative nature of this practice is largely obscured by the 'self-consciously traditionalist' nature of the *domboc* (25–6); it is in the nature of Anglo-Saxon legislation 'to leave even basic principles to be reconstructed from a set of glimpses' but 'a series of suggestive hints' in the legislation from Alfred to Cnut supports the twin hypotheses that, firstly, the oath of loyalty was established in practice as a legal principle by the late ninth century (26), and, secondly, that like the oath recorded in the legislation of Cnut (II Cnut 21), it was 'designed to restrain a whole range of serious crimes, and above all theft' (24). I am grateful to King's College London Archives for permission to cite from this unpublished material, and to the staff thereof for their helpful assistance. Cf. Pratt, *Political Thought*, pp. 232–8.

[58] Foot, *Æthelstan*, p. 141. See also David Pratt, 'Written Law and the Communication of Authority in Tenth-Century England,' *England and the Continent in the Tenth Century: Studies in Honour of Wilhelm Levison (1876–1947)*, ed. David Rollason, Conrad Leyser and Hannah Williams (Turnhout, 2010), pp. 331–50, especially 338–41.

[59] II Æthelstan 1.

> Firstly, that no one spare any thief over twelve years old who is caught red-handed for a theft worth more than 8 pennies.

The term *ærest* here may refer simply to the fact that this is the first law of the collection. It is also possible, however, that there is an echo of the opening of the Alfredian oath-breaking law, and the implication seems to be that the law on theft is first in importance as well as in order. Moreover, like the Alfredian statute, the law on theft also introduces procedural detail: only a theft over the value of 8 pence committed by someone over the age of twelve will incur a capital sentence. And most noticeably, of course, the length of the prison sentence prescribed for convicted thieves mirrors that of the *domboc* exactly: a thief condemned to prison shall 'be forty nights in prison' (*beo XL nihta on carcerne*).

If Wormald is correct in his suggestion that the implications of the Alfredian law on oath-breaking extended to crimes such as theft, then the conclusion that the prescription of imprisonment in the laws of Æthelstan looks back to and builds upon this earlier innovation seems difficult to resist. If this is accepted, however, then the prescription of incarceration in the Alfredian law seems even more striking. Why should the *domboc* specify this apparently uncommon judicial measure in this first, most important, and most influential of its statutes, but not in any other?

A possible explanation for this may be seen in the parallels between the Alfredian law on oath-breaking and ecclesiastical practices of penance in early medieval Europe. As has been frequently noted, the *domboc* as a whole displays a consistent interest in the dual operation of judicial punishment and penitential expiation. Frantzen in particular has argued that the Alfredian legislation is 'the first to make ecclesiastical penance a part of secular punishment.'[60] This is evident in the opening law of the code. As we have seen above, the statute prescribing imprisonment for oath-breakers goes on to state that the prisoner must also make further atonement as prescribed by the bishop (*ðrowige ðær swa biscep him scrife*). The verb *scrifan* used here is part of a well-developed Old English vocabulary relating to the operation of penance.[61] Moreover, both the specification that penance is to be appointed by a bishop and the stipulation that the offender relinquish his weapons (*selle mid eaðmedum his wæpn ⁊ his æhta his freondum to gehealdanne*) mirror the prescriptions associated with the performance of public penance – reserved for the expiation of serious faults – in contemporary Continental documentation.[62]

---

[60] Allen J. Frantzen, *The Literature of Penance in Anglo-Saxon England* (New Brunswick, 1983), p. 126 and n. 11. Cf. Carole Hough, 'Penitential Literature and Secular Law in Anglo-Saxon England,' *Anglo-Saxon Studies in Archaeology and History* 11 (2000), 133–41, at 134. Compare also the essays by Stefan Jurasinski and Nicole Marafioti in this volume.

[61] Catherine Cubitt, 'Bishops, Priests and Penance in Late Saxon England,' *EME* 14 (2006), 41–63, at 44–8.

[62] Sarah Hamilton, 'Rites for Public Penance in Late Anglo-Saxon England,' *The Liturgy of the Late Anglo-Saxon Church*, ed. Helen Gittos and M. Bradford Bedingfield (London, 2005), pp. 65–103, at 66 and 84. See further, Brad Bedingfield, 'Public Penance in Anglo-Saxon England,' *ASE* 31 (2002), 223–55.

Similarly, the sentence of forty nights' imprisonment in the Alfredian code recalls both the common use of the forty-day period in the prescriptions of penitential handbooks, and the Lenten period during which those undertaking public penance were excluded from the Church.[63]

In a general way, the penitential overtones of the Alfredian statute reflect the increasing localization of the penitential experience – most frequently within a monastery – that has been seen as characteristic of Frankish practices during the eighth and ninth centuries.[64] It is, moreover, in the relatively extensive documentation of the Frankish church that the closest parallels for the *domboc*'s association of penitence and incarceration are to be found. The use of incarceration as a disciplinary measure – whilst not sanctioned by the *Rule of St Benedict* – was certainly not unknown in Frankish monasteries during the eighth and ninth centuries.[65] Of perhaps more direct relevance to the Alfredian legislation, however, is the fact that incarceration is also prescribed for members of the secular clergy in the writings of Chrodegang of Metz and Theodulf of Orléans, both of whom also attest the penitential function of the prison.

From the mid-eighth century, Chrodegang's *Regula canonicorum* – ostensibly written for the episcopal community at Metz but perhaps promulgated at the Synod of Ver in 755 – provided one of the first rules for the canonical life.[66] In it, the imprisonment of canons is stipulated for the correction of grave faults such as murder, fornication and theft.[67] Once imprisoned, the miscreant is to be left alone to undertake penance for a duration to be determined by the superior of the community (*solus persistens in poenitentia lucta, quamvis priori visum est*). On his release, he is to continue to undertake public penance at the discretion of the episcopal authorities (*si episcopo vel qui sub eo visum fuerit, agat adhuc publicam poenitentiam*).[68] In the early years of the ninth century, an episcopal statute written by Theodulf similarly attests to the use of incarceration as a corrective measure for wayward clergy, stipulating imprisonment as an alternative to loss of ecclesiastical office for any priest guilty of attempting

---

[63] Hamilton, 'Rites for Public Penance,' pp. 69–83.
[64] Dominique Iogna-Prat, 'Topographies of Penance in the Latin West (c. 800–c. 1200),' trans. Graham Robert Edwards, *A New History of Penance*, ed. Abigail Firey (Leiden, 2008), pp. 149–72, at 152–3. See also Mayke de Jong, 'What Was *Public* About Public Penance? Paenitentia publica and Justice in the Carolingian World,' *Settimane di Studio del Centro Italiano di Studi Sull'Alto Medioevo* 44 (1997), 863–904; Mayke de Jong, 'Monastic Prisoners or Opting Out? Political Coercion and Honour in the Frankish Kingdoms,' *Topographies of Power in the Early Middle Ages*, ed. Mayke de Jong, Frans Theuws and Carine van Rhijn (Leiden, 2001), pp. 291–328.
[65] Pugh, *Imprisonment*, pp. 374–5; Peters, 'Prison Before the Prison,' pp. 27–8. In addition to the examples discussed by Pugh and Peters, in the early 740s the *Concilium germanicum* stipulated the imprisonment of monks and nuns as a punishment for fornication: Albert Werminghoff, ed., *Concilia aevi Karolini*, MGH Conc. 2.1 (Hanover, 1906), p. 4.
[66] Cited from the text in Jerome Bertram, *The Chrodegang Rules: The Rules for the Common Life of the Secular Clergy from the Eighth and Ninth Centuries* (Aldershot, 2005), pp. 27–51.
[67] Bertram, *Chrodegang Rules*, ch. 15.
[68] On the importance of penance in regulations for the canonical life, see Sarah Hamilton, *The Practice of Penance, 900–1050* (Woodbridge, 2001), pp. 98–102.

bribery to obtain a more favourable parish.[69] Moreover, the imprisonment envisaged is again explicitly penitential in conception (*in carceris aerumna longo tempore paenitentiam agendo detinendum*).

Each of these texts was widely influential throughout the period of ecclesiastical reform in Francia during the late eighth and ninth centuries. Chrodegang's rule was a principal source for the *Institutio canonicorum* promulgated by Louis the Pious in 816×17, and in the mid-ninth century an enlarged version of the *Regula* was produced which in turn drew significantly upon the provision of the 816×17 statute.[70] Similarly, the formulation of the episcopal and pastoral responsibilities of the clergy in Theodulf's *Capitulary* were to have 'the most profound influence on his colleagues in the succeeding decades, both as a source for actual prescriptions, and as an inspiration.'[71] Beyond the possibility of the particular influence of these texts, however, it is noteworthy that in both texts the reference to the incarceration of clerics for penitential and disciplinary purposes is introduced without any overt explanation or justification, and without any practical directions regarding how or where the stipulation should be enforced. It seems reasonable to conclude, therefore, that the practice of ecclesiastical incarceration attested in these texts was in fact sufficiently commonplace in Francia during this period for both Chrodegang and Theodulf to assume that their audiences would be familiar with it.

From the later tenth century, both the *Regula canonicorum* and Theodulf's *Capitulary* were apparently well known in England. The Latin text of the enlarged *Regula canonicorum* is preserved to varying degrees of completeness in four insular manuscripts from the tenth and eleventh centuries, the earliest of which can be dated to the final decade of the reign of Æthelstan.[72] The remaining three manuscripts, all of eleventh-century provenance, record not only the Latin text but also an Old English translation of the enlarged *Regula*, apparently undertaken in the mid-tenth century, a single chapter of which also survives independently in one further eleventh-century manuscript.[73] The *Capitulary*, which Sauer describes as 'a fairly popular text in late tenth and eleventh-century England,' also survives in four English manuscripts, the earliest of which is dated to the first half of the eleventh century.[74] The importance of this text in the late Anglo-Saxon period is perhaps suggested by the fact that it was translated into Old English not once, but

---

[69] Peter Brommer, ed., *Capitula episcoporum*, MGH Capit. episc. 1 (Hanover, 1984), p. 114, ch. 16.
[70] See further, Brigitte Langefeld, ed. and trans., *The Old English Version of the Enlarged Rule of Chrodegang* (Frankfurt, 2003), pp. 8–15; Julia Barrow, 'Review Article: Chrodegang, his Rule and its Successors,' *EME* 14 (2006), 201–12, at 201–5.
[71] Rosamond McKitterick, *The Frankish Church and the Carolingian Reforms, 789–895* (London, 1977), pp. 45–79, at 52–3.
[72] Langefeld, *Old English Chrodegang*, pp. 43–50.
[73] For recent opinions on the date of the translation, see Langefeld, *Old English Chrodegang*, pp. 125–44; Michael D. C. Drout, 'Re-Dating the Old English Translation of the Enlarged Rule of Chrodegang: The Evidence of the Prose Style,' *JEGP* 103 (2004), 341–68.
[74] Hans Sauer, ed., *Theodulfi capitula in England* (Munich, 1978), p. 508.

twice, the earlier translation dated by its editor to the second half of the tenth century.[75]

Whether penitential incarceration was in fact ever practised by the Anglo-Saxon Church is, again, uncertain. As the above discussion makes clear, there is no clear documentary or archaeological evidence to support the use of prisons in ecclesiastical discipline in England in this period.[76] It is perhaps suggestive, however, that incarceration is associated with ecclesiastical penitence in two late Old English texts associated with Archbishop Wulfstan, who was certainly familiar with Theodulf's *Capitulary* and probably also knew the *Regula canonicorum* in its revised form.[77]

The first of these Old English texts is the spurious eleventh-century legal 'forgery' known as the Laws of Edward and Guthrum. Probably the work of Wulfstan himself, this text, ostensibly an accord between the West Saxon and Viking rulers agreed during the reign of Alfred and reissued by his son Edward, displays the interest of its compiler in the mutual reinforcement of secular punishment and religious penance, and in the responsibilities and duties of the priesthood.[78] According to the stipulations of this text, a priest who is guilty of a serious offence – which here includes not only adultery and theft, but interestingly also perjury (*forswerigan*) – must make not only legal redress but also spiritual redress in accordance with canonical teaching (*for Gode huru bete, swa canon tæce*).[79] The same statute goes on to state, moreover, that if the offender is unable to provide securities, he is to submit to imprisonment (*carcern gebuge*). Similarly, the short text of the so-called *Handbook for Use of a Confessor* contained in Oxford, Bodleian Library, MS Junius 121 (fols 23v–4r, 54v–7v), which also seems to have been compiled by Wulfstan or by someone close to him, both laments the frequent shortcomings of the clergy and emphasizes their need to undertake penance 'according to canonical prescription' (*æfter canon dome*).[80] The text of the *Handbook* in Junius 121,

---

[75] Sauer, *Theodulfi capitula in England*, pp. 510–13. On possible objections to Sauer's dating, see Malcolm Godden, 'Review: *Theodulfi capitula in England*,' *MÆ* 48 (1979), 262–5.

[76] Excavations of the monastic foundation at Wearmouth have identified a small, sunken structure associated with a building phase dated to the late seventh or early eighth century, which was initially and tentatively identified as 'an external strong room or prison'; see Rosemary J. Cramp, 'Monastic Sites,' *The Archaeology of Anglo-Saxon England*, ed. David M. Wilson (London, 1976), pp. 201–52, at 234. The final report of the excavations, however, identified this feature as 'a storage room or a latrine': Rosemary Cramp et al., *Wearmouth and Jarrow Monastic Sites*, vol. 1 (Swindon, 2005–6), p. 104.

[77] On Wulfstan's knowledge of Theodulf's *Capitulary*, see Hans Sauer, 'The Transmission and Structure of Archbishop Wulfstan's "Commonplace Book",' *Old English Prose: Basic Readings*, ed. Paul E. Szarmach (New York, 2000), pp. 339–93, at 342–3, 349, 361, and 372–3; Wormald, *Making of English Law*, pp. 213–18. On his knowledge of the *Regula canonicorum*, see Langefeld, *Rule of Chrodegang*, pp. 20 and 47–50.

[78] On Wulfstan's authorship of this document, see Dorothy Whitelock, 'Wulfstan and the So-Called Laws of Edward and Guthrum,' *EHR* 56 (1941), 1–21. Wormald dates the composition of the text to c. 1006–8: 'Archbishop Wulfstan: Eleventh-Century State-Builder,' *Wulfstan*, ed. Townend, pp. 9–27, at 10, 15–16, and 26. Cf. Wormald, *Making of English Law*, pp. 389–91.

[79] Edward and Guthrum 3.

[80] Roger Fowler, 'A Late Old English Handbook for the Use of a Confessor,' *Anglia* 83 (1965), 1–34, at 27, line 311. Cf. Allen J. Frantzen, *The Anglo-Saxon Penitentials: A Cultural Database*,

which may represent Wulfstan's original composition,[81] contains a further sentence that is not recorded in other copies of the text, outlining the nature of the penance such clerics might expect to undertake and recommending the use of the prison (*carcern*) alongside measures such as bondage, darkness, scourging, and mutilation.[82]

Whether or not such penitential measures were ever applied, it is clear that a practice of ecclesiastical incarceration associated with penance was known in Anglo-Saxon England from the second half of the tenth century. It is at least possible that this practice was also known in the late ninth century and that its influence might be seen in the innovative legal prescriptions of the *domboc*. Knowledge of the *Regula canonicorum* in the ninth century has been suggested by those who see its influence in the episcopal reforms instituted at Christ Church, Canterbury, by Archbishop Wulfred in 813.[83] Whilst this remains a contentious issue, Wulfred himself, who has been described as a man 'strongly Francophone in his theological tastes and ambitions for the reform of the English Church,'[84] would certainly have observed Frankish practices during the two journeys that he undertook to Rome, and the nature and timing of his reforms seem to indicate close links between ecclesiastical developments in England and on the Continent in this period.

Such links are likely to have been particularly close during the final decades of the ninth century at the court of King Alfred. Strong connections between the house of Wessex and Francia had been established since at least the middle of the ninth century, during the reign of Alfred's father Æthelwulf, as reflected by the latter's marriage to Judith, daughter of Charles the Bald, during the West Saxon king's protracted stay with the Carolingian ruler following a visit to Rome in 855×6.[85] Alfred himself accompanied his father on this visit, and during his own reign recruited the service of Continental scholars such as Grimbald and John the Saxon. Such direct connections with the Continent are apparent in the literary output of the last decade of Alfred's reign. The Anglo-Saxon Chronicle, the origins of which are usually located in Alfred's circle, has been seen as a response to Carolingian models of historiography, and Grimbald himself might have figured largely

---

online at http://www.anglo-saxon.net/penance/index.html, accessed 6 January 2014. On Wulfstan's connection with the *Handbook*, see Joyce Tally Lionarons, *The Homiletic Writings of Archbishop Wulfstan: A Critical Study* (Cambridge, 2010), pp. 133–6.

[81] Lionarons, *Homiletic Writings*, p. 135.
[82] Fowler, 'Handbook for the Use of a Confessor,' p. 27, line 316 and note.
[83] See further Joanna Story, *Carolingian Connections: Anglo-Saxon England and Carolingian Francia, c. 750–870* (Aldershot, 2003), pp. 202–8. Brigitte Langefeld has argued that Wulfred's reforms 'aimed at a monastic restoration based on the familiar *Regula S Benedicti*, rather than a secular innovation on the basis of Chrodegang's Rule': '*Regula canonicorum* or *Regula monasterialis uitae*? The Rule of Chrodegang and Archbishop Wulfred's Reforms at Canterbury,' *ASE* 25 (1996), 21–36, at 35. But cf. Nicholas Brooks, 'Was Cathedral Reform at Christ Church Canterbury in the Early Ninth Century of Continental Inspiration?' *Anglo-Saxon England and the Continent*, ed. Hans Sauer, Joanna Story, and Gaby Waxenberger (Tempe, AZ, 2011), pp. 303–22.
[84] Story, *Carolingian Connections*, p. 202.
[85] Story, *Carolingian Connections*, pp. 224–43.

in its original conception.⁸⁶ Similar arguments have long been made for the apparent Frankish influence on Asser's *Life of King Alfred*.⁸⁷ More recently, the influence of Carolingian literary models has been detected in the construction of the prologues and epilogues to the Old English translation of the *Pastoral Care*, perhaps a work undertaken by the king himself or by one or more of his close followers.⁸⁸ Finally, and perhaps most significantly, Grimbald's influence has also been seen as a motivating factor underlying the incorporation of penitential teaching into the Alfredian legal code.⁸⁹ A monk of St Bertin, Grimbald was sent to England at Alfred's request by a reluctant Fulk of Rheims with a specific view to reforming the English Church in line with Frankish practice.⁹⁰ Through his association with Rheims, Grimbald has been identified as a likely conduit for contemporary Frankish legal ideologies associated with Fulk's predecessor Hincmar, and also as the probable source of the renewal of interest in penitential literature in England evident from the early tenth century, the origins of which might be traced to Alfred's reign.⁹¹

In the light of these connections, it does not seem implausible that the practice of penitential incarceration attested in Frankish sources in the eighth and ninth centuries should have been known in Alfred's court at the close of the ninth century, or that such a practice might – perhaps through the direct agency of Grimbald – have influenced the prescription of incarceration as the penalty for oath-breaking in the first statute of the Alfredian legislation. Such an assumption provides a context for the apparently innovative use of judicial incarceration in this statute. It also accords well with modern critical appreciations of the ideological conception of the *domboc*.

While Wormald was probably overly dogmatic in his assertion that the Alfredian code was 'designed more for symbolic impact than for practical direction,' it is nevertheless clear that the construction of the *domboc* does

---

86 J. M. Wallace-Hadrill, 'The Franks and the English in the Ninth Century: Some Common Historical Interests,' *History* 35 (1950), 202–18, at 212–14; M. B. Parkes, 'The Palaeography of the Parker Manuscript of the *Chronicle*, Laws and Sedulius, and Historiography at Winchester in the Late Ninth and Tenth Centuries,' *ASE* 5 (1976), 149–71, at 163–6. Cf. Alice Sheppard, *Families of the King: Writing Identity in the Anglo-Saxon Chronicle* (Toronto, 2004), pp. 120–5.
87 See Simon Keynes and Michael Lapidge, *Alfred the Great* (London, 1983), pp. 54–5.
88 Malcolm Godden, 'Prologues and Epilogues in the Old English *Pastoral Care*, and their Carolingian Models,' *JEGP* 110 (2011), 441–73.
89 Stefan Jurasinski, 'Violence, Penance, and Secular Law in Alfred's Mosaic Prologue,' *HSJ* 22 (2010), 25–42, especially 40–2. Grimbald's possible influence over the composition of the *domboc* assumes, of course, that it was produced after his arrival in the late 880s. On the traditional dating after 893, see Simon Keynes, 'The Power of the Written Word: Alfredian England, 871–899,' *Alfred the Great*, ed. Reuter, pp.175–97, at 192–3.
90 D. Whitelock, M. Brett and C. N. L. Brooke, eds, *Councils and Synods, with other Documents Relating to the English Church*, vol. 1: *A. D. 871–1204* (Oxford, 1981), pp. 6–12. See further Malcolm Godden, 'Stories From the Court of King Alfred,' *Saints and Scholars: New Perspectives on Anglo-Saxon Literature and Culture in Honour of Hugh Magennis*, ed. Stuart McWilliams (Cambridge, 2012), pp. 123–40, at 135–7.
91 On the influence of Hincmar's conception of secular and divine law, see Wormald, *Making of English Law*, pp. 423–6; Pratt, *Political Thought*, pp. 222–30. For Grimbald's influence on penitential practice, see Frantzen, *Literature of Penance*, pp. 125–7.

indeed reveal an ideological purpose.⁹² The Mosaic preface to the Alfredian laws, complete with its account of the subsequent refinement of the law by the Apostolic Church (Alfred Preface 49.1–5) and by many subsequent synodal decrees (*monega senoðbec*),⁹³ establishes a context for the secular code within 'a continuum of divine law-giving.'⁹⁴ As such, the lengthy preface not only acts as an authorizing device for the following legislation, but also implicitly collapses the distinction between secular law and divine commandment.⁹⁵ In this the first law on oath-breaking may again be seen to be crucial. Not only does this law potentially attest to an innovative connection between crime and breach of fidelity to the king, but, by employing an otherwise uncommon punishment that, as I argue, reflects ecclesiastical penitential practices, it further equates infidelity with sin.

To sum up, my analysis of the evidence for the use of incarceration as a judicial punishment in late Anglo-Saxon England suggests the following conclusions. In the first place, the evidence suggests that imprisonment was not in fact a common measure. This is not to say that the practice was unknown, but it does seem that dedicated prisons were rare and that the custody of criminals or the summary detention of enemies would have habitually taken place without recourse to such facilities. So much is suggested, indeed, by the infrequent references to imprisonment for judicial purposes found in extant legal sources. The inclusion of procedural detail pertaining to incarceration in the Alfredian code strongly implies that such procedures were not well established, and the recognition in Æthelstan's laws that facilities for the incarceration of offenders might not be available in all cases clearly testifies to their scarcity. There is strong reason to believe, therefore, that the stipulation of incarceration in the *domboc* represents an innovative use of a largely unfamiliar judicial punishment.

It has long been suspected that the Alfredian legislation attests to a new development in Anglo-Saxon law-making through its incorporation of penance within secular judgment. In this context it is telling that the closest parallels for the combination of penance and incarceration in the *domboc* occur in Continental prescriptions for ecclesiastical penance. Whilst knowledge of such prescriptions is not attested in Anglo-Saxon England in the late ninth century, it is by no means unlikely that this practice would have been familiar in the cosmopolitan court of King Alfred from which the *domboc* seems to have originated, and I suggest that such prescriptions should be viewed as

---

⁹² Wormald, *Making of English Law*, p. 427.
⁹³ Alfred Preface 49.8
⁹⁴ Pratt, *Political Thought*, p. 222. See also Wormald, *Making of English Law*, p. 426. Wormald's suggestion that this legal ideology should be viewed in the light of a broader 'Alfredian' conception of the English as a chosen race is perhaps more eloquent than convincing. Cf. George Molyneaux, '*The Old English Bede*: English Ideology or Christian Instruction?' *EHR* 124 (2009), 1289–1323.
⁹⁵ Wormald, *Making of English Law*, p. 429: 'Crime could now be perceived as an outrage against God, punishment as the expression of His anger.'

a likely influence on the stipulation of imprisonment in the Alfredian laws. Moreover, if Wormald is correct about the role of the oath-breaking law in the process by which crime came to be seen as a breach of fidelity, then the prominent role of imprisonment here might have significant implications regarding the ideology of kingship that lies behind the Alfredian laws. The construction of the *domboc*, with its Mosaic preface together with its engagement with the idea of penance, gives the king's secular law something of the force of divine teaching; in turn, the first law on oath-breaking implicitly defines the law in relation to the person of the king himself.[96]

The broader implications of this suggestion cannot be pursued further here. For the purposes of the present study, it is sufficient to note that the significant role the stipulation of incarceration plays in the opening of the Alfredian legislation appears to have been recognized by Alfred's immediate successors. The law on oath-breaking is endorsed in the legislation of Edward the Elder, and it has been argued above that the prescription of incarceration for theft in Æthelstan's major Grately legislation also looks back to the Alfredian law. Whilst the prescriptions of Æthelstan's laws are not explicit about the penitential nature of incarceration, the final concern of the Grately code does emphasize the importance of penance as a punishment for oath-breaking, requiring that oath-breakers be refused Christian burial unless their bishop testifies that they have performed the penance assigned to them by their confessor (*swa him his scrift scrife*).[97] Moreover, the prescription of imprisonment in this code not only mirrors the forty-day period appointed for oath-breakers in the *domboc* – the penitential overtones of which have been noted above – but also stipulated a longer period of 120 days' incarceration that is also suggestive of penitential practice. Penance of 120 days' duration is frequently prescribed in early medieval penitential manuals, corresponding to the 'three Lents' – the forty-day fasts associated with Advent, Lent, and Pentecost.[98]

However, whilst the ramifications of the engagement with the idea of penance in the Alfredian laws can be seen in later tenth- and eleventh-century legislation, the innovative use of judicial incarceration in the *domboc* seems not to have had a similarly lasting influence.[99] The testimony of the Old English *Soliloquies* – the starting point of this study – does indicate an expectation that a royal estate might contain a prison, and, whether one wishes to date this text to the later part of the reign of King Alfred or to the first decades of the tenth century, its origins belong to the period during which incarceration featured in the law-codes as a judicial punishment.[100] Such an expectation cannot, however, be taken as evidence for the widespread presence of prisons in late Anglo-Saxon England. There is no unambiguous evidence that judicial

---

[96] Compare the essay by Daniela Fruscione in this volume, pp. 00–00.
[97] II Æthelstan 26.
[98] See Frantzen, *Literature of Penance*, p. 16; Foot, *Æthelstan*, p. 146.
[99] On the increasing visibility of penitential discipline within the post-Alfredian law-codes, see Frantzen, *Literature of Penance*, pp. 146–7.
[100] See above, n. 4.

imprisonment was in fact practised during the successive reigns of Alfred, Edward, and Æthelstan, and incarceration was apparently not prescribed as a judicial measure in law-codes issued after Æthelstan's death.[101] One possible explanation for this state of affairs, hinted at in the contingencies outlined in VI Æthelstan, is that whilst incarceration might have been practical as an exceptional and visible measure reserved for high-status cases such as, perhaps, that of Wulfstan I of York, the wider use of prisons for judicial purposes might have posed both problems of both administration and finance. Howsoever this may be, the evidence seems to suggest that if the normative stipulation of incarceration in the *domboc* does indeed represent an innovation in Anglo-Saxon law, the ideological motivation behind this innovation was not sufficiently strongly felt to leave a lasting mark upon judicial practice in late Anglo-Saxon England.

---

[101] Terminology is again an issue here. The laws of Cnut do perhaps refer to imprisonment in their stipulation that those accused of a crime for whom no-one is prepared to stand surety should be detained before undergoing the ordeal: 'gebuge he hengenne ⁊ þær gebide, oð ðæt he ga to Godes ordale' (II Cnut 35, and cf. *Grið* 16). However, the precise meaning of *hengen* in this context is unclear, and the possibility that this could refer to the stocks, or to some other form of physical detention apart from incarceration, is supported by Alfred 35.2, in which the term is used in the context of personal vendettas. In any case, the detention in II Cnut 35 is clearly custodial in nature.

6

Earthly Justice and Spiritual Consequences: Judging and Punishing in the Old English *Consolation of Philosophy*

Nicole Marafioti

For all the mutilation and execution in this volume, there has been little discussion of the people who issued and implemented judicial sentences in Anglo-Saxon England. While responsibility for the capture, imprisonment, and upkeep of offenders was occasionally assigned to specific individuals in pre-Conquest legislation, corporal penalties rarely designated an agent for the exercise of justice.[1] Instead, the harshest punishments were often articulated with an impersonal construction: let the thieving hand be cut off (*slea mon þa hond*); let the adulteress lose her nose and ears (*heo polige nasa ⁊ earena*); let the traitor's life be forfeit (*si he his feores scyldig*).[2] Although execution cemeteries confirm that both lethal and non-lethal penalties were in fact carried out, it is unclear who exactly oversaw these judicial tasks.[3] The most visible face of justice was the king, who was invariably depicted as the promulgator and enforcer of law in Anglo-Saxon legislation. Even if he was only infrequently involved in the day-to-day work of judging and condemning criminals, the king was consistently portrayed as the source and keeper of the peace.[4] In practice, however, most acts of justice would have been handled on a local level, with lesser magnates initiating legal proceedings on their own authority

---

[1] Patrick Wormald, 'Charters, Law and the Settlement of Disputes in Anglo-Saxon England,' *Legal Culture*, pp. 289–311, at 304–6.

[2] The Anglo-Saxon laws are edited by Liebermann, *Gesetze* I; all subsequent citations follow Liebermann's titles and chapter numbers, unless otherwise noted. The laws quoted above are Alfred 6, II Cnut 53, and V Æthelred 30.

[3] For executed bodies in the archaeological record, see Reynolds, *Deviant Burial*; Andrew Reynolds, 'The Definition and Ideology of Anglo-Saxon Execution Sites and Cemeteries,' *Death and Burial in Medieval Europe: Papers of the 'Medieval Europe Brugge 1997' Conference*, vol. 2, ed. Guy De Boe and Frans Verhaeghe (Zellik, 1997), pp. 33–41; Dawn M. Hadley and Jo Buckberry, 'Caring for the Dead in Late Anglo-Saxon England,' *Pastoral Care*, ed. Tinti, pp. 121–47, at 128–30. Additional recent work on Anglo-Saxon execution sites and cemeteries includes J. L. Buckberry and D. M. Hadley, 'An Anglo-Saxon Execution Cemetery at Walkington Wold, Yorkshire,' *Oxford Journal of Archaeology* 26 (2007), 309–29; Graham Hayman and Andrew Reynolds, 'A Saxon and Saxo-Norman Execution Cemetery at 42–54 London Road, Staines,' *ArchJ* 162 (2005), 215–55; Martin Carver, *Sutton Hoo: A Seventh-Century Princely Burial Ground and its Context* (London, 2005), especially chs 8 and 9.

[4] Patrick Wormald, '*Lex Scripta* and *Verbum Regis*: Legislation and Germanic Kingship, from Euric to Cnut,' *Legal Culture*, pp. 1–43, especially 39–41; Hurnard, *King's Pardon*, pp. 1–5.

and imposing punishments within their jurisdictions.⁵ Yet even in these cases, the king remained the ultimate source of mercy for the condemned, retaining the right to commute or reduce sentences.⁶ Judges might choose from a range of punishments or arbitrate a settlement, but the king could always claim the final word.

So what of the individuals who were responsible for passing judgment in the first place? Whether they were royal reeves, bishops, or other local authority figures, their job cannot have been an easy one. Judges as a group were often chastised by Old English commentators, who complained regularly, if abstractly, about abuses of judicial power. While such general accusations cannot provide an accurate measure of corruption in Anglo-Saxon England, they certainly reflect a stereotype of individuals subverting justice in favor of personal gain. Authors from Alcuin to Ælfric denounced those who issued unjust judgments for their own benefit, affirming that judges who submitted to bribery would 'endure vengeance on Judgment Day' [in Dei judicio vindictam sustinebit] and suffer 'eternal torments with the treacherous devil' [mid þam swicolan deofle þa ecan susle].⁷ More troubling than the greedy judge was the ignorant judge, who did not know which sentence was appropriate and chose the most brutal one; or the bloodthirsty judge, who was so eager to start lopping off body parts that he neglected the truth.⁸ A worst-case scenario is presented in Lantfred's *Miracles of St Swithun*, in which a wrongly accused innocent had much of his body amputated, pierced, poked out, and ripped off – all thanks to the cruel indifference of his judges.⁹ Even members

---

⁵ Shire, hundred, and other local courts are specifically referenced in I Edgar 7, III Edgar 5–5.2, IV Edgar 3–6.2, and II Cnut 18–19: see Patrick Wormald, 'Giving God and King their Due: Conflict and its Regulation in the Early English State,' *Legal Culture*, pp. 333–57, at 346–9; Wormald, 'Charters, Law and the Settlement of Disputes,' p. 304. The role of the aristocracy in administering justice is discussed by Stephen Baxter, *The Earls of Mercia: Lordship and Power in Late Anglo-Saxon England* (Oxford, 2007), pp. 109–18; and royal reeves are treated by Catherine Cubitt, '"As the Lawbook Teaches": Reeves, Lawbooks and Urban Life in the Anonymous Old English Legend of the Seven Sleepers,' *EHR* 124 (2009), 1021–49.

⁶ Hurnard, *King's Pardon*, pp. 1–5.

⁷ The quotations are taken respectively from ch. 20 of Alcuin's *De virtutibus et vitiis*, PL 101, cols 628–9, at 628D; and Ælfric's homily on Ahitophel and Absolom, edited by Skeat, LS I, p. 430, lines 237–8. For Alcuin as a judicial reformer, see Paul Fouracre, 'Carolingian Justice: The Rhetoric of Improvement and Contexts of Abuse,' *Settimane di Studio del Centro Italiano di Studi Sull'Alto Medioevo* 42 (1995), 771–803, at 778–9.

⁸ From the reign of Alfred, there is an emphasis on curbing variation and abuse in judicial sentences, in part through the use of written law. This is discussed extensively in ch. 106 of Asser's *Life of King Alfred*: see William Henry Stevenson, ed., *Asser's Life of King Alfred together with the Annals of Saint Neots* (Oxford, 1959), pp. 92–5; the text is translated by Simon Keynes and Michael Lapidge, *Alfred the Great* (London, 1983), pp. 109–10, with commentary at 275. Concern with just judgment is also articulated in the Mosaic prologue to the *domboc*, particularly in Alfred Prol. 40, 41, 43, and 46: see Michael Treschow, 'The Prologue to Alfred's Law Code: Instruction in the Spirit of Mercy,' *Florilegium* 13 (1994), 79–110, especially 99–102 for Alfred's adaptation of the biblical text in these clauses. The topic also appears prominently in the prologue to I Edward and in III Edgar 3.

⁹ Lantfred's *Miracula* was composed in the 970s; the above-mentioned episode is edited in Lapidge, *Swithun*, pp. 312–13. The relation of this passage to Old English law was established by Dorothy Whitelock, 'Wulfstan *Cantor* and Anglo-Saxon Law,' *Nordica et Anglica: Studies in Honor of Stefan Einarsson*, ed. A. H. Orrick (The Hague, 1968), pp. 83–92.

of the clergy were known to play fast and loose with secular punishments, despite canonical prohibitions against clerical bloodshed. Bishop Theodred of London, for one, reportedly hanged a gaggle of thieves who had been caught robbing the shrine of St Edmund; it was only after their execution that he consulted his books and learned that churchmen were forbidden to issue death sentences.[10] The repeated injunctions in Ælfric's pastoral letters against clergy participating in criminal sentencing indicate that this type of behavior was not simply a hagiographical trope but a point of concern for churchmen whose position in the world required their participation in earthly justice.[11] Each of these texts urged righteous and commensurate justice, but they were all founded on an anxiety – perhaps even an expectation – that judges could not or would not do their jobs well.

Despite their interest in the spiritual consequences of issuing judgments, however, none of these sources explicitly considered how judges themselves might have coped with the moral implications of their work. Given the subjectivity involved in rendering judgment, as well as the potentially fine line between justice and cruelty, there must have been uncertainty about how a lifetime's worth of judicial sentences might affect a judge's soul. In the early eleventh century, the self-consciously merciful (*friðlice*) laws of Archbishop Wulfstan prescribed painful but non-lethal punishments to preserve God's handiwork (*godes handgeweorc*), sparing offenders' lives long enough for them to repent their sins and save their souls.[12] Yet as an archbishop who was deeply involved in worldly affairs, Wulfstan may also have had the souls of judges in mind as he drafted his legislation concerning milder punishments. If an innocent was condemned through a mistaken or corrupt judgment, at least the judge would not face the spiritual consequences of having issued an irreversible capital sentence. Of course, even the life-sparing penalties Wulfstan championed could be abused by those in power. *Swithun's* malicious accusers (*nefandis criminalibus*) convinced a judge to condemn an innocent man to mutilation, a brutal miscarriage of justice which perverted a righteous royal law.[13] For someone like Bishop Theodred, by contrast, who lamented the finality of the death sentences he erroneously issued, the implementation of non-lethal punishments could help ensure that no permanent spiritual harm would be done – to the judge or to the condemned.

The gravity of these examples suggest that for an Anglo-Saxon judge, responsible for a lifetime's worth of difficult or contentious verdicts, earthly

---

[10] The story first appears in Abbo's Latin *Vita* in the mid-980s; it was adapted into Old English by Ælfric some two decades later. The Latin is edited by Michael Winterbottom, *Three Lives of English Saints* (Toronto, 1972), pp. 65–87; the Old English is edited by Skeat, *LS* II, pp. 314–35.

[11] Ælfric's pastoral letters are edited by Bernhard Fehr, *Die Hirtenbriefe Ælfrics in altenglischer und lateinischer fassung* (Hamburg, 1914; repr. 1966). I discuss the letters' treatment of clerical participation in secular judgments in greater depth in 'Punishing Bodies and Saving Souls: Capital and Corporal Punishment in Late Anglo-Saxon England,' *HSJ* 20 (2008), 39–57.

[12] 'Ne forspille for lytlum Godes handgeweorc ꝼ his agenne ceap, þe he deore gebohte': V Æthelred 3–3.1. For Wulfstan's life-sparing punishments, see Whitelock, 'Wulfstan *Cantor*,' pp. 85–6; Marafioti, 'Punishing Bodies,' pp. 51–7; Thompson, *Dying and Death*, pp. 182–4.

[13] Lapidge, *Swithun*, pp. 312–13.

accusations of corruption or cruelty might be the least of his problems. Even the most rigorous judge could make an occasional mistake, just as a well-intentioned law could become an instrument of cruelty instead of order. How would the accidental condemnation of an innocent or an over-zealous application of the law affect the judge's own soul? The remainder of this essay will investigate how concerns about the morality of judging and punishing were addressed in the Old English *Consolation of Philosophy*, a work adapted from Boethius's Latin text in the late ninth or early tenth century, purportedly as part of King Alfred's vernacular translation program.[14] Boethius, writing in the early sixth century, structured his philosophical treatise as a dialogue with the personification of Philosophy. The Old English rendition frames the text as a discussion between Boethius's mind (*Mod*) and the personification of Wisdom, reconfiguring the philosophical themes of the original for a Christian Anglo-Saxon audience.[15]

The following discussion will focus on chapter 38 of the Old English prose text, a discourse on judicial punishment in which Wisdom grapples with the spiritual implications of earthly justice, both for criminals and for judges.[16] In its treatment of the moral hazards faced by judges, the *Consolation* anticipated by more than a century the conflation of earthly and spiritual penalties that would become a defining feature of Archbishop Wulfstan's legislation.[17] While prescriptions for penance in Alfred's *domboc* have been understood as an early attempt to align secular justice with spiritual interests, Wisdom's discourse – which expands significantly on Boethius' original text – uses explicitly penitential rhetoric to construct a nuanced argument about

---

[14] For discussions of Alfred's authorship, see particularly M. R. Godden, 'Did King Alfred Write Anything?' *MÆ* 76 (2007), 1–23; Janet Bately, 'Did King Alfred Actually Translate Anything? The Integrity of the Alfredian Canon Revisited,' *MÆ* 78 (2009), 189–215.

[15] For the adaptation of Boethius's Latin text, see especially Nicole Guenther Discenza, *The King's English: Strategies of Translation in the Old English Boethius* (Albany, 2005), with a discussion of the figure of Wisdom at pp. 88–9. It is significant, in the context of the discussion to follow, that the name Wisdom itself evokes law and judgment (OE *dom*). The concepts of wisdom and wise judgment likewise figure in Alfred's *domboc* and in other texts associated with his reign; see for example Wormald, *Making of English Law*, pp. 427–9.

[16] The full version of the prose text is preserved in MS Oxford, Bodleian Library, Bodley 180 (designated MS B). The standard edition is Godden and Irvine, *OE Boethius*: the text is edited in vol. I, with translation and commentary in vol. II. The following discussion concentrates on lines 50–255 of ch. 38, at pp. 353–7; quotations are cited by the editors' manuscript, chapter, and line numbers. Compare also Walter John Sedgefield, ed., *King Alfred's Old English Version of Boethius, 'De Consolatione Philosophiae'* (Oxford, 1899). Boethius's Latin text is edited by Ludwig Bieler, *Anicii Manlii Severini Boethii Philosophiae Consolatio*, CCSL 94 (Turnhout, 1957), and cited below by book, prose, and sentence number (following Godden and Irvine). All translations are my own, unless otherwise noted. Overviews of the manuscript tradition are provided by Godden and Irvine, *OE Boethius* I, pp. 9–49; Discenza, *King's English*, pp. 7–10.

[17] For the language of penance in Wulfstan's laws, see Carole Hough, 'Penitential Literature and Secular Law in Anglo-Saxon England,' *Anglo-Saxon Studies in Archaeology and History* 11 (2000), 133–41, at 136–8. For a broader look at the convergence of secular and spiritual priorities, see Patrick Wormald, 'Archbishop Wulfstan and the Holiness of Society,' *Legal Culture*, pp. 225–51.

the morality of judging and punishing in the wake of the king's legislative initiative.[18] Accordingly, this chapter of the *Consolation* should be read as a complement to Alfred's laws, illuminating their holistic approach to punishment and providing a striking counterpoint to contemporary complaints about judicial abuse.

As numerous commentators have observed, the Old English *Consolation* offers a more overtly Christian message than the Latin original.[19] Although the author generally followed his source in avoiding explicit references to Christ, Christianity, or the Bible, Boethius's philosophical concepts of good and evil were re-imagined as religious absolutes that would be accessible to an Anglo-Saxon audience.[20] The treatment of earthly justice and punishment was no exception, and the Old English rendition of Boethius's discourse in chapter 38 is marked by a combination of penitential rhetoric and legal terminology. Above all, corporal punishment is conceived as a sort of spiritual cleansing that purges an offender of his sins and allows his soul to be saved. In the case of individuals who harm (*yfelað*) the innocent, for instance, Wisdom asserts:

> Swa swa se sioca ah þearfe þæt hine mon læde to þam læce þæt he his tilige, swa ah se þe þæt yfel deð þæt hine mon læde to þam ricum þæt mon þær mæge sniðan and bærnan his unþeawas.[21]
>
> Just as a sick person needs to be brought to the doctor so that he can take care of him, so a person who commits evil needs to be brought to the judge so that his wrongs can be cut out and burnt.

According to this logic, criminals who are punished for their offenses are better off in the long run than those who get away scot-free; the former are cured of their evils, while the latter are still plagued by them. In both the Latin and the Old English, the judge's objective is not simply to reveal and

---

[18] For the convergence of sacred and secular in the *domboc*, see particularly Wormald, *Making of English Law*, pp. 416–29; Treschow, 'Prologue to Alfred's Law Code.' Penitential aspects of Alfred's laws are examined by Hough, 'Penitential Literature and Secular Law,' pp. 134–5; Allen J. Frantzen, *The Literature of Penance in Anglo-Saxon England* (New Brunswick, 1983), pp. 124–7; Stefan Jurasinski, 'Sanctuary, House-Peace, and the Traditionalism of Alfred's Laws,' *Journal of Legal History* 31 (2010), 129–47, especially at 133–4; Stefan Jurasinski, 'Violence, Penance, and Secular Law in Alfred's Mosaic Prologue,' *HSJ* 22 (2010), 25–42. Alfred's legislative reforms are described by Asser: see Stevenson, *Asser's Life of King Alfred*, pp. 92–5; Keynes and Lapidge, *Alfred the Great*, pp. 109–10 and 275; Wormald, *Making of English Law*, pp. 118–25. See also the essay by Daniel Thomas in this volume.

[19] Godden and Irvine, *OE Boethius* I, pp. 66–8; Discenza, *King's English*, pp. 31–56; Janet Bately, 'Boethius and King Alfred,' *Platonism and the English Imagination*, ed. Anna Baldwin and Sarah Hutton (Cambridge, 1994), pp. 38–44; David A. Lopez, 'Translation and Tradition: Reading the *Consolation of Philosophy* through King Alfred's Boethius,' *The Politics of Translation in the Middle Ages and Renaissance*, ed. Renate Blumenfeld-Kosinski, Daniel Russel, and Luise von Flotow (Ottowa, 2001), pp. 69–84; W. F. Bolton, 'How Boethian is Alfred's *Boethius*?' *Studies in Old English Prose*, ed. Paul E. Szarmach (Albany, 1986), pp. 153–68, at 154.

[20] Godden and Irvine, *OE Boethius* I, p. 67; Discenza, *King's English*, pp. 7 and 41.

[21] B38.234–7. The Latin reads, 'Ad iudicium ueluti aegros ad medicum duci oportebat ut culpae morbos supplicio resecarent': Boethius 4P4.38.

recognize the offense, but to provide a remedy – whether or not the offender is willing. On the surface, this scenario is consistent with the principles of earthly justice, in which criminals must suffer as a consequence of their actions. However, the medical metaphor also plays on a familiar penitential trope, in which sinners are instructed to reveal their sins to a confessor like patients revealing their illnesses to a doctor: though painful or humiliating, the evil must be revealed and probed in order to be cured.[22] In the Old English, the judge (*ricum*) who decrees punishment operates in the same capacity as the confessor who prescribes penance, excising and neutralizing the offender's ills.[23] This passage is not concerned with retributive justice but with the criminal's own well being, and it is significant that the cutting and burning do not remedy any material harm. Rather, the implication is that the judge is mitigating the spiritual illness that inspired the offense. Wisdom's formulation goes further than Philosophy's in equating bodily punishment with care for the soul.[24]

The Old English *Consolation* also considers the potential drawbacks of physical punishments in a way that Boethius did not. In the Latin, Philosophy draws a distinction between perpetrators and victims of injury, stating that those who commit offenses are ultimately unhappier than those on the receiving end, despite all appearances to the contrary: 'infeliciores eos esse qui faciant quam qui patiantur iniuriam' [those who commit an injury are more unhappy than those who suffer the injury].[25] In the Old English, by contrast, this commentary is infused with the language of law and justice. The point seems to apply less to criminals and their victims than to individuals punished by legitimate authorities:

> Ic wat þæt ðis folc his nyle gelefan, þæt is þæt þa bioð gesælegran þe mon witnoð þonne þa bion þe hi witniað.[26]
>
> I know that the people will not believe this – that is, that those who are punished are happier than those who punish them.

This assertion turns on the verb *witnian*. Although it might be broadly rendered 'to injure,' which would be in line with Boethius's Latin *iniuria*, the

---

[22] The metaphor is developed at length in the OE penitential handbook: see Roger Fowler, 'A Late Old English Handbook for the Use of a Confessor,' *Anglia* 83 (1965), 1–34, at 26–8. The trope of the physician would have been familiar to readers of Late Antique and Alfredian texts: see Discenza, *King's English*, pp. 21 and 155 n. 46.

[23] Godden and Irvine translate *ricum* in this passage as 'the powerful person' and regard the word choice as a departure from the Latin *iudex*, 'judge.' However, 'judge' is included in the definitions provided by Bosworth–Toller, p. 794, s.v. 'rica' (n.) and 'rice' (adj.). Given the priorities of the OE author in ch. 38, I would argue that 'judge' is an appropriate rendering of this term and that the passage implies an exercise of earthly justice; see Godden and Irvine, *OE Boethius* II, pp. 79 and 454, and further below.

[24] This formulation prefigures the life-sparing laws of Archbishop Wulfstan: see Dorothy Whitelock, 'Wulfstan and the Laws of Cnut,' *EHR* 63 (1948), 433–52, at 449; Hough, 'Penitential Literature and Secular Law,' pp. 136–8.

[25] Boethius 4P4.32.

[26] B38.210–12. For the concept of happiness, see Godden and Irvine, *OE Boethius* I, p. 76.

Old English term is used consistently throughout this chapter to refer to appropriate and legitimate retribution for harm done, not to unprovoked or criminal offenses.[27] *Witnian* and its cognate *wite* [punishment] appear in fifteen passages in chapter 38,[28] and in thirteen of those passages the word is used in conjunction with *yfel* [evil] to signal punishment for evil deeds or punishment of the wicked.[29] It is not always explicit whether such punishment would be realized in this world or the next, but the consistent use of *wite* in early English legislation, as well as the concern with earthly judges and justice in chapter 38, allows for an interpretation which diverges from Boethius's Latin.[30] While the Old English reference to the punished and their punishers could potentially refer to victims of criminal injury, the author's repeated use of *witnian* – 'those who are punished [*witnoð*] are happier than those who punish them [*witniað*]' – evokes criminal punishment under the law.

The Old English author's introduction of legal terminology thus implies that judges themselves might suffer as a result of their judgments, ending up more unhappy than the offenders they punish. This point is borne out further as the discussion continues. Wisdom establishes that everyone who willingly commits evil is worthy of punishment, and those who punish the innocent are willingly committing evil.[31] This in turn raises the question of who is more deserving of retribution, 'þe þone þe þone unscyldgan witnode,

---

[27] In Bosworth–Toller, the primary definition of *witnian* is 'to punish, torment, plague' and the primary definition of *wite* is 'punishment, pain that is inflicted as punishment, torment': pp. 1257 and 1245. The various meanings of *witnian* elsewhere in the OE corpus are noted by Godden and Irvine, *OE Boethius* II, p. 453. However, the use of the terms is remarkably consistent in ch. 38, referring exclusively to retribution for harm done: see B38.59, 68, 98–9, 103, 118–21, 128, 134, 143, 148, 159, 160, 168, 182, 232, and 243–5.

[28] According to Godden and Irvine's glossary, *witnian* appears a total of twelve times and *wite* a total of forty times in the B-text: for *witnian*, five of these occurrences are in ch. 38 (at lines 168, 211, 212, 217, 221); for *wite*, eighteen are in ch. 38 (lines 59, 68, 98, 99, 103, 118, 120, 143, 148, 159, 160, 214, 218, 220, 221, 230, 243, 245). In addition, *unwitnod* [unpunished] appears a total of six times in the B-text, with five occurrences in ch. 38 (lines 119, 121, 128, 134, 182); and the lone appearance of *witnung* [punishment] in the B-text occurs in ch. 38 (line 225); see Godden and Irvine, *OE Boethius* II, pp. 619 and 626.

[29] There are two instances in ch. 38 in which *wite* is not paired with *yfel*. In one passage, *scyld* [guilt] is used instead of *yfel*: B38.242–6. In the other, Wisdom asserts that he does not wish to inspire good by threatening punishment: B38.100–3, and see further on this passage below, p. 124. *Wite* and *yfel* are also used in conjunction with *wracu* and *wrecan*, which connote vengeance or punishment; and with *riht* and *unriht*, which connote right and wrong in both legal and spiritual contexts: B38.97–100, 133–4, and 164–8.

[30] *Wite* in early Anglo-Saxon legislation is discussed elsewhere in this volume by Valerie Allen, pp. 18–19, and Daniela Fruscione, pp. 36–7 and 46.

[31] 'Ða cwæð he. Hwæþer þu ongite þæt ælc yfelwillende mon and yfelwyrccende sie wites wyrðe? Ða cwæð ic. Genog sweotole ic þæt ongite. Ða cwæð he. Hu ne is se þonne yfelwillende and yfelwyrcende þe þone unscyldgan witnoð? Ða cwæð ic. Swa hit is swa þu segst' [Then he said: do you perceive that every person who desires evil and works evil is worthy of punishment? Then I said: I perceive that clearly enough. Then he said: Is it not true that one who punishes the innocent desires evil and commits evil? Then I said: it is as you say]: B38.213–7. The Latin reads, 'Omnem, inquit, improbum num supplicio dignum negas? Minime': Boethius 4P4.33.

þe ðone þe þæt wite þolode' [the one who punished the guiltless or the one who suffered the punishment].³² The response:

> Ælc unriht witnung sie þæs yfel þe hit doð, næs þas ðe hit þafað, forþam his yfel hine gedeð earmne.³³
>
> Each unrighteous punishment is an evil for the one who commits it, not for the one who suffers it, because his evil makes him wretched.

This concept of unrighteous punishment – *unriht witnung* – is commonplace in Anglo-Saxon warnings against bad judges.³⁴ In the eighth century, Alcuin inveighed against unjust judges (*improbos judices*) who subverted justice and cited inappropriately violent judgments (*uiolentis iudiciis*) as a cause of Viking attacks.³⁵ The tenth-century legal treatise *Iudex* built on Alcuin's work, condemning various behaviors of *unrihtwis* judges: they took bribes; they were blinded by anger; they were too foolish to know the law; they protected evildoers; they harmed the innocent; they were worse than raiding armies; and, in a sinister biblical paraphrase, they were 'swa swa wulfas on æfne, ne læfað nawiht oð morgen' [like wolves in the evening – they leave nothing until morning].³⁶ Like Alcuin, the compiler of *Iudex* was emphatic that unrighteous judges were more concerned with their own interests than with issuing fair judgments. It appears that the author of the Old English *Consolation* was also familiar with this motif, for he departed from Boethius's Latin to follow the same line of reasoning, with Wisdom insisting twice that the worst kind of judge is *yfelwillende* – willing, even eager, to commit evil.³⁷ Whereas undeserved punishments would not harm the souls of the punished,

---

³² B38.220–1; in Latin, 'Cui supplicium inferendum putares, eine qui fecisset an qui pertulisset iniuriam?': Boethius 4P4.35. The use of OE *unscyldig* to describe the punished innocent reinforces the judicial context of this example: there is a clear verbal parallel to the prologue to Alfred's *domboc*, which instructs that 'Soðfastne man ⁊ unscyldigne ne acwele ðu þone næfre' [A trustworthy and innocent man should never be killed]: Alfred Prol. 45; cf. Exodus 23:7. The term *unscyldig* appears two additional times in Alfred's prologue in reference to those who were not guilty under the law: Alfred Prol. 2 and 21. The term *scyldig* is used to connote guilt and liability in Alfred Prol. 17 and 25, and Alfred 3, 5, and 6; compare also Ine 48, 49, 50, 55, 72, and 81; Hlothere and Eadric 8 [12]; Wihtred 8.2 [11], 9–9.1 [12] (the laws of Hlothere and Eadric and of Wihtred are cited according to the numeration in Oliver, *Beginnings of English Law*, with chapter numbers from Liebermann, *Gesetze* I in square brackets).

³³ B38.225–6; the Latin text reads 'Apparet inlatam cuilibet iniuriam non accipientis sed inferentis esse miseriam': Boethius 4P4.37.

³⁴ For *riht* and *unriht* in the context of earthly power, see Lopez, 'Translation and Tradition,' pp. 75 and 78; Daniela Fruscione, '*Riht* in Earlier Anglo-Saxon Legislation: A Semasiological Approach,' *Historical Research* 86 (2013), 498–504.

³⁵ Ch. 20 of Alcuin's *De virtutibus et vitiis* focuses on judges: PL 101, cols 628–9. The complaint about judicial violence appears in Alcuin's letter to King Æthelred of Northumbria after the Viking attack on Lindisfarne in 793; the text is edited by Colin Chase, *Two Alcuin Letter-Books* (Toronto, 1975), pp. 53–6, at 54. For Alcuin's interpretation of the *Consolation* and its influence on Alfred, see Bolton, 'How Boethian is Alfred's *Boethius*?' pp. 161–4.

³⁶ *Iudex* was based on Alcuin's *De virtutibus et vitiis* and is edited in Liebermann, *Gesetze* I, pp. 474–6. The quotation, from *Iudex* 12, is an adaptation of Zephaniah 3:3. Patrick Wormald tentatively dates the Old English text to the reign of Æthelstan or Edgar: *Making of English Law*, pp. 382–3.

³⁷ B38.214 and 216. The correlating Latin, considerably briefer than the OE, is quoted above, n. 31.

those judges who knowingly subverted justice and condemned the innocent deserved the unhappiness they earned for themselves. Spiritually speaking, they were far worse off than their victims.

Yet what about judges who did not willingly commit evil? Wisdom carefully qualifies his statement that the punished are happier than their punishers by explaining that this argument applies only to those who persecute the innocent (*unscyldig*) knowingly, with evil intent.[38] Nevertheless, the logic in this passage is so complex that he and Mod agree that most people – *ðis folc* – would not understand or believe it.[39] Moreover, the assertion that punishers could end up unhappier than the punished seems to imply that a judge could potentially injure his own soul by subjecting offenders to lawful penalties.[40] While such reasoning may seem counterintuitive from a legal standpoint, it is consistent with attitudes towards other types of legitimate violence in penitential literature. The tenth-century *Scriftboc*, for instance, prescribes the following penance:

> Gif man ofslea mannan on folcgefeohte, oððe for nyede, þær he his hlafordes ceap werige, fæste .xl. nihta.[41]

> If someone slays a man in public warfare, or out of necessity when he is the protector of his lord's property, let him fast forty nights.

If public, justifiable killings like these required penitential atonement, judges may well have reasoned that shedding offenders' blood could likewise harm their own souls. Indeed, this conclusion would be consistent with Wisdom's assertion that the punished are happier than their punishers. However, if this were the case, it would mean that royal law was inherently at odds with God's will – a notion antithetical to the model presented in Alfred's *domboc*.[42] If the king's legislation aimed to align secular law with divine interests, how could the need for punishment be reconciled with Christian imperatives?

---

[38] The guiltless (*unscyldig*) appear at B.38.216, 221, and 222; see also above, n. 32.
[39] *Þis folc* appears at B38.171, 210, and 228; see also below, n. 72. For the OE author's departure from Boethius's clean logical style, see Discenza, *King's English*, pp. 68–9.
[40] Compare quotation above, p. 118 and n. 26. This logic contradicts a canon attributed to Jerome, which circulated in England and was included in Archbishop Wulfstan's collection of canon law: 'Homicidas et sacrilegos punire, non est effusio sanguinis sed legum ministerium' [To punish murderers and violators of the sacred is not a shedding of blood but the administration of the laws]: J. E. Cross and Andrew Hamer, eds and trans, *Wulfstan's Canon Law Collection* (Cambridge, 1999), p. 137. The canon also appears in the *Collectio Hibernensis*, edited in Hermann Wasserschleben, *Die Irische Kanonensammlung*, 2nd edn (Leipzig, 1885), p. 87; it was derived from Jerome's *In Hieremiam prophetam*, edited in *PL* 24, col. 811.
[41] The *Scriftboc* (also known as the *Confessionale Pseudo-Egberti*) is edited with commentary by Allen J. Frantzen and available online through *The Anglo-Saxon Penitentials: A Cultural Database*, http://www.anglo-saxon.net/penance/index.html [accessed 6 January 2014]. The above quotation is from MS Oxford, Bodleian Library, Junius 121, fol. 95b; I follow Frantzen's translation of *folcgefeohte* as public warfare. See also Frantzen, *Literature of Penance*, pp. 133–9.
[42] See Wormald, *Making of English Law*, pp. 416–29; Wormald, 'Lex Scripta and Verbum Regis,' p. 34; Treschow, 'Prologue to Alfred's Law Code'; and above, n. 18.

Was it possible for a judge to administer righteous punishment without endangering his own soul?

The *Consolation* does not provide a straightforward answer, but the question is implicitly addressed at two points in chapter 38. One is a discussion of the role of advocates in the judicial process. Following the Latin, Wisdom complains that advocates spend more time lobbying for the victims of crimes than they do prosecuting the perpetrators. Rather than simply securing compensation, he argues, advocates and judges should ensure that the guilty suffer punishments equivalent to the injuries they committed.[43] Yet Wisdom diverges from Boethius's text to qualify this position:

> Ne cweðe ic na þæt þæt yfel sie þæt mon helpe þæs unscyldigan and him foreþingie, ac ic cweðe þæt hit is betre þæt mon wrege þone scyldigan.[44]
>
> I do not say that it is evil to help the guiltless and intervene for him, but I say it is better to accuse the guilty.

As insensitive as this sentiment may seem to modern sensibilities, it is logical from a penitential perspective.[45] The distress of innocent victims was fleeting; however horrible their plight, they would not face eternal consequences for what they suffered at the hands of a wrongdoer. The guilty, by contrast, would certainly be consigned to hell unless they repented properly. If just punishments could help remedy sin, it would be a greater act of Christian kindness to prosecute criminals for the sake of their souls than to provide transitory aid to the oppressed.

By this rationale, the righteous exercise of justice was actually Christian mercy – a position that is elucidated at another point in the text. Wisdom, after discussing the dismal spiritual prospects of offenders who evade punishment, distinguishes between two classes of wrongdoers:

> Ic wille dælan þa yfelan nu on twa, forþam ðe oðer dæl þara yfelena hæfð ece wite, forþam hi nane mildheortnesse ne geearnodon, oðer dæl sceal beon geclænsod and amered on þam heofonlicon fyre swa her bið sylfor, forþam he hæfð sume geearnunga sumere mildheortnesse. Forþam he mot cuman æfter þam earfoðum to ecre are.[46]
>
> I will now divide the evil into two groups, because some of the evil will have eternal punishment, because they earned no mercy. The rest shall be cleansed

---

[43] B38.229–37, following the Latin 4P4.38. As Godden and Irvine note, the OE is more straightforward in this argument than its source, eliminating some of the complex logic of the Latin: *OE Boethius* II, p. 454. The role of advocates in Anglo-Saxon legal procedure is examined by Andrew Rabin, 'Old English *Forespeca* and the Role of the Advocate in Anglo-Saxon Law,' *Mediaeval Studies* 69 (2007), 223–54.

[44] B38.237–9. This sentiment is not explicit in the Latin; see Godden and Irvine, *OE Boethius* II, pp. 454–5. See also Discenza, *King's English*, p. 84, for a discussion of this passage in relation to the legal priorities of Alfred's reign.

[45] For penitential culture in Anglo-Saxon England, see Catherine Cubitt, 'Bishops, Priests and Penance in Late Saxon England,' *EME* 14 (2006), 41–63.

[46] B38.147–52. This passage expands Boethius's Latin to include reward as well as punishment in the afterlife: 'Et magna quidem, inquit, quorum alia poenali acerbitate, alia uero purgatoria clementia exerceri puto; sed nunc de his disserere consilium non est': Boethius 4P4.23. See also Godden and Irvine, *OE Boethius* II, p. 451; Discenza, *King's English*, pp. 37–8.

and purified in the heavenly fire (just as silver is purified here), because they have earned some mercy. For that reason, they can come to eternal glory after that hardship.

According to this formulation, offenders who escaped earthly justice were doomed to eternal punishment, whereas those who began their spiritual cleansing before they died would complete it in the afterlife and eventually attain salvation.[47] The key point, however, is that divine clemency needed to be earned: although earthly punishments did not automatically lead to salvation, they averted outright damnation and helped secure God's mercy. By Wisdom's logic, earthly punishments issued by secular authorities could function as partial penance for an offender's sins.[48]

However, Wisdom implies that unlike ordinary sinners, who were expected to submit to penance willingly and demonstrate true contrition for their misdeeds, criminals would be cleansed (*geclænsod*) against their will.[49] Given the potential severity of judicial punishments, it is no surprise that individuals would make every effort to avoid such penalties. Yet Wisdom sees the situation differently:

> Ac ic wat gif þa scyldigan ænigne spearcan wisdomes hæfdon and be ængum dæle ongitan þæt hi mihtan hiora scylda þurh wite gebetan þe him her on worulde on become, þonne noldan hi na cweþan þæt hit wære wite, ac woldon cweþan þæt hit wære hiora clænsung and heora betrung, and noldon nænne þingere secan, ac lustlice hi woldon lætan þa rican hie tucian æfter hiora agnum willan.[50]

> I know that if the guilty had any spark of wisdom and perceived at all that they might remedy their guilts through the punishment that came to them in the world, then they would not want to say that it was punishment – but they would

---

[47] This image of purgatorial cleansing is found elsewhere in Anglo-Saxon literature: see especially Sarah Foot, 'Anglo-Saxon "Purgatory"', *The Church, the Afterlife and the Fate of the Soul*, ed. Peter Clarke and Tony Claydon, Studies in Church History 45 (Woodbridge, 2009), pp. 87–96; Helen Foxhall Forbes, '*Diuiduntur in quattuor*: The Interim and Judgement in Anglo-Saxon England,' *Journal of Theological Studies* n.s. 61 (2010), 659–84.

[48] The language of this passage is ambiguous enough to apply either to judicial penalties or ecclesiastical penance, and it is certainly possible that the author imagined these two systems of punishment operating in tandem. Such a scenario is hypothesized in the *domboc*: Alfred 1.2, for instance, prescribes both a prison sentence on a royal estate and a penance imposed by the bishop for those who violate oaths; see the discussion by Daniel Thomas in this volume, pp. 000–000. For the penitential aspects of Alfred's laws, see above, n. 18. Overlap between penitential literature and secular law is addressed by Stefan Jurasinski in this volume, pp. 000–000, and more broadly in his 'The Old English Penitentials and the Law of Slavery,' *English Law before Magna Carta: Felix Liebermann and Die Gesetze der Angelsachsen*, ed. Stefan Jurasinski, Lisi Oliver, and Andrew Rabin (Leiden, 2010), pp. 97–118, especially at 103–6; and see also Cubitt, 'Bishops, Priests and Penance.'

[49] See for example Ælfric's *De penitentia*, which outlines the requirements for effective penance, including true repentance and abstention from sin: Benjamin Thorpe, ed., *The Homilies of the Anglo-Saxon Church: The First Part, Containing the Sermones Catholici, or Homilies of Ælfric*, vol. 2 (London, 1846), pp. 602–8, especially at 602–4.

[50] B38.242–8; the Latin reads 'Ipsi quoque improbi, si eis aliqua rimula uirtutem relictam fas esset aspicere uitiorumque sordes poenarum cruciatibus se deposituros uiderent, compensatione adipiscendae probitatis nec hos cruciatus esse ducerent defensorumque operam repudiarent ac se totos accusatoribus iudicibusque permitterent': Boethius 4P4.40.

say that it was their cleansing and their bettering. And they would not seek any advocate, but they would eagerly allow the judge to afflict them according to their own will.

The language used here is significant. Wisdom's hypothetical offenders are clearly submitting to a corporal punishment assigned by a judicial authority; they are not participating in an ecclesiastical process of contrition, penance, and forgiveness.[51] Still, this application of secular justice is unambiguously penitential. The purpose of punishment, in this scenario, is not merely to restore order, exact revenge, or teach miscreants that crime doesn't pay. As Wisdom remarks earlier in the chapter, he does not want 'men þreatian and tihtan to godum þeawum for þam ege þæs wites' [to threaten people and impel them to good customs out of fear of punishment].[52] Instead, offenders should recognize that earthly punishments, like acts of penance, lessen one's suffering in the next life. Whether such penalties were issued in conjunction with ecclesiastical penance or imposed upon those who could not be reconciled with the Church, physical punishment was understood to operate on both body and soul.

Wisdom's ultimate lesson is that earthly mercy does not correspond with divine mercy. A mild sentence might mitigate an offender's physical pain but would not save him from eternal suffering if his soul was not adequately cleansed. A truly merciful judge would assign harsh punishments, for, as Wisdom puts it, 'þæt is þonne hiora mildsung þæt mon wrece hiora unþeawas be hiora gewyrhtum' [that is mercy for the offenders, that their wrongs be avenged according to what they wrought (i.e., as they deserve)].[53] Like a confessor prescribing penance, a judge's sentence ought to be commensurate with the offender's misdeed yet burdensome enough to redeem both the material crime and its attendant sin. Because judicial punishments serve a dual purpose, compensating for an earthly wrong while improving its instigator's chance of salvation, their severity should be recognized as true Christian mercy.[54] This reasoning would allay any concerns a righteous judge might have had about implementing corporal punishments: despite appearances, he was not a tormenter of bodies but a physician of souls.

I would like to address a final aspect of the model of judicial punishment set forth in the Old English *Consolation*: the consequences for serious offenders who managed to evade earthly punishment.[55] The text leaves no doubt that evildoers who are punished in this world are better off than those who get

---

[51] For the practice of penance in Anglo-Saxon England, see Brad Bedingfield, 'Public Penance in Anglo-Saxon England,' *ASE* 31 (2002), 223–55; Sarah Hamilton, 'Remedies for "Great Transgressions": Penance and Excommunication in Late Anglo-Saxon England,' *Pastoral Care*, ed. Tinti, pp. 83–105.
[52] B38.102–3; and above, n. 29.
[53] B38.251–2. Compare Treschow, 'Prologue to Alfred's Law Code,' which illuminates the motif of merciful judgment in the *domboc*.
[54] See above, n. 48.
[55] Discenza, *King's English*, pp. 37–8.

away with their crimes, for Wisdom assures us that those who do not suffer on earth will suffer all the more horribly in the afterlife.[56] Yet the absence of earthly punishment has further implications:

> Þa ðe him bið unwitnode eall hiora yfel on þisse worulde habbað sum yfel hefigre and frecendlicre þonne ani wite sie on þisse worulde. Þæt is þæt him bið ungewitnode hiora yfel on þisse worulde. Þæt is þæt sweotoloste tacn þæs mæstan yfeles on þisse worulde, and þæs wyrstan edleanes æfter þisse worulde.[57]

> Those who go unpunished for all their evil in this world will endure a heavier and more dangerous evil than any punishment in this world. That is, the fact that they go unpunished for their evil in this world – that is the clearest sign of the greatest evil in this world and of the worst retribution after this world.

In other words, an offender who escapes punishment is marked as the worst sinner of all; the lack of earthly consequences signals that his actions have placed him beyond help. An absence of punishment was actually the worst punishment possible.[58]

Nevertheless, Wisdom identifies two potential outcomes for an offender able to evade earthly penalties. One is that he would eventually recognize and willingly repent of the evil he committed. This scenario is characterized as a great gift (*micel gifu*) from God, the highest judge (*hehstan deman*): having been spared debilitating punishments, a criminal would have the opportunity to live, reflect on his wrongs, and repent of his own volition.[59] Yet Wisdom clarifies that this apparent escape from punishment is conditional on the offender's behavior. Serious sinners who evade justice have not been given an eternal gift (*ece gifu*), as some might argue, but simply a second chance – a space of time during which they might 'ongitað hyra yfel and gecyrrað to gode' [understand their evil and turn to good].[60] Unlike those who are cleansed with physical punishments against their will, these offenders face the more challenging task of renouncing evil of their own accord.[61] Although earthly penalties are not a catalyst for contrition in such instances, Wisdom's

---

[56] B38.97–100 and 119–21. See also quotation above: B38.147–52, at n. 46.

[57] B38.119–23. This passage expands on Boethius 4P4.18, but there is no direct Latin equivalent for the above quotation: see Godden and Irvine, *OE Boethius* II, p. 449; Bately, 'Boethius and King Alfred,' p. 44 n. 14.

[58] A similar logic is implicit in Alfred 1.7, which prescribes exile and excommunication for any imprisoned criminals who escaped their punishment; Alfred 1.8 allows the excommunication to be lifted if the escapee compensated according to the law and performed suitable penance.

[59] 'Ða cwæð he ... Þæt is micel gifu þæt he gebit oððæt þa yfelan ongitað hyra yfel and gecyrrað to gode. Ða cwæð ic. Nu ic ongite þæt hit nis ece gifu þæt he gifð þam yflum, ac is hwæthwegu eldung and anbid ðæs hehstan deman' [Then Wisdom said: That is a great gift – that he waits until the evildoers understand their evil and turn to good. Then I said: Now I understand that it is not an eternal gift that he gives to evildoers, but a sort of delay and waiting for the highest judge]: B38.134–9. This passage has no direct Latin equivalent; see Godden and Irvine, *OE Boethius* II, p. 250.

[60] B38.136–7; the Old English is quoted in full above, n. 59.

[61] Compare above, p. 123.

language – once again reminiscent of penitential rhetoric – suggests that a wise offender would seek out an appropriate penance for his misdeeds and make every effort to fully rejoin the Christian community.[62]

The alternative outcome for those who evaded punishment in the world would be considerably less pleasant for everyone involved. In this scenario, the offender is given time to repent but never comes to the realization that he has committed evil; instead, he persists in his wrongdoing for the rest of his life. The illusion that such individuals have gotten away with their crimes offers a starting point for Wisdom's discourse on this topic, as he addresses Mod's objections:

> Đa yflan næfdon nænne anweald ne nænne weorðscipe ne on þisse worulde ne on þære toweardan. Forþam ðe þuhte þæt eallra þinga wyrrest þæt ðu wendest þæt hi hafdon to micelne, and þæt ealne weg siofodest þæt hi ealne weg næron on wite. And ic þe sæde ealne weg þæt hi næfre ne bioð buton wite, þeah þe swa ne þince.[63]

> The evil have no power and no honor in this world or the next. For that seemed to you the worst of all things – that you believed that they had too much, and always complained that they were not always being punished. And I always said to you that they will never be without punishment, even if you do not think so.

Once again, the greatest problem is public perception. Despite Wisdom's insistence that these offenders will suffer eternal punishment, it appears to mortal eyes (like Mod's) that they are being rewarded for their crimes with earthly prosperity. For those who do not know any better, this seems like an ideal situation for the wrongdoer, who is able to do as he likes without any consequences.[64] For the victims of his crimes, by contrast, this seems unjust. Why do offenders not immediately feel the weight of divine judgment for afflicting the innocent? Why are they allowed to continue doing evil on earth, if they have not used their extra time – God's great gift – to amend their ways? According to Wisdom's reasoning, these supposed injustices are part of the divine plan:

> Ic wat þeah þæt ðu wilt siofian þæt hi swa langne fyrst habbað leaf yfel to donne, and ic þe sæde ealne weg þæt se fyrst bið swiðe lytle hwile. And ic þe secge get,

---

[62] For example, exhortations to penance are paired with the phrase *to gode gecyrran* in Ælfric's homily for Quinquagesima (lines 71–3), in Blickling Homily 8 (lines 26–7), and in Vercelli Homily 9 (lines 23–4): see Ælfric of Eynsham, *Catholic Homilies, the First Series: Text*, ed. Peter Clemoes, EETS s.s. 17 (Oxford, 1997), p. 260; R. Morris, ed., *The Blickling Homilies of the Tenth Century*, EETS o.s. 58, 63, 73 (London, 1874–80; repr. 1967), pp. 97–9; D. G. Scragg, *The Vercelli Homilies and Related Texts*, EETS o.s. 300 (Oxford, 1992), p. 160. See also above, n. 49.

[63] B38.155–60. Wisdom expands on the Latin, which reads 'Id uero hactenus egimus ut quae indignissima tibi uidebatur malorum potestas eam nullam esse cognosceres': Boethius 4P4.24.

[64] 'Forþy wenað þa ablendan mod þæt þæt sie sio mæste gesælð þæt men seo alefed yfel to donne, and sio dæd him mote bion unwitnod' [Thus blinded minds think that it is the greatest happiness that a person should be allowed to commit evil and not be punished for the deed]: B38.180–2. The Latin reads 'Nequeunt enim oculos tenebris assuetos ad lucem perspicuae ueritatis attollere ... dum enim non rerum ordinem sed suos intuentur affectus, uel licentiam uel impunitatem scelerum putant esse felicem': Boethius 4P4.27.

swa he lengra bið swa hi bioð ungesæligran, þæt him wære ealra mæst unsælð þæt se fyrst wære oð domes dæg.⁶⁵

I know that you will object that offenders will be allowed to commit evil for such a long time – and I always tell you that the time will be a very little while. And still I tell you: the longer the time is the unhappier they will be, so that it would be the greatest unhappiness for them if that time should last until Judgment Day.

In other words, offenders who do not repent compound the damage to their own souls, making their ultimate punishment all the more severe. Although the suffering they inflict on the innocent is lamentable, it is only transitory; justice will be restored in the next world. Certainly, this would have been an unsatisfying response for individuals concerned only with immediate retribution for earthly misdeeds, as Wisdom notes. For those with insight and patience, however, it should be clear that all offenders will be punished according to their crimes, regardless of whether or not that justice is apparent to their earthly victims.

This logic surely would have resonated with flesh-and-blood judges, since some offenders did find ways to avoid material punishment despite the efforts of earthly authorities. This is the very problem at the heart of Mod's complaint: if judges do not bring wrongdoers to account, those wrongdoers will continue to afflict the innocent. Even if this were only a transitory inconvenience, as it is in Wisdom's reckoning, it would put judges in an awkward position, especially if unpunished criminals were individuals too powerful to be checked.⁶⁶ The illicit seizure of land, for example, would have been perpetrated almost exclusively by landowners.⁶⁷ If local magnates were unwilling or unable to punish such behavior among their peers or betters, it would appear to victims that the authorities were endorsing the oppression of the weak. The king himself might be party to such favoritism. For instance, the relatively lenient sentences issued against the thief Helmstan – presumably as a result of his social status and influential friends – could well have been perceived as evidence of judicial inequity perpetrated by Alfred himself (and later his son, Edward the Elder).⁶⁸ While Helmstan's offenses affected only a limited population, crimes with a wider impact might also go unpunished. In 978,

---

[65] B38.160–4. Wisdom expands on the Latin, which reads 'quosque impunitos querebare uideres numquam improbitatis suae carere suppliciis, licentiam quam cito finiri precabaris nec longam esse disceres infelicioremque fore si diuturnior, infelicissimam uero si esset aeterna': Boethius 4P4.24.

[66] Such a scenario is imagined in III Æthelstan 6 and IV Æthelstan 3; see Julia Barrow, 'Demonstrative Behaviour and Political Communication in Later Anglo-Saxon England,' *ASE* 36 (2007), 127–50, at 136–7.

[67] Wormald, 'Giving God and King their Due,' pp. 351–2.

[68] Helmstan's case is detailed in the Fonthill Letter, edited and translated most recently by N. P. Brooks, 'The Fonthill Letter, Ealdorman Ordlaf and Anglo-Saxon Law in Practice,' *Early Medieval Studies*, ed. Baxter *et al.*, pp. 301–17, at 302–6; the leniency of Helmstan's punishment is addressed at pp. 315–17. Leniency is also discussed by Simon Keynes, 'The Fonthill Letter,' *Words, Texts and Manuscripts: Studies in Anglo-Saxon Culture Presented to Helmut Gneuss*, ed. Michael Korhammer (Cambridge, 1992), pp. 53–97, at 87–8. The role of an influential advocate in Helmstan's legal proceedings is illuminated by Rabin, 'Old English *Forespeca*,' pp. 243–54.

for instance, when King Edward the Martyr was assassinated by his own thegns, the killers were never punished for their act of treason.[69] It seems that the unnamed regicides were influential enough to escape the physical and material consequences that would normally have followed such a serious offense; even Edward's successor, the twelve-year-old King Æthelred, could not or would not bring the killers to justice. If royal authority could not prevail against regicides, how could an ordinary judge compel disproportionately influential individuals to submit to trial and punishment?[70]

For judges faced with overly powerful offenders who could not be brought to justice, the situation would have been fraught. Contemporary critics would have seen a stratified judicial system, in which the weak were punished for minor crimes while the strong faced no consequences for major ones – a perception that Wisdom seeks to rectify throughout this chapter of the *Consolation*. Leaving aside public opinion, however, some judges may have felt the weight of this disparity themselves. What would be the consequences for a judge who failed to uphold earthly justice? Would he be accountable for any future wrongs an unpunished offender might commit against the innocent? Would his inability to enforce earthly law damage his own prospects in the afterlife? According to Wisdom's reasoning, the answer is no. Judges were not responsible for such lapses in earthly justice. It was God, not the judge, who allowed these most serious offenders to live, and it would be God, not the judge, who would determine their eventual – and eternal – punishment.[71]

Notwithstanding the reassurance this logic might provide for judges, there is no expectation in the Old English *Consolation* that this understanding would extend to the rest of the population. Wisdom begins and ends his discourse on earthly punishment with references to those who will not grasp his argument. He articulates his disdain for foolish people (*dysig men*) at the outset

---

[69] The Anglo-Saxon Chronicle blamed the king's kin – presumably his young brother and successor, Æthelred II – for neglecting to avenge his death: 'Hyne noldon his eorðlican magas wrecan, ac hine hafað his heofonlic fæder swyðe gewrecen' [His earthly kin did not want to avenge him, but his heavenly father avenged him very greatly]: ASC D, s.a. 979 (*recte* 978). It is possible that Edward's killers later undertook demonstrative acts of penance in place of punishment; see David Rollason, *Saints and Relics in Anglo-Saxon England* (Oxford, 1989), p. 143.

[70] The clauses on treason and lord-betrayal (*hlafordsearu*) in Alfred's *domboc* indicate that regicide was already a concern a century before Edward's death; see Alfred 1 and 4. It is unclear who would have enforced these laws, however, and it is conceivable that a situation like the one in 978 could have occurred in other cases of regicide.

[71] This very logic was applied to Edward the Martyr's unpunished assassins by Byrhtferth of Ramsey at the turn of the millennium. Although the killers thought that God had not noticed their crime, they had in fact been given a space of life (*spatium uitae*) which they squandered instead of using for penance. Some twenty years later, the killers had begun to feel the weight of divine punishment, and one had already gone blind: 'sicut iustum est, penas sumpsit – non penas quas mortales mortalibus ingerunt, sed tales que animas miserorum inmisericorditer affligunt' [as is just, he received punishments – not punishments which mortals thrust upon mortals, but such punishments as mercilessly afflict the souls of the wretched]. This episode appears in Byrhtferth's *Life of St Oswald* book 4, ch. 20, edited and translated by Michael Lapidge, *Byrhtferth of Ramsey: The Lives of St Oswald and St Ecgwine* (Oxford, 2009), pp. 142–3.

and concludes his discussion by admitting that the people (*þis folc*) rarely comprehend the true meaning of earthly justice; other dismissive mentions of *þis folc* appear throughout the chapter, along with the occasional pointed comment about spiritual blindness.[72] There is no point in trying to convince such people, Wisdom asserts, because their sole interest is immediate, earthly retribution. Their caricature of self-serving judges who oppress the weak and appease the powerful is inconsequential, since it fails to acknowledge God's greater plan of punishment and reward. Although this perception functions as a necessary foil for Wisdom's argument, the misguided concerns of *þis folc* provide more than rhetorical counterpoint. Wisdom is not simply reassuring judges that their work is in line with divine will. He is refuting the notion – seemingly widely held – that justice is an inherently corrupt and partial exercise.

Although the prologue to the Old English *Consolation* names Alfred as its translator, the king's authorship of the text has been questioned, as has its traditional dating to his lifetime.[73] Nevertheless, the argument presented in chapter 38 is very much in line with the judicial priorities of the king's later reign.[74] In the final chapter of his *Life of Alfred*, Asser described a kingdom full of judges who squabbled among themselves and provided conflicting interpretations of the law – an image of judicial chaos that reinforced the importance of Alfred's legal and educational objectives.[75] The king's interest in literacy and written legislation was explicitly linked, in his biographer's reckoning, to a desire to improve the exercise of justice among the Anglo-Saxon nobility.[76] Yet in spite of Asser's damning depiction of contemporary judges, it seems that the greatest problem was a lack of consensus about what constituted righteous justice. Individuals who regarded gifts as an element of honorable social interaction, for instance, might not have seen reciprocal exchange as bribery or corruption.[77] Alternatively, inconsistencies in judicial decisions may have simply reflected a variety of legitimate or

---

[72] The phrase *dysig men* appears at B.38.62, 84, 86, 94, and 185; *þis folc* appears at B.38.171, 210, and 228; and a discussion of spiritual blindness appears at B.38.173–206. See Discenza, *King's English*, pp. 90–4, for the treatment of ignorance in the text; and Godden and Irvine, *OE Boethius* I, pp. 69–70, for *þis folc* as a reference to a general readership.

[73] The earliest extant manuscript is dated c. 950, and Godden and Irvine suggest a composition date between 890 and 930: Godden and Irvine, *OE Boethius* I, pp. 140–6; Godden, 'Did King Alfred Write Anything?' pp. 15–17; and see above, n. 14. However, the text should be understood as a product or continuation of Alfred's translation program, even if it was begun or completed after his death.

[74] Discenza, *King's English*, p. 84.

[75] Stevenson, *Asser's Life of King Alfred*, pp. 92–5; Keynes and Lapidge, *Alfred the Great*, pp. 109–10. In addition, biblical exhortations concerning just judgment were incorporated prominently into the *domboc*'s prologue: see Treschow, 'Prologue to Alfred's Law Code,' pp. 99–102.

[76] Stevenson, *Asser's Life of King Alfred*, p. 94; Keynes and Lapidge, *Alfred the Great*, pp. 109 and 275. See also Wormald, *Making of English Law*, pp. 118–25 and 427–9; Treschow, 'Prologue to Alfred's Law Code,' pp. 81–2; Cubitt, 'As the Lawbook Teaches,' pp. 1039–43.

[77] Fouracre, 'Carolingian Justice,' p. 800.

well-intentioned interpretations of the law; it is not difficult to imagine a clergyman and a lay judge arguing over whether capital punishment was appropriate in a given case. This is not to suggest that there were no abuses of justice for Anglo-Saxon authors to protest, but Asser oversimplifies the problem of judicial misconduct in the same way that Wisdom's *dysig men* do. In the *Life of Alfred*, judges are reduced to caricatures who are at best incompetent and at worst out to serve their own interests. The Old English *Consolation* offers an alternative: an introspective judge who is concerned with moral questions of right and wrong as he administers earthly justice in good faith.

Alfred's attempt to establish a consistent standard of justice in his kingdom reflects this very priority. Although the vernacular rendition of Boethius's seminal Latin work can provide only a sketchy picture of Anglo-Saxon justice at the turn of the tenth century, the language of penance, mercy, and divine retribution that infuses Wisdom's discourse is consistent with the priorities articulated in the king's laws. It is significant that Wisdom acknowledges the need for harsh punishments and the occasional failure to check serious offenders – difficult aspects of earthly justice which could conceivably have become points of contention among judges. For individuals charged with keeping the peace and enforcing the law, the arguments presented in chapter 38 offered a way to reconcile their secular obligations with divine will. At a moment when the *unrihtwis* judge could be cited as a cautionary motif, the Old English *Consolation* offered a nuanced defense of the role of judicial punishment in Christian society. By following Alfred in aligning earthly justice with religious principles, Wisdom confirms that the righteous application of the law is not simply just, but virtuous. Such reassurances would have allayed the conscience of any judge – or, in the case of a lawmaker like Alfred, a king.

7

Osteological Evidence of Corporal and Capital Punishment in Later Anglo-Saxon England*

Jo Buckberry

Recent research by Andrew Reynolds has interrogated the archaeological record for evidence of Anglo-Saxon execution cemeteries.[1] This chapter will discuss how osteological evidence can aid our interpretation of Anglo-Saxon capital punishment and give insight into the types of evidence that might aid in the identification of corporal punishment from skeletal populations. The importance of correctly interpreting skeletal trauma is paramount, but this can be supported by scrutinising the palaeodemographic profile of execution populations, studying burial position, and understanding the decomposition process and the significance of post-depositional disturbance of burials. The essay will lay down a framework for the successful identification of corporal and capital punishments, with reference to Anglo-Saxon documentary sources.

Archaeological Evidence of Capital and Corporal Punishment

Separate execution cemeteries were first founded in the seventh century, and continued to be used throughout the later Anglo-Saxon period, and sometimes as late as the twelfth century.[2] Many of these cemeteries were located close to hundred boundaries, away from community cemeteries and settlements. Prior to this development, during the fifth and sixth centuries,

---

* I thank the following people for their insightful comments and enjoyable discussions on Anglo-Saxon executions, trauma, and decomposition: Dawn Hadley, Andrew Reynolds, Annia Cherryson, Steve Symes, Ericka L'Abbé, João Pinheiro, Chris Knüsel, Anthea Boylston, Rob Janaway, Emma Brown, Lorna Felix, Rachel Holgate and Michelle Williams-Ward. Thank you to Simon Mays for discussing the amputation at School Street, Ipswich, and suggesting a suitable image for this paper. Finally, my thanks to Edward Faber for patiently listening to me on this subject for a number of years and for commenting on this manuscript.

1 Reynolds, *Deviant Burial*.
2 For example at Staines in Surrey: Andrew Reynolds, 'The Definition and Ideology of Anglo-Saxon Execution Sites and Cemeteries,' *Death and Burial in Medieval Europe: Papers of the 'Medieval Europe Brugge 1997' Conference*, vol. 2, ed. Guy De Boe and Frans Verhaeghe (Zellik, 1997), pp. 33–41, at 34–5; Graham Hayman and Andrew Reynolds, 'A Saxon and Saxo-Norman Execution Cemetery at 42–54 London Road, Staines,' *ArchJ* 162 (2005), 215–55; Reynolds, *Deviant Burial*.

deviant burials were usually found within normal community cemeteries, rather than in liminal locations.[3]

The introduction of separate execution cemeteries during the seventh and eighth centuries has been linked to the conversion to Christianity in the seventh century, and the rise of churchyard burial in the eighth.[4] From this time onwards it was no longer the norm to include wrongdoers in community cemeteries.[5] Although this has been linked to the influence of the Church, it is generally agreed that the early English Church showed little interest in enforcing churchyard burial, at least in the centuries immediately following the conversion.[6] Indeed, the first law code referring to the exclusion of criminals from burial in consecrated ground, II Æthelstan 26, dates to the early tenth century.[7] Churchyards appear to have been consecrated from the tenth century onwards,[8] and from this date it is legitimate to argue that the unbaptised, suicide victims, and criminals were excluded from burial in consecrated ground; however, in practice such people were already buried away from churchyards and other community cemeteries at a much earlier date.[9] The foundation of execution cemeteries in the seventh and eighth centuries suggests that the process of state formation, rather than the influence of the Church, governed their development.[10]

Later Anglo-Saxon execution cemeteries have been defined as having several of the following characteristics:[11]

- Varied burial alignments
- Unusual burial positions
- Prone burials
- Evidence of decapitation or other trauma (e.g. amputation of hands or feet)
- Evidence of tied hands and/or feet

---

[3] Helen Geake, 'Burial Practice in Seventh- and Eighth-Century England,' *The Age of Sutton Hoo*, ed. Martin Carver (Woodbridge, 1992), pp. 83–92, at 87; Reynolds, 'Definition and Ideology,' p. 37.

[4] Reynolds, 'Definition and Ideology,' p. 37.

[5] Annia Kristina Cherryson, 'Normal, Deviant and Atypical: Burial Variation in Late Saxon Wessex,' *Deviant Burial in the Archaeological Record*, ed. Eileen M. Murphy (Oxford, 2008), pp. 115–30.

[6] Donald Bullough, 'Burial, Community and Belief in the Early Medieval West,' *Ideal and Reality in Frankish and Anglo-Saxon Society: Studies Presented to J. M. Wallace-Hadrill*, ed. Patrick Wormald (Oxford, 1983), pp. 177–201, at 186; Richard Morris, *The Church in British Archaeology*, Council for British Archaeology Research Report 47 (London, 1983), p. 50; Helen Geake, 'Persistent Problems in the Study of Conversion-Period Burials in England,' *Burial in Early Medieval England and Wales*, ed. Sam Lucy and Andrew Reynolds (London, 2002), pp. 144–55, at 153; Helen Gittos, 'Creating the Sacred: Anglo-Saxon Rites for Consecrating Cemeteries,' *Burial in Early Medieval England and Wales*, ed. Lucy and Reynolds, pp. 195–208, at 202.

[7] Wormald, *Making of English Law*, pp. 307–8 and 339–40; Gittos, 'Creating the Sacred,' p. 201.

[8] Gittos, 'Creating the Sacred,' p. 208.

[9] Reynolds, 'Definition and Ideology,' p. 38.

[10] Reynolds, 'Definition and Ideology'; Reynolds, *Deviant Burial*.

[11] John J. Wymer, 'The Excavation of a Ring Ditch at South Acre,' *Barrow Excavations in Norfolk, 1984–88*, ed. John. J. Wymer, East Anglian Archaeology Report 77 (Dereham, 1996), pp. 58–89, at 89; Reynolds, 'Definition and Ideology'; Reynolds, *Deviant Burial*.

Osteological Evidence

- Shallow and undersized graves
- Evidence of intercutting graves
- Multiple interments
- Presence of low-status dress fittings
- Predominantly adult male populations
- Pre-existing earthworks, especially prehistoric barrows
- Location close to boundaries, especially of hundreds
- Proximity to routeways

The identification of those receiving corporal punishment is more problematic archaeologically, as there is no indication that they were necessarily buried in a distinctive manner. This means that we must look for evidence of the skeletal manifestations of punishments in the osteological record. Amputations, for example, are clearly evident in skeletal remains, although their identification may have been less accurate in early osteological reports.

Osteological Evidence of Capital Punishment

Capital punishment is first documented in the laws of Ine, and is present in many Anglo-Saxon law codes.[12] The mode of execution is not always given, but prescribed executions include decapitation, hanging, drowning, stoning, and burning. In many cases convicted criminals were denied burial in consecrated ground, but this punishment was not reserved for those executed for their crimes: also included were those who died unbaptised, suicides, excommunicates,[13] and possibly even strangers, who were occasionally listed as being denied burial in consecrated ground in later medieval documents.[14]

Osteologically, decapitation is usually clearly evident providing the skeleton is well-preserved (see Figure 7.1 for the anatomical regions discussed in this chapter). Severing of the neck would usually be undertaken with a heavy bladed weapon, e.g. an axe or a sword. Any injury caused by a bladed weapon is described as sharp-force trauma; this group of trauma includes incisions (created by running a blade along a body part or bone), puncture injuries (caused by the tip of a bladed weapon, for example during stabbing), and chopping trauma, where a blade is swung towards the victim, often resulting in a cleft in the bone.[15] Sharp-force trauma can be identified in bone by the linearity of the lesion, the presence of a smooth, often polished

---

[12] Ine 5.
[13] Andrew Reynolds, *Later Anglo-Saxon England: Life and Landscape* (Stroud, 1999), p. 103; Reynolds, *Deviant Burial*, pp. 23–6 and 214.
[14] Christopher Daniell, *Death and Burial in Medieval England* (London, 1997), p. 201; Gittos, 'Creating the Sacred.'
[15] Steven A. Symes et al., 'Interpreting Traumatic Injury to Bone in Medicolegal Investigations,' *A Companion to Forensic Anthropology*, ed. Dennis Dirkmaat (Chichester, 2012), pp. 340–89.

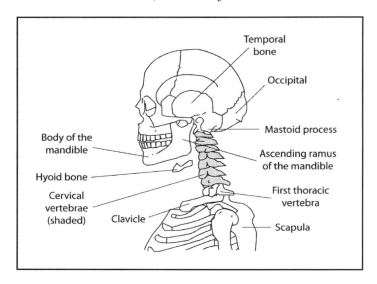

FIG. 7.1 Anatomical regions and bones discussed in this chapter (drawn by Dan Bashford)

surface on the acute side, and a defined, clean edge to the injury.[16] Decapitation will usually be caused by chopping trauma, but care must be taken to differentiate this from incised trauma, which may be present if bodies were dismembered, for example to facilitate the display of heads following a different mode of execution, such as hanging. Microscopy and Scanning Electron Microscopy (SEM) can be used to identify striations in the surface of sharp-force trauma in bone and can be used to infer direction of force; irregularities in the edge of the blade will leave striations running parallel to the direction of the blow.[17] Occasionally these striations are visible with the naked eye or with the use of a magnifying glass, but they are much more difficult to identify and interpret in the trabecular (spongy) bone that forms vertebral bodies (among other areas) than in the dense cortical bone found on the shafts of long bones, the neural arches of vertebrae, the mandible, and the outer and inner tables of the cranium. Where a significant force is applied, the trauma can result in additional fractures that radiate away from the point of impact, caused by failure of the bone. These blunt-force fractures continue beyond the point where the blade itself comes to a stop.[18]

---

[16] Anthea Boylston, 'Evidence for Weapon-Related Trauma in British Archaeological Samples,' *Human Osteology in Archaeology and Forensic Science*, ed. Margaret Cox and Simon Mays (London, 2000), pp. 357–80.
[17] Boylston, 'Evidence for Weapon-Related Trauma'; Symes *et al.*, 'Interpreting Traumatic Injury.'
[18] Symes *et al.*, 'Interpreting Traumatic Injury.'

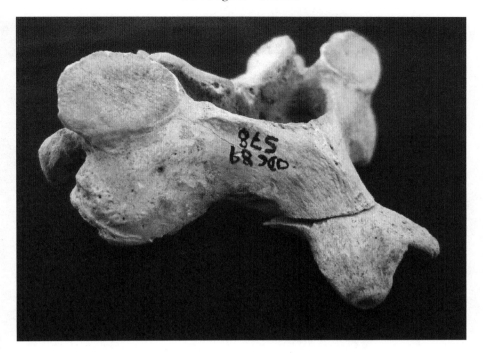

PLATE 7.1 Sharp-force trauma to the posterior of a cervical vertebra, consistent with decapitation (Skeleton 578 from Old Dairy Cottage) (photograph © Jo Buckberry)

This type of trauma has been described as sharp-blunt trauma, reflecting the two different mechanisms of injury.[19]

Injuries that result in decapitation can be delivered from any angle, but evidence suggests that many decapitations were from behind. Blows aimed to decapitate usually affect the cervical (neck) vertebrae (Plate 7.1).[20] However, if a blow is delivered high up on the neck, or is angled upwards, the cranial base may also be involved, particularly the occipital bone at the back of the cranium and the mastoid processes of the temporal bone, which project inferiorly just behind the ear. In addition, many decapitations from behind will also involve the mandible, with injuries ranging from small v-shaped nicks to the ascending ramus, to more substantial sharp-blunt trauma affecting the inferior portion of the mandibular body. Decapitation at a lower level can result in trauma to the clavicles and/or upper thoracic (chest) vertebrae. Not all decapitation is from behind the victim. Sharp-force trauma has occasionally been observed on vertebral bodies, which are on the

---

[19] João Pinheiro, pers. comm.
[20] A. K. Cherryson et al., '"He Shall Be Slain and Buried in Unconsecrated Ground": The Anglo-Saxon Execution Cemetery at Old Dairy Cottage, Winchester' (in prep).

front of the spine. Chopping trauma to the anterior vertebral body would be expected in cases of decapitation from the front, whereas incision wounds may be observed on the anterior of vertebrae belonging to individuals who have been dismembered or, possibly, had their throats cut. These injuries can be expected to be long and narrow with a v-shaped cross-section, and there would be no evidence of associated blunt-force trauma. If the injury affects an area with well-preserved cortical bone, striations may be visible on the bone surface, allowing for the differentiation between an incision or chopping trauma.

At sites with poor levels of bone preservation, it is possible that sharp-force trauma may be obscured either by degradation of the bone surface, or by complete loss of the affected elements. However, if the head was displaced, but buried before decomposition occurred, it may be possible to infer decapitation. The soft tissues of the neck will hold the mandible, hyoid, and any vertebrae above the level of decapitation in place. Thus, if excavation reveals the deposition of the cranial extremity (i.e., the articulated bones of a head or head and neck) rather than of just the cranium, we can assume that it was deposited while sufficient soft tissue remained to hold the additional bones in articulation. This was seen at Walkington Wold, where four disarticulated heads, identified by the presence of articulating mandibles and cervical vertebrae, were excavated (Plate 7.2).[21] Of course, care must be taken not to mistake a case of decapitation for a largely disturbed burial where only the head has remained in a grave, a phenomenon which is often seen in crowded cemeteries with lots of inter-cutting of graves.

Death by hanging rarely leaves any mark on the skeleton. Occasionally, in cases of long-drop hanging, the second cervical vertebrae will fracture, separating the anterior body from the posterior neural arch (Plate 7.3).[22] But cervical fracture is rare; an examination of the cervical vertebrae of victims of judicial hanging in England dating from 1882 to 1945 showed that just six out of thirty-four individuals had a fracture to the second cervical vertebrae (axis), and only one further fracture was identified (to the body of a congenitally abnormal third cervical vertebra). This suggests that the so-called 'hangman's fracture' is relatively rare in cases of judicial hanging, even when a long drop was employed.[23] The few images of early medieval hangings suggest gallows with a short drop were used; in these cases death was more likely to occur by asphyxiation than spinal fracture, leaving no direct evidence in the osteoarchaeological record. Recent investigation into

---

[21] J. L. Buckberry and D. M. Hadley, 'An Anglo-Saxon Execution Cemetery at Walkington Wold, Yorkshire,' *Oxford Journal of Archaeology* 26 (2007), 309–29; J. L. Buckberry, 'Off With Their Heads: The Anglo-Saxon Execution Cemetery at Walkington Wold, East Yorkshire,' *Deviant Burial in the Archaeological Record*, ed. Murphy, pp. 148–68.

[22] S. O'Connor et al., 'Exceptional Preservation of a Prehistoric Human Brain from Heslington, Yorkshire, UK,' *Journal of Archaeological Sciences* 38 (2011), 1641–54; T. Waldron, 'Legalized Trauma,' *International Journal of Osteoarchaeology* 6 (1996), 114–18.

[23] R. James and R. Nasmyth-Jones, 'The Occurrence of Cervical Fractures in Victims of Judicial Hanging,' *Forensic Science International* 54 (1992), pp. 81–91.

PLATE 7.2 Skull associated with Skeleton 1 from Walkington Wold, Barrow 1, East Yorkshire. This disarticulated head was buried with the mandible and several cervical vertebrae in articulation with the cranium, suggesting the presence of soft tissue at the time of deposition. (photograph © Hull and East Riding Museum: Hull Museums)

causes of hyoid fracture has shown that the greater horns of the hyoid can dislocate or fracture during manual strangulation and suicidal hanging; however, these fractures are not ubiquitous in either cause of death, and are also seen in a variety of accidental deaths. Thus, in the absence of soft tissue or other contextual information, hyoid fractures should not be used to infer strangulation or hanging in a modern forensic setting.[24] The hyoid bone is small and fragile and rarely recovered from archaeological sites; it is unlikely that hyoid fractures will be identified with confidence in archaeological material, and if they are identified, interpretation should be cautious.

Execution by stoning would result in multiple traumatic lesions distributed across the body. These would be blunt-force injuries, which are infrequently discussed in the osteological literature. In part, this is because peri-mortem trauma to the post cranial skeleton can be easily mistaken for post-mortem

---

[24] Symes *et al.*, 'Interpreting Traumatic Injury,' p. 355; Ericka L'Abbé, pers. comm.

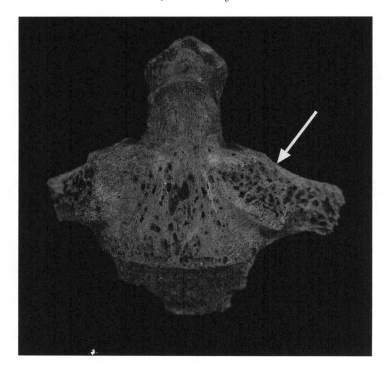

PLATE 7.3 Second cervical vertebra with peri-mortem 'hangman's fracture', from Iron Age Heslington, York (photograph © Jo Buckberry)

damage, unless the observer has some experience with peri-mortem trauma.[25] The broken edges do not have the polished appearance or straight margins of sharp-force trauma; thus they were frequently missed in older osteological reports. However, in recent years osteologists have become more adept at identifying peri-mortem blunt-force injuries, taking a lead from data collected from forensic cases, and reanalysis of skeletal collections has identified many

---

[25] Ante-mortem refers to injuries sustained before death; in palaeopathology we identify this based on seeing evidence of healing, which can take several weeks to be visible on bone. Post-mortem refers to things that occurred after death, but as osteoarchaeologists we can only identify breaks that have occurred when the bone no longer responds like living bone, i.e. it is still flexible and breaks in predictable ways. However, bone can retain its elastic qualities for weeks or even months after death. Peri-mortem means around the time of death. While it is tempting to believe this means 'at the time of death,' what we observe is bone that behaves like living bone and shows no sign of healing. Thus breaks that occur post-mortem but while the bone is still elastic are recorded as peri-mortem injuries. Similarly an individual can survive an injury for a number of hours, or even days, and then die, leaving evidence of 'peri-mortem trauma' in the archaeological record. In the case of decapitation, however, we can rule out a period of survival without evidence of healing!

Osteological Evidence

peri-mortem blunt-force injuries that had been missed in earlier studies.[26] Thus, older osteological reports should be interpreted carefully, and ideally skeletal material should be re-examined for evidence of trauma, especially where aspects of the burial suggest some form of deviancy. It has recently been argued that fractures to the scapulae (shoulder blades), which are covered by a thick layer of muscle tissue, protecting them from injury, might be suggestive of beatings, especially with clubs or sticks;[27] stoning might be an alternative interpretation.

Burning, either as an execution or as the result of an accidental fire, would result in characteristic changes to bone. Charred bones are blackened, but with increasing heat and/or duration of burning, bone changes colour from black/blue-black, through grey, and finally to white when it is fully calcined (complete loss of the organic component). During this process the bones warp and crack. Curved transverse fractures of long bones in particular are characteristic of the burning of a body (rather than of dry bone), and are thought to result from the burning away and receding of the soft tissue, thus they can be used to infer the direction of burning.[28] As the body burns, muscles and ligaments shrink; the flexor muscles contract more than the extensors, which means that joints bend and burned bodies will take on a characteristic contracted, 'pugilistic pose.'[29] Therefore, if a burnt body is buried with some soft tissue remaining, the excavated skeleton might be expected to be in the pugilistic pose, and some of the bones, especially those of the extremities, would show signs of burning.[30] The pugilistic pose without evidence of burning might represent cadaveric spasm, or possibly live burial.[31]

Decomposition and Display

Another feature of Anglo-Saxon execution cemeteries that should be considered is the display of criminals, or the heads of criminals, as a deterrent

---

[26] See, for example Rick J. Schulting and Linda Fibiger, eds, *Sticks, Stones, and Broken Bones: Neolithic Violence in a European Perspective* (Oxford, 2012); J. L. Buckberry, 'Peri-Mortem Trauma at Stirling Castle' (in prep).

[27] J. Blondiaux et al., 'Bilateral Fractures of the Scapula: Possible Archeological Examples of Beatings from Europe, Africa and America,' *International Journal of Paleopathology* 2 (2012), 223–30.

[28] Christopher W. Schmidt and Steven A. Symes, eds, *The Analysis of Burned Human Remains* (London, 2008).

[29] Schmidt and Symes, *Burned Human Remains*; D. H. Ubelaker, 'The Forensic Evaluation of Burned Skeletal Remains: A Synthesis,' *Forensic Science International* 183 (2009), pp. 1–5.

[30] While most of the extremities would show the highest degree of burning, the fingers would be curled into, and protected by the palms of the hand. Thus distal hand phalanges are often less well burnt than other elements.

[31] See the debate on G41, Sewerby: S. M. Hirst, *An Anglo-Saxon Inhumation Cemetery at Swereby East Yorkshire*, York University Archaeological Publications 4 (York, 1985); T. Anderson, 'Palaeopathology: More than Just Dry Bones,' *Proceedings of the Royal College of Physicians of Edinburgh* 24 (1994), 554–80; C. J. Knüsel, R. C. Janaway and S. E. King, 'Death, Decay and Ritual Reconstruction: Archaeological Evidence of Cadaveric Spasm,' *Oxford Journal of Archaeology* 15 (1996), 121–8.

to others. Indeed, it has been argued that this might be why many execution cemeteries are located close to important routeways.[32] If an entire body was left on the gallows for any period, it would start to decompose. One of the most important factors in the decomposition of exposed bodies is the position of the remains; areas that are exposed are more accessible to insects and therefore are likely to decompose more rapidly than those in contact with the ground or protected in some way. Overall it is agreed that the decomposition of cadavers is highly variable, with ambient temperatures, humidity, insects, and scavengers (among other factors) all having a part to play in the decomposition process, and influencing especially the rate and sequence of decomposition.[33] As such, it is difficult to establish a 'standard' sequence of decomposition for human remains, although it has been suggested that humans broadly follow the same disarticulation pattern as large mammals.[34] In large ungulates, which were presumably lying on their sides, this pattern of disarticulation starts with the shoulder joint, followed by those between the cranium and atlas, and cranium and mandible. After this, the joints between major long bones and within the extremities disarticulate, followed by those joints of the body supported by large areas of muscle mass or strong ligaments, such as the intervertebral joints of the thoracic and lumbar regions, the articulations between the thoracic vertebrae and ribs, and the two articulations between the radius and ulna in the forearm. The sacro-iliac joint (at the back of the pelvis) and the cervical intervertebral joints often endure the longest.[35] In cases of hanging, the process of disarticulation is different, as the body is not supported by the surface it is lying on. Modern forensic cases of hanging have shown that the first joint to disarticulate is usually in the neck, causing the body to be released from the noose and to fall to the ground. Often the head will roll away, especially if the ground is sloped.[36] The body would then skeletonise from the position it fell in.

Patterns of decomposition and disarticulation have been used to interpret the post-mortem fate of archaeological human remains.[37] Labile joints are

---

[32] Andrew Reynolds, 'The Geography of Burial in Later Anglo-Saxon England: Expressions of Status in Unfurnished Burials,' paper presented at the International Medieval Congress at Leeds, 8–11 July 2002.

[33] R. W. Mann, W. M. Bass and L. Meadows, 'Time Since Death and Decomposition of the Human Body: Variables and Observations in Case and Experimental Field Studies,' *Journal of Forensic Sciences* 35 (1990), 103–11; Alison Galloway, 'The Process of Decomposition: A Model from the Arizona-Sonoran Desert,' *Forensic Taphonomy: The Postmortem Fate of Human Remains*, ed. William D. Haglund and Marcella H. Sorg (Boca Raton, FL, 1997), pp. 139–50.

[34] Douglas H. Ubelaker, 'Taphonomic Applications in Forensic Anthropology,' *Forensic Taphonomy*, ed. Haglund and Sorg, pp. 77–90, at 77.

[35] A. Hill and A. K. Behrensmeyer, 'Disarticulation Patterns of Some Modern East African Mammals,' *Paleobiology* 10 (1984), 366–76.

[36] Rob Janaway, pers. comm.

[37] A. Boddington, 'Chaos, Disturbance and Decay in an Anglo-Saxon Cemetery,' *Death, Decay and Reconstruction: Approaches to Archaeology and Forensic Science*, ed. A. Boddington, A. N. Garland and R. C. Janaway (Manchester, 1987), pp. 27–42; Henri Duday, 'Archaeothanatology or the Archaeology of Death,' *The Social Archaeology of Funerary Remains*, ed. Rebecca Gowland and Christopher Knüsel (Oxford, 2006), pp. 30–56; Henri Duday and Mark Guillon,

those that disarticulate rapidly, whereas persistent joints remain articulated for longer during the decomposition process. By recording the level of articulation of both labile and persistent joints it is possible to infer how well-preserved a body was at the time of burial, although it must be noted that voids in the burial environment will also allow disarticulation to occur.[38] For most burials during the later Anglo-Saxon period, the body will have been buried when the soft tissues were sufficiently well-preserved for joints to have remained in articulation. Some of these joints are likely to disarticulate in the grave, especially if they were placed in a coffin, which created a void around the body until the coffin had decayed.[39] In an unenclosed inhumation burial, if disarticulation is faster than the infilling with soil of the void produced as soft tissue decomposes, bones will become displaced within the grave. If there is material supporting the joints, such as infilling soil or some form or wrapping, more joints remain articulated.[40] Thus, individuals inhumed in a coffin will show a higher degree of disarticulation than individuals placed directly into the grave. Individuals who are exposed for a period of time before inhumation will display a higher degree of disarticulation than those interred rapidly, but these individuals may retain articulation at the persistent joints.[41] In a hanging–display scenario, the labile joints will disarticulate more readily, and individual bones will fall from the suspended body. This process will be accelerated if scavengers can reach the remains. If an individual was buried after a period of exposure, but before the major joints became disarticulated, one might expect the hands, feet and possibly clavicles to have been lost prior to burial. After a longer period of display, larger joints such as the shoulder, knee or neck may disarticulate. Interestingly, it has been noted that the atlanto-occipital joint (between the atlas and occipital) is more persistent than the cervical intervertebral joints, and that initial disarticulation at the neck often occurs at the atlas–axis articulation, or at the axis–third-cervical articulation.[42] If a body was decapitated prior to burial, one would expect the first, and possibly the second, cervical vertebra to be articulated with the cranium, and the remainder of the cervical vertebrae to be with the torso. Future excavations of Anglo-Saxon execution cemeteries could utilise the archaeothanatological approach to better understand the post-mortem

---

'Understanding the Circumstances of Deposition when the Body is Skeletonised,' *Forensic Anthropology and Forensic Medicine: Complementary Sciences from Recovery to Cause of Death*, ed. Aurore Schmitt, Eugénia Cunha, and João Pinheiro (Totowa, NJ, 2006), pp. 117–58; Henri Duday, *The Archaeology of the Dead: Lectures in Archaeothanatology* (Oxford, 2009); K. Gerdau-Radonic, 'Archaeological Insights into the Disarticulation Pattern of a Human Body in a Sitting/Squatting Position,' *Proceedings of the Twelfth Annual Conference of the British Association for Biological Anthropology and Osteoarchaeology*, ed. P. D. Mitchell and J. L. Buckberry, BAR International Series 2390 (Oxford, 2012), 151–60.

[38] Duday and Guillon, 'Understanding the Circumstances of Deposition.'
[39] Boddington, 'Chaos, Disturbance and Decay.'
[40] Duday and Guillon, 'Understanding the Circumstances of Deposition.'
[41] Duday and Guillon, 'Understanding the Circumstances of Deposition.'
[42] Duday, 'Archaeothanatology or the Archaeology of Death'; Gerdau-Radonic, 'Disarticulation Pattern of a Human Body.'

deposition sequence of individuals who may have been displayed for a period before burial.

If the body decomposes to a point that bone is exposed, it may be possible to observe weathering of the bone surface, such as cracking and flaking of the bone cortex.[43] Care must be taken here, as the cortex of buried bone can also display taphonomic alteration.[44] At Cottam, East Yorkshire, a combination of weathering on the frontal bone of a disarticulated cranium and a discrepancy between the radiocarbon date for the bone compared with the stratigraphic date for its deposition have been used to argue that this individual's head might have been displayed. Only the cranium was recovered; the mandible and cervical vertebrae were not in articulation. The cranium was radiocarbon dated to AD 647 to 877 (cal 2 sigma), whereas the pit it was deposited in contained a coin dating to AD 858 to 862.[45] This was interpreted as possible evidence for the use of head stakes (*heafod stoccan*), sometimes explicitly linked to the treatment of criminals, in Anglo-Saxon written sources, including charter boundaries.[46] This cranium did not show any evidence of trauma or damage to the cranial base, but cranial base damage has been interpreted as possible evidence of display on a stake at the later Bronze Age cemetery of Runnymede on the Surrey/Berkshire border.[47] Here, the fragmented remains of a cranium (without a mandible) were found in a pit which also contained a stake. Reconstruction of the cranium revealed the absence of the base of the cranium, with a roughly circular hole in the occipital bone, although it was difficult to assess if this area had been removed deliberately. The direct association of this cranium with a stake, and the location of the pit close to a possible entranceway, were used to support the interpretation of display.[48] However, isolated crania should not automatically be interpreted as evidence of display; at Walkington Wold, two of the isolated crania had claw marks consistent with a badger, somewhat unsurprising given that the cemetery had been partially disturbed by a badger sett.[49] Thus, evidence of post-mortem damage can also be important for the interpretation of remains.

[43] Ubelaker, 'Taphonomic Applications.'
[44] Jane E. Buikstra and Douglas H. Ubelaker, *Standards for Data Collection from Human Skeletal Remains*, Arkansas Archaeological Survey Research Series 44 (Fayetteville, 1994); Jacqueline I. McKinley, 'Compiling a Skeletal Inventory: Disarticulated and Co-mingled Remains,' *Guidelines to the Standards for Recording Human Remains*, ed. Megan Brickley and Jacqueline I. McKinley, Institute of Field Archaeologists Paper 7 (Southampton, 2004), pp. 14–17.
[45] J. D. Richards, 'Cottam: An Anglian and Anglo-Scandinavian Settlement on the Yorkshire Wolds,' *ArchJ* 156 (1999), 1–110, at 34–7 and 92–4.
[46] S 430 and 501; Skeat, *LS* I, p. 492; Stanley Rypins, ed., *Three Old English Prose Texts in MS Cotton Vitellius A xv*, EETS o.s. 161 (1924), p. 161; A. L. Meaney, 'Pagan English Sanctuaries, Place-Names and Hundred Meeting-Places,' *Anglo-Saxon Studies in Archaeology and History* 8 (1995), 29–42, at 30.
[47] A. Boylston, S. Norton and C. Roberts, 'Ritual or Refuse? Late Bronze Age Mortuary Practices at Runnymede,' unpublished osteological report, Biological Anthropology Research Centre, Department of Archaeological Sciences, University of Bradford (1995).
[48] Boylston *et al.*, 'Ritual or Refuse?' p. 15.
[49] Buckberry, 'Off With Their Heads.'

The Demography of Execution

It has been argued that Anglo-Saxon execution cemeteries contain a high proportion of adult males, and that many of these were relatively young.[50] Indeed, of the 813 individuals buried in Anglo-Saxon execution cemeteries identified by Andrew Reynolds, 259 were identified as male and just 67 as female. The remaining 487 were either unsexed, or no mention of their sex was present in the original excavation reports. The number of females is skewed by data from South Acre, where 36 of the 70 individuals (51.4%) who could be sexed were identified as female or possibly female.[51] It should be noted that at two of the sites discussed by Reynolds in *Anglo-Saxon Deviant Burial Customs*, reanalysis of the skeletal material has reduced the number of females: from 1 to 0 at Walkington Wold, and from 2 to 1 at Old Dairy Cottage.[52] The recent publication of evidence from the cemetery at St John's College, Oxford, adds an additional 33 males, and no females.[53] Thus, using the most up-to-date data available, there are 294 males and 65 females, providing a sex ratio of 4.5:1 for Anglo-Saxon execution cemeteries. There is clearly a bias towards males, but the full extent of this needs to be confirmed through reassessment of the sex of the individuals excavated a few decades ago. If the sex imbalance is shown to be true, then the reasons behind this imbalance should be investigated. Were males more likely to commit a crime that carried a harsh penalty, or were women more likely to be given a lenient sentence? The suggestion that the age-at-death profile of execution cemeteries is skewed towards younger individuals should also be investigated further. The identification of older individuals is notoriously difficult from skeletal remains[54] and it is now recognised that many age estimation methods will predict a demographic profile that mimics that of the population the method was developed on.[55] Bayesian modelling of age-at-death profiles at execution sites may allow us to investigate this further, as it will remove the biases inherent in traditional age-estimation methods. It will also facilitate more nuanced interpretations of the age-at-death structure, allowing us to investigate whether the profile is characteristic of a normal, attritional population, or whether other factors may be behind biases in age profile; factors such as

---

[50] Wymer, 'Ring Ditch at South Acre'; Buckberry, 'Off With Their Heads'; Reynolds, *Deviant Burial*.
[51] Wymer, 'Ring Ditch at South Acre.'
[52] Buckberry and Hadley, 'An Anglo-Saxon Execution Cemetery'; Cherryson et al., 'He Shall Be Slain.'
[53] A. M. Pollard et al., '"Sprouting Like Cockle Amongst the Wheat": The St Brice's Day Massacre and the Isotopic Analysis of Human Bones from St John's College, Oxford,' *Oxford Journal of Archaeology* 31 (2012), 83–102.
[54] Andrew Chamberlain, 'Problems and Prospects in Palaeodemography,' *Human Osteology*, ed. Cox and Mays, pp. 101–16; Margaret Cox, 'Ageing Adults from the Skeleton,' *Human Osteology*, ed. Cox and Mays, pp. 61–81.
[55] J. P. Bocquet-Appel and C. Masset, 'Farewell to Palaeodemography,' *Journal of Human Evolution* 11 (1982), 321–33.

catastrophic events, immigration, or, in the case of execution cemeteries, social reasons.[56]

Osteological Evidence of Corporal Punishment

Corporal punishments, as listed in Anglo-Saxon law codes, often included amputation of the hand or foot. Most other forms of corporal punishment or judicial ordeal, such as burning, scalding, whipping, or the mutilation of eyes, ears, and nose,[57] would have affected the soft tissue rather than the skeleton, and are therefore unlikely to be identifiable in the archaeological record. Thus, this section will specifically deal with the osteological evidence of amputation.

Many individuals would survive the amputation of a limb, and one would expect to see evidence of a healed stump; a bony callus forms at the ends of the bone, covering the exposed medullary cavity, and over time the bone surface would appear smooth and rounded (Plate 7.4).[58] Secondary infections might be expected; in these cases deposits of uneven bone might be present overlying the original bone cortex, and/or drainage holes for pus (cloacae) might be present if the bone marrow in the medullary cavity was involved (osteomyelitis). If the amputee survived for a long time, there may be wasting of the affected limb (disuse atrophy), and an increase in robusticity on the opposite side may also be present.[59] If an individual did not survive, the severed bone would display peri-mortem (unhealed) sharp-force trauma, running approximately perpendicular to the shaft of the bone. The distal (removed) portion is unlikely to be recovered from the same context. Striations would be evident on the cut surface from the tool used for the amputation (Plate 7.5).[60] In the case of a peri-mortem injury, it is extremely difficult to determine from the osteological evidence if an individual was alive when a limb was severed but subsequently died of a complication, such as haemorrhage, or if the individual was mutilated after death. Interpretation would

---

[56] R. L. Gowland and A. T. Chamberlain, 'Detecting Plague: Palaeodemographic Characterisation of a Catastrophic Death Assemblage,' *Antiquity* 79 (2005), 146–57; Andrew Chamberlain, *Demography in Archaeology* (Cambridge, 2006); R. C. Redfern and A. T. Chamberlain, 'A Demographic Analysis of Maiden Castle Hillfort: Evidence for Conflict in the Late Iron Age and Early Roman Period,' *Journal of Paleopathology* 1 (2011), 68–73.

[57] Reynolds, *Deviant Burial*, pp. 21–6.

[58] S. Mays, 'Healed Limb Amputations in Human Osteoarchaeology and their Causes: A Case Study from Ipswich, UK,' *International Journal of Osteoarchaeology* 6 (1996), 101–13.

[59] P. Ponce, I. Arabaolaza and A. Boylston, 'Industrial Accident or Deliberate Amputation? Three Case Studies from a Victorian Population in Wolverhampton, West Midlands,' *Proceedings of the Seventh Annual Conference of the British Association for Biological Anthropology and Osteoarchaeology*, ed. S. R. Zakrzewski and W. White, BAR International Series 1712 (Oxford, 2007), pp. 36–42.

[60] Louise Fowler and Natasha Powers, *Doctors, Dissection and Resurrection Men: Excavations in the 19th-Century Burial Ground of the London Hospital, 2006*, MOLA Monograph 62 (London, 2012), pp. 166–9 and 175–85.

Osteological Evidence

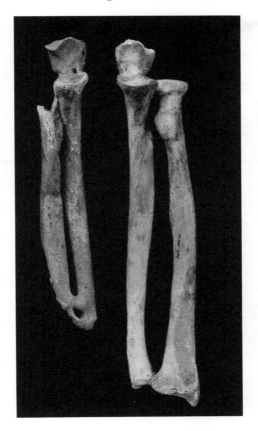

PLATE 7.4 Healed amputation from later medieval Ipswich; note the rounded, healed ends of the bones (photograph © English Heritage)

rely on evidence from the burial context, but strong conclusions may not be forthcoming.[61]

Crucially, those who had a judicial amputation may not have been buried alongside execution victims, and thus we need to look at patterns of amputation in the entire population, bearing in mind that it will be difficult to ascertain if amputations were judicial, medical, or the result of accidents or battle trauma.[62] Osteologically, amputations are comparatively uncommon, but they have been identified in a variety of populations in Britain; most

---

[61] See the discussion of this issue at a nineteenth-century hospital site in London in Fowler and Powers, *Doctors, Dissection and Resurrection Men*, pp. 166–9.
[62] Mays, 'Healed Limb Amputations'; Fowler and Powers, *Doctors, Dissection and Resurrection Men*.

PLATE 7.5 Nineteenth-century peri-mortem amputation from the Royal London Hospital. This amputation was done with an amputation saw, leaving obvious grooves and striations on the cut surface. As Anglo-Saxon amputations were likely to have been undertaken with a sword or axe, the peri-mortem cut surface would be smoother, with small striations from imperfections in the blade edge. (photograph © Museum of London Archaeology)

reported examples show evidence of healing.[63] There is, however, scant evidence for amputation dating to the early medieval period in England. Of the two amputations attributed to the Anglo-Saxon period in *Health and Disease in Britain from Prehistory to the Present Day*[64] (which collated evidence from a huge number of osteological reports), one was wrongly identified, having been recovered from a cemetery now dated AD 1263 to 1548.[65] The second case was from Tean Island in the Scilly Isles off the coast of Cornwall.

---

[63] Charlotte Roberts, 'Trauma in Biocultural Perspective: Past, Present and Future Work in Britain,' *Human Osteology*, ed. Cox and Mays, pp. 337–56; Charlotte Roberts and Margaret Cox, *Health and Disease in Britain from Prehistory to the Present Day* (Stroud, 2003).
[64] Roberts and Cox, *Health and Disease*, pp. 216–17.
[65] Mays, 'Healed Limb Amputations'; and pers. comm.

Only a short summary of the case has been published.[66] Interestingly, from an osteological perspective, peri-mortem amputations may be under reported, as taphonomic damage to the cut surface could remove all direct evidence of amputation.[67] In contrast, amputation and mutilation are probably over reported in the archaeological record, as missing extremities are frequently noted and sometimes interpreted as evidence of amputation or mutilation, especially in older excavation reports. A recent study of skeletons recorded in excavation reports to have suffered amputation or mutilation found no osteological evidence to support those findings.[68] Care must be taken that reliable evidence of amputation, in the form of either a healed stump or a cut surface, is present before further interpretations are made, as hands and feet in particular are often disturbed post-mortem.

The severed hand or foot, if excavated, would also provide evidence that amputation took place. These elements would also display unhealed sharp-force trauma, but it is uncertain where they would ordinarily be disposed. It is possible that amputated hands or feet may have been deposited with refuse, and thus that an articulated hand might be recovered from a midden context. There is documentary evidence that suggests an alternative fate for a severed limb. II Æthelstan 26 indicates that in the case of moneyers who issued false coin, the severed hand was to be displayed above the mint.[69] Over time the displayed hand would decompose, separating the individual bones, and it is therefore unlikely that they would have been deposited as a group. The author is unaware of any hands (with or without evidence of trauma) recovered from any Anglo-Saxon settlement site. Amputated limbs and dissected bodies have been recovered from a variety of post-medieval deposits, many of which are thought to be the medical waste from anatomy schools.[70] There is no reason why amputated hands and feet would not survive in the archaeological record, but it is well known that these smaller bones are more likely to be missed during excavation.[71] Even if they were recovered, the cut surface may not survive, making interpretation extremely difficult.

We have a growing body of archaeological and osteological evidence of capital punishment in later Anglo-Saxon England; however, it is apparent that detailed osteological and palaeopathological analysis is crucial to our understanding of these sites. It is essential that older osteological assemblages

---

[66] D. Brothwell and V. Møller-Christensen, 'Medio-historical Aspects of a Very Early Case of Mutilation,' *Danish Medical Bulletin* 10 (1963), 21.
[67] Roberts, 'Trauma in Biocultural Perspective.'
[68] L. Felix, 'Osteological Evidence of Judicial Mutilation in Anglo-Saxon Execution Cemeteries' (unpublished MSc dissertation, University of Bradford, 2009).
[69] Compare the essay by Daniel O'Gorman in this volume.
[70] For example, P. D. Mitchell et al., 'The Study of Anatomy in England from 1700 to the Early 20th Century,' *Journal of Anatomy* 219 (2011), 91–9; Fowler and Powers, *Doctors, Dissection and Resurrection Men*.
[71] T. Waldron, 'The Relative Survival of the Human Skeleton: Implications for Palaeopathology,' *Death, Decay and Reconstruction*, ed. Boddington et al., pp. 55–64.

are revisited and reanalysed, if they are still extant. Osteology has successfully identified decapitation as a common mode of execution; evidence for hanging is more ephemeral, and is more likely to be inferred from a combination of cemetery characteristics, the demography of the individuals within the cemetery, the presence of fully articulated burials, and, possibly, post holes that may relate to gallows. The nature and biomechanics of bone trauma associated with hanging means that osteological evidence of hanging, at a time when long drops do not appear to have been utilised, is less likely.

The lack of direct evidence of amputation in the archaeological record is intriguing. Clearly corporal (and capital) punishment would have only affected a small proportion of the living population, as only a small proportion of any population is likely to resort to crime. This is borne out by the small number of individuals excavated from Anglo-Saxon execution cemeteries, compared with the overall number of skeletons excavated from other contexts. Good evidence of amputation is virtually non-existent, but this could be explained in part by evidence of unhealed amputations being missed in early osteological reports, and by post-mortem disturbance of burials removing some evidence. But even taking this into consideration, there is a real mismatch in the documentary sources and the osteological record. Archaeological evidence also suggests that execution was a rare punishment; many Anglo-Saxon execution cemeteries appear to have been in use for a long period, yet contain relatively few individuals. Both Sutton Hoo and Stockbridge Down appear to have been in use for up to 500 years, but they contain just thirty-nine and forty-one burials respectively, suggesting executions took place approximately once every decade.[72] At Walkington Wold, a total of thirteen individuals were buried over a period of between 220 and 390 years, suggesting just one or two executions per generation.[73] This may account for the varied locations of decapitation blows at this cemetery, and the presence of two individuals with injuries quite high up on the back of the cranium, perhaps suggesting they were struck by an inexperienced executioner.[74] It is quite likely that the corporal and capital punishments in Anglo-Saxon law codes constitute a deterrent rather than a reality. Most individuals were fined for their crimes, whereas more severe punishments appear to have been meted out infrequently. Thus it could be argued that Anglo-Saxon law codes were effective in preventing the most serious crimes from being committed on a regular basis.

---

[72] Reynolds, *Deviant Burial*, p. 247.
[73] Buckberry and Hadley, 'Anglo-Saxon Execution Cemetery.'
[74] Buckberry and Hadley, 'Anglo-Saxon Execution Cemetery.'

8

Mutilation and Spectacle in Anglo-Saxon Legislation

Daniel O'Gorman

This chapter explores a particular type of corporal punishment, one that has elements unique to later Anglo-Saxon England. It makes its first appearance in the Grately code of King Æthelstan, likely promulgated in the late 920s.[1] This punishment, which targeted minters who struck coins in an unauthorized fashion, is found in a section that appears to have been part of an earlier code that had been incorporated into the Grately edict.[2] Denoted as clause 14.1 in its modern edition, the law states:

> If a moneyer is found guilty, let the hand with which he performed the crime be cut off, and set up on the mint. If there is a charge and he wishes to clear himself, then he shall go to the hot iron and clear the hand with which he is accused of performing the evil. If he then is found guilty at that ordeal, do the same as is said here before.[3]

---

[1] The sobriquet comes from the epilogue to this code, which begins 'All this was ordained at the great synod at Grately' [Ealle ðis wæs gesetted on ðam miclan synoþ æt Greatanleage]. Felix Liebermann reprints this epilogue from William Lambarde's Ἀρχαιονομια (London, 1568), the *editio princeps*. Although it appears in the vernacular in no extant manuscript, Liebermann believed that Lambarde ('Ld') had taken it from one of a series of manuscripts to which he had had access but had since been lost: see Liebermann, *Gesetze* I, pp. 166 and xxxiii–iv. Patrick Wormald demonstrates that, in this instance, either Lambarde or his mentor in Old English, Laurence Nowell, likely supplied the epilogue by retranslating from the Latin translation found in the *Quadripartitus* ('Quadr'), an early twelfth-century compilation of Anglo-Saxon laws: Wormald, 'The Lambarde Problem: Eighty Years On,' *Legal Culture*, pp. 139–78, at 159. Liebermann also prints the epilogue as it appears in *Quadripartitus*, 'The whole of this was instituted and confirmed at the great synod at Grately' [Totum hoc institutum (et confirmatum) est in magna synodo apud Greateleyam]: *Gesetze* I, p. 167. Liebermann follows Reinhold Schmid, *Die Gesteze der Angelsachsen: in der Ursprache mit Übersetzung*, 2nd edn (Leipzig, 1858) in indentifying this code as 'II Æthelstan.' For the dating, see Wormald, *Making of English Law*, pp. 439–40. Unless otherwise noted, all translations are my own.

[2] Successive ordinals ('second, third, ... seventh') introduce clauses 13.1 to 18, suggesting that they represent a previous code that has been preserved in Grately.

[3] '[Gif se] mynetere ful wurðe, slea mon þa hand of, ðe he ðæt ful [mid wor]hte, ꝥ sette upp an þa mynetsmyðþan. Gif hit þonne [tyhtle] sie, ꝥ he hine ladian wille, þonne ga he to hatum isene ꝥ ladie [þa hand, m]id þe man tyhð, þæt þæt facen worhte. Gif he þonne on þam or[dale ful] wurþe, do man þæt ylce swa hit her beforan cweð.' This code survives in two versions. That quoted is from MS BL Cotton Otho B. XI ('Ot'), an early eleventh-century manuscript nearly destroyed in the 1731 Cottonian fire; for details of the manuscript and its preservation of the laws, see Wormald, *Making of English Law*, pp. 172–81. The emendations enclosed in brackets are as in Lieberman, taken from MS Canterbury, Cathedral Library, Lit.

149

The same condign justice is directed towards those minting debased coins in the code now known, rather misleadingly, as IV Æthelred, conventionally dated to the early 990s.[4] Clause 5.3 decrees, with regard to those who produce coins that are either of impure metal or deficient weight: 'And they have ordained that moneyers shall lose a hand and that it shall be set up over that mint.'[5]

In arranging for the display of the severed hand, these two clauses added a new aspect to an established form of punishment. Judicially sanctioned mutilation, in the form of the amputation of a thief's hand, first appeared in the Anglo-Saxon law codes at the end of the ninth century in Alfred's *domboc*, both in his own laws and in those which he attributes to his predecessor Ine.[6] Provisions for such mutilations became both more varied and more frequent in the legislation of the later tenth and early eleventh centuries, eventually incorporating the foot, tongue, nose, ears, upper lip, and scalp and dealing with crimes as varied as swearing falsely, adultery and, most commonly, theft.[7]

A rationale for these multiple prescriptions for bodily disfigurement is found in the laws of Cnut, which state: 'thus one might punish and at the same time preserve the soul.'[8] However, other interpretations of the

---

B. 2 ('So'), a transcript of Otho B. XI made before the fire that he attributed to seventeenth-century antiquarian William Somner, but which has since been recognized as a product of Nowell's. See Liebermann, *Gesetze* I, p. xl; Wormald, *Making of English Law*, p. 262 n. 380.

[4] Benjamin Thorpe, *Ancient Laws and Institutes of England* (London, 1840), pp. 127–9, was the first to so identify this code, based on the arrangement found in *Quadripartitus*, in which what we now know as IV Æthelred 5–9 – a coherent block of statutes primarily given over to the kingdom's coinage – is inserted with some miscellaneous ordinances, along with the tolls and customs provisions that constitute IV Æthelred 1–4.2, after Æthelred's Wantage code (III Æthelred). Thorpe wedded the two parts under the rubric 'De Institutis Lundonie.' The code's dating is derived from an apparent reference to its provisions contained in III Æthelred 8, which can be rather securely fixed to 997, but it could be much older and even originate with one of Æthelred's predecessors.

[5] 'Et constituerunt, monetarii cur manum perdant, et ponatur super ipsius monetae fabricam.' Found only in *Quadripartitus*, this code does not survive in the vernacular. 'They' in this text refers to the 'sapientibus omnibus,' mentioned earlier in the ordinance.

[6] Ine 18 and 37 (in both cases either a hand or a foot), and Alfred 6 (specifying theft from a church).

[7] See Alfred 25.1 (castration, for a slave who rapes another slave); Alfred 32 (tongue, for slander); III Edmund 4 (scalp and little finger, for theft); III Edgar 4 (tongue, for false accusations); II Cnut 16 (tongue, for false accusations); II Cnut 30.4 (hand or foot, for twice-convicted thieves); II Cnut 30.5 (nose, ears and upper lip or scalp, for more serious offenses); II Cnut 36 (hand, for perjury); II Cnut 53 (nose and ears, for committing adultery against one's husband). See also the essay by Valerie Allen in this volume.

[8] 'Swa man mæg styran ⁊ eac thære sawle beorgan': II Cnut 30.5. Interestingly, the biblical injunction, found in Matthew 5:30 and repeated in Mark 9:42, that might seem to offer the clearest justification for such measures – that if your hand offends, you should cut it off – is not cited here or anywhere else in the kingdom's legislation. Indeed, a search of the *Fontes Anglo-Saxonici* indicates that neither verse was drawn upon by Anglo-Saxon authors. Ursula Lenker finds that most, but not all, Anglo-Saxon sources followed Roman tradition in using Mark 9:38–48 as the pericope for the ninth Wednesday after Pentecost: *Die westsächsische Evangelienversion und die Perikopenordnungen im angelsächsischen England* (Munich, 1997), pp. 327 and 330. Matthew 5:30 was not so employed, although Matthew 5:25–9 (which included the similar sentiment that if your eye offends, you should pluck it out) is the pericope

Mutilation and Spectacle

significance of this corporeal scarring have also been offered. Michel Foucault famously argued that the mutilated bodies of criminals (whether alive or dead) functioned as spectacles, reminding all who viewed them of the power of the sovereign.[9] More recently, Katherine O'Brien O'Keeffe, addressing a specifically Anglo-Saxon context, contended that such bodies also served as a constant declaration of the guilt of the perpetrator.[10] In this chapter, I focus not on the criminal body as a whole, but on the detached body part. I wish to explore the spectacle that would have been constructed by the prominent display of a severed hand. If, as Foucault and O'Brien O'Keeffe have argued, the bodies of malefactors served as a text upon which both guilt and the justice of the state were to be inscribed, how were these excised pages intended to be read?

A natural place to begin our search would be with other legislation that contains provision for such spectacles. Unfortunately, a survey of contemporary laws offers little in the way of close parallels. The relevant clause of Æthelstan's Grately code nicely illustrates the combination of borrowing and originality present in much Anglo-Saxon legislation. Seventy years ago, Robert Lopez noted the appearance in several early medieval texts of the principle that a counterfeiter should pay with his hand, which he speculated had been transmitted to the West from Byzantine law sometime in the seventh century.[11] It is found in a Visigothic clause attributed variously to Chindaswinth (r. 642–53) or his successor Receswinth (r. 653–72), which states 'he who debases money whether by clipping or shaving, when first the judge recognizes this, he shall immediately be seized, and if he is a slave, his right hand removed.'[12] At roughly the same time, the code issued by the Lombard Rothari (r. 636–52) contained the similar provision that 'if anyone should shape gold or fabricate money without the command of the king, his hand shall be cut off.'[13]

---

for the fourth Wednesday after Pentecost in all but one list, again in accord with Roman usage. In sum, while no doubt familiar, there is no evidence that this dictum was stressed to Anglo-Saxon audiences.

[9] Michel Foucault, *Surveiller et punir: Naissance de la prison* (Paris, 1975).

[10] Katherine O'Brien O'Keeffe, 'Body and Law in Late Anglo-Saxon England,' *ASE* 27 (1998), 209–32, at 214–18.

[11] R. S. Lopez cites the appearance of this provision in these codes, which he attributes to a lost code of Heraclius (r. 610–41): 'Byzantine Law in the Seventh Century and its Reception by the Germans and the Arabs,' *Byzantion* 16 (1942–3), 445–61, at 450–1. Michael Hendy accepts a Byzantine origin for these laws, but questions the need for an otherwise unrecorded code to serve as their source: *Studies in the Byzantine Monetary Economy, c. 300–1450* (Cambridge, 1985), p. 328.

[12] VII.6.2: 'Qui solidos adulteravit, cirucumciderit sive raserit, ubi primum hoc iudex agnoverit, statim eum conprehendat, et si servus fuerit, eidem dextera manu abscidat': Karl Zeumer, ed., *Leges Visigothorum*, MGH LL nat. Germ. 1 (Hanover, 1902), p. 310. Provisions for the amputation of a hand appear in two other locations in these codes: VII.5.1, for those who forge royal documents or the royal seal, limited to 'minor persona'; and VII.5.9, for all who knowingly dictate spurious material to a notary. The former provision offers the rationale that the hand should be removed because that is the member by which the crime was committed ('per quam tantum crimen admisit').

[13] 242: 'Si quis sine iussionem regis aurum figuraverit aut moneta confinxerit manus ei incidatur': George Pertz, ed., *Leges Langobardum*, MGH LL 4 (Hanover, 1868), p. 60. This clause,

Similar provisions for counterfeiters appear in the 818–19 *Capitula legibus addenda* of Louis the Pious (r. 814–40), which reads: 'Concerning false money, we command: the hand of he who had allowed it to be struck shall be cut off.'[14] In the capitulary collection he assembled in 827, Abbot Ansegisus of St. Wandrille incorporated this language nearly verbatim, and in 864, Charles the Bald (r. 840–77) cited this capitulary by book and chapter in the Edict of Pîtres, when he prescribed the same punishment for counterfeiters.[15] While there is no evidence that Anglo-Saxon legislation was influenced by Visigothic or Lombard precedent, the same cannot be said of these Carolingian decrees. Pîtres may well have been known to Anglo-Saxon lawmakers, and Ansegisus's collection certainly was.[16]

Frisian law constitutes yet another possible source of inspiration. A similar regulation appears in some versions of the Old Frisian *Seventeen Statutes*. The sixteenth statute reads, in part, 'at the command of the judge and with the permission of the emperor or from his representative, for him found guilty and sentenced of counterfeiting coins or reducing coins in size, because of both these deeds the right hand shall be cut off upon the court-platform.'[17] This is not the only instance of parallels between Anglo-Saxon and Frisian law. Based on strong similarities between their respective injury tariffs, Lisi Oliver has argued the case for Frisian influence on the *domboc* issued by Alfred.[18] Alfred's code only predates Grately by some thirty years, so the

  and its immediate successor on false charters, are the only ones which impose this penalty in Rothari's edict.

[14] 19: 'De falsa moneta iubemus: qui eam percussisse conprobatus fuerit, manus ei amputetur': Alfred Boretius, ed., *Capitularia regum Francorum*, MGH Capit. 1 (Hanover, 1883), p. 285. Jean Lafaurie surveys Carolingian measures against forgery, including legislation: 'The *Novi Denarii* and Forgery in the Ninth Century,' *Studies in Numismatic Method Presented to Philip Grierson*, ed. C. N. L. Brooke *et al.* (Washington, D.C., 1983), pp. 137–46.

[15] *Collectio capitularium Ansegisi*, 4.31: 'De falsa moneta iubemus, ut qui eam percussisse conprobatus fuerit, manus ei amputetur': Gerhard Schmitz, ed., *Die Kapitulariensammlung des Ansegis*, MGH Capit. n.s. 1 (Hanover, 1996), pp. 641–2. For the Edict of Pîtres, see Boretius and Krause, *Capitularia regum Francorum* 2, p. 315, no. 273.13. Pîtres cites 'libro IV. capitulorum XXXIII' (or in some manuscripts, 'XXVIII'), but in all extant versions of Ansegisus it is IV.31. Clause 8 of the same code (on the refusal to accept good money) similarly refers to IV.32 as IV.30.

[16] Components of Ansegisus can be found in two English Manuscripts: MS Oxford, Bodleian Library, Hatton 42, a mid-ninth-century compilation that includes Book 1 and elements of Book 2 of Ansegisus's capitularies; and MS Cambridge, Corpus Christi College 265, a Worcester book compiled in the mid-eleventh century that contains excerpts from these two books; see Helmut Gneuss, *Handlist of Anglo-Saxon Manuscripts: A List of Manuscripts and Fragments Written or Owned in England up to 1100* (Tempe, AZ, 2001), p. 159. Clauses 8–24 of Pîtres present a blueprint for Charles's *renovatio* of the coinage, addressing many of the same themes, albeit in greater detail, as IV Æthelred 5–9.

[17] 'Bi skeltata bonne and bi keyseres orloui ieftha sines weldiga boda fon falske tha fon fade sa hach ma sine ferra hond opa tha thingstapule of to slande umbe tha twa deda': Wybren Jan Buma and Wilhelm Ebel, eds, *Das Rüstringer Recht* (Göttingen, 1963), pp. 40–1. The passage is translated by the editors as 'auf Befehl des Skeltata und mit der Erlaubnis des Kaisers oder von dessen Bevollmächtigtem schuldig gesprochen und verurteilt wegen Münzfälschung oder Münzverringerung, so soll man ihm wegen dieser beiden Taten die rechte Hand auf dem Dingstapel abhauen.'

[18] Oliver, *Body Legal*, pp. 235 and 237.

possibility of a continuing Frisian legacy cannot be discounted. However, the earliest surviving written versions of the *Seventeen Statutes* only date to the end of the thirteenth century, and while the statutes as written may incorporate some ninth-century elements, as the reference to the (Carolingian) emperor suggests, establishing a time of composition for any specific piece entails substantial conjecture.[19]

Regardless of the immediate source, if the decree mandating the amputation of a forger's hand had a Continental provenance, the highly visible display of the mutilated body part was a uniquely Anglo-Saxon addition to these laws. Even in England it was not consistently stipulated. Indeed, while juridical mutilation for a wide variety of offenses becomes increasingly common in the kingdom's tenth- and eleventh-century codes, the two clauses on counterfeiters in Grately and IV Æthelred represent the only instances in which the severed pieces of the body are used in such an admonitory fashion.

In the absence of contemporary legal parallels, any attempt to discern the intent behind such a display will have to draw upon a wider range of sources. Literary and archaeological evidence both provide hints that the practice may not have been quite as exceptional as it first seems. We can begin with arguably one of the most famous of early medieval dismembered limbs – the arm that had formerly been attached to Grendel in *Beowulf*, and which briefly adorned the roof of Heorot. Working from the perspective of the poem, both Rolf Bremmer and Gale Owen-Crocker have noted similarities between *Beowulf* and Æthelstan's code.[20] Although the lexical parallels are not precise, the two instances resonate with one another in some significant ways. After Beowulf has wrenched the arm from the monster, its significance as a trophy is trumpeted several times in the poem. The first instance is immediately after the confrontation: 'That was a clear symbol, after the warrior laid down the hand, arm and shoulder – there was Grendel's grasp all together – under the wide roof.'[21] The next morning we are told that 'many a bold-minded man went to the high hall to see the strange wonder.'[22] As for Hrothgar, the king, 'he went to the hall, stood on the platform, saw the steep roof shining with

---

[19] Buma and Ebel, *Rüstringer Recht*, pp. 11–19, discuss the dating and composition of the 'Riustring' manuscript, MS Oldenburg, Niedersäachsisches Staatsarchiv 24.1, Ab. 1, from which the quoted text was taken. Nikolaas Algra fixes the origins of the sixteenth statute to the 'Rule of Charlemagne': 'The Relation Between Frisia and the Empire from 800–1500 in the Light of the Eighth of the *Seventeen Statutes*,' *Approaches to Old Frisian Philology*, ed. Rolf H. Bremmer Jnr, Thomas S. B. Johnston and Oebele Vries (Amsterdam, 1998), pp. 1–76, at 73.

[20] Rolf H. Bremmer Jnr, 'Grendel's Arm and the Law,' *Studies in English Language and Literature: Doubt Wisely: Papers in Honour of E. G. Stanley*, ed. M. J. Toswell and E. M. Tyler (New York, 1996), pp. 121–32, at 126–7; Gale R. Owen-Crocker, 'Horror in *Beowulf*: Mutilation, Decapitation and Unburied Dead,' *Early Medieval English Texts and Interpretations: Studies Presented to Donald G. Scragg*, ed. Elaine Treharne and Susan Rosser (Tempe, AZ, 2003), pp. 81–100, at 94 n. 23.

[21] 'Þæt wæs tacen sweotol, / syþðan hildedeor hond alegde / earm ond eaxle – þær wæs eal geador / Grendles grape – under geapne hr(of)': *Beowulf*, lines 833b–36.

[22] 'Eode scealc monig / swiðhicgende to sele þam hean / searowundor seon': *Beowulf*, lines 918b–20a.

gold and Grendel's hand.'²³ Finally, a more minute inspection is carried out 'when nobles, by the warrior's courage, scrutinized the hand, the foe's fingers, over the high roof.'²⁴ The poem's ambiguities about the precise location of the arm within (or outside) the hall need not detain us here. What matters is the clear similarity to the laws on counterfeiters. In each case, the limb is displayed at the place where the original wrongdoing was committed. In both epic and law, the arm or hand is mounted up high, in such a fashion as to catch the attention of any passer-by; the *Beowulf* poet's repeated insistence on this point leads Bremmer to observe that 'the emphasis on the visibility of the arm makes it clear that the exhibited limb fulfills a function as signal and testimony.'²⁵

A further point also suggests itself: in each case the guilty party has been distanced from the limb in such a way as to suggest that the misdeed lies in the severed element that is on display, and not in the body as a whole. The focus is now on the culpable body part rather than the rest of the person, who is no longer present. Indeed, although in the case of *Beowulf* the audience is made aware of Grendel's subsequent death as a result of the wound, the truncated limb does not in itself inevitably herald the death of the malefactor. Instead, the display of this culpable body part serves to call attention to the specific nature of the transgression, while at the same time providing evidence of the nullification of the threat represented by that limb. Thus, that arm (and by proxy, that individual) would no longer commit murder, just as that hand (and again, given the dexterity required for the striking of hand-hammered coinage, that minter) would no longer falsify coins. This triumphant proclamation of security is explicitly challenged in *Beowulf* when Grendel's mother reclaims her son's bloodied arm the next night and takes it away with her.²⁶ The removal of the arm demonstrates that the implied guarantee of safety represented by the severed limb no longer held, and that the threatening conditions that were in effect prior to Grendel's defeat had returned.

How meaningful are these comparisons? I am by no means so reckless as to suggest that Æthelstan's law was drafted with the specific example of *Beowulf* in mind, or, depending on one's position on the date of its composition, that the epic deliberately included a reference to this provision, whether in Grately or IV Æthelred.²⁷ At a minimum, however, I would claim that themes that would resonate with the poem's audience – namely the forcible amputation

---

²³ 'He to healle geong, / stod on stapole, geseah steapne hrof / golde fahne ond Grendles hond': *Beowulf*, lines 925b–27. I follow Bremmer in understanding the *stapol* neither as the steps leading up to the hall nor as a supporting pillar within the hall, but as an external platform upon which the king carried out many of his duties: 'Grendel's Arm,' pp. 127–8. Bremmer also notes the potential similarity between Beowulf's *stapol* and the Frisian *thingstapul* from the statute on counterfeiters.
²⁴ 'Siþðan æþlingas eorles cræfte / ofer heanne hrof hand sceawedon / feondes fingras': *Beowulf*, lines 982–4a.
²⁵ Bremmer, 'Grendel's Arm,' p. 128.
²⁶ *Beowulf*, lines 1302b–03a.
²⁷ For the most recent discussion on this question, see the essays in L. Neidorf, ed., *The Dating of Beowulf: A Reassessment* (Cambridge, forthcoming). As its title suggests, this volume,

of a transgressor's offending limb, that limb's prominent display at the location where the transgression occurred, and the assertions of authority and communal security inherent in this display – would strike a similar chord among those who encountered this legislation.

The fate of the seventh-century Northumbrian saint and king Oswald presents a second instance of the triumphant display of a vanquished foe's arm. In his *Ecclesiastical History*, Bede writes that after Oswald was defeated at Maserfelth by Penda of Mercia, 'the king who had him slain ordered the head and the hands with the arms shorn from the body and hung on stakes.'[28] As Bremmer notes, the ninth-century Old English translator of Bede develops this passage a bit.[29] In this version we are told 'the king who slew him ordered his head to be set on a stake, and his hand with the arm, which had been struck off the body, he ordered to be hung up.'[30] Here, head and (just one) hand are disposed of in different ways, with the hand hung up so that it might be exhibited, in a fashion not too dissimilar from that described in either *Beowulf* or the coinage laws. Around the millennium, Ælfric, in the homily he wrote for Oswald's feast-day, provided further detail, stating 'then the heathen king ordered his head be struck off, and his right arm, and that they be set up as a trophy.'[31] In this telling the treatment of head and hand is the same, but Ælfric clarifies which of the saint's arms is hung up, and makes explicit that through mounting the head and arm, Penda is proclaiming his victory over Oswald. The similar usage of Oswald's head suggests that such display need not be limited to hands. Here too, a parallel with Beowulf can be discerned; after dispatching the mother, Beowulf struck Grendel's head from its corpse and four men carried it back on a stake to Heorot, where it was dragged by the hair across the floor and exhibited to those assembled within.[32]

We will revisit Oswald's arm presently; for now we turn to the archaeological record, which also offers some hints about the nature of bodily punishment and subsequent display in this period. Society's undesirables, and wrongdoers in particular, ran the very real risk of interment in unconsecrated ground, distant from any churchyard. In his survey of such nontraditional Anglo-Saxon burials, Andrew Reynolds catalogs bodies that have undergone

---

emphasizing the preponderance of evidence pointing to a relatively early date of composition, may be viewed as a response to Colin Chase, ed., *The Dating of Beowulf* (Toronto, 1981).

[28] 'Caput et manus cum brachiis a corpore praecisas iussit rex, qui occiderat, in stipitibus suspendi': Bede, *Ecclesiastical History of the English People*, ed. Bertram Colgrave and R. A. B. Mynors (Oxford, 1969), p. 250.

[29] Bremmer, 'Grendel's Arm,' pp. 125–6.

[30] 'Heht se cyning, se ðe hine slog, his heafod on steng asetton; ⁊ his hond mid þy earme, þe of his lichoman aslegen wæs, het to ahoon': Thomas Miller, ed. and trans., *The Old English Version of Bede's Ecclesiastical History of the English People*, vol. 1, EETS o.s. 95–6 (1890–1, repr. 1959), p. 188.

[31] 'Þa het se hæþena cyningc his heafod of-aslean and his swiðran earm and settan hi to myrcelse': Skeat, *LS* II, p. 136.

[32] *Beowulf*, lines 1637b–39, and 1647–50. Bremmer offers some suggestions on the *wælsteng* upon which Grendel's head was borne: 'Grendel's Arm,' pp. 124 and 130 n. 16.

a range of amputations, including arms, hands, legs, and feet.[33] The concentration of these remains in execution cemeteries suggests a judicial context for such mutilation. This evidence is not unequivocal; the passage of time, the imperfect preservation of most sites, and the imprecise nature of osteological analysis combine to make it extremely difficult to determine when and under what circumstances a given body part was severed, or indeed whether it was separated after death.[34] Further, it is impossible to know whether the specific instances noted by Reynolds constitute amputations for forgery, theft, swearing false oaths, wounding, or for some other crime altogether – although the extant laws only provided for the loss of a hand for these offenses. Taken as a whole, however, their existence strongly indicates that legislation sanctioning such punishments did not exist in theory alone, and indeed was, at least occasionally, put into practice.

Cemetery remains offer no proof as to what was actually done with amputated hands. Reynolds, however, in his survey of those who appear to have been decapitated, assesses the evidence for a display somewhat analogous to that described in Grately. He notes the large proportion of bodies in execution cemeteries in which the skull is missing; in addition he points to the occurrence of the phrase *heafod stoccan* in various charter bounds that describe lands bordering these cemeteries, and concludes that it refers to stakes upon which the severed heads of criminals were mounted.[35] Support for this interpretation comes from Ælfric's homily of the Seven Sleepers, in which, describing the perpetrators of the Decian persecution, he writes: 'and the headless they hung on the town-walls and they set their heads, just like those of other thieves, outside the town-walls on the head-stakes.'[36] This *stocc* also has a parallel in the *steng* on which Oswald's head was placed in the Old English Bede.

As a sign both of the criminality of the malefactors, and of the justice and authority of the king, such heads would have offered a message similar to that of a severed hand, perhaps one that was even more emphatic. Nevertheless, there is a significant difference between these heads and the hands of forgers. Anglo-Saxon execution cemeteries were, as a rule, located away from population centers and often in regions that served as boundaries between parishes, hundreds, and even counties.[37] Their function as cemeteries, and further as cemeteries for those who had been excluded from the life and death of the rest of the community, would have rendered them even more liminal. In contrast with the post-Conquest era, which seems to have witnessed the

---

[33] Reynolds, *Deviant Burial*, pp. 173–4 and 268.
[34] J. L. Buckberry and D. M. Hadley, 'An Anglo-Saxon Execution Cemetery at Walkington Wold, Yorkshire,' *Oxford Journal of Archaeology* 26 (2007), 309–29, at 323–7.
[35] Reynolds, *Deviant Burial*, pp. 223–4, from the suggestion by Percy Reaney of 'a stock or post on which the head of a criminal was fixed after beheading' for *heafod-stocc*: *The Origin of English Place-Names* (London, 1960), p. 158.
[36] 'And ða heafod-leasan man hengc on ða port-weallas and man sette heora heafda swilce oþra ðeofa buton ðam port-weallon on ðam heafod-stoccum': Skeat, *LS* I, p. 492.
[37] Reynolds, *Deviant Burial*, pp. 241–50.

interment of criminals in designated hospitals or parishes, these execution cemeteries were, by every measure, on the periphery, and thus any heads displayed there were unlikely to have been observed on a regular basis by many people.[38] Ælfric too, apparently considered the proper place for such an array to be 'outside the walls' – that is, at a distance (albeit an undefined one) from the community. Obviously, this isolation would not preclude a general knowledge of such an exhibition, but it was not as likely to function as edifying 'spectacle.'

Mints, in contrast, were both ubiquitous and integral to the Anglo-Saxon community. From just a handful at the time of the death of Alfred, they continued to proliferate throughout the tenth and eleventh centuries, and roughly 100 pre-Conquest locations where coins were struck have been identified on the basis of mint signatures.[39] Not only were they common to most significant settlements, they appear also to have been restricted to such settlements, as indicated by the clause that immediately succeeds IV Æthelred's restatement of Grately, which is directed against those who mint in 'forests or similar places,' decreeing that they shall forfeit their lives unless the king elects to show them mercy.[40] Therefore, unlike the decapitated heads impaled upon stakes at relatively remote execution cemeteries, severed hands mounted upon the smithies at which coins were struck would have constituted a spectacle encountered much more regularly by a far broader swathe of the populace.

The notion that such visibility would have been desirable, however, raises the question of why provision for this kind of display is not found elsewhere in the kingdom's laws. One possible explanation is that the mint, which functioned not only as a workshop but also as a venue at which individuals could exchange old coins for new, occupied a more public space than that where many other crimes would have been perpetrated; if a thief's hand were to be mounted at the place where the theft occurred, or a married woman's

---

[38] Christopher Daniell, 'Conquest, Crime and Theology in the Burial Record: 1066–1220,' *Burial in Early Medieval England and Wales*, ed. Sam Lucy and Andrew Reynolds (London, 2002), pp. 241–54, at 243–7. Jay Paul Gates shows how the early eleventh-century death of Eadric Streona becomes a public spectacle, with a subsequent display of his head in London, when it is taken up by Anglo-Norman historians: see 'Imagining Justice in the Anglo-Saxon Past: Eadric *Streona*, Kingship and the search for community,' *HSJ* 25 (forthcoming); and also his essay in this volume.

[39] H. Bertil Petersson presents a census of 44,350 Anglo-Saxon pennies of the late tenth and eleventh centuries found in Scandinavian hoards. He finds 107 different mint signatures, three of which he can only tentatively place, and seventeen of which cannot be geographically located at all: 'Coins and Weights: Late Anglo-Saxon Pennies and Mints, c. 973–1066,' *Studies in Late Anglo-Saxon Coinage in Memory of Bror Emil Hildebrand*, ed. Kenneth Jonsson, Svenska numismatiska foreningen numismatiska meddelanden 35 (Stockholm, 1990), pp. 207–433, at 213–14.

[40] 'Et monetarii, qui in nemoribus operantur uel alicubi similibus fabricant, uitae suae culpabiles sint, nisi rex uelit eorum misereri.' A nearly identical reading can be found at the end of Æthelred's Wantage code (III Æthelred 16), dated to the late 990s: '⁊ þa myneteres þe inne wuda wyrceð oððe elles hwær, þæt þa bion heora feores scyldig, buton se cyning heom arian wille.'

nose or ears at the site where she committed adultery, they were unlikely to have been quite so conspicuous. Another, perhaps more compelling, reason may lie in the nature of the crime. In later Anglo-Saxon England, every coin bore the name of the king. The ruler's portrait was featured with increasing frequency as well; after Edgar's reforms in the early 970s, with the exception of the extremely limited *Agnus Dei* issue, it too became a constant.[41] A moneyer who created impure or underweight coinage was in effect falsifying the king's name and image. In this respect, it may be significant that seventh-century Visigothic and Lombard law also mandated the loss of a hand for those who forged royal charters, but for no other offenses. The striking of bad money seems to have fallen into a restricted class of misdemeanors that were construed as a direct assault on royal dignity and probity.

This hypothesis can be tested by examining the continued evolution of legal measures taken to combat counterfeiting after the Conquest. One particularly notorious event indicates that mutilation of minters of false or adulterated coin endured at least into the 1120s. Henry of Huntingdon, Symeon of Durham, Robert of Torigni, and the Anglo-Saxon Chronicle, among others, all record that at the order of Henry I, many counterfeiters (a somewhat later source, the Margam Chronicle, gives the number as ninety-four) had their right hands removed – although none indicate what, if anything, was done with the hands after they were severed – and were castrated as well.[42] In succeeding generations, later commentators supply further details on punishment, and, more usefully, rationales as to why striking and circulating debased or clipped coins were considered particularly serious crimes.

Towards the end of the twelfth century, *Glanvill* places falsifying – a broad category into which fall the creation of false charters, measures, money, and 'other similar acts that comprise such falsification' – in the restricted list of criminal acts to be adjudicated in a royal court, along with others such as homicide, rape, and arson.[43] All such crimes incur the penalty of loss of limb or death.[44] The author goes on to state that the forgery of royal charters, as opposed to private ones, is a form of *lèse-majesté*, which the text had earlier defined as plotting or acting against the king's life, or betrayal of the realm

---

[41] Kenneth Jonsson offers a detailed treatment of Edgar's reform, and usefully contrasts pre- and post-reform monetary regimes: *The New Era: The Reformation of the Late Anglo-Saxon Coinage* (Stockholm, 1987). Simon Keynes reviews the context and possible motivation for the production of the *Agnus Dei* penny: 'An Abbot, an Archbishop and the Viking Raids of 1006–7 and 1009–12,' *ASE* 36 (2007), 151–220.

[42] Henry of Huntingdon, *Historia Anglorum*, ed. and trans. Diana Greenway (Oxford, 1996), p. 474; Symeon of Durham, 'Historia Regum,' in Thomas Arnold, ed., *Symeonis Monachi opera omnia*, vol. 2 (London, 1882–5), p. 281; Elisabeth Van Houts, ed. and trans., *Gesta Normannorum ducum*, vol. 2 (Oxford, 1992–5), pp. 236–8; ASC E, s.a. 1125; H. R. Luard, ed., 'Annales de Margan,' *Annales monastici*, vol. 1 (London, 1864-9), p. 11. This event is discussed in some detail by Mark Blackburn, 'Coinage and Currency under Henry I: A Review,' *ANS* 13 (1991), 49–81, at 64–8.

[43] 'Alia similia que talem falsitatem continent': G. D. G. Hall, ed. and trans., *The Treatise of the Laws and Customs of the Realm of England Commonly Called Glanvill* (London, 1965), p. 176.

[44] Hall, *Glanvill*, pp. 3 and 177.

or the army.[45] By the middle of the next century, Bracton was willing to countenance the addition of counterfeiting and coin clipping to forging the royal seal as acts that, 'touch the crown of the king,' and thus also constitute *lèse-majesté*.[46] Bracton describes this as a transgression which exceeds all others in its punishment; those found guilty are to be drawn, broken, and hanged, their goods confiscated and their heirs disinherited.[47] Two additional works of the later thirteenth century expand on this. *Britton* confirms that, just as with plotting against the king's life or crown, falsifying the royal seal and counterfeiting or clipping coin is high treason, for which the penalty is drawing and death, or, in the case of women, burning.[48] Elsewhere in this text, an extended list of offenses against the coinage includes not only counterfeiting and clipping, but debasing coins, striking coins of whatever quality without royal permission, and importing counterfeit.[49] Finally, *Fleta* also agrees that forgery of the royal seal, counterfeiting, and coin clipping are all *lèse-majesté*, no less than designs against the king's life, realm or army.[50] The penalties for such betrayal are those found in Bracton, with an additional provision for 'intensified bodily pain.'[51]

Two conclusions can be drawn from this survey. The commentators are unanimous in associating forgery of the king's seal (and, by extension, the production of documents with such a seal) with the forgery of the king's money. Further, both crimes are regarded as of the gravest category of offenses – on a level with conspiring against the king's person – in a way that separates them from almost all other wrongdoings.[52] This connection was codified in the Treason Act of 1351, in which counterfeiting the royal seal or money and knowingly importing false money were included among the seven offenses to be considered high treason.[53] The supposition, then, that counterfeiting was viewed as a particularly egregious act, and a direct affront to the crown, seems well supported. What are absent are instances of display analogous to those prescribed for the severed hands of Anglo-Saxon counterfeiters.

---

[45] Hall, *Glanvill*, pp. 171–2 and 176–7.
[46] 'Tangit coronam domini regis': Henry de Bracton, *On the Laws and Customs of England*, vol. 2, ed. George Woodbine, trans. Samuel Thorne (Cambridge, MA, 1968–77), pp. 334–8.
[47] Bracton, *Laws and Customs of England*, pp. 318 and 334–5.
[48] Francis Morgan Nichols, ed. and trans., *Britton*, vol. 1 (Oxford, 1865), pp. 40–1.
[49] Nichols, *Britton*, p. 25.
[50] H. G. Richardson and G. O. Sayles, eds and trans, *Fleta*, vol. 2 (London, 1955–82), p. 46.
[51] 'Cum pene aggrauacione corporalis': Richardson and Sayles, *Fleta*, p. 56. The crimes of coin-clipping and counterfeiting are defined at great length in this text at pp. 55 and 58–9 respectively. In the latter instance, the penalty is given as drawing and hanging for men, and burning for women.
[52] Richardson and Sayles, *Fleta*, p. 46, marks the only instance in these commentaries in which another crime is elevated to this category: concealing the discovery of treasure-trove is here grouped with forgeries as one of the transgressions which 'personam regis tangut principaliter.'
[53] 25 Edward III stat. 5, cap. 2. The others were: plotting against or attempting the life of the king, his queen or his eldest son; violating the queen, the king's eldest unmarried daughter, or the wife of the king's eldest son; levying war against the king in his realm; aligning with or providing aid and comfort to the king's enemies; and slaying royal officials in the course of carrying out their duties.

The association with treason, however, suggests a connection to such display. From the mid-thirteenth century, England witnessed instances in which the most notorious of offenses, almost always associated with *lèse-majesté*, were punished not merely with drawing and hanging, but also the partition of the criminal's body, with the removal of the head and the division of the body into separate pieces. Matthew Paris relates an early example. In 1238 an attempted assassin of Henry III was caught and

> torn limb from limb by horses at Coventry, a frightful warning and sorrowful spectacle to show to all daring to plot such deeds. First he was pulled apart, afterwards beheaded, and the body was divided into three parts. Each was dragged through one of the great English cities and afterwards hung on a stake in the manner of a thief.[54]

In 1242 a similar fate befell the assassin's co-conspirator William Marisco, although his body was divided into four parts which were sent to the four principal cities of the realm.[55] Quartering of the body appears to have been the subsequent rule, although there was some latitude in the eventual disposition of the parts; in some instances there is a discernable intent to send them to regions where this display would have the greatest impact. Thus, in 1283, the left arm and the left leg of David ap Gruffydd were sent to Bristol and Hereford respectively, the two largest cities proximate to Wales, while in 1305 the remains of William Wallace went to Newcastle, Berwick, Perth, and Aberdeen – locales either in northern England or Scotland proper.[56] As with Anglo-Saxon mints, this triumphant exhibition of pieces of a transgressor's body takes place in locations where it would be most meaningful to witnesses. Katherine Royer has described the high medieval execution ritual as a form of 'spectacular justice' and sees its development originating in the thirteenth century, but the observed movement of execution from the periphery to the urban center at the time of the Conquest suggests the seeds were planted earlier, and indeed, the punishment that Anglo-Saxon law prescribed for counterfeiting can be viewed as a precocious articulation of the same phenomenon.[57]

Returning to the pre-Conquest era, if the evidence just surveyed offers some insights into the motivation behind the display of an amputated hand, particularly in the case of extremely serious offenses such as counterfeiting,

---

[54] 'Membratim laniatum equis apud Coventre, exemplum terribile et spectaculum lamentabile præbere [jussit] omnibus audentibus talia machinari. Primo enim distractus, postea decollatus, et corpus in tres partes divisum est. Quælibet enim pars per unam de majoribus Angliæ civitatem pertracta est, et postea cruci appensa latronali': Matthew Paris, *Chronica majora*, ed. H. R. Luard, vol. 3 (London, 1872–83), p. 498.

[55] Matthew Paris, *Chronica majora*, vol. 4, p. 196. Marisco also suffered disemboweling, followed by the burning of his viscera, before he was quartered.

[56] J. Stephenson, ed., *Chronicon de Lanercost* (Edinburgh, 1839), pp. 112–13 and 203. In both instances the heads remained on display in London.

[57] 'Thirteenth-century English kings were not doing anything not done before to enemies of the state. What changed was that executions became an urban spectacle': Katherine Royer, 'The Body in Parts: Reading the Execution Ritual in Late Medieval England,' *Historical Reflections* 29 (2003), 319–39, at 327.

Cnut's great law code complicates matters a bit. This code was issued at Christmas in either 1020 or 1021, and is by far the most comprehensive instance of Anglo-Saxon legislation.[58] II Cnut 8.1 states: 'and he who after this makes counterfeits, loses the hand with which he made the counterfeit, and he shall not buy it back with anything, not with gold nor with silver.'[59] The provision for subsequent mounting of the hand is conspicuous by its absence. Why was it dropped from Cnut's code? One possibility is that the earlier legislation which contained this element was unknown to Archbishop Wulfstan of York, the primary architect of Cnut's laws, who referred instead to some earlier, Continental precedent, such as Ansegisus's capitulary (which was known to him). Patrick Wormald's analysis of the sources for Cnut's code makes this supposition fairly easy to investigate.[60] There is little positive evidence that Wulfstan would have been aware of the relevant section of IV Æthelred; it survives today only in the twelfth-century Latin translation made by the compiler of *Quadripartitus*. Although Wormald adduces one other possible borrowing in Cnut's code from this part of IV Æthelred, it is not an exact parallel, nor is it a particularly distinctive or innovative clause, and Wulfstan may well have arrived at it independently.[61] At first glance, Grately does not fare much better, with only one extant pre-Conquest witness, but, although its clauses are infrequently echoed in Cnut's laws, there are instances that exhibit similarities not only in content but in syntax, suggesting the earlier decree was known and used in the composition of Cnut's code.[62]

If, then, Wulfstan kept Grately's amputated hands, why did he not also retain the display of these hands? He may have preferred to rely on Continental precedents, considering Grately's addition an unwarranted innovation. Alternatively, his exclusion of this element can be seen as consonant with a preference for punishment that was in some way salvific; indeed, Wulfstan's dictum 'thus one might punish and at the same time preserve the soul,' to which we have already referred, is taken from the same code. The large number of instances of amputation prescribed in Cnut's code indicates that Wulfstan clearly was comfortable with the notion that mutilation aided a wrongdoer's atonement, but he may well have deemed the display of the mutilated part to serve no such purpose, although this interpretation admittedly puts a lot of weight on the absence of six words.

---

[58] Wormald, *Making of English Law*, p. 345, discusses the date of the promulgation of this code.

[59] '⁊ se ðe ofer ðis fals wyrce, ðolie ðara handa, ðe he þæt fals mid worhte, ⁊ he hi mid nanum ðingum ne bycge, ne mid golde ne mid seolfre.' This is the reading found in MS Cambridge, Corpus Christi College 383 ('B'), dated to the turn of the twelfth century. Differences between this and the other two extant versions are trivial.

[60] Wormald, *Making of English Law*, pp. 356–61.

[61] Wormald, *Making of English Law*, p. 358. This clause is IV Æthelred 7.3, which states that reeves complicit in counterfeiting shall suffer the same punishment as the perpetrators, unless they are pardoned by the king or clear themselves by oath or the full ordeal. II Cnut 8.2 states that a reeve so accused is to clear himself by the threefold purgation, and that if he fails, he is to suffer the same penalty as the counterfeiter.

[62] Compare, for instance, II Æthelstan 22 and 22.2 with II Cnut 28–28.1.

There was, of course, one other circumstance under which bodies and bodily parts might commonly be displayed in Anglo-Saxon England. The religious landscape was decorated with the relics of holy men and women, and in some ways these dismembered saintly bodies can be seen as the inverse of dismembered criminal ones. True, the remains themselves were not, as a rule, exhibited, but the reliquaries in which they were kept often were, and their lavish ornamentation had the potential of amplifying the effect they had on those who viewed them.[63] A hand discussed earlier, that of Oswald of Northumbria, exemplifies this category.

Bede writes of Oswald that Bishop Aidan, deeply moved by an act of munificence on the part of the king, 'grabbed his right hand and said "let this hand never age".'[64] The fulfillment of this pious wish is described immediately thereafter:

> For when he was killed in battle, his hand with his arm was cut from the rest of his body, and it has come to pass that they have remained incorrupt to this day. Indeed, they are preserved in an enclosed silver reliquary in the church of Saint Peter in the royal city which, from the name of the former queen, is called Bebbe [Bamburgh], and are venerated with appropriate honor by all.[65]

Bede also places Oswald's head at Lindisfarne, and the rest of his body at Bardney.[66] Each would become a locus of devotion, as would the site where the dying king's blood was spilled, but I would like to concentrate on the saint's uncorrupted hand. Like the severed hand of a counterfeiter, Oswald's hand offered multiple messages to those who viewed it. The hand itself signified the king's propensity for charitable giving, whereas its dismembered condition represented the suffering he had endured. The lack of decay advertised the saintly state to which Oswald had since ascended, a message reinforced by the ornate silver casket in which the relic was contained as well as the

---

[63] Note, however, the reservations expressed by William of Malmesbury towards the claim by the monks of Peterborough that they had come into possession of St. Oswald's arm: M. Winterbottom and R. M. Thompson, eds, *William of Malmesbury: Gesta pontificum Anglorum, The History of the English Bishops*, vol. 1 (Oxford, 2007), pp. 480–2. The mere possession of a reliquary, without any evidence that it contained what was claimed of it, was not necessarily convincing.

[64] 'Adprehendit dexteram eius et ait: "Numquam inueterescat haec manus"': Bede, *Ecclesiastical History*, p. 230.

[65] 'Nam cum interfecto illo in pugna manus cum brachio a cetero essent corpore resectae, contigit ut hactenus incorruptae perdurent. Denique in urbe regia, quae a regina quondam uocabulo Bebba cognominatur, loculo inclusae argento in ecclesia sancti Petri serunatur ac digno a cunctis honore uenerantur': Bede, *Ecclesiastical History*, p. 230. Bede provides a somewhat less elaborated version of these events a bit later in his narrative: a year after Penda had Oswald's head and hands displayed as a trophy of his victory, 'his successor to the kingdom, Oswiu, coming with an army, took them away and buried the head in the cemetery of the church at Lindisfarne, but the hands with the arms in the royal city' [deueniens cum exercitu successor regni eius Osuiu abstulit ea, et caput quidem in cymiterio Lindisfarnensis ecclesiae, in regia uero ciuitate manus cum brachiis condidit]: *Ecclesiastical History*, p. 252.

[66] This story is repeated in its essentials by Miller, *Old English Bede*, pp. 166 and 188; and Skeat, *LS* II, pp. 130–2 and 136. The latter also notes the early tenth-century translation of the body from Bardney to Gloucester: Skeat, *LS* II, p. 142.

ecclesiastical milieu in which it was set. Possession of this hand in turn redounded to the glory of the church in Bamburgh where it was ensconced, a glory that was successfully contested by the monks of Peterborough in the eleventh century, when they stole it, claiming it had been neglected in its former location.[67]

Oswald, while better documented and more prominent than most, was but one of a multitude of English saints, the veneration of whom dated back to the introduction of Roman Christianity among the Anglo-Saxons. Bede notes that Pope Gregory I dispatched relics to the island soon after Augustine's arrival, along with sacred vessels, altar cloths, and other items that 'were necessary to the ministry and worship of the Church.'[68] Although it apparently was not present in Bede's exemplar, most versions of Gregory's *Libellus responsorium* also represent him sending genuine relics of a martyred St Sixtus to Augustine so that that bishop might supplant a pre-existing cult that he deemed likely spurious.[69] While these early instances were almost certainly contact relics rather than corporeal ones, over time they would be augmented by a multitude of indigenous saints.[70] Their bodies, whether intact or in pieces, existed in an environment in which their exhibition conveyed multiple, overlapping meanings to those who witnessed them.

A final question that needs to be broached is that of the actual application of the laws against counterfeiting. Although this paper has endeavored to place the display of severed hands in a broader legal, literary, and religious context, none of the connections that have been suggested go very far in resolving the debate over whether the laws promulgated in Anglo-Saxon codes were actually enforced – and if so how extensively – or if they were primarily ideological expressions designed to proclaim the authority and ideals of those who issued them, but with little practical impact on the day-to-day ordering and regulation of society. There is evidence to suggest that in later centuries at least some counterfeiters and clippers were punished to the fullest extent of the law.[71] For our period, however, a dearth of records

---

[67] W. T. Mellows, ed., *The Chronicle of Hugh Candidus, a Monk of Peterborough* (Oxford, 1949), pp. 52 and 70; Reginald of Durham, 'Vita Sancti Oswald Regis et Martyris,' in Arnold, *Symeonis Monachi opera omnia*, vol. 1, pp. 373–5.

[68] 'Cultum erant ac ministerium ecclesiae necessaria': Bede, *Ecclesiastical History*, p. 104.

[69] A few variants of this *obsecratio Augustini* are printed in Margaret Deanesly and Paul Grosjean, 'The Canterbury Edition of the Answers of Pope Gregory I to St. Augustine,' *Journal of Ecclesiastical History* 10 (1959), 1–49, at 28–9; the authors suggest that the Sixtus in question is most likely Pope Sixtus II (d. 258). Paul Meyvaert summarizes the manuscript tradition of the *Libellus*, concluding that the *obsecratio*, although absent from Bede, was original to the letter: 'Bede's Text of the *Libellus responsionum* of Gregory the Great to Augustine of Canterbury,' *England before the Conquest: Studies in Primary Sources Presented to Dorothy Whitelock*, ed. Peter Clemoes and Kathleen Hughes (Cambridge, 1971), pp. 15–33.

[70] John Blair catalogs well over 200 of these 'homegrown' saints culted in England prior to the Conquest: 'A Handlist of Anglo-Saxon Saints,' *Local Saints and Local Churches in the Early Medieval West*, ed. Alan Thacker and Richard Sharpe (Oxford, 2002), pp. 495–565.

[71] Blackburn suggests that the large number of moneyers whose names disappear from later coins of Henry I makes plausible the Margam annals' number of ninety-four counterfeiters punished in the 1120s: 'Coinage and Currency,' pp. 65–8. Zerifa Entin Rokéah cites a selection of entries from the Gaol Delivery Rolls and the Pipe Rolls during the reign of Edward

documenting legal proceedings makes it impossible to detect any similar enforcement. In short, we cannot say whether the doorways of mints were commonly ornamented with amputated hands. It just might be significant that, considering the number of coins of this era that have been uncovered, forgeries (as distinct from coins designed to mimic Anglo-Saxon issues but produced elsewhere and not intended to circulate within England) are quite rare, although any claim to a causal relationship between the ordinances and this scarcity would be speculative at best.[72] Nevertheless, I do believe that we have a number of indications that the pre-Conquest audience was well equipped to receive the variety of messages that this sort of display would encompass. As in later cases of drawing and quartering, it need not have happened often to have served as a powerful deterrent.[73] To paraphrase Voltaire's epigram on a notorious eighteenth-century instance of spectacular justice, it would not have required many transgressing minters to provide sufficient discouragement to the others.

Note: Elements of this chapter were first presented at the 2010 International Medieval Congress at Leeds. My thanks go to Jay Paul Gates and Nicole Marafioti for their initiative in organizing the series of sessions that gave rise to this book and for their abundant encouragement and patience as editors. I am further indebted to them, as well as Allen Frantzen, for providing comment and suggestions on earlier drafts of this paper.

I which record the drawing and hanging of males and the burning of females found guilty of transgressing the laws on coinage: 'Money and the Hangman in Late-13th-Century England: Jews, Christians and Coinage Offences Alleged and Real (Part I),' *Jewish Historical Studies* 31 (1988–90), 83–109, at 107–8 n. 69.

[72] For a useful caution against the too-ready acceptance of a link between the notoriety and severity of punishments and the incidence of crime, see Timothy Reuter, 'The Insecurity of Travel in the Early and High Middle Ages: Criminals, Victims and their Medieval and Modern Observers,' *Medieval Polities and Modern Mentalities*, ed. Janet Nelson (Cambridge, 2006), pp. 38–71, at 49–51 and 69–71.

[73] Lantfred's 'Translatio et miracula S. Swithuni' attributes precisely this aim of 'ad deterrendos' to Edgar when referring to a (no longer extant) law promulgated by that king which punished thieves and robbers with torture and extreme mutilations: Lapidge, *Swithun*, pp. 310–13.

9

The 'Worcester' Historians and Eadric *Streona*'s Execution

Jay Paul Gates

For the post-Conquest historians Eadric *Streona* was 'the destroyer of many monasteries and the savage oppressor of all.'[1] He was inherited as a narrative figure from Anglo-Saxon sources as the great English traitor during Cnut's conquest, a synecdoche for the English nation during the Danish conquest, and a figure emblematic not just of a failure by the nobility to fulfill their social responsibilities, but also of a predatory aristocracy and the consequences of their actions for the nation.[2] As such, he proves a useful model for the critique of bad practices in the Anglo-Norman period without necessarily having to call out contemporaries by name. Eadric was made ealdorman of Mercia in 1007, was one of Æthelred's closest counselors, and was married to Æthelred's sister Eadgyth.[3] As ealdorman, he was a powerful figure able to muster an army, and although his responsibility was to raise his army in support of the English king, he is recorded as repeatedly switching sides during the Danish invasions between 1009 and 1016. In fact, in 1015, the Anglo-Saxon Chronicle records that he raised an army to challenge the rebellious Edmund Ironside, not in defense of the king, but in his own interests. Although it is tempting here to see him contemplating a bid for the throne, he did not, in the end, battle Edmund, but he did take his army and forty of the king's ships and submitted to Cnut. Then in the entry for 1017, the Anglo-Saxon Chronicle records that with Cnut's accession to the throne the new king made Eadric ealdorman of Mercia, and within a year ordered that he be killed (*ofslægen*).

---

[1] 'Multorum monasteriorum destructor, et cunctorum fere extiterat oppressor': T. Hearne, ed., *Hemingi chartularium ecclesiæ Wigorniensis* (Oxford, 1723), p. 281.
[2] Jay Paul Gates, 'A Crowning Achievement: The Royal Execution and Damnation of Eadric Streona,' *Heads Will Roll: Decapitation in the Medieval and Early Modern Imagination*, ed. Larissa Tracy and Jeff Massey (Leiden, 2012), pp. 53–72; Alice Sheppard, *Families of the King: Writing Identity in the Anglo-Saxon Chronicle* (Toronto, 2004), pp. 94–120; Ryan Lavelle, *Aethelred II: King of the English, 978–1016* (Stroud, 2002), pp. 131–3; Simon Keynes, 'A Tale of Two Kings: Alfred the Great and Æthelred the Unready,' *TRHS* 36 (1986), 195–217, at 216; Frank Stenton, *Anglo-Saxon England*, 3rd edn (Oxford, 1971), pp. 381–2 and notes; Edward A. Freeman, *The History of the Norman Conquest of England, its Causes and its Results*, vol. 1 (Oxford, 1870), p. 413.
[3] ASC E, s. a. 1007; Keynes, 'A Tale of Two Kings,' p. 214; Keynes, *Diplomas*, p. 213.

The post-Conquest authors who address Eadric do not simply repeat the story as it appears in their sources; they elaborate it, especially his betrayal of king and country, his execution, and the disposal of his body. In fact, the Anglo-Norman sources that mention Eadric divide neatly on how they depict his execution. Most make graphic Eadric's crimes and display him both figuratively as a political actor, and literally as an executed body.[4] However, there are exceptions in two sources produced at Worcester as a part of St Wulfstan's historiographical project. Hemming's Cartulary and the Worcester Chronicle erase Eadric's identity. He is denied Christian burial, his body is cast out of the city and left to the ravages of nature, and in the very account of his crimes and execution, he is written out of history, a narrative process through which the community is unified. It is the significance of his erasure that I pursue here.

This essay diverges slightly from the others in this volume by considering how post-Conquest, Anglo-Norman historians looked back to performative violence in Anglo-Saxon England in order to establish claims on their community going forward.[5] In this sense, it is really about Anglo-Norman concerns. However, because they look to the Anglo-Saxon past as their inheritance and choose to develop it, we should consider that past as living and productive for them. In fact, the Anglo-Norman historians' treatment of Eadric's execution should catch our attention because between 1076 and 1312 'not a single English earl, and indeed hardly a single baron, was executed (or murdered) in England for political reasons.'[6] Certainly, we should not underestimate the impact of the Norman Conquest on the English. 'The devastating experience of 1066 had meant that the correspondence between a kingdom and a people, a community of tradition, custom, law, and descent ... no longer applied in England.'[7] However, there was continuity, particularly in institutions that shaped the community, even if in forms that were not immediately recognizable. Most relevant to the discussion at hand, Emma Mason has shown continuity in the expropriation of Church lands by kings and royal agents, whether Anglo-Saxon ealdormen or Norman sheriffs.[8] St Wulfstan

---

[4] I have discussed Eadric in the pre-Conquest Anglo-Saxon Chronicle and the *Encomium Emmae Reginae* in Gates, 'A Crowning Achievement.' I examine the Anglo-Norman histories not produced at Worcester that treat Eadric in 'Imagining Justice in the Anglo-Saxon Past: Eadric Streona, Kingship and the Search for Community,' *HSJ* 25 (forthcoming).

[5] Julia Barrow has discussed how demonstrative behavior, including performative violence, was deployed in late Anglo-Saxon England: 'Demonstrative Behaviour and Political Communication in Later Anglo-Saxon England,' *ASE* 36 (2007), 127–50.

[6] David Carpenter, *The Struggle for Mastery: The Penguin History of Britain, 1066–1284* (London, 2003), p. 127.

[7] John Gillingham, 'Henry of Huntingdon and the Twelfth-Century Revival of the English Nation,' *The English in the Twelfth Century: Imperialism, National Identity and Political Values* (Woodbridge, 2000), pp. 123–44, at 128. Gillingham is citing Susan Reynolds on the kingdom, people and community: Susan Reynolds, *Kingdoms and Communities in Western Europe, 900–1300* (Oxford, 1984), p. 250.

[8] Emma Mason, 'Change and Continuity in Eleventh-Century Mercia: The Experience of St Wulfstan of Worcester,' *ANS* 8 (1985), 154–76. Additionally, Patrick Wormald has shown that post-Conquest England looked back to the Anglo-Saxon period for its model legislation. In fact, he goes even further, arguing that the legislation Archbishop Wulfstan of York

certainly perceived this continuity, having himself witnessed the depredations at Worcester by the eleventh-century Anglo-Saxons, even extending to his own bishop, Ealdred, and by the Normans after the Conquest.[9] Here I focus solely on the treatment of Eadric, his crimes, and execution in Hemming's Cartulary and the Worcester Chronicle. I argue that they deploy historiography in defense of their community and its ancient privileges, and that they shape their accounts of Eadric to encourage Anglo-Norman kings to reject elements of the English past that had failed, and to establish continuity with a worthy English past instead.

Before turning to the histories themselves, it is worth considering the context and purposes for historiography in the Anglo-Norman period, particularly at Worcester. As has been suggested, history as written in the Middle Ages was an expression of community and 'the maintenance and creation of traditions and histories is one way in which societies, communities, seek social order.'[10] The English historiographical revival began about a generation after the Norman Conquest[11] in a context of profound changes in language, culture, and government.[12] The Latin textual culture generally in England was used 'to bridge the religious, social and cultural fissures opened by the Conquest,'[13] and the Anglo-Norman historians particularly 'sought tactful mediations between Norman and English points of view.'[14] Moreover, the context of those writing established broad and common goals that shaped an English historiographical tradition, which R. W. Southern has proposed grew up across England as a means to preserve English monasteries, their religious and intellectual traditions, and a position in the world. English historians extracted 'from unpromising documents a new picture of antiquity,'[15] and their use of those documents affected their narrative focus,[16] especially as

wrote for Æthelred and Cnut acted as the foundation for English law through the twentieth century: Wormald, 'Archbishop Wulfstan: Eleventh-Century State-Builder,' *Wulfstan*, ed. Townend, pp. 9–27. It is notable that William I made a particular effort to depict his succession as legitimate and his rule as continuing practices as they were in *tempore regis Edwardi*: George Garnett, *Conquered England: Kingship, Succession and Tenure, 1066–1166* (Oxford, 2007), pp. 9–17. C. Warren Hollister has discussed how such a model was developed to shape the institutions of government that would define social structures during the reign of Henry I: *Henry I* (New Haven, CT, 2001), pp. 21–9.

[9] Emma Mason, *St Wulfstan of Worcester, c. 1008–1095* (Oxford, 1990), chs 3–4, with Ealdred at pp. 85–7.
[10] Leah Shopkow, *History and Community: Norman Historical Writing in the Eleventh and Twelfth Centuries* (Washington, D.C., 1997), pp. 5–6.
[11] Elisabeth van Houts, 'Historical Writing,' *A Companion to the Anglo-Norman World*, ed. Christopher Harper-Bill and Elisabeth van Houts (Woodbridge, 2002), pp. 103–22, at 120–1; R. W. Southern, 'Presidential Address: Aspects of the European Tradition of Historical Writing: 4. The Sense of the Past,' *TRHS*, 5th series 23 (1973), 243–63, at 246.
[12] Southern, 'The Sense of the Past,' p. 246.
[13] Christopher Baswell, 'Latinitas,' *The Cambridge History of Medieval English Literature*, ed. David Wallace (Cambridge, 1999), pp. 122–51, at 122.
[14] Andrew Galloway, 'Writing History in England,' *Cambridge History of Medieval English Literature*, ed. Wallace, pp. 255–83, at 263.
[15] Southern, 'The Sense of the Past,' p. 249.
[16] Galloway, 'Writing History in England,' pp. 256–7.

they worked to establish a community identity through an ideologically imagined past.[17] Gabrielle Spiegel explains that

> historical writing, precisely to the degree that it claimed to be free of imaginative elaboration, served as a vehicle of ideological elaboration. The prescriptive authority of the past made it a privileged locus for working through the ideological implications of social changes in the present and the repository of contemporary concerns and desires.[18]

Exactly such imaginative ideological elaboration is evident in the historiographical project put forward by St Wulfstan of Worcester. As has been noted, 'Of all the Old English monasteries, Worcester was the most successful in preserving its links with the past.'[19] However, such links through Wulfstan's project pursued two approaches to community. On the one hand there is a local and practical concern aimed at curbing abuses, regaining alienated properties, and maintaining the community's resources, particularly notable in the collection and compilation of charters. Such an approach is evident in Hemming's Cartulary.[20] On the other is the promotion of 'the enlargement of monastic history from a local to a universal setting,'[21] represented by the Worcester Chronicle. Eadric, as ealdorman of Mercia – both specific to Worcester and a national actor – may be seen as a figure in whom these two approaches enter into dialogue. His betrayals of Kings Æthelred and Edmund, as well as of the English, in battle make evident his place in the universal setting. But his role is equally relevant to the local environment: the community at Worcester suffered a long history of the alienation of its properties, and it seems they took personally the crimes of Eadric, the ealdorman who should have protected them. It is, after all, the Worcester historians who record Eadric's cognomen *streona*, 'the acquisitor,' indicating their understanding of his relationship to the community. Thus the historiographical project at Worcester is specific to that community and its concerns, but also follows the model of their pre-Conquest sources in extending the particular to the general, encompassing and defining the larger nation.

Hemming's Cartulary

Probably the earliest of the post-Conquest histories to treat Eadric is Hemming's Cartulary, produced c. 1096. It was compiled at the command of St Wulfstan to document the pre-Conquest properties designated for the sustenance of the monks at Worcester,[22] and likely to support them during

---

[17] Sheppard, *Families of the King*, p. 12.
[18] Gabrielle Spiegel, *Romancing the Past: The Rise of Vernacular Prose History in Thirteenth-Century France* (Berkeley, 1993), p. 5.
[19] R. W. Southern, 'The Place of England in the Twelfth-Century Renaissance,' *Medieval Humanism and Other Studies* (New York, 1970), pp. 158–80, at 168.
[20] Southern, 'The Sense of the Past,' p. 249–50; Francesca Tinti, 'From Episcopal Conception to Monastic Compilation: Hemming's Cartulary in Context,' *EME* 11 (2002), 233–61.
[21] Southern, 'The Sense of the Past,' p. 250.
[22] Ann Williams, 'The Spoliation of Worcester,' *ANS* 19 (1997), 383–408, at 383.

the reign of William Rufus (r. 1087–1100).[23] Although it is called a cartulary, the manuscript goes beyond earlier cartularies compiled at Worcester in providing detailed narrative texts. These texts, including the one dealing with Eadric, are an innovative means of documenting Worcester's past, and they are important because they indicate to the reader the reason for the production of the Cartulary.[24] In his *Enucleatio libelli*, an explanatory note on the Cartulary which immediately follows the treatment of Eadric, Hemming states,

> If anything useful will come out of this work of mine, God, to whom I commend everything, in His goodness, knows better; in as far as my intention is concerned, this is that if the king's heart, with God's favor, is ever consolidated in doing justice, which is currently withering, and if law, which is now confounded by unjust leaders, is made firm through the support of justice, either the bishop or dean, or any other officer of this monastery, provided a suitable occasion is found, may know in what way he should claim and demand those lands, to avoid that, hidden in clouds of ignorance, they are altogether deleted from memory.[25]

This would appear to be a significant deployment of historiography in defense of the Worcester community's rights and corporate survival.[26] As is evident in the assertion of the value of historiography, it is not only backward-looking, but is intended to be productive in the present. There is a clear statement regarding the goal that lands not be deleted from memory. However, as becomes clear, Hemming is not opposed to deleting from memory those who expropriate the lands. In this, Hemming is elaborating the terms for his history and which aspects will define the community. The Cartulary should thus be understood in the framework that Gabrielle Spiegel lays out for historical texts: they 'both mirror *and* generate social realities, are constituted by *and* constitute the social and discursive formations which they may sustain, resist, contest, or seek to transform' (italics original).[27] Hemming invokes a past that must be rejected in order for a sense of community to be regained. Moreover, in the clear concern with law and justice (*iustitia*), and with the king's responsibility to support justice, the Cartulary is a pointed commentary on kingship; in its focus on the present moment, on William Rufus's kingship, it demands the correction of ongoing practices.

---

[23] Francesca Tinti, '*Si litterali memorię commendaretur*: Memory and Cartularies in Eleventh-Century Worcester,' *Early Medieval Studies*, ed. Baxter *et al.*, pp. 475–97, at 476.
[24] Tinti, 'From Episcopal Conception to Monastic Compilation,' p. 235.
[25] 'Quid uero utilitatis hoc meo labore exerceatur, Dei pietas melius nouit, cui totum committo; quantum tamen ad meam attinet dispositionem hec est, ut, si quando Dei gratia concedente cor regis iustitia qua nunc marcescit consolidetur, lexque quę nunc iniustis principibus confusa est, iustitia fulcietur stabilietur, sciat siue episcopus, siue decanus, uel aliquis prelatus huius monasterii, dum tempus aptum inuenerit, quomodo eas proclamet, quomodo eas expetat, ne ignoratię nebulis absconsę, penitus ex memoria deleantur': Hearne, *Hemingi Chartularium*, pp. 282–3. The translation is from Tinti, '*Si litterali memorię commendaretur*,' pp. 492–3.
[26] Southern, 'The Sense of the Past,' p. 249.
[27] Gabrielle Spiegel, 'History, Historicism, and the Social Logic of the Text in the Middle Ages,' *Speculum* 65 (1990), 59–86, at 77; cf. Susan Reynolds, *Kingdoms and Communities*, p. 2.

Hemming's ideological elaboration acts as a reflection on the passage immediately preceding it and provides a way to interpret the Eadric narrative in relation to William Rufus's reign. Essentially, Hemming shows Eadric in a land-grab permitted by two kings, although he is eventually executed:

> In this time, a certain Eadric, nick-named *Streona*, that is, the acquisitor, for the first time under king Æthelred and afterward for some time under Cnut who held power over all the English, ruled as if under the king [*quasi sub rege dominabatur*] in so far as he took control of vills and provinces when he pleased (for instance, Winchcombshire, as it was then, he attached to Gloucestershire); supported by such force, his power and his might, he stole three vills, which were called by the names Batsford and Eisey, and *Keingaham*,[28] from the possession of the monastery, when Leofsige was bishop. But not long after this same man lost everything along with his life. For, by the command of King Cnut, he was killed [*occisus*], then ignominiously thrown [*ignominiose projectus*] outside the walls of London, nor is he even judged [*judicatus*] worthy of a tomb, with God himself rendering a worthy vengeance; he who proved the destroyer [*destructor*] of many monasteries, and the savage oppressor of all, was by all now denied a tomb.[29]

Hemming's treatment of Eadric is brief and particular. He is concerned with Eadric's expropriation of monastic lands, for which he is first given his moniker, *streona*. However, what is less clear is the role of each king in his actions. There is ambiguity in the phrase *quasi sub rege dominabatur*. Elsewhere, I translated this as 'had dominion as if a sub-king.'[30] However, on reflection, it seems that there is a question of responsibility embedded in the grammar. If we understand the phrase as 'as a sub-king,' we can understand that Eadric ruled Mercia as a petty king, abandoning his responsibilities to protect the community, maintain peace and social order, and enforce good law – a set of responsibilities clearly associated with kingship and good governance.[31] Although these are the duties of an ealdorman as much as of a king, the rhetoric of 'sub-king' would, perhaps, suggest Eadric's transgressions. He violates his responsibilities both the ealdordom and to his king in that he is not supporting royal interests. In this case, the *sub-* is vital: Hemming stresses Eadric's obligations to the actual king, despite his disproportionate

---

[28] Williams notes that *Keingeham* has not been identified: 'The Spoliation of Worcester,' p. 385 n. 18.

[29] 'Eo tempore, quo Edric, cognomento Streona, id est, adquisitor, sub rege primitus Athelredus, et postea aliquandiu sub Cnut omni Anglorum regno præerat, et quasi sub rege dominabatur, in tantum, ut villulas vilis et provincias provinciis pro libito adjungeret, (nam vicecomitatum de Wincelcumb, que per se tunc erat, vicecomitatui Gloeceastre adjunxit) hic, tanta fretus potentia, ab hujus monasterii possessione, Leofsigo episcopo existente, vi et fortitudine sua. iii^{es}. villas abstulit, que his nominibus appellantur, Bæcces-hofre, ˥ Æsige, ˥ keingaham. Sed non multo post ipse etiam omnia sua cum vita perdidit. Namque, jubente Cnut rege, occisus, atque extra murum Lundonie ignominiose projectus, nec etiam sepulture judicatus est dignus, Deo sibi dignam ultionem reddente, ut, qui multorum monasteriorum destructor, et cunctorum fere extiterat oppressor, a cunctis etiam ad sepulturam sperneretur': Hearne, *Hemingi Chartularium*, pp. 280–1. My translation.

[30] Gates, 'A Crowning Achievement,' p. 59, following a translation of Keynes, 'A Tale of Two Kings,' p. 214.

[31] Richard Kaeuper, 'Social Ideals and Social Disruption,' *The Cambridge Companion to Medieval English Culture*, ed. Andrew Galloway (Cambridge, 2011), pp. 87–106, at 91.

power.³² A similar conclusion may be reached if we understand the phrase to mean 'he ruled as if he were under the king,' i.e., he represented himself as if he were working for the king but was really out for himself. However, in this reading, both kings, first Æthelred and later Cnut, are implicated by failing in their obligations to promote good ealdormen and administrators, and to protect the Church. Whether the kings truly allowed Eadric to despoil Worcester, Eadric represents his actions as being permitted by royal authority, and so as reflecting on the king.

It would seem that both Æthelred and Cnut are to blame for not stopping Eadric, yet they are never said to approve of his actions. Indeed, Cnut's command to execute him stands in opposition to Æthelred's inaction as an example of the king fulfilling his obligations by punishing injustice, and possibly punishing transgressions against his royal reputation and royal authority. In any case, his command proves to be a moment of community unification. Although the conclusion appears straightforward, the passage merits close stylistic examination to appreciate the richness of its logic and the many themes it invokes: the legal language used for Eadric's exposure; the alignment of earthly and divine judgment; the spiritual implications of the denial of consecrated burial; the shame involved, not least in the slow, public disintegration of the body; the equation of the consecrated tomb and the secure monastery; the overall tone of vengeance.

The legal language invites an examination of who commands and who enacts the punishment, and eventually aligns earthly and divine judgment. There is a grammatical conflation of agents – king, God, community – in the working together towards a legal outcome. First, 'jubente Cnut rege' [by the command of King Cnut] invokes the king's role; second, 'Deo sibi dignam ultionem reddente' [with God himself rendering a worthy vengeance] provides spiritual justice; third, Eadric was judged (*judicatus*) by the community as a whole (*a cunctis*). The grammar here is interesting. The emphasis is on the ablatives, not the nominatives: by Cnut, with God, by all. Eadric is buried in participles (*occisus, judicatus*) until the end, at which point he is finally labeled as *destructor* and *oppressor*. Eadric is defined by his crimes. The punishments are presented as consequences, and those who enforce them, human and divine, work together to achieve the correct outcome.

In the conflation of earthly and divine judgment, denying Eadric Christian burial should further be understood as damning him. Although Nicole Marafioti demonstrates that capital punishment would not necessarily result in the damnation of the criminal, denial of Christian burial, which was considered a Christian right by at least the late tenth century, was certainly perceived to increase the likelihood.³³ Moreover, in the denial of burial there

---

³² Stephen Baxter, *The Earls of Mercia: Lordship and Power in Late Anglo-Saxon England* (Oxford, 2007), p. 107. On the Anglo-Saxon Chronicle's treatment of Eadric's violation of lordship obligations, see Sheppard, *Families of the King*, pp. 94–120.

³³ Nicole Marafioti, 'Punishing Bodies and Saving Souls: Capital and Corporal Punishment in Late Anglo-Saxon England,' *HSJ* 20 (2008), 39–57, at 50. Helen Gittos suggests that this was

is an echo of an Old English formula for excommunication to which Elaine Treharne has drawn attention. In it, excommunicates are 'to be dumped, unceremoniously, in an unmarked grave – one distinct even from a heathen grave – so that eternal damnation is guaranteed.'[34] Reading God's 'worthy vengeance' against Marafioti's point and the excommunication charter, the denial of burial must certainly be seen as a judgment of Eadric to damnation.

Yet there is a visual paradox to the disposal of the body: it is visible to the point of humiliation, but only temporarily; once the body has disintegrated and been consumed by wild animals, Eadric's only memorial will be the memory created for him by the spectacle and the texts that preserve his crimes and punishment. Familiar from the placement of executed criminals' bodies at boundaries, Eadric's rotting body would have acted as an assertion of law and royal authority and as a warning to those entering London.[35] Moreover, the shame of the disposal would have been understood, as is implied in the adverb *ignominiose*. However, this should not only be understood as 'shamefully' or 'disgracefully,' but literally 'without name.' In death and punishment, as his body disappears, Eadric is stripped of identity and removed from memory except in so far as the histories record his actions. As noted above, he comes to be identified only by his crimes, *destructor* and *oppressor*.

Finally, the vengeance for his crimes equates the consecrated tomb with the security of the monastery and then extends outward to the security of the nation. Cnut gives the command, after which the whole community that had been injured by Eadric enacts God's own vengeance and denies him consecrated burial, thus leaving him vulnerable to damnation. Although Cnut may have initially been culpable for not protecting the community against Eadric, when he does have Eadric executed, he is depicted as doing God's will and unifying the community.[36] Æthelred gets no such redemption. His reputation remains fixed and is tied to Eadric in that he apparently allowed Eadric's outrages.[37] In Eadric's disappearance from view, the only memorial

customarily the case earlier, but that it is codified in II Æthelstan 26 and I Cnut 22.5: 'Creating the Sacred: Anglo-Saxon Rites for Consecrating Cemeteries,' *Burial in Early Medieval England and Wales*, ed. Sam Lucy and Andrew Reynolds (London, 2002), pp. 195–208, at 201. See also the Introduction to this volume, pp. 8–9 and nn. 46–7.

[34] E. M. Treharne, 'A Unique Old English Formula for Excommunication from Cambridge, Corpus Christi College 303,' *ASE* 24 (1995), 185–211, at 197–8.

[35] Andrew Reynolds has extensively examined the placement of execution sites at geographical boundaries: 'The Definition and Ideology of Anglo-Saxon Execution Sites and Cemeteries,' *Death and Burial in Medieval Europe: Papers of the 'Medieval Europe Brugge 1997' Conference*, vol. 2, ed. Guy De Boe and Frans Verhaeghe (Zellik, 1997), pp. 33–41; *idem*, 'Burials, Boundaries and Charters in Anglo-Saxon England: A Reassessment,' *Burial in Early Medieval England and Wales*, ed. Lucy and Reynolds, pp. 171–94.

[36] Williams 'The Spoliation of Worcester,' pp. 383–4, notes that one of Hemming's great complaints regards the losses the Church faced in the payment of geld, especially in the early years of Cnut's reign.

[37] Sheppard addresses the Anglo-Saxon Chronicle's treatment of Eadric in relation to Æthelred and Cnut to argue that 'the annalist's focus on the ethos of lordship transforms what we are accustomed to reading as a story of rupture into one of continuity': *Families of the King*, p. 95. In this, Hemming is apparently working from an existing model of representing the relationship between lord and community.

allotted to him is in the form of his crimes and how his complete removal brought justice for the community, both local and national.

As powerful a treatment as this may be, it is worth noting that Eadric is not alone in this chapter. There is another despoiler: the Norman Roger de Juri. By invoking him along with Eadric, Hemming juxtaposes Anglo-Saxon and Anglo-Norman, and draws parallels that put significant demands on William Rufus without actually calling him by name.

> In the same way [*simili modo*], at the time of King William [I], Roger de Juri seized the land in Gloucestershire which is called Hamton, from lord bishop Wulfstan who was acting as the king's ambassador at Chester, and whose rule was disturbed at this time; and there was also a dispute regarding the episcopate between Archbishop Thomas and our lord. None of this was able to be examined at that time. Hence this was done such that the monastery has been despoiled ever since. But he did not rejoice over the plunder without punishment. For, living as though he were the richest and dearest cupbearer to the king, he incurred the king's anger, and only barely protected his life by flight, and lost all his possessions, and, shamefully [*ignominiose*] exiled from his country, after a short time died.[38]

In this, we can see gestures to both Anglo-Saxon antiquity and the recent post-Conquest past to make common claims. By beginning with Eadric and turning to Roger, Hemming is able to draw parallels. As Eadric despoiled Worcester, in the same way (*simili modo*), Roger seized lands in Gloucestershire. As Eadric was punished by the king, the community, and God, so Roger incurred William I's anger, was excluded from the community, and was left to God's judgment in death. And, again like Eadric, he reaches his end outside of the community, shamefully (*ignominiose*), and he disappears from the rest of the account. Even though his name is remembered, his identity is effaced with exile. Thus there is a common model put forward for how William Rufus and subsequent kings are expected to treat despoilers. Eadric's actions in the past are marked out as injustices in need of correction in the present. The claim to antiquity is then to a connection to a just past, before Eadric's crimes against the community; and it is a call on the king to choose between the two models – Æthelred and Cnut – to promote justice, and to protect the community in the present. Moreover, because the historiographical project is promoted by Wulfstan, and because it rejects the excesses of a failed Anglo-Saxon past, Hemming's criticisms and calls upon the king, particularly upon William Rufus, would likely have been received with relative equanimity. After all, Wulfstan was in favor with both William

---

[38] 'Simili modo, tempore Willelmi regis, Rocgerius de Juri invasit terram in Gloeceastrescire, que Hamtun nominatur, domino Wlstano episcopo existente in legatione regis apud Ceastram, et quia regnum erat adhuc turbatum, et de episcopatu etiam inter Thomam archiepiscopum et dominum nostrum altercatio, nulla hinc eo tempore poterat esse discussio. Hinc factum est, ut usque hodie monasterium inde spoliatum est. Nec ipse impune super rapina gavisus est. Nam vivens, cum esset ditissimus et pincerna regis carissimus, regalem incurrit iram, vixque fuga vitam ad modicum protexit, omnesque suas possessiones permaximas perdidit, et exul a patria ignominiose post parvum tempus obiit': Hearne, *Hemingi Chartularium*, p. 281.

I and William Rufus, held an important administrative role, and 'assisted in suppressing the baronial revolts of 1075 and 1088.'[39] He was certainly in a strong position to influence the kings, protect Worcester locally, and possibly effect national reform.

The Worcester Chronicle

Like Hemming's Cartulary, the Worcester Chronicle, now generally attributed to the monk John,[40] was composed at the command of St Wulfstan, and was possibly begun before his death in 1095.[41] In this, the chronicle is participating in Worcester's program of historiography; however, from the beginning it was also engaged in a larger historical project, and it was developed in dialogue with other histories over a long period. The chronicle was begun as a continuation of the world chronicle of Marianus Scotus,[42] but its main interest is in recounting events in England, continuing up to 1140.[43] It was written in three stages, the first two to 1131, then the third to at least 1140, but possibly as late as 1143.[44] For the annals of the tenth and eleventh centuries a particular tone is set by supplementing the historical material, drawn mainly from the Anglo-Saxon Chronicle, with content from *vitae* and other sources.[45] Moreover, in developing over such a long period, John's work overlaps with that of other contemporaries of whom he was aware and who were aware of his work, including Eadmer of Canterbury and William of Malmesbury.[46] Such overlap supports the view of a widespread historiographical project emerging in England.[47] Although John's chronicle should be viewed as very much a part of the Worcester program, its scope extends beyond Worcester to the entire English Christian community.[48]

John's generic conflation of *vita* and annals in his work ensconces its history firmly in political life.[49] In this, the chronicle promotes an idea that support for the English Church is what defines inclusion in the community. As Gransden

---

[39] Antonia Gransden, 'Cultural Transition at Worcester in the Anglo-Norman Period,' *Medieval Art and Architecture at Worcester Cathedral: The British Archaeological Association Conference Transactions for the Year 1975*, ed. G. Popper (Leeds, 1978), pp. 1–14, at 1–2.
[40] Gransden, 'Cultural Transition at Worcester,' pp. 6–7.
[41] JW, p. xviii.
[42] Martin Brett, 'John of Worcester and his Contemporaries,' *The Writing of History in the Middle Ages: Essays Presented to Richard William Southern*, ed. R. H. C. Davis and J. M. Wallace-Hadrill (Oxford, 1981), pp. 101–26, at 110.
[43] JW, p. xix.
[44] JW, pp. lxvii–lxxxi. For a full discussion of the stages of development, see Brett, 'John of Worcester.'
[45] JW, pp. xix–xx.
[46] Brett, 'John of Worcester,' pp. 111–14.
[47] Southern, 'The Sense of the Past,' p. 249.
[48] St Wulfstan's historiographical program at Worcester seems to have had a broad influence: in addition to his *Gesta regum Anglorum*, *Gesta pontificum Anglorum*, and *Historia novella*, William of Malmesbury also wrote a *Vita Wulfstani*.
[49] On the conflation of *vita* and chronography, see Spiegel, 'History, Historicism, and the Social Logic of the Text in the Middle Ages,' p. 79.

notes, the chronicle 'has a pro-English bias, although not so markedly.'[50] John seems to develop a view of the English community as fundamentally shaped by its past saints, a matter that supports the idea that the English monasteries were trying to maintain their traditions, and especially their Anglo-Saxon saints.[51] God and the English saints from the past are on the side of the English.[52] The only thing that undermines English success is treachery from within. The two figures marked out for this in relation to the Danish conquest are Æthelred and Eadric, a point that, if we assume the elaboration of a common ideology within the histories from Worcester, suggests the ambiguous grammar in Hemming's Cartulary was indeed intended to implicate Æthelred along with Eadric.[53] Each is associated with an important figure of the English Church: Æthelred with Dunstan, one of the heroes of the monastic reform movement; and Eadric with Archbishop Ælfheah, possibly the most memorable martyr of the Danish invasions.

On Æthelred's death, John records an early prophecy from Dunstan, which he draws from Osbern's and William of Malmesbury's *vitae*.[54] Dunstan explains the many tribulations of Æthelred's life:

> These St Dunstan had prophetically announced would come upon him when he, on the day of his coronation, had placed the crown upon his head: 'Because,' he said, 'you obtained the kingdom through the death of your brother, whom your mother killed; hear therefore the word of the lord. Thus saith the Lord, "The sword shall not depart from thine house, raging against thee all the days of thy life", slaying those of your seed until your kingdom is given to an alien power whose customs and tongue the people you rule do not know; and your sin and your mother's sin and the sin of the men who committed murder at the wicked woman's advice will not be expiated except by long-continued punishment.'[55]

In this prophecy we can see a divine plan. God is clearly punishing the English for Æthelred's betrayal of his own brother. Yet it is Eadric's conniving and plotting, often in conjunction with Cnut's, that finally bring about the

---

[50] Antonia Gransden, *Historical Writing in England*, vol. 1: *c. 550–1307* (Ithaca, NY, 1974), p. 147. For instance, William Rufus is compared unfavorably with the Anglo-Saxon kings because, where they supported the Church, he robbed it.

[51] Southern, 'The Place of England,' p. 168. Although Southern believes that the Normans were skeptical of Anglo-Saxon saints, Susan Ridyard has argued persuasively that both English and Norman abbots recognized and even exploited the political utility of Anglo-Saxon saints: S. J. Ridyard, '*Condigna veneratio*: Post-Conquest Attitudes to the Saints of the Anglo-Saxons,' *ANS* 9 (1987), 179–206.

[52] A particularly vibrant example of this occurs when, after his conquest, Swein attempts to demand tribute from the town where St Edmund was buried and his sanctity, whereupon Edmund's apparition attacks and kills him: *JW*, pp. 476–7, s.a. 1014.

[53] See above, pp. 170–1.

[54] *JW*, p. 484, s.a. 1014 and nn. 1–2.

[55] 'Quas super illum uenturas, regalis consecrationis sue die, post impositam coronam, prophetico spiritu, sanctus ei predixerat Dunstanus: "Quoniam", inquit, "aspirasti ad regnum per mortem fratris tui, quem occidit mater tua, propterea audi uerbum Domini. Hec dicit Dominus: 'non deficiet gladius de domo tua, seuiens in te omnibus diebus uite tue,' interficiens de semine tuo, quousque regnum tuum transferatur in regnum alienum cuius ritum et linguam gens cui presides non nouit: nec expiabitur nisi longa uindicta peccatum tuum et peccatum matris tue et peccatum uirorum qui interfuere consilio eius nequam"': *JW*, pp. 484–5, s.a. 1016.

conquest of the English. As will become clear, the prophecy sets Æthelred's crimes as one of the reasons the English will suffer, creates a connection between Æthelred and Dunstan, and establishes a structure for Cnut, with Eadric's aid, to effect divine retribution.

Eadric is introduced in the chronicle in the year 1006, the same year that Bishop Ælfheah of Winchester was elevated to the archiepiscopate of Canterbury. John retains the cognomen *streona* that Hemming applied to Eadric (although he does not translate it into Latin) and also refers to him as *dolosus et perfidus* [crafty and treacherous].[56] Indeed, John stresses his treacherous character through the repetition of *perfidus*, twelve times, right up until the line narrating his execution in 1017.[57] And although we get a clear sense of his character when he is introduced in the midst of a plot to murder Ealdorman Ælfhelm by inviting him to a feast in order to ambush him, John seems to have adopted the description of Eadric's character from Osbern's post-Conquest *Vita Elphegi*, which he quotes when he narrates Eadric's elevation to the ealdormanry. For the year 1007, Eadric is described as follows (the portions of the passage in italics are taken directly from Osbern's *Vita Elphegi*):[58]

> In that year also *the king* made the *Eadric* mentioned above (son of Æthelric that is Leofwine), ealdorman of the Mercians. *He was indeed a man of low birth but his tongue had won for him riches and rank; ready of wit, smooth of speech, he surpassed all men of that time, both in malice and treachery and in arrogance and cruelty.*[59]

Thus Eadric is depicted as low, scheming, and nasty, and is subtly associated with the martyrdom of Archbishop Ælfheah and the undermining of the English Church by being described from Ælfheah's *vita*.[60] Although it is not clear that the audience for the chronicle would have recognized the allusion, when the texts are compared it is evident that John is making a direct connection. Even if an audience did not recognize the reference, Eadric is structurally associated with Ælfheah by being introduced to the history in the year of Ælfheah's elevation to archbishop. Moreover, although John cannot directly associate Eadric with Ælfheah's martyrdom, he does, in the same year that Ælfheah is martyred, mark out the *perfidus* Eadric from among the other leading English nobles who were gathered in London to pay a tribute to the Danes. Eadric's behavior here may be read as another form of treachery: rather than fighting the Danes, Eadric wants to pay them off, which would give them the opportunity to come back later. This is in contrast to Ælfheah,

---

[56] JW, pp. 456–7, s.a. 1006.
[57] JW, pp. 456, 462, 470, 478, 480, 488, 490, 492, 494, 502, and 504. He is *perfidissimus* once: p. 486. From the introduction of Eadric until his death, *perfidus* is used only in relation to him: pp. 456–504.
[58] Osbern, *Vita Sancti Elphegi*, ch. 7, PL 149, cols 380–381. Darlington and McGurk note such borrowings in their edition of JW.
[59] 'Quo etiam anno *rex Edricum* supra memoratum, Ægelrici uel Leofuuini filium, *hominem humili quidem genere, sed cui lingua diuitias ac nobilitatem comparauerat, callentem ingenio, suauem eloquio, et qui omnes id temporis mortales tum inuidia atque perfidia, tum superbia et crudelitate superauerat*, Merciorum constituit ducem': JW, pp. 460–1, s.a. 1007.
[60] JW, pp. 470–1.

who is martyred because he refuses both to tax his flock any more to appease the Vikings, and to allow anyone to pay his ransom.[61]

Beyond being an enemy of the Church. Eadric is depicted as a national traitor. On several occasions he undermines English military victories. Although John mostly follows the Anglo-Saxon Chronicle entry for 1012 in his narration, one case stands out:

> But the treacherous ealdorman Eadric Streona, his [Æthelred's] son-in-law, for he had married his daughter [Eadgyth], labored by all means, by wiles and baffling arguments, that they should not join battle but permit their enemy, on that occasion, to depart, and so as a traitor to his country he urged and persuaded and snatched the Danes from the hands of the English and allowed them to get away.[62]

This is a particularly damning presentation when compared with the Anglo-Saxon Chronicle at this point, which simply states, 'But it was ealdorman Eadric who stopped it, as it always was.'[63] In comparison, John heightens the judgment, showing Eadric to be a traitor to his king and father-in-law, a traitor to his country, and an aid to the Danish army.[64] This seems to run parallel with the betrayal of King Edward by his brother Æthelred and his mother, for which Dunstan prophesies the conquest of the English. Moreover, it is 'the treacherous ealdorman Eadric Streona and certain others'[65] who will not allow Edmund and Cnut to finally fight, but counsel instead the partition of the kingdom; and because Eadric is the only one named, he appears, if not the leader, the most culpable.

John emphasizes Eadric's treachery, but unlike Hemming, he presents Cnut as a conniving figure who exploits Eadric's willingness to behave deceitfully and later kills him for it.[66]

> In July King Cnut married Ælfgifu, that is Emma King Æthelred's widow, and at Christmas, when he was at London, he ordered the treacherous [*perfidum*] Ealdorman Eadric to be killed in the palace because he feared that some day he

---

[61] On nobles not fighting when they should, see Malcolm Godden, 'Apocalypse and Invasion in Late Anglo-Saxon England,' *From Anglo-Saxon to Early Middle English: Studies Presented to E. G. Stanley*, ed. Malcolm Godden, Douglas Gray and T. F. Hoad (Oxford, 1994), pp. 130–62.

[62] 'At perfidus dux Edricus Streona, gener eius, habuit enim in coniugio filiam eius Edgitham, et insidiis et perplexis orationibus ne prelium inirent, sed ea uice suos hostes abire permitterent, modis omnibus allaborauit, suasit et persuasit et a manibus Anglorum Danos, ut patrie proditor, eripuit et abire permisit': JW, pp. 462–5, s.a. 1009. John errs in identifying Eadgyth at Æthelred's daughter rather than his sister.

[63] 'Ac hit wæs þuruh Eadric ealdorman gelet swa hit gyt æfre wæs': ASC C, s.a. 1009.

[64] On the possible expansiveness of such a violation of the relationship between a lord and his man, Sheppard notes, 'historians of the medieval period frequently use the word "lordship" in such varied contexts as medieval social relations and social identity, land tenure, aspects of kingship and legal theory, obligations of military service, issues of royal protection, and the difficult social and political structures evoked in explorations of vassalage and fiefs. All these areas of inquiry are linked by a common understanding of the existence of a personal and political relationship between lord and man, an acceptance of the importance of that relationship, and a realization that the lordship tie can productively illuminate other areas of medieval political and social life': *Families of the King*, pp. 13–14.

[65] 'Perfidus dux Edricus et quidam alii': JW, pp. 492–3, s.a. 1016.

[66] JW, pp. 494–505, s.a. 1016–17.

would be entrapped by Eadric's treachery, just as Eadric's former lords Æthelred and Edmund, that is Ironside, were frequently deceived, and he ordered his body to be thrown over the city wall, and left unburied.[67]

As with Hemming's account, the method of Eadric's execution is left unstated. However, there is no kind of judicial process. Eadric here is not *judicatus*, as in the Cartulary: this is a political murder. As Cnut shores up his own rule by eliminating possible pretenders to the throne, either through murder or exile, he also removes the traitor who made his conquest possible. Cnut appears to be acting purely practically and John does not show any affection for him. Indeed, the only positive thing said about Cnut after his accession comes in the account for 1031, when he went to Rome and secured protections for English pilgrims and swore to amend his life.[68] Still, the specific order to dump Eadric outside the city wall and to leave his body unburied is significant. Eadric is cast out of the city, suggesting the exile of a criminal, and he is denied Christian burial, and, ostensibly, salvation. But unlike Hemming's account, it is not the community that denies him burial; it is Cnut. As Cnut unwittingly fulfills Dunstan's prophecy by subjugating the English to foreign rule, so he also punishes the English traitor who helped to effect it.

Paired with the execution of Eadric is the dismantling of Æthelred's kin group in a single sentence. Æthelred and Edmund Ironside are both dead, and Æthelred's widow Emma moves to a new kin group and joins a new royal house. This seems to close the frame begun by Dunstan's prophecy. As Æthelred and his mother were guilty of the betrayal of Edward, setting in motion the divine plan of retribution, the betrayal by Eadric – a son by marriage – brings about the complete collapse of Æthelred's kin group, including the removal of Emma, the female figure whose innocence places her in contrast to Æthelred's mother.[69]

Developing the history through the frames of *vitae*, and aligning the accounts of the two figures responsible for treachery with major English saints – Æthelred with Dunstan, Eadric with Ælfheah – John shapes his history as a political commentary that shows a divine plan for the English community, and so promotes support for the English Church as a means to inclusion within it. The Normans are not excluded from this possible community; rather, their support for the English Church and good governance

---

[67] 'Iulio rex Canutus derelictam regis Ægelredi reginam Alfgiuam, scilicet Emmam, in coniugium accepit, ac in Natiuitate Domini, cum esset Lundonie perfidum ducem Edricum in palatio iussit occidere quia timebat insidiis ab eo aliquando circumueniri sicut domini sui priores Ægelredus et Eadmundus, scilicet Ferreum Latus, frequenter sunt circumuenti et corpus illius super murum ciuitatis proici ac insepultum precepit dimitti': *JW*, pp. 504–5, s.a. 1017.

[68] *JW*, pp. 512–13, s.a. 1031.

[69] Although Æthelred and Emma's sons Alfred and Edward were still alive, they were in exile at the Norman court. Alfred would later return to an ambush by Godwine in which he was blinded, which resulted in his death. And although Edward would eventually return at the invitation of Cnut and Emma's son Harthacnut, Harthacnut welcomed him as a brother, suggesting that even Edward was adopted into the new royal house. Regardless of how we read the two *æþelings*, at the point of Eadric's betrayal, the English royal family was dismantled.

would ostensibly give them a place in the divine plan, as is suggested by the Norman Emma's removal from the dismantled kin group to the new royal house. In this, the 'universal' approach to historiography moves beyond the simple goals of protecting a church's or monastery's property, and even beyond making claims on a particular king; it proposes a choice between two models of behavior within a divine framework. As in Hemming's Cartulary, the bad model of Anglo-Saxon history is rejected; in its place is a good model of history grounded in English saints, and a community defined by the traditions of the English Church.

What is certainly clear in Wulfstan's project is that historiography is assumed to be an active and demanding genre that engages its contemporaries with positive and negative models, in the classical sense, for moral imitation,[70] and with interpretations of the past through which to view and shape the present. If, as a figure of Anglo-Saxon community, Eadric represents a rapacious Anglo-Saxon aristocracy that plundered Church lands, St Wulfstan's project then looks to an earlier period of Anglo-Saxon history to ensure property claims and to an earlier form of Anglo-Saxon community as a model on which to go forward in the present. However, through the insistent emphasis on Eadric's execution and the treatment of his corpse, the Worcester historians largely dispose of that history. Eadric is judged and rejected by the community, left without Christian burial, and damned.

Nevertheless, the model is not simply based on rejection of history. It is intended to be productive. Through their treatment of Eadric, the Worcester historians are able to elaborate an ideology of community dependent on the king and his agents fulfilling their responsibilities, and to comment on the failures or wrongs of administrators and kings in the present, without necessarily having to rebuke them directly or by name. Moreover, the positive models associated with the English Church give the English a place in post-Conquest England and assert a strong continuity from the Anglo-Saxon past to the Anglo-Norman present. In this, they present a possible vision of Anglo-Norman community, one that rejects the bad Anglo-Saxon past and embraces the Normans, provided the Normans support the values of the community and uphold their responsibilities to it.

Focusing on the figure of Eadric as he was treated within St Wulfstan's narrowly defined historiographical project allows for two significant levels of analysis. First, a comparison of the two works from Worcester to recount Eadric's part in history indicates the ideological goals underpinning the project. The corrupt past is blamed for the conquest of the English, first by the Danes and later by the Normans, a point that is highlighted by the pairing of Eadric and Roger de Juri in Hemming's Cartulary. However, that past is also rejected and the historiographers look to a worthy, imagined Anglo-Saxon past to maintain their identity in the present. And it is in the

---

[70] Southern, 'The Sense of the Past,' p. 243.

positive claims that the second level becomes clear. Historiography can act as an ideological tool to construct a narrative not only to explain the past, but to shape community identity in the present and establish the terms for new social relationships. Such was certainly clear to William I – and the Norman aristocracy who followed his model – when he insisted on the fiction of the continuity of English traditions from the *tempore regis Edwardi* into his rule. But this also opened the door for historical claims on Norman kings, guided by the politically astute and flexible St Wulfstan, to acknowledge that past, learn from it, and become more just rulers in protecting the local communities like Worcester and promoting a larger Anglo-Norman community.

10

Capital Punishment and the Anglo-Saxon Judicial Apparatus: A Maximum View?

Andrew Rabin

In the final volume of his *Commentaries on the Laws of England*, Sir William Blackstone praised what he saw as the 'most remarkable' achievements of pre-Conquest English law: 'the constitution of parliaments,' 'the election of their magistrates by the people,' and the development of the 'most important guardian both of public and private liberty,' the jury.¹ Equal to these accomplishments, in Blackstone's view, was Anglo-Saxon law's 'great paucity of capital punishments,' particularly for first offenses.² Although Blackstone's version of pre-Conquest legal history has been largely discredited, his assertion that legislators often restricted, if not abandoned entirely, the use of the death penalty came to form part of a scholarly consensus on early English criminal prosecution.³ This consensus assumed its most durable form in the work of Frederic William Maitland, who argued that capital punishment played only a small role in Anglo-Saxon law; according to Maitland, it was not until the latter half of the twelfth century that 'the doctrine of felony was developed [and] capital punishment supplanted the old wites.'⁴ Among

---

1 Sir William Blackstone, *Commentaries on the Laws of England*, vol. 4, ed. Thomas A. Green (Chicago, 1979), pp. 405–7.
2 Blackstone, *Commentaries on the Laws of England*, p. 406. It should be noted that Blackstone's comment here is one of a series of observations found throughout the *Commentaries* offering thematic support for increased limitations on capital sentences in eighteenth-century English law: See Daniel J. Boorstin, *The Mysterious Science of the Law: An Essay on Blackstone's Commentaries* (Chicago, 1941), pp. 143–4; Richard A. Cosgrove, *Scholars of the Law: English Jurisprudence from Blackstone to Hart* (New York, 1996), p. 39.
3 On Blackstone's view of Anglo-Saxon law, see Wormald, *Making of English Law*, pp. 4–6. Wormald does point out, though, that several of Blackstone's arguments, 'had more substance than Maitland or any historian of his or later times have been ready to allow': *Making of English Law*, p. 5. For an example of Blackstone's influence on this topic, see Henry Adams, 'The Anglo-Saxon Courts of Law,' *Essays in Anglo-Saxon Law* (Boston, 1876), p. 32. Adams follows Blackstone's formulation nearly *verbatim*, although he does not cite his source.
4 Pollock and Maitland, *History of English Law* I, p. 606, and see also I, p. 104, and II, p. 482. Variations on Maitland's claim recur in, among others, Julius Goebel, *Felony and Misdemeanor: A Study in the History of Criminal Law* (New York, 1937, reprinted 1976), pp. 237–8; John Hudson, *Land, Law, and Lordship in Anglo-Norman England* (Oxford, 1994), pp. 20–6; J. B. Post, 'Local Jurisdictions and the Judgment of Death in Later Medieval England,' *Criminal Justice*

Anglo-Saxonists, Maitland's arguments have led to analyses of a perceived ambivalence towards execution in pre-Conquest courtly and ecclesiastical culture.[5] Tracing inconsistencies in the legislative definition of capital crime as well as objections to the death penalty raised by such prominent writers as Ælfric of Eynsham, those studying this issue have suggested that the Anglo-Saxon attitude towards the execution of criminals was complex, contradictory, and subject to considerable debate. For such scholars, the legal and conceptual problems posed by capital punishment may perhaps best be summed up by Archbishop Wulfstan's famous declaration in V Æthelred: 'it is the judgment of our lord and his council that Christian men shall not be sentenced to death for minor crimes; but instead, more mild penalties shall be assessed to meet the needs of the people, so that the handiwork of God and what he purchased dearly for himself not be destroyed for minor offenses.'[6]

Recently, however, excavations of what have been labeled 'execution cemeteries' by Andrew Reynolds, Jo Buckberry, Dawn M. Hadley, Craig Cessford, Graham Hayman, and others have uncovered evidence that capital punishment may have been far more widespread than traditionally thought.[7] These scholars draw on the work of historians arguing for a 'maximalist' account of Anglo-Saxon state-formation in order to suggest that such cemeteries provide evidence for the early centralization of pre-Conquest judicial practices.[8] For

---

History 4 (1983), 33–49, at 3; Elizabeth Vodola, *Excommunication in the Middle Ages* (Berkeley, CA, 1986), p. 190; Hurnard, *King's Pardon*, pp. 1–30; R. C. Van Caenegem, *The Birth of the English Common Law*, 2nd edn (Cambridge, 1988), p. 64; Trisha Olson, 'The Medieval Blood Sanction and the Divine Beneficence of Pain: 1100–1450,' *Journal of Law and Religion* 22 (2007), 63–128, at 68–9.

[5] See, for instance, Katherine O'Brien O'Keeffe, 'Body and Law in Late Anglo-Saxon England,' *ASE* 27 (1998), 209–32, at 215; Wormald, *Making of English Law*; Thompson, *Dying and Death*, pp. 174–5, 180, and 186; Dorothy Whitelock, 'Wulfstan *Cantor* and Anglo-Saxon Law,' *Nordica et Anglica: Studies in Honor of Stefan Einarsson*, ed. A. H. Orrick (The Hague, 1968), pp. 83–92, at 86; Nicole Marafioti, 'Punishing Bodies and Saving Souls: Capital and Corporal Punishment in Late Anglo-Saxon England,' *HSJ* 20 (2008), 39–57.

[6] '⁊ ures hlafordes gerædnes ⁊ his witena is, þæt man Cristene men for ealles to litlum to deaðe ne fordeme; ac elles geræde man friðlice steora folce to þearfe, ⁊ ne forspille for litlum Godes handgeweorc ⁊ his agene ceap þe he deore gebohte': V Æthelred 3. All quotations from the Old English laws are taken from Liebermann, *Gesetze*. All translations are my own.

[7] Reynolds, *Deviant Burial*; Graham Hayman and Andrew Reynolds, 'A Saxon and Saxo-Norman Execution Cemetery at 42–54 London Road, Staines,' *ArchJ* 162 (2005), 215–55; Andrew Reynolds, 'The Definition and Ideology of Anglo-Saxon Execution Sites and Cemeteries,' *Death and Burial in Medieval Europe: Papers of the 'Medieval Europe Brugge 1997' Conference*, vol. 2, ed. Guy De Boe and Frans Verhaeghe (Zellik, 1997), pp. 33–41; Craig Cessford *et al.*, 'Cambridge Castle Hill: Excavations of Saxon, Medieval, and Post-Medieval Deposits, Saxon Execution Site and a Medieval Coinhoard,' *Proceedings of the Cambridge Antiquarian Society* 94 (2005), 73–101; Aliki Pantos, 'The Location and Form of Anglo-Saxon Assembly Places: Some "Moot Points",' *Assembly Places and Practices in Medieval Europe*, ed. Aliki Pantos and Sarah Semple (Dublin, 2004), pp. 155–80; J. L. Buckberry and D. M. Hadley, 'An Anglo-Saxon Execution Cemetery at Walkington Wold, Yorkshire,' *Oxford Journal of Archaeology* 26 (2007), 309–29; Sarah Semple, 'A Fear of the Past: The Place of the Prehistoric Burial Mound in the Ideology of Middle and Later Anglo-Saxon England,' *World Archaeology* 30 (1998), 109–26.

[8] On maximalism, see James Campbell, 'The Late Anglo-Saxon State: A Maximum View,' *The Anglo-Saxon State* (London, 2000), pp. 1–30, especially at 2, 4, and 30. On the implications of execution cemetery excavations for the maximalist thesis, see Reynolds, *Deviant Burial*,

instance, in their study of the cemetery uncovered at 42–54 London Road in Staines, Reynolds and Hayman claim that the sustained use of the site between the eighth and twelfth centuries reveals 'a centrally organized judicial system during the growth period of the major early Anglo-Saxon kingdoms.'[9] Likewise, in his provocative book *Anglo-Saxon Deviant Burial Customs*, Reynolds contends that execution sites reflect a 'fearsome judicial system' at work as early as the seventh century.[10] Implicit in such claims is a methodological argument for the subordination of textual evidence to the archaeological record. As Reynolds writes, 'many of the aspects of the fully developed Late Anglo-Saxon judicial system are present before their inter-relationships and detailed functions are more clearly revealed in documents of the tenth and eleventh centuries.'[11] The work of Reynolds and his colleagues thus raises a series of significant historical and interpretive problems for students of Old English law and governance: first, how to reconcile the textual and archaeological evidence for capital punishment; second, how to understand the relationship between textual and archaeological evidence in the study of pre-Conquest law; and finally, how to situate debates about the death penalty within larger discussions concerning the degree of centralization of the Anglo-Saxon state. As I argue in this article, re-examining the textual evidence for capital punishment in light of the archaeological record will enable us to better address these issues. In particular, I suggest that while archaeological evidence reveals capital punishment to have been more common than previously realized, the documentary record indicates that the application of the death penalty, as well as the centralization of law more generally, were far more politically fraught than maximalist claims recognize.

Drawing on both legislation and other forms of legal records including wills, charters, and dispute records, this article surveys the textual evidence for judicial execution in pre-Conquest law in order to understand the disjunction between the documentary and archaeological evidence more clearly. In doing so, it follows the work of those historians who, in Warren Brown's formulation, seek to understand 'the relationship between royal authority and local social processes as seen through the lens of dispute.'[12]

pp. 1–33 and 235–50; Hayman and Reynolds, 'A Saxon and Saxo-Norman Execution Cemetery,' pp. 215 and 51–2; Reynolds, 'Definition and Ideology,' pp. 37–41; Cessford et al., 'Cambridge Castle Hill,' p. 78; Pantos, 'Location and Form,' p. 155; Buckberry and Hadley, 'An Anglo-Saxon Execution Cemetery,' pp. 324–5; D. M. Hadley, *The Vikings in England: Settlement, Society, and Culture* (Manchester, 2006), p. 91. For a specific discussion of the implication of the execution cemetery excavations for the Maitland hypothesis, see Patrick Wormald, 'Frederick William Maitland and the Earliest English Law,' *Law and History Review* 16 (1998), 1–25, at 17–18.

[9] Hayman and Reynolds, 'A Saxon and Saxo-Norman Execution Cemetery,' p. 215.
[10] Reynolds, *Deviant Burial*, p. 1.
[11] Reynolds, *Deviant Burial*, p. 32. On this point, see also Andrew Reynolds, *The Emergence of Anglo-Saxon Judicial Practice: The Message of the Gallows*, The Agnes Jane Robertson Memorial Lectures on Anglo-Saxon Studies (Aberdeen, 2009), pp. 2–6.
[12] Warren Brown, *Unjust Seizure: Conflict, Interest, and Authority in an Early Medieval Society* (Ithaca, NY, 2001), p. 5.

The picture that emerges from these texts is one of a judicial system far less centralized – and far less centrally *controlled* – than necessarily indicated by a maximalist analysis. In particular, I suggest that the highly conditional and carefully limited rhetoric applied to the circumstances surrounding royal intervention in capital cases marks the death penalty as a site of dispute where the centralizing agenda of an increasingly aggressive monarchy comes into conflict with decentralized practices of regional legal communities eager to maintain traditional, locally specific judicial customs.[13] In other words, the rhetorical sensitivity of the textual record concerning the king's application of the death penalty highlights the fissure between an ideology of royal power and the political realities of legal practice.

Capital Punishment in Royal Legislation

Among the most influential claims in Patrick Wormald's seminal essay, '*Lex Scripta* and *Verbum Regis*: Legislation and Germanic Kingship from Euric to Cnut,' is his controversial observation concerning the seeming disjunction between Anglo-Saxon legislating and legal practice: 'I have (I hope) read all the Anglo-Saxon charters recording judicial decisions, and even on matters of criminal law where written law might have helped there is not a single direct reference to, still less a quotation from, the extant texts.'[14] This claim has met considerable resistance since the essay's initial publication in 1977, and Wormald himself subsequently suggested that he may have overstated his case.[15] However, whether or not Wormald is right that written law played little role in the adjudication of legal disputes, his observation highlights that royal legislation formed only one component – and not necessarily the primary or decisive one – of law as understood and practiced in pre-Conquest civil and criminal proceedings. The authority of royal law appears to have been particularly ambiguous in capital cases. The high value placed on reconciliation and consensus in early medieval judicial practice, as well as the emphasis on the avoidance of feud, meant that courts often preferred negotiated settlements to penalties imposed by an external authority.[16] As Thomas

---

[13] Reynolds alludes to the possibilities of such an approach in his observation that the picture of pre-Conquest law in such Old English literary texts as 'The Gifts of Men' is 'very much one of a combination of local custom amended by royal decree': Reynolds, *Deviant Burial*, p. 8.

[14] Patrick Wormald, '*Lex Scripta* and *Verbum Regis*: Legislation and Germanic Kingship, from Euric to Cnut,' *Legal Culture*, pp. 1–43, at 21.

[15] A comprehensive account of the disagreement over Wormald's arguments would be too lengthy to include here; however, an excellent, recent summation of the debate as well as a response to Wormald's claims may be found in Catherine Cubitt, '"As the Lawbook Teaches": Reeves, Lawbooks and Urban Life in the Anonymous Old English Legend of the Seven Sleepers,' *EHR* 124 (2009), 1021–49, especially 21–2. Wormald's own comments on the subject may be found in his *Legal Culture*, pp. x–xv and 42–3.

[16] Wendy Davies and Paul Fouracre, 'Dispute Processes and Social Structures,' *The Settlement of Disputes in Early Medieval Europe*, ed. Davies and Fouracre (Cambridge, 1986), pp. 228–40, at 233–7; Hyams, *Rancor and Reconciliation*, pp. 71–110; Andrew Rabin, 'Old English

Andrew Green argued in his study of post-Conquest jury nullification, the common practice of acquitting a defendant rather than sentencing him to death resulted from 'deeply ingrained notions of how social harmony was to be maintained through composition with, rather than ultimate rejection of, the offender.'[17] This ambivalence towards the penalties dictated by the king is expressed in royal legislation through what one scholar has described as 'a conscious degree of ambiguity' in death-penalty clauses.[18] As we shall see, this ambiguity – or, to be more precise, conditional rhetoric – reserves the king's prerogative to assess capital penalties even as it characterizes variant regional practices as also under the aegis of royal authority. In doing so, the laws express the ideological aspirations of the crown's centralizing agenda while recognizing the limits of its practical authority.

The extent of the legal ambiguity surrounding the death penalty is indicated both by the relative scarcity of capital punishments throughout most royal law, and by the ratio between those clauses which mandate execution and those which merely reserve it as a judicial prerogative.[19] Regulations concerning capital punishment take up only a small fraction of Anglo-Saxon royal law: in the thirty-eight pre-Conquest law-codes attributed to specific kings, references to the death penalty occur in just seventy-eight clauses, the earliest of which appear in the seventh-century West Saxon laws of Ine and Kentish laws of Wihtred, and the latest in the eleventh-century laws of Cnut. However, even this number over-represents the frequency of capital penalties, since a disproportionate number of these clauses – twenty-eight, or approximately 36% – is concentrated in the laws promulgated during the fifteen-year reign of Æthelstan (r. 924–39). Taken as a whole, the corpus of death penalty clauses may be divided into three categories. The smallest of these, containing fifteen clauses (approximately 19% of the total), treat capital punishment as simply a condition for further action, as in Wihtred 22.1 [27]: 'If [a slave] is executed, to his master shall be paid half his value' (*gif hine man acwelle, þam agende hine man healfne agelde*).[20] Those in the

---

Forespeca and the Role of the Advocate in Anglo-Saxon Law,' *Mediaeval Studies* 69 (2007), 223–54; Maurizio Lupoi, *The Origins of the European Legal Order*, trans. Adrian Belton (Cambridge, 2000), pp. 224–31; Reynolds, *Emergence of Anglo-Saxon Judicial Practice*, p. 44.

[17] Thomas Andrew Green, *Verdict According to Conscience: Perspectives on the English Criminal Trial Jury, 1200–1800* (Chicago, 1985), p. 64.

[18] Thompson, *Dying and Death*, p. 182.

[19] The data presented in this paragraph are based on the clauses reprinted in Reynolds, *Deviant Burial*, pp. 251–61, which he collected from Attenborough, *Laws* and Robertson, *Laws*. I have checked these against the editions of the laws in Liebermann, *Gesetze* I and Oliver, *Beginnings of English Law*, pp. 59–82, 125–34, and 151–64, from which I have gathered several further clauses not listed in Reynolds. I have limited myself to legislation explicitly attributed to specific kings or reigns based on the assumption – admittedly problematic – that these are more likely to reflect the legal attitudes and priorities of the royal court than regional 'laws' or anonymous political tracts, the function and provenance of which are even more contestable.

[20] Wihtred's code is cited by the numeration provided in Oliver, *Beginnings of English Law*, with the numeration from Liebermann, *Gesetze* I, in square brackets. All other laws follow the numeration in Liebermann, *Gesetze* I.

second category, containing twenty-seven clauses (approximately 34% of the total), reserve the death penalty as a possible sentence for criminal activity; however, other potential actions – including a lesser punishment or royal pardon – are specified also. For instance, Ine 6 decrees: 'If anyone fights in the house of the king, he shall forfeit all that he owns and it will be according to the king's judgment whether he lives or not' (*Gif hwa gefeohte on cyninges huse, sie he scyldig ealles his iefes, Ᵹ sie on cyninges dome hwæðer he lif age þe nage*). In the final category, containing thirty-seven clauses (approximately 47% of the total), are those clauses in which the death penalty is ruled to be the required punishment for criminal activity, as in Alfred 4: 'If anyone conspires against the king's life … he must give up his life and all that he owns' (*Gif hwa ymb cyninges feorh sierwe … sie he his feores scyldig Ᵹ ealles þæs ðe he age*). On the surface, then, it appears that the primary role of capital punishment in royal legislation is as a sentence mandated for serious crimes, and one which cannot be replaced by lesser penalties or set aside according to the will of the court; however, as before, these numbers also are skewed by the anomalous emphasis on capital sentences in Æthelstan's legislation. If one omits the exceptionally draconian law-codes of Æthelstan, a very different picture emerges: of the fifty remaining clauses, only twenty (40%) prescribe death as a mandatory sentence; in contrast, the majority of the clauses – twenty-five (50%) – now list the death penalty as only one among several possible juridical responses to a criminal action. Accordingly, a more accurate interpretation of these numbers suggests that, in those instances when capital punishment was deemed appropriate, the predominant practice was to leave king or judge considerable leeway in its application. Though the laws reserve the king's right to sentence offenders to death, they ensure that other options – ranging from fine or imprisonment to full pardon – are available also. In doing so, the laws proclaim the king's jurisdiction over the lives of his subjects while also limiting the circumstances under which the exercise of that jurisdiction might provoke a challenge to royal authority.

This comparatively flexible, even tentative, treatment of the death penalty in royal legislation suggests that capital sentences may have been construed more as discursive instruments servicing an ideology of centralized kingship than as legal prescriptions carrying the expectation of regular enforcement. Understanding death-penalty clauses in this fashion helps explain the development of Anglo-Saxon legislative rhetoric surrounding capital punishment. As early as the laws of Wihtred and Ine – the oldest surviving legislation to contain capital sentences – clauses condemning offenders to death provide legislators with a means of claiming new juridical prerogatives and extending the reach of royal authority. On the one hand, the tentative, even contradictory treatment of the death penalty in Wihtred's and Ine's legislation preserves considerable latitude in its application: Wihtred's laws leave capital sentences entirely to the king's discretion while Ine's more complicated legislation initially decrees that a thief must be executed, yet then allows his life to be redeemed by the payment of wergild and later rules that the proper penalty for theft is not death after all but mutilation.[21] At the same time, though, the rhetoric of capital punishment in these texts suggests that their compilers viewed death-penalty clauses as a means of expanding the scope of royal jurisdiction. For example, according to a clause found with slight variations in both Wihtred's and Ine's legislation, 'If a man from afar or a stranger should leave the road and neither calls out nor blows a horn, he shall be considered a thief to be put to death (*to sleanne*) or ransomed.'[22] It is unclear whether the phrase *to sleanne* connotes formal judicial execution or simply a withdrawal of royal protection from the foreigner enabling his killer to act without fear of legal penalty. In either case, however, the clause's implication is the same: the king here claims the prerogative to classify someone as a thief – whether an actual theft has occurred or not – and, in doing so, to subject even a foreigner to his authority. While it is true that requiring a stranger to 'loudly announc[e] his friendly intentions is quasi-universal,'[23] equally important here is the exploitation of this custom to assert the king's right to define an individual's status as a subject. In claiming the right to identify an individual as a thief – independent of his actions, beliefs, or origins – the king declares his absolute jurisdiction over that person's life and freedom.[24] Whether or not executions were ever carried out under this provision – and there is no evidence that any were – claiming the right to define an individual in a manner that licenses a capital sentence allows the king to emphasize the scope of his jurisdiction and the absolute authority of his justice.

The incorporation of nearly identical capital clauses into the laws of Ine and Wihtred reflects the correspondence between the two courts as well as the increasing sophistication of eighth-century legislation; however, it may also indicate a response by the kings and their courts to competition from regional judicial authorities operating outside the purview of royal law. Although Reynolds lists the erection of execution apparatus, such as gibbets or gallows, as one of the 'formulaic physical characteristics' that serve as 'evidence for centralized royal power from the seventh and eighth centuries,'[25] formal execution was not a penalty found exclusively in royal law. Studies of later pre- and post-Conquest execution sites and practices have shown that gallows were erected for personal use by local lords as symbols of their capacity – often more aspirational than actual – to compete

---

[21] Wihtred 21, 22 [26, 27]; Ine 12, 37. Hurnard goes so far as to suggest that the purpose of such clauses, particularly in the laws of Wihtred, was to assert the authority of the royal pardon over the capital sentences passed by lower courts: Hurnard, *King's Pardon*, pp. 1–3.

[22] 'Gif feorran cumen man oþþe fræmde buton wege gange ⁊ he þonne nawðer ne hryme ne he horn ne blawe, for ðeof he bið to profianne: oþþe to sleanne oþþe to alysenne': Wihtred 23 [28]; cf. Ine 20.

[23] Oliver, *Beginnings of English Law*, pp. 179–80.

[24] On the legal authority to classify someone as a thief and the implications of such a classification, see Andrew Rabin, 'Testimony and Authority in Old English Law: Writing the Subject in the "Fonthill Letter",' *Law and Sovereignty in the Middle Ages and the Renaissance*, ed. Robert Sturges, Arizona Studies in the Middle Ages and Renaissance 28 (Tempe, 2011), pp. 153–72, at 166–8.

[25] Reynolds, *Deviant Burial*, p. 237.

with or even supersede royal authority.²⁶ Although possession of a gallows could, as Reynolds and Hayman have argued, function as a physical sign of 'the king's authority over life and death,' gallows also served as symbols of communities' capacity to resolve their own disputes and maintain their legal autonomy.²⁷ More suggestively, the occurrence in the eighth century of formal executions outside of the purview of royal law, and the threat such executions were thought to pose to the king's authority, is indicated by a passage in Bede's commentary on Genesis in which he complains about the frequency of unsanctioned hangings, characterized as a violation of divine justice. Asking, 'how many have shed men's blood and their blood is not shed?' (*Quanti effuderunt sanguine humanum, et sanguis eorum effuses non est?*), Bede writes that whoever kills men by hanging (*occid[it] hominem ... suspendio*), 'his blood shall be shed for he squanders his eternal life by sinning' (*fundetur sanguis illius quia peccando uitam perdit aeternam*).²⁸ Although more suggestive than conclusive, the evidence of later practice alongside Bede's reference to hangings occurring outside of royal jurisdiction raises the possibility that the inclusion of capital clauses in Ine's and Wihtred's legislation does not reflect a new aggressive policy of judicial enforcement by a strong, centralized monarchy; rather, writing the death penalty into royal legislation may have served as a way of incorporating pre-existing regional practice into the purview of royal law.²⁹ Implicitly, framing capital punishment as a royal prerogative characterizes executions carried out by regional authorities as extensions of the king's power rather than alternatives to it.³⁰ The capital clauses in the laws of Ine and Wihtred thus might be better understood as a royal means of asserting primarily ideological claims regarding the supercessionary authority of the king's jurisdiction than as records of the actual enforcement practices of a centralized government.

Throughout much of the ninth and early tenth centuries, capital sentences in royal legislation remained relatively static. Alfred largely reiterates the capital clauses of earlier laws, while the surviving legislation of Edward the Elder omits mention of the death penalty entirely.³¹ The legislation of Æthelstan, however, not only puts new emphasis on capital punishment,

---

[26] The symbolic erection of gallows has been discussed in Pollock and Maitland, *History of English Law* I, p. 607; Post, 'Local Jurisdictions,' p. 7; Robin Fleming, 'Rural Elites and Urban Communities in Late-Saxon England,' *Past and Present* 141 (1993), 3–37, at 11–12; Robert Bartlett, *The Hanged Man: A Story of Miracle, Memory, and Colonialism in the Middle Ages* (Princeton, NJ, 2004), pp. 17, 42–3.

[27] Hayman and Reynolds, 'A Saxon and Saxo-Norman Execution Cemetery,' p. 251; Reynolds, *Deviant Burial*, pp. 236–7.

[28] Charles W. Jones, ed., *Bedae Venerabilis opera*, part 2,1: *Opera exegetica: Libri quatuor in principium genesis usque ad nativitatem Isaac et eiectionem Ismahelis adnotationum (in Genesim)*, CCSL (Turnhout, 1967), II.ix.5–6, p. 133.

[29] Attempts to subject regional practice to the king's jurisdiction by writing it into royal legislation occur elsewhere in the pre-Conquest legal corpus also, as in III Edgar 1–2. On this point, see Andrew Rabin, 'Female Advocacy and Royal Protection in Tenth-Century England: The Legal Career of Queen Ælfthryth,' *Speculum* 84 (2009), 261–88, at 266–8.

[30] On this point, see also Hyams, *Rancor and Reconciliation*, pp. 84–7.

[31] Cf. Alfred 4 and 7; Ine 6.

but also replaces much of the conditional rhetoric of the earlier laws with more aggressive language identifying the death penalty as a primary judicial instrument of a strong, centralized monarchy. The first indications of this new approach to capital punishment appear in Æthelstan's earliest surviving law-code: lacking a prologue, II Æthelstan begins with the decree that 'one shall not spare any thief over twelve years old if he is taken in the act and [the stolen goods are] over eight pence.'[32] Subsequent clauses sentence to death those who attempt to flee following a crime, who plot against their lords, who commit murder through witchcraft, who disrespect the king's wishes, and who resist arrest.[33] Later laws add that those guilty of thefts committed since the promulgation of II Æthelstan 'shall not be deemed worthy of life in any way' (*nullo modo vita dignus habeatur*), that women sentenced to death shall be 'pushed from a cliff or drowned' (*præcipitetur de clivo vel submergatur*), that slaves guilty of capital crimes shall be stoned to death by other slaves, and that death sentences shall be passed against those who harbor criminals, fail to report encounters with fugitives, and attempt to defend suspects resisting arrest.[34] Increasing the number of capital crimes in this fashion reflects, in Wormald's words, the 'enhanced ambitions and upgraded techniques' of Æthelstan's approach to lawmaking:[35] Æthelstan's harsh sentences indicate the extent to which violations of the peace had come to be seen as affronts to the king's authority. That sheltering and offering assistance to fugitives – or even simply failing to report a fugitive's presence in a region – have now come to be classified as capital crimes suggests that hindering royal justice is an offense equal in severity to the theft of property or the taking of life. Underlying these provisions is the implication that bonds of loyalty to the king now supersede bonds of kinship or regional affiliation.[36] Further, the high proportion of clauses classifying the death penalty as mandatory rather than subject to judicial discretion – eighteen of the former in comparison to only two of the latter – effectively subordinates the sentencing decisions of regional officials to the written authority of royal legislation.[37] The capacity to mandate the death penalty for a broad range of offenses thus serves as an expression of the king's overarching authority.

Yet, if the capital clauses in Æthelstan's legislation reflect an attempt to consolidate judicial power under a strong, centralized monarchy, such clauses

---

[32] 'Mon ne sparige nænne þeof þe æt hæbbendre honda gefongen sy, ofer XII winter ⁊ ofer eahta peningas': II Æthelstan 1.
[33] II Æthelstan 1.2, 2.1, 4, 6, and 20.6. For a sense of the comparative severity of Æthelstan's laws, compare the clauses dealing with similar crimes in the laws of Alfred: Alfred 1–16.
[34] IV Æthelstan 6, 6.1, 6.2, 6.3, 6.4, 6.5, and 6.7; V Æthelstan Prol. 2 and Prol. 3; VI Æthelstan 1.1, 1.2, 1.3, 1.4, 1.5, and 6.3.
[35] Wormald, *Making of English Law*, p. 304.
[36] Hyams, *Rancor and Reconciliation*, p. 81. David Pelteret points out that a similar negotiation of loyalties takes place in the legislation regulating the executions of slaves: *Slavery in Early Mediaeval England* (Woodbridge, 1995), p. 87.
[37] See the statistics above, pp. 185–6. This point has also been made in a more general fashion by Victoria Thompson, who points out that 'prior to the tenth century, execution is rarely specified as an automatic punishment': *Dying and Death*, p. 181.

also appear to have evoked sufficient controversy to force the king to mitigate some of his harsher decrees. In part, modifications to the capital clauses of Æthelstan's later legislation reflect theological opposition to their severity;[38] yet the changes also suggest underlying concerns over the royal usurpation of traditionally regional or ecclesiastical prerogatives. The possibility that the expanded use of the death penalty would raise objections had been anticipated in Æthelstan's earlier legislation: for instance, clauses concerning the compensation to be paid for executed slaves seem designed to appease masters fearful of losing their property, while provisions removing convicts from their kin-group and designating special penalties for those who seek vengeance following an execution protect those carrying out capital sentences against the threat of lawsuit or feud.[39] While there is little evidence to indicate the extent to which such concerns were warranted, revisions to the death penalty provisions in Æthelstan's later laws suggest that the king's aggressive centralization of judicial authority did encounter resistance. The complaint with which V Æthelstan opens, that 'our protection has been less respected than I desired,' implies that previous assertions concerning the extent of royal jurisdiction and the efficacy of royal justice remained more aspirational than actual.[40] More revealing is an appendix to Æthelstan's final set of laws in which the king asks Bishop Theodred of London to inform Archbishop Wulfhelm of Canterbury that, following consultation with his councilors, 'it appears cruel to him that young persons should be executed for such little crimes, which he has learned is done everywhere' and, consequently, the minimum age for execution is to be raised from twelve to fifteen.[41] Apparently added after VI Æthelstan's initial promulgation, the appendix characterizes the execution of those under fifteen as an extra-judicial practice which the king seeks to curb rather than as a lawful penalty explicitly permitted by his previous legislation.

The appendix raises a number of questions, among the most important of which involves the reasons for this change in policy: despite the king's claim, it seems disingenuous for him to profess surprise or chagrin at the execution of minors given his earlier death penalty provisions.[42] Doing so,

---

[38] On this point, see Marafioti, 'Punishing Bodies,' pp. 39–57.
[39] III Æthelstan 6; IV Æthelstan 3, 6.6. On these clauses, see Hyams, *Rancor and Reconciliation*, p. 81; Pelteret, *Slavery in Early Mediaeval England*, p. 87.
[40] 'Ure frið is wyrs gehealden ðonne me lyste': V Æthelstan Prologue. On Æthelstan's difficulty in asserting his authority, see Simon Keynes, 'Crime and Punishment in the Reign of King Aethelred the Unready,' *People and Places in Northern Europe, 500–1600: Essays in Honour of Peter Hayes Sawyer*, ed. Ian Wood and Niels Lund (Woodbridge, 1991), pp. 67–81, at 69–70.
[41] 'Him to hreowlic þuhte þæt manswa geonge mancwealde oððe eft for swa lytlan swa he geaxod hæfde þæt man gehwær dyde': VI Æthelstan 12.1. VI Æthelstan was promulgated c. 935×9; it is instructive to note that a similar ban on juvenile executions did not enter United States federal law until the Supreme Court's 2005 decision in *Roper v. Simmons* (no. 03–0633).
[42] It should be noted here that no evidence survives of an actual increase in executions – either of minors or of those who had already reached their majority – during Æthelstan's fifteen-year reign: Reynolds, *Deviant Burial*, p. 237. Wormald points out that the earliest charter to reference an execution explicitly is dated to Æthelstan's reign (S 443). However – as he also observes – this text is patently a forgery: Wormald, *Making of English Law*, p. 307.

however, allows him to characterize the change in policy as a magnanimous concession to the petitions of council and church, instead of as an attempt to dissociate himself from a controversial and (if V Æthelstan's prologue is to be believed) ineffective policy. That the policy change resulted from ecclesiastical intervention is suggested by the fact that the appendix is composed, not in a traditional clausal structure, but as a memorandum to Theodred and Wulfhelm. The mention of these two prelates in particular indicates that VI Æthelstan's appendix may have arisen out of a conflict between royal and ecclesiastical jurisdiction.[43] Wulfhelm repeatedly features in Æthelstan's legislation as a defender of ecclesiastical prerogatives, especially those related to the exercise of criminal justice. Among the clauses attributed to him is that placing the ordeal under the king's and archbishop's joint jurisdiction in II Æthelstan as well as that equating royal and archiepiscopal sanctuary protections in IV Æthelstan.[44] On the other hand, Theodred's later reputation as an opponent of ecclesiastical participation in capital punishment suggests that his objections were grounded as much in theology as in concerns over ecclesiastical governance.[45] Attributing opposition to Æthelstan's policies specifically to Wulfhelm and Theodred thus suggests the appendix may have developed out of an attempt to protect ecclesiastical prerogatives, particularly those in conflict with the sentencing practices of secular law. However, this analysis is conjectural and evidence of opposition to Æthelstan's policies remains more allusive than explicit; nonetheless, the manner in which his legislation initially frames and later revises those policies suggests that attempts to use capital clauses as a means of extending the scope of royal authority were conditioned and ultimately limited by political considerations.

Reinforcing the sense that the death penalty proved an ineffective tool for the consolidation of judicial authority is the decline in capital clauses in the legislation of Æthelstan's successors. The laws of Edmund refer to mandatory execution in only a single clause, where it is reserved for slaves guilty of leading other slaves in robber-bands, while Edgar's laws omit mention of mandatory execution entirely.[46] Moreover, the penalties for certain crimes punished by mandatory execution in Æthelstan's legislation, such as theft or the violation of royal protection, revert to royal or judicial discretion in

---

[43] Julius Goebel has suggested that it was just such a conflict that led to the diminishing use of the death penalty in the later Anglo-Saxon period: 'although the courtkeeper's power to impose the death penalty is in practice established in the course of the tenth and eleventh centuries, so much of the jurisdiction over crimes is controlled by ecclesiastical immunities that this penalty is to be dormant until the thirteenth century': *Felony and Misdemeanor*, pp. 237–8.

[44] II Æthelstan 23.2, and IV Æthelstan 6.1. See also Nicholas Brooks, *The Early History of the Church of Canterbury* (London, 1984), pp. 217–18; Wormald, *Making of English Law*, pp. 299–30.

[45] See, for instance, Theodred's depiction in the narrative of the seven thieves preserved in Ælfric's life of the martyred King Edmund: Marafioti, 'Punishing Bodies,' pp. 43–4; Thompson, *Dying and Death*, p. 184.

[46] III Edmund 4.

the laws of Edmund and Edgar.⁴⁷ This trend continues in the legislation of Æthelred and Cnut, especially those laws composed by Archbishop Wulfstan of York, in which mandatory execution comes to be replaced by royal discretion or judicial mutilation.⁴⁸ Wulfstan's explicit rejection of the death penalty in V Æthelred 3, quoted above and repeated in both VI Æthelred and II Cnut, suggests that the reasons behind this movement away from capital punishment were, in part, theological.⁴⁹

Wormald, Whitelock, and O'Brien O'Keeffe have all discussed the influence on Wulfstan of the Continental Latin canon transcribed in MS BL Cotton Nero A. I: 'There are in these times secular judges who for a small crime condemn men immediately to death, thinking of no account the admonition of the apostle, saying "Punish and do not put to death".'⁵⁰ However, the shift from death to mutilation also highlights the latter penalty's political utility. By the eleventh century, restraint in the face of wrongdoing had come to be figured as one of the royal virtues, while the precariousness of the later years of Æthelred's reign and the earlier years of Cnut's circumscribed both men's ability to exercise unchecked judicial power.⁵¹ The usefulness of disfigurement as a penalty is indicated by Cnut's mutilation of English hostages in 1014: mutilating his prisoners allowed Cnut to mediate between mercy (which might have been taken as weakness) and execution (which might have risked overextending his authority).⁵² Significantly, the loss of hands, ears, and noses suffered by the 1014 hostages closely resembles the forms of mutilation decreed in the penalty clauses of II Cnut.⁵³ Political concerns and theological considerations thus appear to have conspired to limit the circumstances under which the king could legitimately claim the right of execution.⁵⁴ If the increase in capital clauses in Æthelstan's legislation served as a strategy to extend royal authority, the retraction of these clauses in the laws of later kings suggests that this strategy met with only limited success.

---

⁴⁷ See, for instance, II Edmund 6, III Edgar 7.3, IV Edgar 1.2. On these clauses, see Whitelock, 'Wulfstan Cantor,' p. 85.
⁴⁸ O'Brien O'Keeffe, 'Body and Law,' pp. 216–17; Wormald, *Making of English Law*, p. 126.
⁴⁹ See above, p. 182. See also VI Æthelred 10, II Cnut 21.
⁵⁰ 'Sunt namque his temporibus iudices seculares qui pro modico commisso homines statim morti adiudicant, parui pendentes monita apostoli, dicentis: castige et non mortificate': text and translation taken from O'Brien O'Keeffe, 'Body and Law,' p. 216. See also *EHD* 1, p. 443 n. 1; Patrick Wormald, 'Archbishop Wulfstan and the Holiness of Society,' *Legal Culture*, pp. 225–51, at 240.
⁵¹ On the virtues of royal restraint, see Hyams, *Rancor and Reconciliation*, pp. 129–30; Olson, 'Medieval Blood Sanction,' p. 63; Paul R. Hyams, 'What Did Henry III of England Think in Bed and in French about Kingship and Anger?' *Anger's Past*, ed. Rosenwein, pp. 92–124, at 116–20. On the precariousness of Æthelred's and Cnut's reigns, see M. K. Lawson, *Cnut: The Danes in England in the Early Eleventh Century* (New York, 1993), pp. 82–9.
⁵² The hostage episode is recorded in *ASC* C, s.a. 1014. On the political implications of Cnut's actions, see Ryan Lavelle, 'The Use and Abuse of Hostages in Later Anglo-Saxon England,' *EME* 14 (2006), 269–96, at 293.
⁵³ II Cnut 8.1, 8.2, 30.4, 30.5, 36, 48.1, and 53. See also Lawson, *Cnut*, p. 208. Although the similarities between Cnut's mutilation of the English hostages and the clauses on mutilation in II Cnut are striking, it is worth noting that the king's motivations in the earlier instance were almost certainly other than purely legal; see Lavelle, 'Use and Abuse,' pp. 269–96.
⁵⁴ Cf. Wihtred and Ine's laws, above p. 186–7.

Capital Punishment and Judicial Apparatus

As the above survey suggests, the evolution of capital clauses in Anglo-Saxon legislation is neither linear nor indicative of the steady emergence and consolidation of royal authority. The relative scarcity of capital clauses, the predominance of conditional syntax, and the retreat from mandatory death sentences following the reign of Æthelstan together indicate that disputes over the death penalty participated in a larger negotiation between the king, church, and regional aristocracy over the nature and extent of royal authority: even as kings sought to extend their jurisdiction by claiming the right to execute offenders, such efforts appear to have met opposition from those seeking to stem the advance of royal power. The politically fraught nature of capital punishment emerges still more clearly if we turn from royal legislation to surviving charters and dispute records. The depiction of the king's authority in these texts sheds light on how the political concerns underlying royal legislation influenced the ways in which capital crimes were investigated, prosecuted, and recorded.

Capital Punishment in Pre-Conquest Dispute Records: A Case Study

Although the archaeological evidence gathered by Reynolds suggests that executions occurred with some frequency, relatively few capital cases are preserved in the charters and chronicle entries recording Anglo-Saxon legal disputes.[55] In part, the paucity of textual evidence reflects the nature of the sources: most surviving records involve disputes over land, and the risk of royal forfeiture led charter drafters to overlook or downplay any criminal activity that may have influenced the suit.[56] Even so, while crimes such as theft, kidnapping, rape, murder, and violence in the king's hall all occur with some regularity in the records of Anglo-Saxon legal disputes, the perpetrators seldom receive the ultimate penalty.[57] Of the few executions which are recorded in Anglo-Saxon charters, most either appear in documents of dubious authenticity[58] or, as in the famous case of the widow drowned as a witch, occur in circumstances that raise questions about the legality of the proceedings.[59] Domesday Book preserves a single, obscure reference to 'a

---

[55] For a summary of the archaeological evidence, see Reynolds, *Deviant Burial*, pp. 262–71.
[56] Rabin, 'Old English *Forespeca*,' pp. 244–9; Patrick Wormald, 'A Handlist of Anglo-Saxon Lawsuits,' *Legal Culture*, pp. 253–87, at 284–6.
[57] See, for instance, S 916, 923, 926, 927, 934, 1026, 1211, 1229, 1445, 1447, 1448a and 1457. The most detailed account of someone drawing his weapon in the presence of the king (in this case, Alfred) occurs in the twelfth-century life of Saint Edburga of Winchester by Osbert of Clare; despite the penalty set out in Alfred 7, the malefactor is spared. The text is edited in Susan J. Ridyard, *The Royal Saints of Anglo-Saxon England* (Cambridge, 1988), pp. 253–309, with the relevant passage at 270–1.
[58] See n. 42 above.
[59] Anthony Davies, 'Witches in Anglo-Saxon England: Five Case Histories,' *Superstition and Popular Medicine in Anglo-Saxon England*, ed. Donald Scragg (Manchester, 1989), pp. 41–56, at 50–2; Andrew Rabin, 'Anglo-Saxon Women before the Law: A Student Edition of Five Old

smith who was put to death for theft' in the half-hundred of Harlow, yet no other details survive.[60] Perhaps the most complete pre-Conquest death penalty prosecution is recorded in S 877, a charter of c. 996 documenting the disposition of lands forfeited by a nobleman executed for his defiance of the king's authority.[61] Significantly, the narrative preserved in this charter reveals an awareness of the potential political complexities involved in a capital prosecution. Indeed, as I will argue, the arc of the charter's narrative is principally determined by anxiety over its portrayal of the exercise of royal authority. The manner in which this anxiety shapes the legal record reflects both the concerns capital punishment evoked and the challenges confronted by the king when seeking to use it to further his agenda.

In the details it preserves as well as those it omits, S 877 illustrates the extent to which the king's capacity to sentence offenders to death was circumscribed by the norms of later Anglo-Saxon legal practice. In the settlement of disputes, as John Hudson has argued, formal procedure often played a less important role than the expectations, traditions, and beliefs that provided the context within which legal arguments transpired:

> Apart from formal claims and denials, procedure and argument displayed considerable informality and flexibility. Personality and power, honour and shame came into play, implicitly or explicitly. Argument did not focus on legal rules; indeed the legal was not clearly distinguished, if distinguished at all, from the social or the religious.[62]

These norms influenced both the informal negotiations shaping the treatment of disputes by the court, and the manner in which disputes would be recorded by the victors following their resolution.[63] The ambiguities surrounding S 877's narrative indicate the potential for conflict between such norms and the necessities, both practical and ideological, of royal justice. The charter records that a certain Wulfbald, following his father's death, seized first his stepmother's land and then that of his kinsman. When the king, Æthelred *unræd*, demanded that Wulfbald return the property, the latter refused and the court fined him the full value of his wergild. Following three subsequent trials for defiance of the king's authority, Wulfbald's case was referred to

---

English Lawsuits,' *Old English Newsletter* 41 (2008), 33–56, at 43–4; Andrew Rabin, 'Law and Justice,' *The Blackwell Handbook of Anglo-Saxon Studies*, ed. Jacqueline Stodnick and Renée Trilling (Oxford, 2012), pp. 85–98. For a different view of the legality of this case, see Reynolds, *Deviant Burial*, p. 1.

[60] Ann Williams and H. G. Martin, eds, *Domesday Book: A Complete Translation* (New York, 1992), p. 970.
[61] S 877 has been edited as no. 31 in Sean Miller, *Charters of the New Minster, Winchester*, Anglo-Saxon Charters 9 (Oxford, 2001), pp. 144–57.
[62] John Hudson, 'Court Cases and Legal Arguments in England, c. 1066–1166,' *TRHS* 6th series 10 (2000), 91–115, at 92.
[63] On these issues, see Sarah Foot, 'Reading Anglo-Saxon Charters: Memory, Record, or Story?' *Narrative and History in the Early Medieval West*, ed. Elizabeth M. Tyler and Ross Balzaretti (Turnhout, 2006), pp. 39–67; Paul R. Hyams, 'Norms and Legal Argument before 1150,' *Law and History*, ed. Andrew Lewis and Michael Lobban (Oxford, 2004), pp. 41–61, especially 44–5; Rabin, 'Old English *Forespeca*,' pp. 231–6; Rabin, 'Testimony and Authority,' pp. 169–71.

the king's council, which forfeited 'all of Wulfbald's lands and his person also for the king to do with as he wished, either for life or for death.'[64] The charter records little of relevance to Wulfbald's prosecution beyond these few details, and these do as much to muddy the narrative as to clarify it. Particularly ambiguous is the nature of Æthelred's participation in the dispute: the account omits any justification for the king's intervention in what appears to be just a regional dispute over inheritance, any explanation for Wulfbald's willingness and ability to repeatedly defy the king's authority, any clarification concerning the king's personal involvement in the meeting of the royal council that finally resolved the dispute, and – perhaps most importantly – any indication of whether the king ultimately executed Wulfbald or spared his life. Indeed, the narrative's Rorschach-like quality is indicated by the fact that it has been cited to support claims concerning the strength as well as the weakness of Æthelred's rule.[65] However, in that the account's ambiguities involve the scope of the king's participation in the dispute, and that these ambiguities should resonate so closely with the ambivalence underlying the capital clauses of royal legislation, the concerns behind S 877's problematic narrative appear to extend beyond Æthelred's personal authority to royal involvement in capital sentencing itself.[66] In other words, when confronted with the unusual circumstances of the dispute, the drafters of S 877 seem anxious to depict Æthelred as adhering to the norms of royal practice, rather than to risk portraying the king as overly aggressive in exercising his authority.

Particularly suggestive of the conflict between Æthelred's decision to intervene in the dispute and the traditional norms governing royal behavior is the apparent ease with which Wulfbald defied the king's authority. Wulfbald's ability to repeatedly reject Æthelred's rulings indicates the extent to which regional privileges, however informal, restricted the king's prerogative to intervene in local disputes. S 877 records that it was immediately following Wulfbald's initial seizure of his step-mother's lands that 'the king sent to him and ordered that he restore that which he stole' (*send se cyng him to ⁊ bead him þæt he agefe þæt reaflac*).[67] Four successive trials follow, each of which results in Wulfbald being condemned and fined the full value of his wergild. Peter Kitson suggests that Wulfbald did acknowledge the king's judgment by paying the fines, even if he did retain the stolen property.[68] This reading

---

[64] 'Ealle Wulboldes ære ⁊ hine silfne to þam þe se cynge wolde swa to life swa to deaþe': Miller, *New Minster*, p. 145.
[65] Cf. Keynes, 'Crime and Punishment,' pp. 78–80; *EHD* 1, pp. 47 and 575.
[66] On this point, see also Keynes: 'it is possible that Wulfbald's defiance of authority reflects weaknesses inherent in the legal system itself, rather than the inability of a particular king to enforce the law': 'Crime and Punishment,' p. 79.
[67] Miller, *New Minster*, p. 151, suggests that the king may not actually have been involved in the initial attempts to bring Wulfbald to justice; however, the charter is quite explicit about Æthelred's early involvement, and the king's ultimate forfeiture of the property suggests a royal interest in the lands under dispute.
[68] Peter Kitson, *A Guide to Anglo-Saxon Charter Boundaries* (forthcoming); cited in Miller, *New Minster*, p. 151.

seems unlikely, though: not only does the charter explicitly state that Wulfbald 'ignored' (*forset*) the ruling, but after the second trial he compounded his crime by seizing the lands of a second kinsman at Brabourne. It is more probable that Wulfbald felt little obligation to heed the king's judgment on a matter of only regional importance. Indeed, he may even have been acting on legal precedent, as provisions in the laws of both Æthelstan and Edgar suggest that repeated refusals by local landholders to acknowledge the judgments of royal courts were a regular occurrence.[69] Studies of jury-nullification in post-Conquest courts similarly indicate that local authorities often failed to enforce royal judgments when these were seen as infringing on local rights or interests.[70] Moreover, the king's swift intervention in the dispute appears to have been at variance with the traditional practices of royal justice. That the king possessed only a limited right of intervention is suggested by a charter of c. 992 in which Æthelred was prevented from ruling on a dispute after one of the litigants protested that the suit more properly should be referred to a shire court.[71] II Cnut, promulgated nearly thirty years after the Wulfbald case, sets out a four-appeal procedure to be used in lawsuits concerning land seizures that closely resembles the progress of the dispute in S 877; however, according to this provision, it is only after these appeals have passed through the hundred and shire courts that the king may intervene.[72] Patrick Wormald has suggested that kings of the tenth and eleventh centuries viewed regional criminal activity as a justification for the strategic forfeiture of property, and it is possible that a maneuver of this sort lay behind Æthelred's decision to involve himself in the dispute.[73] Whether this is the case or not, Æthelred's intervention reframes the dispute as one concerned as much with the extent of royal jurisdiction as it is with the disposition of property. Æthelred's failure to enforce his judgment serves as an indicator of the limits of his personal authority and of the normative constraints on the prerogatives of the king.[74]

Æthelred's overreaching may explain one of the dispute's more puzzling features: the king's absence from the gathering of the royal council in London at which the dispute was finally resolved. According to the charter, a 'great

---

[69] I Edgar 3, II Æthelstan 25.2.
[70] Fleming, 'Rural Elites,' 11–12; Thomas A. Green, 'Societal Concepts of Criminal Liability for Homicide in Mediaeval England,' *Speculum* 47 (1972), 669–94, at 688; Henry Summerson, 'Attitudes to Capital Punishment in England, 1200–1350,' *Thirteenth-Century England VIII: Proceedings of the Durham Conference, 1999*, ed. Michael Prestwich, Richard Britnell, and Robin Frame (Woodbridge, 2001), pp. 123–33, at 133.
[71] S 1454, edited as no. 66 in A. J. Robertson, *Anglo-Saxon Charters*, 2nd edn (Cambridge, 1956), pp. 136–9.
[72] II Cnut 19.
[73] Rabin, 'Old English *Forespeca*,' p. 245; Patrick Wormald, 'Giving God and King their Due: Conflict and its Regulation in the Early English State,' *Legal Culture*, pp. 333–57, at 339–41. On this point, it is worth noting that the property does ultimately devolve to Æthelred, who then grants it to his mother Ælfthryth.
[74] On this point, cf. P. A. Stafford, 'The Reign of Æthelred II: A Study in the Limitations on Royal Policy and Action,' *Ethelred*, ed. Hill, pp. 15–46.

meeting' (*miclan sinoþ*) was held in London at which 'all of the councilors who were there, both ecclesiastical and lay' (*ealle þæt witan þe þær wæron ge gehadode ge læwide*) deemed Wulfbald's property and life forfeit to the king. The charter then lists two archbishops, thirteen bishops, four ealdormen, one earl, seven abbots, and twenty-three laymen of unspecified rank as participants. The text does not identify who presided at the gathering – although Simon Keynes speculates that it may have been Ealdorman Æthelwine of East Anglia, the highest-ranked nobleman among those listed[75] – or whether the king was present.[76] However, the king's actual attendance at the meeting may have been less important than his being seen to be absent, particularly given the crime for which Wulfbald was likely being prosecuted. The charter omits the specific charge brought against Wulfbald, but it is doubtful that a meeting of this sort would have convened merely to address a family dispute over a relatively small (approximately sixteen-sulung) estate. It is more probable that the trial centered on Wulfbald's defiance of the king's authority: not only is this crime more likely to have attracted the attention of the royal council, but the penalty assigned to Wulfbald by the lower courts corresponds to that set by Æthelred's law-codes for opposition to the king's rulings.[77] If the dispute's central issue has become the proper exercise of royal authority, particularly in matters normally adjudicated by local courts, relinquishing the prosecution of Wulfbald to the royal council effectively shields Æthelred from the accusation of exceeding the king's traditional jurisdiction, an accusation to which he was especially vulnerable during this period in his reign.[78] Even if political considerations necessitated Æthelred's absence from the meeting itself, it is unlikely that such a gathering of the secular and spiritual aristocracy would have occurred without the king being, at the very least, in the vicinity.[79] Moreover, as Paul Hyams points out, the primary work of dispute resolution often transpired in contexts more informal than traditional court proceedings: 'much of the talk by which courts were informed took place before the trial or in between formal hearings. Consequently, much of the real business of deciding cases happened outside court.'[80] Æthelred could thus influence the council's deliberations without appearing to dictate its decision.

Æthelred's omission from the trial record foreshadows the ambiguity surrounding the penalty Wulfbald ultimately suffered for his crimes. Although the council grants Æthelred the right to put Wulfbald to death, the charter does not specify whether the execution took place. According to the charter, the council 'forfeited … all of Wulfbald's lands and his person also for the king to do with as he wished, either for life or for death. And he possessed all

---

[75] Keynes, *Diplomas*, p. 214 n. 16.
[76] For different views on this question, see Keynes, *Diplomas*, p. 129 n. 56; Miller, *New Minster*, pp. 151–2.
[77] V Æthelred 31.
[78] Keynes, *Diplomas*, pp. 176–7.
[79] Æthelred is not known to have missed any other meeting of the *witan* until the final years of his reign, when his attendance was limited by his failing health: Keynes, *Diplomas*, p. 214.
[80] Hyams, 'Norms and Legal Argument,' p. 44.

this [property] without correction until he died' (*getæhton ... ealle Wulboldes ære ⁊ hine silfne to þam þe se cynge wolde swa to life swa to deaþe. ⁊ he hæfne ealle þis ungebet oþe he forþferd*). Left unclear in this passage is whether Wulfbald held the stolen property unpunished (*ungebet*) by civil authority until he finally died of natural causes, or whether an unrepentant (*ungebet*) Wulfbald clung to the property until finally executed by the king with the approval of his council.[81] The question has divided readers of the charter: Dorothy Whitelock and Simon Keynes, for instance, both speculate that Æthelred spared Wulfbald, while more recent readers such as Sean Miller and Peter Kitson have argued for Wulfbald's execution.[82] Once again, however, it may be that the charter's evasiveness on this point – embodied in such cryptic, formulaic phrases as *swa to life swa to deaþe* that recall the 'conscious degree of ambiguity' characterizing the capital clauses of royal legislation[83] – reflects a deliberate choice by S 877's drafters. As with the account of Wulfbald's trial, here too the shape of the legal record appears to be determined by political concerns over the seeming overextension of the king's power: if the emphasis on conciliar deliberation during the trial precludes any allegation of arbitrary royal action, the ambiguity concerning Wulfbald's punishment fosters the impression that juridical authority resides more with the gathering of regional aristocrats and church leaders who determined the sentence than with the king who administered it. An emphasis on procedure rather than penalty allows the narrative to characterize the forfeiture of Wulfbald's property, not as the result of the king's unilateral exercise of his powers as prosecutor and executioner, but as the just verdict of the lords spiritual and temporal. Implicitly, Wulfbald's execution comes to be less important than the disposition of his estates. In framing the dispute's resolution in this fashion, the charter legitimizes Æthelred's forfeiture of Wulfbald's lands while avoiding any portrayal of the king's actions as an attempt to expand royal landholdings or jurisdiction through the capricious use of capital punishment.

S 877 cannot be described as a 'typical' Anglo-Saxon criminal prosecution, if such a thing may even be said to exist;[84] however, the fact that a dispute of this sort should have been viewed as atypical highlights the extent to which royal involvement in local criminal prosecution had come to be seen as politically fraught, even in the later Anglo-Saxon period. The image evoked by the drafters of S 877 is not one of a coherent judicial system consolidated under a centralized monarchy. Rather, the prosecution of Wulfbald reveals an ongoing tension between regional and royal judicial authorities. The conditional rhetoric characterizing the capital clauses of royal legislation here finds its echo in the ambiguities surrounding royal involvement in the

---

[81] On the range of possible meaning for *ungebet*, see Bosworth–Toller.
[82] Keynes, *Diplomas*, pp. 201–2; Keynes, 'Crime and Punishment,' p. 79; Miller, *New Minster*, p. 152; *EHD* 1, p. 47.
[83] Thompson, *Dying and Death*, p. 182; and see above, n. 18.
[84] Patrick Wormald, 'Charters, Law and the Settlement of Disputes in Anglo-Saxon England,' *Legal Culture*, pp. 289–311, at 292.

(possible) execution of a criminal. Taken together, the capital clauses and records of capital cases suggest a need to further nuance the maximalist account of the early Anglo-Saxon state: if the archaeological evidence of the last decade has shown capital punishment to have been far more common during the Anglo-Saxon period than hitherto recognized, the textual evidence suggests that the similarities between execution sites may be more indicative of analogous regional practices than a homogeneous or homogenizing judicial system. The picture of royal power that emerges from the royal legislation and lawsuit records is one in which kings may have aspired to centralized authority, yet found their ability to exercise that authority checked by competing constituencies, regional politics, and a limited institutional infrastructure. Re-examining the rhetoric surrounding the pre-Conquest death penalty thus offers, if not proof of a fully constituted 'Anglo-Saxon state,' then at the very least a better sense of the political challenges attendant upon that state's creation.

Index

Page numbers in bold type refer to illustrations and their captions.

accident 43–4, 46, 67, 137, 139, 145
adultery 107, 113, 150, 158
advocate, advocacy 122, 124, 127 n.68
Ælfheah, saint, archbishop of Canterbury and bishop of Winchester (*Elphegi*) 6, 175–6, 178
Ælfric, abbot of Eynsham 6, 114–15, 123 n.49, 126 n.62, 155–7, 182, 191 n.45
Ælfthryth, mother of Æthelred II 177–8, 196 n.73
Æthelberht II, king of the East Anglians (d. 794) 4 n.15
Æthelberht, king of Kent (d. 616?) 11–12, 18–19, 21–2, 25, 30, **31**, 35, 37–8, 40–41, 46, 48–55, 62 n.45, 63, 65, 67, 69, 70–2, 76–7, 83–4, 85 n.43, 88
Æthelred I, king of the Northumbrians (d. 796) 120
Æthelred II '*Unræd*', king of the English (r. 978–1016) 1, 4, 9, 95, 128, 150 n.4, 165, 166–7 n.8, 168, 170–3, 175–8, 192, 194–8
Æthelred, king of the Mercians (r. 674/5–704) 18
Æthelstan, king of the English (r. 924–39) 3, 8, 12, 25, 97, 100–1 n.44, 103–4, 106, 110–12, 120 n.36, 149, 151, 153–4, 185–6, 188–93, 196
Æthelwulf, king of the West Saxons (r. 839–58) 108
afterlife 72–3, 124, 188
Alamani 42, 82 n.31
Alcuin of York 114, 120
Alfred, king of the Anglo-Saxons (r. 871–99) 2, 4 n.15, 11, 13, 19–20, 25, 27, 30, 40–7, 48–54, 62–3, 70, 75, 83–4, 86–90, 93, 96–7, 100–1, 103, 107–12, 114 n.8, 116–17, 118 n.22, 120 n.35, 122 n.44, 127, 129–30, 150, 152, 157, 188, 189 n.33, 193 n.57

amputation 2, 7, 13–14, 51, 66, 114, 132–3, 144, **145**, **146**, 147–8, 150–6, 160–1, 164
Anglo-Saxon Chronicle (ASC) 4–5, 71, 95, 98–9, 108, 128 n.69, 158, 165, 166 n.4, 171 n.32, 172 n.37, 174, 177, 192 n.52, 100, 100–1 n.44
Ansegisus, abbot of St Wandrille 152, 161
arson 97, 158
Asser, *Life of King Alfred* 109, 114 n.8, 117 n.18, 129–30
Augustine, archbishop of Canterbury 40, 163

Bamburgh 162–3
baptism 132–3
beating 5, 76, 85 n.46, 87, 89–90, 139 *see also* flogging
Bede 18, 32, 40, 55–7, 71, 80 n.24, 81–2, 85 n.44, 155, 162–3, 188
Bede, *Historia Ecclesiastica*, Old English 155–6, 162
Beonna, king of the East Angles (fl. 749–94) 23, **62**
Beowulf see under poetry, Old English
Bible 6–7, 13, 41, 47, 63, 66–7, 74–6, 78–9, 85, 114 n.8, 117, 120, 129 n.75, 150 n.8 *see also* Heptateuch, Old English
binding 4 n.15, 5, 7, 93
bishops 2–3, 13, 80–1 n.25, 96, 104–6, 111, 114, 123 n.48, 169, 191, 197
blinding 1, 4–5, 128 n.71, 144, 178 n.69
blood, bloodshed 6, 11, 13, 18, 20–1, 25, 27, 84 n.42, 114–15, 121, 154, 162, 188
Boethius *see Consolation of Philosophy*, Old English
Boniface (Wynfrith), saint 57
Book of Durrow 58, **60**

201

Index

bot, gebetan [compensation] 1, 19, 26–7, 30, 35, 41, 44, 49, 97, 107, 123, 198
  see also compensation (monetary); restitution
boundaries 32, 64–5, 131, 133, 142, 156, 172
branding 2
bruise 64, 84
burial, consecrated 4, 8–9, 132–3, 155, 171–2
burial, unconsecrated 9, 132–3, 155, 171–2
burning 65, 133, 139, 144, 159, 160 n.55, 163–4 n.71
Byzantium 21–2, 55, 151

capital punishment *see* execution
Carolingian 52, 54, 103, 108–9, 152–3 *see also* Franks; law, Frankish
castration 27, 50–1, 67 n.68, 70, 150 n.7, 158
cemeteries, consecrated 8, 132, 155, 162 n.65 *see also* burial, consecrated
cemeteries, execution 8, 14, 113, 131–2, 136, 139–44, 148, 156–7, 182–3 *see also* 'deviant burial'
Charlemagne, emperor 23, 45 n.75, 52, 63 n.49, 153 n.19
Charles the Bald, emperor 108, 152
charters 4, 9, 32, 100–1 n.44, 101 n.46, 142, 151–2 n.13, 156, 158, 168, 172, 183–4, 190 n.42, 193–8
  S 430 142 n.46
  S 443 4 n.14, 190 n.42
  S 501 142 n.46
  S 877 4 n.14, 194–8
  S 883 4 n.14, 9
  S 1454 196
Chrodegang of Metz, *Regula Canonicorum* 105–6, 108 n.83
churchyard *see* cemeteries, consecrated; burial, consecrated
Cnut, king of the English (r. 1016–35) 1, 4, 15, 29, 103 n.57, 112 n.101, 150, 161, 165, 166–7 n.8, 170–3, 175–8, 185, 192
coinage 11, 14, 19–32, 56, **61**, **62**, 142, 147, 149–52, 154–5, 157–9, 164
coinage, counterfeit 14, 22, 31–2, 45, 147, 149–54, 156, 158–9, 160–4
compensation (monetary) 2 n.8, 11–12, 17–30, **31**, 32–3, 35–47, 48–50, **51**, 52–4, 66–71, 76, 80 nn24–5, 81–4, 86–90, 122, 125 n.58, 190 *see also bot*; restitution

confession, confessor 13, 80–1 n.25, 89, 111, 118, 124
confiscation 9, 42, 159 *see also* forfeiture of property
conquest of England, Danish 165, 175–9
conquest of England, Norman 3, 15, 20, 93, 98–9, 158, 160, 166–7, 179
Consolation of Philosophy, Old English 13, 116–30
counterfeiter 31–2, 151–4, 158–63 *see also* coinage, counterfeit
court, hundred 4, 114 n.5, 196
court, shire 4, 114 n.5, 196
crime, as legal concept 3, 6, 9, 12, 34–5, 38 n.23, 39, 44–7, 103–4, 110–11, 115, 119, 181–2, 184, 189, 191, 193, 198
crime, as wrongdoing 2, 5, 14–15, 31, 35 n.9, 45, 67, 94, 96–7, 103–4, 110, 112, 119, 122, 124–8, 133, 143, 148, 149–50, 151 n.12, 156–9, 164 n.72, 166–8, 171–3, 176, 182, 186, 189–93, 196–7
criminals 1–3, 5–6, 9–10, 45, 95, 110, 113, 116–19, 122–3, 125, 127, 132–3, 139, 142, 151, 156–7, 160, 162, 171–2, 178, 182, 189, 199
cruelty 3, 114–16, 176, 190

'deviant burial' 7–8, 14, 132
damnation 7, 92, 123, 171–2, 179
Danes 4 n.15, 18–19, 165, 175–7, 179 *see also* conquest of England, Danish
death penalty *see* execution
decapitation 4 n.15, 6–7, 132–4, **135**, 136, **137**, 138 n.25, 141, 148, 155–7, 160, 162
decomposition, bodily 7–8, 131, 136, 139–42, 147, 162
disability 9, 36, 66–7 n.67, 83
disfigurement (*womwlite*) 55, 64–5, 76, 84–6, 89
display of body parts and executed bodies 7–8, 14–15, 134, 139–42, 147, 149–57, 159–64, 166
doctor *see* physician
domboc *see under* law, Anglo-Saxon
Domesday Book 4, 193
drawing 159–60, 164
drinctinbeag [fine] 36–7, 46 *see also* fine; *wite* [fine]
drowning 133, 189, 193
Dunstan, archbishop of Canterbury 6, 175–8

Eadberht, king of the Northumbrians (r. 737–58) 23

202

Index

Eadgyth, sister of Æthelred II 165, 177
Eadred, king of the English (r. 946–55) 4, 99–100, 100–1 n.44
Eadric Streona, ealdorman 4–5, 15, 95, 157 n.38, 165–80
East Anglia 4 n.15, **62**, 197
Ecgfrith, king of the Northumbrians (r. 670–85) 18, 94
Edgar, king of the English (r. 959–75) 4, 6, 8 n.42, 18, 24, 120, 158, 164 n.73, 191–2, 196
Edmund Ironside, king of the English (r. 1016) 95, 165, 168, 177–8
Edmund, king of the English (r. 939–46) 12, 100 n.40, 103, 191–2
Edmund, saint, king of the East Angles (r. 855–69) 115, 175 n.52, 191 n.45
Edward I, king of England (r. 1272–1307) 163–4 n.71
Edward the Confessor, king of the English (r. 1042–66) 99, 178 n.69, 180
Edward the Elder, king of the Anglo-Saxons (r. 899–924) 96–7, 101 n.46, 107, 111–12, 127, 188
Edward the Martyr, king of the English (r. 975–78) 128, 177–8
Emma (Ælfgifu) of Normandy, queen 177–9
Encomium Emmae Reginae 5 n.20, 166 n.4
excommunication 9, 42, 102, 125 n.58, 133, 172
execution 1–9, 12, 14–15, 36–8, 41–2, 45–8, 94, 97, 104, 113, 115, 130–1, 133–4, 137, 145, 147–8, 160, 165–7, 171, 176, 178–9, 181–94, 197–9
execution burials and cemeteries 8–9, 14, 113, 131–48, 156–7, 182–3
execution sites 8–9, 143, 172 n.35, 183, 187, 199
executioner 2, 7–9, 14, 148, 198
exile 2, 9 n.49, 39, 93, 96–7, 102, 125 n.58, 173, 178

feaxfang [hair-pulling] 63–5 *see also* hair
felony 181
feud 9–12, 17–18, 36, 184, 190
fine 2, 9, 12, 19–20, 36–7, 39–41, 42–6, 48–53, **54**, 55, 63–4, 66, 69, **70**, 148, 186, 194–5 *see also* drihtinbeag [fine]; *wite* [fine]
flight 36, 173, 189
flogging 2, 6, 39, 101 n.45 *see also* beating

forfeiture of property 2, 9 n.49, 41, 101, 186, 193–8
forgery *see* coinage, counterfeit; counterfeiter
Francia 50, 57, 62, 106, 108
Franks 20, 22, 56 n.28, 57, 58 n.42, 62–3, 70, 80–1, 94 n.9, 105, 108–9
Frisia 18, 48, 52–8, 61–72, 84, 88, 152–3, 154 n.23

gallows 5, 7, 136, 140, 148, 187–8
gifts 21, 125–6, 129
Gloucestershire 170, 173
Gregory I, pope 40, 56, 163
Grimbald of St Bertin 108–9
guilt, as legal concept 29, 34 n.4, 44, 47, 119 n.29, 120 n.32, 151

hair 5, 22, 63–4, 155 *see also feaxfang*
hanging 4 n.15, 5–7, 13, 115, 133–4, 136–7, **138**, 140–1, 148, 159–60, 163–4 n.71, 188
Harold Harefoot, king of the English (r. 1035–40) 5
Harthacnut, king of the English (r. 1040–42) 178 n.69
head stakes (*heafod stoccan*) 7–8, 142, 155–7, 160
hell 12, 36, 122
Hemming's Cartulary 166–79
Henry I, king of England (r. 1100–35) 89 n.57, 99, 158, 163 n.71, 167 n.8
Henry III, king of England (r. 1216–72) 160
Heptateuch, Old English 75–6, 86, *see also* Bible
Hincmar of Rheims 45, 109
homicide 67, 158, 80–1 n.25, 83, 121
hostages 192
humiliation 8, 37, 86, 88–90, 118, 172

incarceration 2, 4–6, 13, 92–112, 113, 123 n.48, 125 n.58, 186
Ine, king of the West Saxons (r. 688–726) 23, 53 n.17, 101, 150, 185
injury 10–11, 13, 19–20, 26–8, 30–1, 35–7, 39, 41, 43, 48–54, 62–4, 66–7 n.67, 67, 69–70, 74–81, 83–6, 86 n.47, 88–9, 118–19, 121, 133–9, 144, 152, 172
innocence 75 n.9, 79, 87, 114–17, 119–22, 126–8, 178
intentionality (*geweald*) 43–4, 46–7, 53 n.17, 64, 66–7, 121, 153
Ireland 57, 74, 77, 80–1, 86–7

203

Index

John of Worcester 100, 100–1 n.44, 174–8
judges 1–2, 6, 13, 15, 38, 113–30, 150, 152, 186, 192
Judgment Day 114, 127
jury 181, 185

Kent 2, 4 n.15, 21–3, 35–6, 38–40, 46, 50 n.6, 52, 58, 64, 77 n.16, 185
kidnapping 193
kinship 9–10, 17, 35–7, 40, 46, 83, 97, 128 n.69, 178–9, 189, 190

Laesae maiestatis see treason
Lantfred, *Translatio et miracula S. Swithuni* 6, 8 n.42, 18 n.6, 30 n.65, 94, 114–15, 164 n.73
law, Anglo-Saxon (by code)
   Æthelberht 11–12, 18–19, 22, 30, **31**, 35–8, 40, 48–53, **54**, 55, 62 n.45, 63–5, 67, 69, **70**, 71–2, 76–7, 83–4, 85 n.43, 88
   III Æthelred (Wantage) 9, 150 n.4, 157 n.40
   IV Æthelred 150, 152 n.16, 153–4, 157, 161, 192
   V Æthelred 1–2, 113, 115, 182, 192, 197 n.77
   VI Æthelred 2, 192 n.49
   II Æthelstan (Grately) 8, 13 n.57, 28, 31, 97, 103, 111, 132, 147, 149, 151–4, 156, 161 n.62, 171–2 n.33, 189, 191, 196 n.69
   III Æthelstan 127 n.66, 190 n.39
   IV Æthelstan 127 n.66, 189 n.34, 190 n.39, 191
   V Æthelstan 3, 189 n.34, 190–1
   VI Æthelstan 3, 25, 97, 112, 189 n.34, 190–1
   Alfred (*domboc*) 2, 11, 19, 26–7, 30, **31**, 32, 40–7, 48–53, **54**, 63–4, 69, **70**, 75, 83–4, 86–9, 93, 96–8, 100–5, 108–12, 113 n.2, 114 n.8, 116–17, 120 n.32, 121, 123 n.48, 124 n.53, 125 n.58, 128 n.70, 129 n.75, 150, 152, 186, 188, 189 n.33, 193 n.57
   I Cnut 171–2 n.33
   II Cnut 1–2, 4 n.12, 13, 18, 29 n.64, 31 n.74, 103 n.57, 112 n.101, 113, 114 n.5, 150, 161, 192, 196
   I Edgar 114 n.5, 196 n.69
   III Edgar 2 n.8, 4 n.12, 114 nn5 and 8, 150 n.7, 188 n.29, 192 n.47
   IV Edgar 2 n.8, 114 n.5, 192 n.47
   II Edmund 2 n.8, 192 n.47
   III Edmund 103, 150 n.7, 191 n.46
   I Edward 96, 114 n.8
   II Edward 96–7, 100, 102–3
   Edward and Guthrum 107
   Grið 112 n.101
   Hloþere and Eadric 36, 38, 120 n.32
   Ine 23, 26, 101, 120 n.32, 133, 150, 185–8, 192 n.54
   Iudex 120
   Wihtred 38–40, 46–7, 120 n.32, 185–8
law, Burgundian 64
law, divine 10, 109 n.91, 110
law, English post-Conquest
   Assize of Clarendon 99
   Bracton 159
   Fleta 159
   Glanvill 158
   Leges Henrici Primi 89
   Leis Willelme 76–7, 87, 90
law, Frankish 50 n.7, 50 n.10, 51, 103, 152–3
law, Frisian 43 n.66, 48, 51–3, **54**, 62–9, **70**, 71–2, 85 n.46, 88, 152–3, 154 n.23
law, Irish 65 n.62, 68 n.69, 74, 76 n.14, 77 n.18, 78, 80, 82–4, 86–7
law, Lombard 36 n.11, 42, 152, 158
law, Mosaic 41, 47, 74, 78, 41–2, 101
law, Saxon 51, 64–7, **70**
law, Swabian 66–7, **70**
law, Visigothic 42 n.59, 151–2, 158
lawsuits 4, 190, 196, 199
lex talionis see talion
liability, as legal concept 34 n.4, 42–4, 53 n.17, 74, 77, 120 n.32
Lindisfarne 120 n.35, 162
live burial 7, 139
Lombards 57, 151 *see also* law, Lombard
London 6, 56, 97, 115, 145 n.61, 157 n.38, 160 n.56, 170, 172, 176–7, 190, 196–7
Louis the Pious, emperor 106, 152

maiming 30 n.68, 48, 50, 66, 79, 80
Maitland, Frederick William 43, 46, 96 n.19, 181–2, 182–3 n.8, 188 n.26
Margam Chronicle 158, 163 n.71
martyrdom 5–6, 128, 163, 175–7, 191 n.45
maximalism 14–15, 182–4, 199
mediation 11, 18–19, 24, 26, 36, 114
medical practice 7 n.38, 69, 74–5, 77, 79–82, 87, 118, 145, 147
memory 8, 169, 172
Mercia 18, 23, 155, 165, 168, 170, 176

Index

mercy 1, 3, 9 n.44, 41, 114, 122–4, 130, 157, 192
minimalism 14–15
mints, minters 14, 21–4, 28–9, 31–2, 56, 147, 149–50, 154, 157–8, 160, 163 n.71, 164
monasticism 7, 13, 96, 105, 107 n.76, 108 n.83, 165, 167–73, 175, 179
money *see* coinage
Moses 41, 110–11, 114 n.8 *see also* law, Mosaic
multiple burials 133
murder 36, 41, 68–9, 80–1 n.25, 105, 121 n.40, 154, 166, 175–6, 178, 189, 193
mutilation 1–5, 7, 9, 14–15, 18, 48–71, 96, 108, 113, 115, 144, 147, 149–64, 187, 192

Norman Conquest *see* conquest of England, Norman
Northumbria 4, 23, 28, 100, 100–1 n.44, 155

oath 36, 41, 43, 68, 95–7, 100–4, 109–11, 123 n.48, 156, 161 n.61
Offa, king of the Mercians (r. 757–96) 4 n.15, 21 n.21, 23–4
Old Dairy Cottage, Winchester **135**, 143
ordeal 29–31, 97, 112 n.101, 144, 149, 161 n.61, 191
Osbern of Canterbury 175–6
osteology *see* punishment, osteological evidence for
Oswald, saint, king of the Northumbrians (r. 634–42) 155–6, 162–3
Oswine, king of Deira (r. 642–51) 5 n.15
Oswiu, king of the Northumbrians (r. 642–70) 4 n.15, 162 n.65

paganism 5, 21, 56 n.32, 57, 71, 73
pain 8, 13, 17–18, 33, 88, 115, 118, 119 n.27, 124, 159
pardon 9, 15, 161 n.61, 186, 187 n.21
peace 1–3, 11–12, 15, 17–19, 25–6, 40, 45–6, 103, 113, 130, 170, 189
penance 2, 13, 79–82, 85–6, 89, 91, 104–11, 116, 118, 121–6, 128 nn69 and 71, 130
Penda, king of the Mercians (d. 655) 155, 162 n.65
penitentials 13, 76, 78–87, 89–91, 105, 107–9, 111, 118 n.22, 121, 123 n.48
perjury 107, 150 n.7
physician 13, 75–6, 77 n.18, 79, 85, 90, 117–18, 124

poetry, Old English
 Battle of Maldon 71
 Beowulf 5, 18, 71, 153–5
 Dream of the Rood 5
 Fates of Mortals 5
 Fates of the Apostles 5
 Gifts of Men 184 n.13
 Judith 6
 Juliana 5
 Maxims I 85
 Maxims II 5
prison *see* incarceration
prone burial 7, 132
property 9, 35, 38 n.26, 42, 80–1 n.25, 121, 179, 189–90, 194–8
protection 1–2, 14, 32, 40, 42 n.59, 45–7, 64 n.52, 99, 120–1, 139–40, 168, 170–4, 177 n.64, 178–80, 187, 190–1
punishment *see* amputation; beating; binding; blinding; branding; burning; decapitation; drawing; drowning; execution; fine; flogging; forfeiture of property; hanging; incarceration; mutilation; stoning
punishment, non-lethal (*friðlice*) 1–2, 9, 113, 115, 118 n.24, 182
punishment, osteological evidence for 14, 131–48, 156
purgatory 17, 123 n.47

rape 27, 150 n.7, 158, 193
reeves 9, 96, 102, 114, 161 n.61
relics 78, 94, 162–3
repentance 1, 6, 10, 115, 122, 123 n.49, 125–7, 198
restitution 5, 12, 26, 35–9, 42, 44, 46, 51, 66, 69, 75 n.9, 79–81, 84, 86–7 *see also bot*; compensation (monetary)
riht, *unriht* 12, 39–40, 47, 96, 119 n.29, 120, 130
Rome 42 n.58, 56–7, 108 178
Rule of St Benedict 105, 108 n.83

salvation 1–2, 18, 123–4, 161, 178
Saxony 45 n.75, 64–7 *see also* law, Saxon
Scandinavia 29, 50 n.8, 55, 56 n.32, 58 n.42, 88, 157 n.39
settlement (judicial) 11–12, 20–1, 114, 184, 194
Seven Sleepers of Ephesus 7 n.33, 156
shame 9, 11, 15, 64, 81, 84 n.42, 85, 88–9, 171–3, 194
shire court 4, 114 n.5, 196
sick-maintenance 13, 74–91

Index

sin 6, 47, 79, 80 n.23, 80–1 n.25, 83, 89, 110, 115, 117–18, 122–3, 124, 175
slander 27 n.54, 45–6, 150 n.7
slavery 23, 25–7, 39, 46, 56, 82, 84 n.42, 87, 89, 150 n.7, 151, 185, 189–91
Soliloquies of St Augustine, Old English 92–3, 98, 111
sorcery 97
soul 1–2, 7, 10, 12–14, 18, 47, 80, 83, 87, 115–18, 120–2, 124, 127, 128 n.71, 150, 161
spectacle 8, 151, 157, 160, 164, 172
Staines (Surrey) 131, 183
stoning 133, 137, 139, 189
suicide 132–3
surety 95, 97, 112 n.101
Sutton Hoo 21–2, 56, 58, **59**, 148
Swein 'Forkbeard', king of the English (r. 1013–14) 175 n.52
Symeon of Durham 100 n.42, 158

talion 10–11, 18, 27, 45, 67
tariffs 11–12, 19–21, 25–6, 30–2, 35, 52, 53 n.17, 63, 64 n.52, 66–7 n.67, 70, 84, 152
theft, thieves 3, 5–6, 9–10, 12–13, 31, 35–6, 39, 45–6, 80–1 n.25, 94, 97, 99, 101 n.45, 103–5, 107, 111, 115, 127, 150, 156–7, 160, 164 n.73, 186–7, 189, 191, 193–4
Theodred, bishop of London 6, 115, 190–1
Theodulf of Orléans 105–7
tonsure 88, 96
treason, traitors 5, 15, 41–2, 45–6, 100 n.42, 103, 113, 128, 158–60, 165, 175–8

vengeance 5, 10–12, 17–19, 25, 27, 36 n.11, 39, 46, 97, 114, 119 n.29, 124, 170–2, 190
victims of crimes 10–13, 15, 35–6, 48–51, 53, **54**, 66–8, 74, 76–91, 118–19, 121–2, 126–7
Vikings 10, 24, 29, 48, 107, 120, 177
violence 3, 5 n.21, 9–12, 15, 17, 45, 79, 87–91, 120 n.35, 121, 166, 193

Wales 56, 65 n.62, 160
Walkington Wold (Yorkshire) 136, **137**, 142–3, 148

warfare 10, 37, 46, 48, 121, 159 n.53
wergild (*wergeld*) 19–20, 22, 26, 36, 39, 41–3, 45, 50–1, 53, **54**, 66, 66–7 n.67, 69, **70**, 71, 80 n.25, 83, 186, 194–5
Wessex 12, 23, 40, 50, 52–3, 57, 62, 93 n.5, 99, 101, 107–8, 185
Wihtred, king of Kent (r. 690–725) 38–40, 46–7, 186
Wijnaldum Brooch 58, **59**
Wilfrid, bishop of Northumbria 57, 94–5
William I 'the Conqueror', king of England (r. 1066–87) 76, 166–7 n.8, 173–4, 180
William II 'Rufus', king of England (r. 1087–1100) 169–70, 173–4, 175 n.50
William of Malmesbury 100, 162 n.63, 174–5
Winchester 94, 99
wisdom 20, 92, 116, 123 *see also Consolation of Philosophy*, Old English
witan [council] 100, 197
witchcraft 189, 193
wite [fine] 12, 19, 36–7, 43–4, 46, 53 n.17 *see also* fine; *drihtinbeag* [fine]
wite [punishment] 12, 36, 119–20, 122–6, 181
witness (legal) 30, 32, 38, 44, 77 n.19, 100–1 n.44
womwlite see disfigurement
Worcester 15, 152 n.16, 165–80
wound 11, 30, 35 n.9, 43, 48–9, 51, 53, 66–8, 76–7, 80 n.24, 82–4, 86, 88–91, 136, 154, 156
Wulfhelm, archbishop of Canterbury 190–1
Wulfred, archbishop of Canterbury 108
Wulfstan I, archbishop of York 99–100, 101–1 n.44, 112
Wulfstan II, archbishop of York and bishop of Worcester 1–3, 10, 13, 107–8, 115–16, 118 n.24, 121 n.40, 161, 182, 192
Wulfstan, saint, bishop of Worcester 166–8, 173–4, 179–80

ANGLO-SAXON STUDIES

Volume 1: The Dramatic Liturgy of Anglo-Saxon England
M. Bradford Bedingfield

Volume 2: The Art of the Anglo-Saxon Goldsmith: Fine Metalwork in Anglo-Saxon England: Its Practice and Practitioners
Elizabeth Coatsworth and Michael Pinder

Volume 3: The Ruler Portraits of Anglo-Saxon England
Catherine E. Karkov

Volume 4: Dying and Death in Later Anglo-Saxon England
Victoria Thompson

Volume 5: Landscapes of Monastic Foundation: The Establishment of Religious Houses in East Anglia, c. 650–1200
Tim Pestell

Volume 6: Pastoral Care in Late Anglo-Saxon England
edited by Francesca Tinti

Volume 7: Episcopal Culture in Late Anglo-Saxon England
Mary Frances Giandrea

Volume 8: Elves in Anglo-Saxon England: Matters of Belief, Health, Gender and Identity
Alaric Hall

Volume 9: Feasting the Dead: Food and Drink in Anglo-Saxon Burial Rituals
Christina Lee

Volume 10: Anglo-Saxon Button Brooches: Typology, Genealogy, Chronology
Seiichi Suzuki

Volume 11: Wasperton: A Roman, British and Anglo-Saxon Community in Central England
edited by Martin Carver with Catherine Hills and Jonathan Scheschkewitz

Volume 12: A Companion to Bede
George Hardin Brown

Volume 13: Trees in Anglo-Saxon England: Literature Law and Landscape
Della Hooke

Volume 14: The Homiletic Writings of Archbishop Wulfstan
Joyce Tally Lionarons

Volume 15: The Archaeology of the East Anglian Conversion
Richard Hoggett

Anglo-Saxon Studies

Volume 16: The Old English Version of Bede's *Historia Ecclesiastica*
Sharon M. Rowley

Volume 17: Writing Power in Anglo-Saxon England: Texts, Hierarchies, Economies
Catherine A. M. Clarke

Volume 18: Cognitive Approaches to Old English Poetry
Antonina Harbus

Volume 19: Environment, Society and Landscape in Early Medieval England: Time and Topography
Tom Williamson

Volume 20: Honour, Exchange and Violence in *Beowulf*
Peter S. Baker

Volume 21: *John the Baptist's Prayer* or *The Descent into Hell* from the Exeter Book: Text, Translation and Critical Study
M. R. Rambaran-Olm

Volume 22: Food, Eating and Identity in Early Medieval England
Allen J. Frantzen